D1606016

BECOMING BYZANTINE

BECOMING BYZANTINE

Children and Childhood in Byzantium

Edited by Arietta Papaconstantinou and Alice-Mary Talbot

Published by DUMBARTON OAKS RESEARCH LIBRARY AND COLLECTION

Distributed by Harvard University Press, 2009

Copyedited, designed, and typeset by Princeton Editorial Associates, Inc., Scottsdale, Arizona

Cover illustrations: Front: Chora Church, Constantinople (1316/21), Caresses of the Virgin (see Fig. 1, p. 176); Back: Terracotta wheeled horse, fourth century, Agora excavations, Athens (see Fig. 20, p. 223)

Library of Congress Cataloging-in-Publication Data

Becoming Byzantine : children and childhood in Byzantium / edited by Arietta Papaconstantinou and Alice-Mary Talbot.
    p.   cm.   —   (Dumbarton Oaks Byzantine Symposia and Colloquia)
Includes bibliographical references and index.
ISBN 978-0-88402-356-2
1. Children—History. 2. Children—Byzantine Empire—Social conditions. 3. Family—Byzantine Empire. 4. Byzantine Empire—Social conditions. 5. Byzantine Empire—Social life and customs. I. Papaconstantinou, Arietta. II. Talbot, Alice-Mary Maffry.
    HQ767.87.B43   2009
    305.2309495'0902—dc22
    2008048054

www.doaks.org

CONTENTS

INTRODUCTION

Homo Byzantinus in the Making

Arietta Papaconstantinou

A British nanny must be a general!
The future empire lies within her hands.
"The Life I Lead," *Mary Poppins,* 1964

U PON ITS RELEASE IN 1964, *Mary Poppins* became what we have come to call a cult film. Along with its many other qualities, it is arguably one of Hollywood's strongest statements in the area of the history of childhood. Produced only four years after the famous book by Philippe Ariès that gave birth to this new field,[1] here is a film that paints a pathetic picture of the straitjacket educational principles of Edwardian England, offering as the proper alternative an education based on play, making expert use of one of the characteristics traditionally attributed to childhood—belief in the "marvelous"—and giving children a voice in their own upbringing:[2] The Banks children want a nanny who has "a cheery disposition, rosy cheeks, no warts," and plays all sorts of games—and they get her. To the father's cry that "children must be molded, shaped and taught / That life's a looming battle to be faced and fought," Mary Poppins ironically replies that "they must feel the thrill of totting up a balance-book, / A thousand ciphers neatly in a row. / When gazing at a graph that shows the profits up, / Their little cup of joy should overflow!"[3] Instead of being the expected "general" who will mercilessly train for their future task the children she is entrusted with, heirs to the dominion and thus strategic assets of

---

1   P. Ariès, *Centuries of Childhood* (London, 1962), a translation of *L'enfant et la vie familiale sous l'Ancien Régime* (Paris, 1960). Interestingly, the difference between the French and English titles reflects the fact that most English-speaking scholars have indeed generally neglected both that the book is meant to deal with the ancien régime and that it includes a section on family life.
2   These were the educational principles popularized in the 1960s by figures like Benjamin Spock, reaching a zenith in the 1970s with such cultural icons as Ivan Illich's *Deschooling Society* (New York, 1971) and Supertramp's "Logical Song" (1979).
3   "A British Bank," from the soundtrack of *Mary Poppins.*

empire, this untypical "British nanny" bows to principles that very recognizably belong to the spirit of the 1960s.

Mary Poppins the film seriously distorted the novel on which it was based, written in 1934 and set in its own time, which presented a much less playful Mary Poppins. Its author, Pamela Travers, is known to have disapproved of the film version of her sterner and more irritable character.[4] What Disney's *Mary Poppins* shares with the contemporary work by Philippe Ariès is the view that people in the past did not understand childhood and had to somehow "discover" it with the help of an agent. The two works place that past at very different moments and identify very different agents, but both espouse the progressive paradigm according to which the condition of children has steadily improved throughout history. Ariès tackles the question in the long term, situating the discovery of childhood in the seventeenth and eighteenth centuries, as a by-product of the developments that gave rise to the Enlightenment. He states bluntly that "in medieval society the idea of childhood did not exist"—adding that this was not to be confused with lack of affection for children.[5] His thesis has been much discussed and repeatedly refuted, especially by medievalists who seem almost offended to have been deprived of a historical object.[6] The flourishing state of the history of childhood in ancient and medieval studies today is probably one of Ariès's greatest achievements. Scholarship often advances through controversy, and this is one of the most obvious cases in point.

The purported absence of childhood posited by Ariès has been refuted by his critics and replaced with a depiction of historical parents as universally loving and nurturing, a position epitomized in the final sentence of Nicholas Orme's introduction to his *Medieval Children:* "And, as the reader will by now have realized, I believe them to have been ourselves, five hundred or a thousand years ago."[7] Even though his erasure of difference between childhood in the past and childhood today is an obvious overstatement, in milder forms the same idea runs through a number of recent studies that downplay the negative aspects of childhood in the past.[8]

---

4   P. L. Travers, *Mary Poppins* (London, 1934). This very successful novel was followed by several sequels. On Travers and her disagreement with Disney, see C. Flanagan, "Becoming Mary Poppins: P. L. Travers, Walt Disney, and the Making of a Myth," *New Yorker,* 19 December 2005.
5   Ariès, *Centuries of Childhood,* 128.
6   See the references given by Dimiter Angelov in this volume, esp. nn. 4–6.
7   N. Orme, *Medieval Children* (New Haven, 2001), 10.
8   See the remarks made by Isabelle Cochelin in her review of Orme's *Medieval Children* in *Medieval Review* 04.02.06 (2004) (http://hdl.handle.net/2027/spo.baj9928.0402.006).

This optimistic picture ultimately rests on a positive view of childhood in today's world. The reverse perspective also exists, however. It is based not on the paradigm of progress but on the equally pervasive notion of a lost golden age set in indistinct "earlier times," *autrefois*. Stemming from an increased awareness of the dangers of existence, this pessimistic view, perhaps a backlash against the optimism that preceded it, is very popular and massively circulated by the press as well as by a steady flow of books aimed at the general public and emphasizing the darker side of childhood and family life.[9]

> Children across the world seem to be the victims of biogeographical dislocations that unnerve the adults around them. If they are not being abused or raped, then they are apparently starved and murdered in larger numbers than hitherto. If not the subject of physical violence, then alternatively, in the developed world they are so appallingly spoiled and pampered that by puberty, we are told, they sink into adolescent depression persuaded they have little to live for. . . .
>
> On what foundations are we so shocked? What has been the past of childhood that makes us so confident we are the first generation to witness these calamities? Are the changes we read about genuinely without precedent?

These observations are made by Laurence Brockliss and George Rousseau in a short essay explaining the rationale for the establishment of a Centre for the History of Childhood at the University of Oxford.[10] They capture the essence of a vision of decline that is a recurring historical model and touches perceptions of childhood as it does all other areas. We thus find ourselves confronted with two different motivations for studying the history of childhood: one is to show that it was as good then as it is now, and the other is to show that it is not worse now than it was then. The former mirrors the late twentieth-century, politically correct, antievolutionist view of the past, whereas the latter reflects

---

9 See, for instance, "Kalashnikov Kids," *The Economist,* 8 July 1999; J. R. Kincaid, *Erotic Innocence: The Culture of Child-Molesting* (Durham, N.C., 1998); G. Sereny, *Cries Unheard: The Story of Mary Bell* (London, 1998), published in the United States with *Why Children Kill* added to the title. Interestingly, the recent theater stagings of *Mary Poppins* in London (2004) and on Broadway (2006) adopted the darker mood of the novel, as against Disney's adaptation of it.

10 L. Brockliss and G. Rousseau, "The History Child," *Oxford Magazine,* Michaelmas 2003, 4–7; available online at www.history.ox.ac.uk/research/clusters/history_childhood/HoC_ox_mag.pdf.

the fin de siècle and early twenty-first-century concern with the evils of hyper-modernization.

So where is Byzantium in all that? Byzantium is absent from the debates, indeed from the field in general—in all fairness, however, it is, in its absence, in larger company than those who are present. In a recent overview of the history of childhood, Peter Stearns identified as one of its most urgent challenges its extension to societies beyond Western Europe and North America.[11] Indeed, very little work has been done outside the Western world; and even for the West, research has mainly flourished in and on those regions and cultures where emotional investment in childhood is very high.[12] The lack of comparative material has acted as a brake to the emancipation of the field's theoretical framework from the question posed by Ariès, which still underpins much of the work on the subject.

The call to expand geographically and thematically comes at a time when the gradual rise of interest in other periods and regions has already raised some intriguing new questions.[13] To some extent, this book is an attempt to add to this literature and to contribute to those questions by opening up a virtually unknown world. However, it also—and perhaps primarily—aims to introduce those debates to Byzantine history and to advance our understanding of Byzantine society. If "childhood is the protean state where identities are formed and the destinies of nations and peoples defined," as has been recently claimed, then studying how a society deals with it can bring enormous insights into its aspirations and self-image.[14]

The absence of studies on Byzantine childhood is admittedly only relative. Phaidon Koukoules first wrote an article on the care of children in 1938, and

11   P. N. Stearns, "Challenges in the History of Childhood," *Journal of the History of Childhood and Youth* 1 (2008): 38; see also P. Fass, "The World Is at Our Door: Why Historians of Children and Childhood Should Open Up," ibid., 11–31.

12   See the surveys of literature for the decade 1990–2000 in *AnnalesDH* 102 (2001), by V. Dasen for antiquity (6–17, bibliography 47–73) and D. Lett for the Western Middle Ages (17–25, bibliography 73–85). Both show very clearly how the themes and approaches in the history of childhood are informed by contemporary concerns, often in a much more straightforward manner than in other historical fields.

13   Very interesting work has been done on China, for instance: see among others A. B. Kinney, *Representations of Childhood and Youth in Early China* (Stanford, 2004), and the general survey by Ping-Chen Hsiung, "Treading a Different Path? Thoughts on Childhood Studies in Chinese History," *Journal of the History of Childhood and Youth* 1 (2008): 77–85.

14   Fass, "The World Is at Our Door," 13.

ten years later he devoted more than 180 pages in his magnum opus on Byzantine daily life to the practices related to children and childhood.[15] In the 1970s, Évelyne Patlagean investigated aspects of childhood related to questions of family law, kinship, and the place of the child in social networks and family strategies.[16] These are areas in which legal sources, canonical and secular, are comparatively rich, and they were later also exploited by Ruth Macrides to investigate adoption and symbolic kinship.[17] These works have shown the breadth of the social network into which a child was introduced through its birth and baptism, and on occasion its subsequent adoption, and the strength of those ties, not only socially but also in law.[18] The more specific question of relations between children and parents has been tackled from the legal side in a monograph by Anastasios Christophilopoulos that remains little known, and from the social point of view by Alexander Kazhdan, who based his observations on the two models offered by hagiography: that of a saint's respect and obedience to parents and that of breaking with the family.[19]

Hagiography, as well as literary biography and literature in general, has also been used to examine Byzantine representations of childhood[20] and the moral

15   Ph. Koukoules, "Περὶ τῆς τῶν ἀνήβων τροφῆς καὶ ἐπιμελείας παρὰ Βυζαντινοῖς," Ἐπετηρὶς τῆς Ἑταιρείας Βυζαντινῶν Σπουδῶν 14 (1938): 310–30; idem, Βυζαντινῶν βίος καὶ πολιτισμός, vol. 1.1, Collection de l'Institut Français d'Athènes 10 (Athens, 1948), 1–184.

16   É. Patlagean, "L'enfant et son avenir dans la famille byzantine (IVe–XIIe siècles)," AnnalesDH 10 (1973): 85–93; eadem, "Christianisation et parentés rituelles: le domaine de Byzance," AnnalesESC 33 (1978): 625–36. See also eadem, "Familles et parentèles à Byzance," in Histoire de la famille, ed. A. Burguière, C. Klapisch, and F. Zonabend (Paris, 1986), 1:421–41.

17   R. J. Macrides, "The Byzantine Godfather," BMGS 11 (1987): 139–62; eadem, "Kinship by Arrangement: The Case of Adoption," DOP 44 (1990): 109–18; eadem, "Dynastic Marriages and Political Kinship," in Byzantine Diplomacy, ed. J. Shepard and S. Franklin (Aldershot, 1992), 380–410; eadem, "Substitute Parents and Their Children in Byzantium," in Adoption et fosterage, ed. M. Corbier (Paris, 2000), 1–11.

18   See also H. Antoniadis-Bibikou, "Quelques notes sur l'enfant de la moyenne époque byzantine (du VIe au XIIe siècle)," AnnalesDH (1973): 77–84.

19   A. P. Christophilopoulos, Σχέσεις γονέων καὶ τέκνων κατὰ τὸ Βυζαντινὸν δίκαιον (Athens, 1946); A. Kazhdan, "Hagiographical Notes," Byzantion 54 (1984): 188–92.

20   D. Abrahamse, "Images of Childhood in Early Byzantine Hagiography," Journal of Psychohistory 6 (1979): 497–517; C. Jouanno, "Le Roman d'Alexandre ou l'enfance d'un héros," in Enfants et enfances dans les mythologies: Actes du VIIème colloque du Centre de Recherches Mythologiques de l'Université de Paris-X (Chantilly, 16–18 septembre 1992), ed. D. Auger (Paris, 1995), 269–89; eadem, "Récits d'enfances dans la littérature byzantine d'imagination," Pris-ma: Bulletin de liaison de l'Équipe de Recherche sur la Littérature d'Imagination au Moyen Âge 12 (1996): 39–56; N. Kalogeras, "What Do They Think about Children? Perceptions of Childhood in Early Byzantine Literature," BMGS 25 (2001): 2–19.

and religious status of newborns, especially during the ambivalent period between birth and baptism.[21] The same sources tell us most of what we know about childhood education, a subject recently studied by Nikos Kalogeras, if only for the period leading up to Iconoclasm.[22] Recent studies on child illnesses, on orphans, and on children in art demonstrate a fast-growing interest in the subject.[23]

However, despite an undeniable and sustained interest in the question, there is as yet no comprehensive treatment of the history of Byzantine children and childhood, except an important and insightful but necessarily short article by Ann Moffatt dating back to 1986.[24] Many of the works cited above do not place their object in the category of the history of childhood and have remained aloof from debates in that field. Furthermore, they generally focus not on the children but on the social institutions in which those children played a role, namely the family or kin group, the educational environment, the church, the medical world, or charitable institutions. Even though this volume, which evolved from a Dumbarton Oaks symposium in May 2006, is not the much-needed comprehensive monograph, its contributors have attempted to cover their subjects as systematically as the space of an article allows. The selected papers cover essential questions such as legal definitions of childhood and adolescence, procreation, death, breastfeeding patterns, material culture, and ideal views of children from the political and religious perspectives. One essay examines their place in monasteries, which were among Byzantium's central institutions. By looking into as-yet neglected aspects of childhood in medieval Byzantium and by addressing some general issues, we hope to provide not only an impetus but also a solid basis for further studies.

Much of the information on Byzantine childhood is found in holy biographies and *enkomia,* highly rhetorical works in which topoi tend to take precedence over direct description, leaving us with some "realities" so obvious that they are historically meaningless: that children like to play, that they have acci-

21   M.-H. Congourdeau, "Regards sur l'enfant nouveau-né à Byzance," *REB* 51 (1993): 161–75; J. Baun, "The Fate of Babies Dying before Baptism in Byzantium," in *The Church and Childhood,* ed. D. Wood, Studies in Church History 31 (Oxford, 1994): 115–25.

22   N. M. Kalogeras, "Byzantine Childhood Education and its Social Role from the Sixth Century until the End of Iconoclasm" (PhD diss., University of Chicago, 2000).

23   C. Hummel, *Das Kind und seine Krankheiten in der griechischen Medizin: Von Aretaios bis Johannes Aktuarios (1. bis 14. Jahrhundert)* (Frankfurt, 1999); T. S. Miller, *The Orphans of Byzantium: Child Welfare in the Christian Empire* (Washington, D.C., 2003); C. Hennessy, *Images of Children in Byzantium* (Aldershot, forthcoming).

24   A. Moffatt, "The Byzantine Child," *Social Research* 53 (1986): 705–23.

dents, and that they are noisy and not always obedient—and from the point of view of literary construction, even those function as topoi. However, a close look at the evolution over time of a number of stories, such as the Lives of Constantine and Alexander and the rewritings of late antique hagiographical accounts in later centuries, highlights considerable changes in the treatment of childhood. These trends are clearly demonstrated in the articles by Dimiter Angelov and Béatrice Caseau.

Another difficulty with using sources of a biographical nature is that they always conform to the traditional model according to which elements in childhood prefigured what the individual was to become in later life. This purely rhetorical device worked not only in panegyric but also in the rhetoric of blame (*psogos*): while some children showed signs of their future greatness, others displayed the unfortunate symptoms of a more negative development. The rhetoric worked because it rested, as it still does, on the concept of a fundamental continuity in an individual's personality, which entailed the construction of a linear and unified life story—what Pierre Bourdieu has aptly named "the biographical illusion."[25] Here again, it is only by confronting the varying stress and value placed over time on some qualities rather than others that one can circumvent the stereotyped nature of the sources.

As the subject of Byzantine childhood is arguably still in its early stages, it has seemed appropriate to several contributors to tackle the Ariès thesis in the specific context of Byzantium. This enterprise is much less vain than it may initially seem. When one looks at Byzantine ideals of childhood, it is difficult at first sight not to agree with Ariès. The all-pervading theme of the *puer senex,* implying that a "good" child is one that behaves like an adult, indeed supports his point that little value was accorded to childhood as such and that children were treated as miniature adults. In the words of Manuel Holobolos, a future leader would ideally have "an adult mind (*presbeutikon phronema*)" in what was still a puerile soul or body.[26] This expression is strikingly reminiscent of the ideal of holiness once applied to women, who were said to have male hearts under their female traits or even to *be* men despite their (female) physical form.[27] It is as if

25   P. Bourdieu, "L'illusion biographique," *Actes de la recherche en sciences sociales* 62–63 (1986): 69–72.

26   Quoted by Dimiter Angelov, below, 102, n. 68, and 114, n. 121.

27   Gregory of Nazianzos, Carmina 2.1.1, De se ipso 119, PG 37:979: ἄρσενα θυμὸν ἔχουσα ἐν εἴδει θηλυτεράων; Palladios, Dialogue on the Life of John Chrysostom 16.186–187, ed. A.-M. Malingrey, SC 341–42 (Paris, 1988), 318–19, on Olympias: ἀνὴρ γάρ ἐστι παρὰ τὸ τοῦ σώματος σχῆμα.

the Byzantines had some difficulty admitting that their ideals could be attained by any category of humans other than adult males—and, indeed, as if Ariès's thesis were perfectly fitted to Byzantium. However, tested by several contributors, this conclusion proves to be no more than an illusion.

Ariès founded much of his argument on the absence of a specific vocabulary related to childhood in the premodern West. The legal definitions of childhood and youth analyzed by Günter Prinzing in the opening chapter clearly show that Byzantine legislators and the society to which they belonged not only defined childhood but also subdivided it into several stages with vocabulary specific to each, showing a subtle interplay between generic and specific terms. Byzantine laws and other regulations also recognized a series of turning points in the status of children and young people, several of which were important enough to be marked by specific rites of passage in the church.[28] Predictably, as in most traditional societies, responsibility in penal matters was imposed at a much earlier age than today—but, also typically, in economic and patrimonial matters, full independence was achieved much later than in modern society.

The existence of a specific concept of childhood is an issue more explicitly addressed in the article by Dimiter Angelov on the models of ideal childhood that were circulated through the biographies of emperors and patriarchs, and in the parallel article by Béatrice Caseau on the childhood ideal in the Lives of saints. Analyzing a large amount of material over several centuries, both articles show that those texts define their ideal in opposition to *normal* childhood. Their authors constantly refer to this concept, if sometimes only to say it needs amending. Behaving like grown-ups was the sign of exceptional children, whose superior qualities were interpreted as God-given and thus totally unnatural. Even if it is left unexpressed, there is room in this discourse for normal, natural childhood, which evidently is taken for granted by most authors. It is not the consciousness of childhood that seems to become more acute over time, but that of the family, as biographies, both holy and secular, became more aristocratic and lineage-oriented, clearly departing from the initial late antique model that emphasized a break with the family and detachment from family ties as the path to success.

Another argument made by Philippe Ariès was that premodern children lived in a world that was materially identical to that of adults, albeit in miniature.

---

28 See the examples in A. Papaconstantinou, "L'enfance," in *Économie et société à Byzance (VIIIe–XIIe siècle): Textes et documents,* ed. S. Métivier (Paris, 2007), 203–9.

This is the point on which he has been most thoroughly criticized, not only in publications but also in exhibitions devoted to children and childhood, which have demonstrated the existence of a material culture conceived especially for children.[29] Brigitte Pitarakis shows that this was equally true in Byzantium. There was indeed a substantial production of artifacts designed for children, not only toys and clothes but also jewels—a consequence, perhaps, of the early ages of betrothal and marriage, occasions when most jewelry was presented. There were also special baby foods, an important part of children's material environment.

Pitarakis goes beyond the simple question of the concept of childhood to argue that the Byzantines had strong feelings for their children and that the material culture she describes is the product of that affection. This argument is perhaps aimed less at Ariès, who, as we saw, made a clear distinction between the lack of a concept of childhood and the lack of affection, than at a more general trend among historians to portray parents of preindustrial societies as cruel and indifferent. Her argument, based on the indirect evidence of the material environment, is powerfully reinforced by Alice-Mary Talbot's study of the death and burial of children and the effect of such events on the families. It is not easy to investigate this question for a society in which the expression of feelings was codified and ritualized, giving the impression that those feelings were totally artificial. Death was, however, the one situation about which feelings were very commonly expressed, often in an extreme way. Even if, like all Byzantine literature, the funerary oration (*epitaphios logos*) was a highly rhetorical genre filled with topoi, the very creation of these topoi shows a need to express certain emotions, and Talbot cites some gripping texts that one cannot imagine being produced by indifferent individuals. The death of a child was generally less dramatized than it is today, in great part because, like most traditional societies, the Byzantines had more children and placed less emotional weight on each one individually, clearly expecting some of them to die early. Nevertheless, such a death, especially after infancy, evidently remained an unnatural event.

Marie-Hélène Congourdeau describes the considerable activity deployed by women, and families in general, to secure the conception and survival of a child,

---

29   Examples include the exhibitions *L'enfance au moyen âge,* at the Bibliothèque Nationale in Paris in 1994, and *Coming of Age in Ancient Greece: Images of Childhood from the Classical Past,* at the Hood Museum at Dartmouth College, New Hampshire, the Onassis Cultural Center in New York, the Cincinnati Art Museum, and the J. Paul Getty Museum in Los Angeles. Both were accompanied by splendid catalogues, edited by, respectively, D. Alexandre-Bidon and P. Riché (Paris, 1994) and J. Neils and J. H. Oakley (New Haven, 2003).

and the various social and religious registers within which those practices took place. She highlights in passing the vulnerability of women, who always somehow bore the ultimate responsibility for infertility or other difficulties. Evidently children were deemed to be a completely female business. This attitude was reinforced by the fact that their main source of food in the first year was breastfeeding. This continued well into the third year, as Chryssi Bourbou and Sandra Garvie-Lok were able to ascertain through their very stimulating study of stable nitrogen isotopes in preserved skeletons. Comparative material makes clear that the Byzantines weaned their children considerably later than some Western societies, including Frankish populations in Greece, although the technique used cannot detect the difference between maternal breastfeeding and wet-nursing.

Wanting a child and breastfeeding it for a long period are of course relatively ambivalent signs of affection. Considering the importance of lineage continuity, the social pressure to have children was high, and the desire for children was also a function of a woman's need to provide an heir for the family and to conform to a social model. As for breastfeeding, promoted today as the locus of essential "bonding" between mother and child, it probably had very different connotations in Byzantium. Medical literature and other sources indicate that wet-nursing was the preferred model, even though it did come at a cost and was consequently mainly accessible to the elites.[30] The role of breastfeeding in birth control and providing immunity from infection were probably important factors in its success, undoubtedly more so than its emotional value.

Feelings toward children who were clearly perceived as such certainly existed in Byzantine families. However, such feelings are not incompatible with practices we consider today to be signs of indifference, cynicism, or even cruelty. As in most societies other than the postwar West, children functioned primarily as assets to their families and the other social groups of which they were part. They were used in the alliance strategies of the elites, on the farms of the peasantry, and in the workshops of the urban artisans. Childhood, as Peter Stearns has tried to show, depends first and foremost on the prevailing economic system, and this is as true today as it was in the Middle Ages—only we consider consumerism a better fate for children than work on farms.[31] That a child was expected

---

30   See J. Beaucamp, "L'allaitement: Mère ou nourrice ?" in *XVI. Internationaler Byzantinistenkongress: Akten* 2, no. 2 (= *JÖB* 32, no. 2 [1983]: 549–58) on the late antique period.
31   P. N. Stearns, *Childhood in World History* (London, 2006), 131–32 and passim.

to share in the family's hardships did not necessarily signal a lack of affection, and the fact that grief at the death of a child could include worry about the family's economic future did not make that grief less real. The anthropologist Bernard Vernier has convincingly shown how feelings, even the most sincere, often follow preconceived social patterns, especially within kin groups, and how they are linked both to set naming practices and to the circulation of wealth within families.[32]

To this point I have presented only one part of the story. Several of the papers here show that there was also a grimmer side to the picture. As Alice-Mary Talbot shows, mortality rates in Byzantium were very high, as in most premodern societies. This affected children in many ways: first because they were the primary victims of many diseases, but also because of the deaths of the adults who cared for them, which left behind a comparatively high proportion of orphans. This category is strikingly present in our sources, the more so as these sources usually do not distinguish between orphans and children who were abandoned in infancy.[33]

Günter Prinzing's overview of legal literature reveals that children were also considered legally and criminally responsible from a very early age, usually around seven. The penalties they had to suffer were no different from those of adults who had committed the same crimes, although some legal collections were more forgiving than others, raising the age of responsibility to ten or even fifteen years of age.

It is, however, the article by Richard Greenfield that presents a more consistently negative picture. This unconventional study of children in monasteries opens up a world of child abuse on which most other sources are silent. When one reads what monastic founders or authors had to say about children, sexual abuse seems to have been not only widespread but considered entirely normal and not in the least prejudicial to the child. Abuse, however, does not seem to have been a category recognized by the Byzantines. Indeed, the problem as presented by monastic writers is not the damage done to a child by a monk who could not control his libido, but rather the damage done to the monk's claim to impassibility (ἀπάθεια) by some charming, overly desirable child. It is precisely

---

32   B. Vernier, *La genèse sociale des sentiments: Aînés et cadets à Karpathos* (Paris, 1992).
33   The sources are brought together in Miller, *Orphans of Byzantium*, which does not, however, address the issue statistically. Abandonment is a topic on which much has been written for the ancient and medieval worlds: see J. Boswell, *The Kindness of Strangers: The Abandonment of Children in Western Europe from Late Antiquity to the Renaissance* (New York, 1988).

this concern that reveals the practice to us so bluntly, and presumably it was not entirely confined to the monastic world. Secular laws punishing young passive homosexuals confirm that the practice was quite common. Some form of sexual abuse may also have hidden behind tales of guardians who treated their orphaned wards abusively, reflecting what was probably a cruder reality than the idyllic stories we find in holy biographies.

This is not to say that child abuse was a universal practice, in monasteries or elsewhere. As Greenfield argues, monastic literature tends to overstate and overrepresent a number of obsessions that were part of the monastic state, as well as topoi of monastic literature from its very beginnings in late antiquity. The fact that sexual abuse of children is not otherwise mentioned in Byzantine sources rather indicates that it was the object of some form of taboo and thus not entirely endorsed by prevailing social values.

This issue brings us back to some of the broader questions evoked earlier. Perhaps Nicholas Orme's assertion that medieval society was "ourselves" a thousand years ago does contain some truth, albeit not—or not only—in the sense intended by the author. Human societies at all times exhibit both the best and the worst in moral terms, and what historians choose to highlight or insist on depends on a number of complex factors. Childhood history evidently remains an emotionally charged field, where identification still prevails over distantiation, and where the historicization of concepts has not yet reached full maturity.

A society's manner of dealing with children is used to pass value judgments and to assess its degree of humanism or civilization. One example of such an assessment that is central to the study of the late antique and medieval worlds argues for a "discovery" of childhood brought about not by the Enlightenment but by Christianity. The idea has circulated for some time but has never been expressed quite as explicitly as in Odd Bakke's recent book, with the telling title *When Children Became People: The Birth of Childhood in Early Christianity*.[34] Until the Christian era, we are told, on the basis of the writings of Aristotle and other philosophers, children were considered more like animals than like humans, and a child's opinion counted no more than that of an animal.[35] Children were more easily abandoned, killed, or sexually abused because there were no church fathers to stir people's consciences about such matters.[36] Only with

---

34   O. M. Bakke, *When Children Became People: The Birth of Childhood in Early Christianity*, trans. B. McNeil (Minneapolis, 2005).
35   Ibid., 16.
36   Ibid., 15–55 and passim.

the Christian idea that the newborn child has an individual soul did children at last become full members of humanity.

Needless to say, this analysis is as biased an interpretation as that of Ariès, but without the extenuating circumstance of pioneering an uncertain new field. Taking philosophical and theological arguments to be the driving principles of a society gives an image of it that is as removed from reality as an ivory-tower intellectual's existence is from life in Las Vegas, if not more so. Any society—even ours—happily disregards children's opinions (witness the use of words like *childish* and *infantile*) and considers that most of the time they talk nonsense (literally the Aristotelian ἄλογον), but this tendency is obviously not made into a social or existential principle; and there were Greek moralists well before Christianity who condemned abandonment and infanticide, as Archibald Cameron showed as early as 1932.[37] Evidently, too, things went on much as they had done in the areas targeted by Bakke well into the Christian centuries, and, as Richard Greenfield's solid evidence shows, even at the heart of the most Christian of institutions. It is important to dismantle the myth that children's lives were transformed with the coming of Christianity that underpins many accounts of the history of childhood in late antiquity, even when they make but a cursory appearance in studies devoted to other subjects.

Despite the similarities in the ways, good and bad, that various societies have viewed and treated children, there is something recognizably Byzantine about the children who have occupied the authors of this volume. What makes the attitudes of this specific society different? Obviously children are desired; they cry, play, die, and are mourned; they are noisy and disruptive; and they are retrospectively constructed as early prodigies when in later life they have become important. These tendencies are hardly different from what we see in our own societies or in scores of others. It is the specific ways in which these things are done—the choices made among a host of possibilities for contraception, baby food, toys and games, mourning—the intricate pattern woven by the combination of all those elements, and the relative value a society puts on them, that create a culture's unique and recognizable flavor. In Byzantium, the subtle interaction of Roman law, Christian principles, Greek language, and the Eastern Mediterranean cultural substratum resulted in a wealth of vocabulary to describe

---

37   A. Cameron, "The Exposure of Children and Greek Ethics," *Classical Review* 46 (1932): 105–14. Yet still in the influential *Late Antiquity: A Guide to the Post-classical World*, ed. O. Grabar, G. Bowersock, and P. Brown (Harvard, 1999), 373, s.v. *children, exposure of,* one reads that with Christianity such practices "ceased to be morally neutral."

the first stages of life that neither Ariès nor even his critics could find in Western medieval societies. The all-pervading, if artfully adapted, model of Constantine and the ever-present Cappadocian fathers, the very particular relationship to the dominating presence of Constantinople, the links to the Christian world of the former eastern provinces, and the role played in people's lives by the Theotokos combined to make their world Byzantine beyond doubt. Constant interaction with adults, the unconscious interiorization of the cultural values observed and acted out as natural, allowed every child to be inculturated and thus to contribute to the identity of Byzantium as a distinct state and culture. Well beyond the touching, exasperating, or sometimes even revolting anecdotes about children that are scattered throughout this volume, well beyond the history of childhood as a subject in its own right, understanding the first stages of life and the ways in which they were handled can help us to better comprehend Byzantine culture and society in general and can open up new avenues to a closer definition of the *Homo byzantinus*—or rather of the *homines byzantini,* as we must certainly make room for much chronological and regional variation.

University of Oxford

OBSERVATIONS ON THE LEGAL STATUS OF CHILDREN AND THE STAGES OF CHILDHOOD IN BYZANTIUM

Günter Prinzing

T HE OVERALL TOPIC OF THIS ESSAY is extremely complex and cannot be treated exhaustively and comprehensively in the space of an article.[1] Therefore I have chosen to focus on the status of legitimate children (γνήσιοι παῖδες) in Byzantium, leaving out illegitimate children (φυσικοὶ [νόθοι] παῖδες),[2] orphans,[3] and the children of slaves.[4] In addition, this paper does not deal with the various forms of adoption (υἱοθεσία).[5]

The author expresses his gratitude to Arietta Papaconstantinou and Alice-Mary Talbot for their kind support and many suggestions on improving the text, to the anonymous readers for their helpful critical remarks, and finally to John Michael Deasy in Mainz for the translation.

1 For a general introduction to the history and sources of Byzantine law, see K. E. Zachariä von Lingenthal, *Geschichte des griechisch-römischen Rechts,* 3rd ed. (1892; repr. Aalen, 1955); P. E. Pieler, "Byzantinische Rechtsliteratur," in H. Hunger, *Die hochsprachliche profane Literatur der Byzantiner* (Munich, 1978), 2:341–480; Pieler, "Byzantinisches Recht," *LMA* 2:1221–27; S. Troianos, *Οι πηγές του βυζαντινού δικαίου: Δεύτερη έκδοση συμπληρωμένη* (Athens, 1999). On more specialized topics, see A. Kazhdan, "Law, Civil," *ODB* 2:1191–93; M. T. Fögen, "Law, Roman, " *ODB* 2:1193–94; A. Schminck, "Ehe. D. Byzantinisches Reich," *LMA* 3:1641–44; idem, "Canon Law," *ODB* 1:372–74; L. Burgmann, "Strafe, Strafrecht. B. Spätantike und Byzanz," *LMA* 8:197–98.

2 See, for instance, J. Zepos and P. Zepos, eds., *Synopsis Basilicorum, ex editione C. E. Zachariae v.Lingenthal,* ed. *Jus graecoromanum* (Athens, 1931; repr. Aalen, 1962)*,* vol. 5 (hereafter Syn. Bas.) Π. 1.1 (= H. J. Scheltema, D. Holwerda, and N. van der Wal, eds., *Basilicorum libri LX, series A; Textus librum I–LX* [Groningen, 1953–88]) (hereafter Bas.), 28.4.57); J. Zhishman, *Das Eherecht der orientalischen Kirche* (Vienna, 1864), 719–23; H. Antoniadis-Bibicou, "Quelques notes sur l'enfant de la moyenne époque byzantine (du VIe au XIIe siècle)," *AnnalesDH* (1973): 80–81.

3 See T. Miller, *The Orphans of Byzantium: Child Welfare in the Christian Empire* (Washington, D.C., 2003).

4 G. Prinzing, "Sklaverei V. Byzanz," *Der Neue Pauly: Enzyklopädie der Antike,* ed. H. Cancik and H. Schneider (Stuttgart, 1996–2002), 11:630–32; Y. Rotman, *Les esclaves et l'esclavage de la Méditerranée antique à la Méditerranée médiévale, VIe–XIe siècles* (Paris, 2004).

5 See Antoniadis-Bibicou, "Quelques notes," 81; R. J. Macrides, "Kinship by Arrangement,"

Several contributions have already been made to the topic by Hélène Antoniadis-Bibicou, Évelyne Patlagean, and Ann Moffatt, and some aspects are covered in lexica and encyclopedia entries, to which I refer the reader for additional information. The excellent monograph by Antonia Kiousopoulou on the family in thirteenth-century Epiros also throws much light on legal questions.[6] The observations presented here are intended merely as an attempt to impose some order on the mass of relevant sources, which include collections of Byzantine civil and canon law (between which there is not always a clear distinction) and texts dealing with the administration of justice. This paper first surveys the terminology describing the stages of childhood in medical and common language and then examines the various regulations on the legal status of children and adolescents.

The Terminology of the Stages of Childhood

Before dealing with the specifically legal aspects, it seems appropriate to take a brief look at the vocabulary used in Byzantium to describe the stages of childhood and youth. In a recent book on childhood illnesses in Greek medicine, Christine Hummel examines the medical vocabulary pertaining to childhood and adolescence and shows that in antiquity childhood was defined as continuing until the fourteenth year.[7] This period was subdivided into four distinct stages:

1. Birth to first dentition, ca. 12 months
2. First dentition to weaning, ca. 2 years

DOP 44 (1990): 109–18; A. Kiousopoulou, *Ο θεσμός τῆς οἰκογένειας στὴν Ἥπειρο κατὰ τον 130 αἰώνα* (Athens, 1990), 158–62; and R. J. Macrides and A. Cutler, "Adoption," *ODB* 1:22; R. J. Macrides, "Substitute Parents and their Children in Byzantium," in *Adoption et fosterage,* ed. M. Corbier (Paris, 2000), 1–11.

6   Antoniadis-Bibicou, "Quelques notes" (above, n. 2); É. Patlagean, "L'enfant et son avenir dans la famille byzantine (IVe–XIIe siècle)," *AnnalesDH* (1973): 85–93; eadem, "L'entrée dans l'âge adulte à Byzance aux XIIIe–XIVe siècles," *Actes du colloque international "Historicité de l'enfance et de la jeunesse," Athènes, 1–5 octobre 1984* (Athens, 1986), 263–70; A. Moffatt, "The Byzantine Child," *Social Research* 53 (1986): 705–23; Kiousopoulou, *Θεσμός,* 131–43 (on the role of children within the family); A. Kazhdan, "Kind, II: Byzantinisches Reich," *LMA* 5:1145–47; J. Herrin, A. Kazhdan, and A. Cutler, "Childhood," *ODB* 1:420–21; M. Klijwegt and R. Amedick, "Kind," *RAC* 20:865–947, especially 866–98 and 904–39 (basic); J. Gaudemet, "Familie I (Familienrecht)," *RAC* 7:319–22, 336–37, 339–44, 346–52; J. Wiesehöfer, "Kind, Kindheit," *Der Neue Pauly* 6:464–66 (above, n. 4).

7   C. Hummel, *Das Kind und seine Krankheiten in der griechischen Medizin: Von Aretaios bis Johannes Aktuarios (1. bis 14. Jahrhundert)* (Frankfurt am Main, 1999), 300.

---

3. Third year to second dentition, 6–7 years
4. 6–7 years to puberty, ca. 14 years[8]

Hummel also briefly discusses the most common terms used by the Greeks to refer to children. It immediately becomes apparent that those very familiar terms βρέφος, παιδίον, παιδάριον, and παῖς, νήπιος were related to age, albeit in a very approximate way, and a term such as παῖς had almost as generic a connotation as *child* in English today—as well as metaphorical uses. The same was true of the term κόρη, used to refer to young girls or virgins.[9]

For Byzantinists, it might be of special interest here to mention one model of the stages of life that may be considered a Byzantine version of the ancient paradigm. It is described by the patriarch Photios in a poem written for an otherwise unknown Markellos.[10] The poem, formally presented as a hymn (ᾠδή), speaks of nine ages of human life. The first four ages cover childhood and youth. These are βρέφος (up to the age of 4), παιδίον (covering ages 4–10), βούπαις (from 10 to 18), and μειράκιον (between 18 and 20). The next age, ἀκμή, extends from 20 to 35, so that for Photios, childhood and youth are over by the twentieth year. This is precisely the end of childhood and youth in the Old Testament, a very likely source for Photios's scheme.[11]

In Byzantium, according to the tradition of Roman law, the age of 25 legally marked the end of childhood and youth.[12] Before that age, individuals were considered ἀφήλικες (or -λικοι).[13] However, Patlagean has correctly emphasized

8   Ibid., 97 but see there n. 247, about a different model for the stages of life, found in the *Corpus Hippocraticum* (Hp. hebd. 5). Dividing life into periods of no more than seven years, the model distinguishes the following early phases of the development of a man: παιδίον, up to the age of 7 years; παῖς, from the age of 7 to the first ejaculation; μειράκιον going up to the growth of beard (about 21), and νεανίσκος, in which the fully developed young man is formed.

9   Ibid., 97. For Byzantine legal definitions (or explanations) of the term παῖς, see also Bas. 2.2.53 (p. 28, lines 20–21) (= CIC *Dig* 50.16.56). Cf. Syn. Bas. P.1. 93; Bas. 2.2.196 (= CIC *Dig* 50.16.200 = Syn. Bas. P.1.124); Bas. 2.2.212 (p. 45, lines 11–12) (= CIC *Dig* 50.16.212 = Syn. Bas. P.1.125) (all above, n. 2).

10   N. B. Tomadakes, "Φωτίου, Ἡλικίαι ἀνθρώπων," Ἐπιστημονικὴ Ἐπετηρὶς Φιλοσοφικῆς Σχολῆς τοῦ Πανεπιστημίου Ἀθηνῶν 23 (1972–73): 9–16, esp. 10–14, text: 13–14. (The text of the poem is reproduced in T. Detorakes, Βυζαντινὴ φιλολογία: Τὰ πρόσωπα καὶ τὰ κείμενα [Heraklio, 2003], 2:569–70.)

11   See Klijwegt and Amedick, "Kind," 895 (above, n. 6); see also below on traces of Old Testament influence on legislation concerning children and juveniles.

12   See Fögen, "Law, Roman" (above, n. 1). Cf. also Kleijwegt and Amedick, "Kind," 890.

13   Patlagean, "L'entrée" (above, n. 6), 264–65, erroneously includes, besides ἀφῆλιξ and ἀφήλικος, also ἀνήλικος; but this term designates a minor under the age of 12/14; see table 2.1. See

that children were referred to as ὑπεξούσιοι so long as they remained dependent on or under the control of the father (or grandfather), unless they had been declared independent (αὐτεξούσιοι) by an act of emancipation.[14] Even in that case, young women remained legally disadvantaged in many respects compared to men.[15] The category of ὑπεξούσιοι includes, without distinction, all male and female members of the group of children and juveniles, because they were subject either to parental authority or, if the father (or grandfather) was no longer alive, to that of a guardian or curator.[16] A certain modification to these regulations, however, was introduced by novel 25 of Leo VI, which ruled "that the son who established an independent household should be granted legal independence (αὐτεξούσιον) regardless of any formal procedure of emancipation."[17]

Some further terms referring to Byzantine children and juveniles between ages 1 and 25 are given by Antoniadis-Bibicou; others can be found in Kiousopoulou's book, as well as in Erich Trapp's *Lexikon zur byzantinischen Gräzitat* (= *LBG*).[18] Nurslings and infants of ages approximately 1 to 3 years are described

also Antoniadis-Bibicou, "Quelques notes" (above, n. 2), 77; Moffatt, "Byzantine Child" (above, n. 6), 705–6. Cf. also E. Eyben, "Jugend," *RAC* 19, esp. 411–18, 421–22, 430–36.

14   Patlagean, "L'entrée," 265; cf. also Herrin, Kazhdan, and Cutler, "Childhood" (above, n. 6), 421. However, Romano-Byzantine law also refers to the category of αὐτεξούσιοι as still being children, viz. minors, in need of a *tutor* or *curator:* see Zachariä von Lingenthal, *Geschichte* (above, n. 1), 106, and n. 16 below.

15   See J. Beaucamp, "La situation juridique de la femme à Byzance," *Cahiers de civilisation médiévale* 20 (1977): 145–76; eadem, *Le statut de la femme à Byzance (4e–7e siècle),* 2 vols. (Paris, 1992); eadem, "La christianisation du droit à Byzance: L'exemple du statut des femmes," *Cristianità d'Occidente e cristianità d'Oriente (secoli VI–XI)* (Spoleto, 2004) (= *Settimane* 51, special issue), 2:917–55; A. Laiou, "Frau. d. Byzantinisches Reich," *LMA* 4:867–73, and J. Herrin, A. Kazhdan, and A. Cutler, "Women," *ODB* 3:2201–4.

16   In Justinan's *Corpus Juris Civilis,* the guardian was called *tutor* (ἐπίτροπος) if he took care of children under 12–14, or *curator* (κουράτωρ) if he took care of juveniles between 12–14 and 25 years old (see, e.g., *Institutiones* 1, 22, and 23); see also Zachariä v. Lingenthal, *Geschichte* (above, n. 1), 120. The differences between *tutor* and *curator* later disappeared. Cf. also N. van der Wal, ed., *Manuale Novellarum Justiniani: Aperçu systématique du contenu des novelles de Justinien* (Groningen, 1998), 65 n. 59.

17   See Herrin, Kazhdan, and Cutler, "Childhood" (above, n. 6), 421; cf. also Zachariä von Lingenthal, *Geschichte,* 125. For the text of the novel, see P. Noailles and A. Dain, *Les Novelles de Léon VI le Sage: Texte et traduction* (Paris, 1944), 99, lines. 26–101, 5. On the novels of Leo VI in general, see *Regesten der Kaiserurkunden des Oströmischen Reiches von 565–1453,* ed. F. Dölger, part 1, vol. 2, *Regesten von 867–1025,* 2nd rev. ed., ed. Andreas A. Müller and Alexander Beihammer (Munich, 2003), no. 513a (with further references).

18   Antoniadis-Bibicou, "Quelques notes" (above, n. 2), 77 n. 1. All additions to her list are taken from *LBG* and thus denoted. Kiousopoulou, Θεσμός (above, n. 4), 132–33 (terms and expressions taken from there are designated by *K*).

as νεογνὸν παιδίον (newborn), ὑπομάσθιον,[19] or ὑπομάζιον παιδίον (nursling). A term such as νήπιον (infant) seems to be broader in meaning, as it is used both for children in their very early years and for 4- to 7-year-olds. Thus the expressions ἐκ νηπίας ἡλικίας[20] and νηπιόθεν usually mean "from childhood [infancy] onward" without indicating exact age.[21] This usage overlaps with terms like μειράκιον (boy, youth) and νεανίσκος (juvenile, young man), which, like κόρη, probably designate children of ages approximately 6 to 14 years as well as those of ages 14 to approximately 18 or 20.[22] Τέκνον (child) is another general term that covers several age groups, as a counterpart to παῖς.[23] Other terms found are νηπίαχον (*LBG,* infant), μικρὸν παιδίον (K, child aged 8), παίδιος (*LBG,* boy, lad), παιδίσκος, παιδίτζιν (*LBG, K,* both meaning *child* in the sense of ἄνηβος), υἱός (son), and θυγάτηρ (daughter).

These terms from the common vocabulary in Byzantium were supplemented by terms more specific to the legal vocabulary. Other than the classic history of Byzantine law by Karl-Eduard Zachariä von Lingenthal, the most helpful works for this search are the excellent glossary, in the edition by Konstantinos Pitsakes, of the late Byzantine compendium of secular Byzantine law compiled by Konstantinos Harmenopoulos (1320–1383), titled *Hexabiblos;*[24] a paper by Menelaos Tourtoglou about minors in Byzantine criminal law;[25] the comprehensive monograph by Joëlle Beaucamp on the legal status of women in the early Byzantine period;[26] and the older Λεξιλόγιον ἐκκλησιαστικοῦ δικαίου by E. Roussos.[27] The additional terms identified from these sources are listed in table 1.

19   See Antoniadis-Bibicou, "Quelques notes," 77 n. 1 (probably erroneously given as ὑπομάσγιον).

20   Beaucamp, *Statut de la femme* (above, n. 15), 2:120.

21   *LBG,* s.v., rendered by Trapp as "von Kindheit an," that is, "from childhood on," but perhaps more precise would be "von früher Kindheit an," that is, "from infancy on."

22   See Klijwegt and Amedick, "Kind" (above, n. 6), 866.

23   Originally, τέκνον probably designated the child as the mother's "offspring, born"; see Hummel (above, n. 7, 97), and Klijwegt and Amedick, "Kind," 866. According to Bas. 2.2.101 (= CIC *Dig* 50.16.104) = Syn. Bas. P.1.151 (above, n. 2), the term *teknon* applies also to grandchildren. Finally, the term is also used neutrally of "spiritual children," who can be adults.

24   *Κωνσταντίνου Ἁρμενοπούλου Πρόχειρον Νόμων ἢ Ἑξάβιβλος,* ed. K. Pitsakes (Athens, 1971), 387ff., whose book I, titles 12, 13, and 17 (= pp. 69–82, 89–91) is extensively cited by Patlagean, "L'entrée" (above, n. 6), 264 n. 1. On Harmenopoulos and his work, see below. On the author, see P. E. Pieler, "Konstantinos 3. K. Armenopulos," *LMA* 5:1398; M. T. Fögen, "Harmenopoulos, Constantine," *ODB* 2:902.

25   M. Tourtoglou, "Οἱ ἀνήλικοι στὸ βυζαντινὸ καὶ μεταβυζαντινὸ ποινικὸ δίκαιο," Πρακτικὰ τῆς Ἀκαδημίας Ἀθηνῶν 60 (1985): 362–82.

26   Beaucamp, *Statut de la femme* (above, n. 15); see especially the index in vol. 2.

27   E. Roussos, Λεξιλόγιον ἐκκλησιαστικοῦ δικαίου, Βυζαντινὸν δίκαιον (Athens, 1948).

If we take into account the terms already presented, we can distinguish three categories (apart from ἐνήλικος/ἐνῆλιξ, which designate adults), each describing a relatively specific age or status group among children and juveniles:

terms applied to the group of children aged from approximately 3 to 7: ἄνηβος, νήπιος, -ον, and ἴμφας[28]

terms applied to children aged from 7 to 12–14: ἄνηβος, ἀνήλικος/ἀνῆλιξ, and ἐλάττων

terms applied to children or juveniles aged from 13–15 to 25: ἔφηβος, ἀφῆλιξ/ἀφήλικος, and νέος[29]

Note that in this list, ἄνηβος is the opposite of ἔφηβος, and ἀνῆλιξ is the opposite of ἀφῆλιξ.

This lexically oriented part of the paper concludes with a brief look at the Latino-Greek legal lexica from the Byzantine period, which have been published in volumes 6 and 8 of the Frankfurt *Fontes minores*. Here we find, for example, in the lexicon for the *Hexabiblos aucta,* compiled around 1400, the note that the term υἱός "covers all παῖδες, male and female," and that "the designation ὑπεξούσιοι also includes grandchildren (ἔγγονοι)."[30] The Lexicon ἄδετ (compiled between the ninth and the thirteenth centuries) translates *infans* by ὁ ἑπταέτης, "the 7-year-old"; the *proximos infanti* as ἐγγὺς τῶν ιβ' ἐτῶν, thus as an "almost 12-year-old"; and the *proximos pubertati* as δεκατεσσάρων ἐτῶν, that is to say as an (almost) "14-year-old."[31] In the so-called Lexicon αὐσηθ (tenth–eleventh centuries) and its

28   Concerning this group of young children, we owe an important reference to a brief passage on the delimitation of age groups among children to Spyros Troianos's article about the penalties in Byzantine law: S. Troianos, "Die Strafen im byzantinischen Recht: Eine Übersicht," *JÖB* 42 (1992): 55–74. The text he quotes at 59 n. 22 is found in a version of the *Institutiones* paraphrase by Theophilos (3. 9.10) in Cod. Sinait. 1117 and states: "The age of the orphan is subdivided into three stages: because there are the ἴμφαντες . . . θηλάζοντες, who are still nurslings, and a little older (thus the approximately 1–3-year olds), then the so-called πρόξιμοι ἴμφαντες, that is those who are beginning to speak well, and finally the πρόξιμοι πουβερτάτοι, namely those approaching puberty." Accordingly our group of young children is seen here as subdivided into the two groups mentioned above, while the third group mentioned in the text is to be identified with the following group of children, ages 7 to 12/14. But cf. also my discussion in the following paragraph!

29   See also the paragraph summarizing the various terms for children and adolescents in Tourtoglou, "Οἱ ἀνήλικοι" (above, n. 25), 367 (with further references to sources).

30   See M. T. Fögen, "Das Lexikon zur Hexabiblos aucta," *FM* 8 (1990): 211 (Y 2): "Τῇ τοῦ υἱοῦ προσηγορίᾳ πάντες οἱ παῖδες καὶ ἄρρενες καὶ θήλειαι περιέχονται, καὶ τῇ τῶν ὑπεξουσίων καὶ οἱ ἔγγονοι περιέχονται" (with app. font.).

31   L. Burgmann, "Das Lexikon ἄδετ: Ein Theophiloskommentar," *FM* 6 (1984): 46, I. 39; 56, Π. 57–58 (in line 58 the word ἐγγὺς from line 57 should be [mentally] added before δεκατεσσάρων). Concerning the translation of *infans*, see also the Lexikon αὐσηθ.

TABLE I

Byzantine legal terms for childhood and adolescence

Term	Definition	Sources and literature
ἄνηβος	*Impubes;* still immature, not yet pubescent (also: minor); aged between 7 (or even 3) and 14 (in the case of girls, 12)	Pitsakes, *Hexabiblos,* 389 Roussos, 49
ἀνηβότης	*Impubertas;* not adult, of minority age *(Unmündigkeit, Minderjährigkeit)*	Roussos, 49 Trapp, *LBG*
ἔφηβος	*Pubes;* pubescent, sexually mature, marriageable, (qualified) major, but still in minority: aged between 12–14 and 25	= ἀφῆλιξ, cf. *Michaelis Pselli Poemata,* ed. L. G. Westerink (Stuttgart, 1992), poem 8, p. 134, lines 270–71; see Tourtoglou, 367; Roussos, 219; Pitsakes, *Hexabiblos,* 392 (s.v. *aphelix*)
ἐφηβότης, τελεία ἐφηβότης	Maturity: *Reifezeit, Mannbarkeit* (age of full maturity, 18 onward)	Trapp, *LBG* Antoniadis-Bibicou, "Quelques notes," 78
ἀνήλικος/ ἀνῆλιξ	*Impubes; nondum adultus, minor;* immature (in the sense of ἄνηβος), minor under 15 or 13 (*Ecloga* 5.1)	Cf. *Ecloga* 2.5.2–3, 2.8.1, 5.1; Roussos, 50; Pitsakes, *Hexabiblos,* 389, 392; Tourtoglou, 367 n. 17; cf. Zachariä von Lingenthal, *Geschichte,* 122, and Trapp, *LBG*
ἀνηλικιότης	*Aetas infirma;* age of minority, *Unmündigkeit, Minderjährigkeit*	Roussos, 50; Trapp, *LBG*
ἀφῆλιξ, ἀφήλικος	*Pubes;* minor in the sense of ἔφηβος	Roussos, 97; Pitsakes, *Hexabiblos,* 392
ἀφηλικιότης	*Minderjährigkeit*	Trapp, *LBG*

(*continued next page*)

TABLE I (*continued*)

ἐνήλικος, ἐνῆλιξ	*Major, pubes;* adult, of full age (25) becoming adult	Roussos, 174; Beaucamp, *Le statut,* 2:166 n. 56
ἐνηλικιότης	*Matura aetas;* majority (age of majority)	Roussos, s.v. ἐνῆλιξ, 174; Trapp, *LBG*
ἀτελής ([τῆς] ἡλικίας)	Minor	Cf. Beaucamp, *Le Statut,* 2:377–78; Roussos, 91; Pitsakes, *Hexabiblos,* 392
ἐλάττων	Minor in the sense of ἀνῆλιξ, -ικος	Roussos, 165; Pitsakes, *Hexabiblos,* 398
ἔννομος ἡλικία	Age of maturity (*gesetzliches Alter, Volljährigkeit*)	*Ecloga,* 2.5.2 (210)
ἥττων, ἥττονες	Minor in the sense of ἀφῆλιξ, in contrast to: μείζων, the adult. (But, according to Roussos, s.v., ἥττων = *anhelikos.*)	Roussos, 225; Pitsakes, *Hexabiblos,* 402
ἴμφας	Infant under 7 years old (similarly νήπιος), or 7-year-old	Tourtoglou, 367; Pitsakes, *Hexabiblos,* 403
νέος	*Juvenis;* juvenile, but also minor in the sense ἀνῆλιξ, -ικος, ἥττων (see Roussos)	Pitsakes, *Hexabiblos,* 409; Roussos, 310; Patlagean, "L'entrée," 264

derivatives, the term *infans* (or *infati*) is explained by its Greek counterparts as νήπιον/-ς or ἑπταετής[32] or νήπιος, ἑπταετής.[33] In the same lexicon, ἄνηβος (ἄρρην [male]), given only in Greek without its Latin counterpart, is explained, depending on the version, as κατώτερος τῶν ιδ' χρόνων, thus as "someone under 14 years old"[34] or as ὁ μήπω πληρώσας τὸν <ι>δ' χρόνον, ἐπὶ δὲ τῶν θηλειῶν τὸν ιβ', consequently as "one who has not yet attained the age of 14 years, or 12 years for girls,"[35]

32   L. Burgmann, "Das Lexikon αὐσηθ," *FM* 8 (1990): 249–337, here 270 I-2, and (in the *Laurentianus* Lexikon) 307, I-3, and 308, I-20.

33   Ibid., 335, I-2 (Lexikon *adnoumion*).

34   Ibid., 262, A-5.

35   Ibid., 297, A-31 (*Laurentianus* Lexikon; according to the app. font. based on Theophilos, 1.22 prooemium).

whereas ἔφηβος is rendered there as ὁ ἐπέκεινα τῶν ιε' ἐτῶν, thus as "someone over 15 years old."[36] Striking here is the explanation of the term ἥβη (sexual maturity) as ἡ τρίχωσις τοῦ σώματος ἢ τὸ ὑπερβεβηκέναι τὸ ιδ' ἔτος, ἐπὶ δὲ τῶν θηλειῶν τὸ ιβ', thus "the body's becoming hairy or being older than 14, however, in the case of girls, older than 12."[37] Finally, in the Lexikon Μαγκίπιουν, whose origin (Crete?) and date are hard to determine, the term μινόριβους (minoribus) is to be found rendered simply as ἔλαττον, ἥττον, that is, "minor."[38]

Regulations on the Legal Status of Children and Adolescents

What follows is a survey of regulations regarding children and adolescents from two principal groups of sources. The first consists of the ecclesiastical canons up to the eighth century; the second group consists of secular legal texts (including novels), from the *Ecloga* (741) up to the aforementioned *Hexabiblos*. (My comments on these texts also include a short remark on the possible influence of the Bible on Byzantine regulations concerning children's rights and duties.) Thus I refer in detail only occasionally to the legal regulations of Justinian I, although they formed the basis for much of the Byzantine legal system.[39]

The references here are divided into two main groups: those concerning minors in the sense of ἄνηβοι, that is, children under the ages of 12 (girls) or 14 (boys), and those concerning children or young people virtually in their majority (ἀφήλικες), thus those over 12/14 years.[40]

Minor Children/ἄνηβοι up to the Age of 12/14

Some general rules concerning this group are found in two canons from church synods. In canon 15 of the synod of Gangra (around 340, Cappadocia), those who forsake their children (τέκνα) and do not educate them in respectful piety,

36   Ibid., 306, E-81 (*Laurentianus* Lexikon); cf. there also 280 Π-19 (and equally 320, Π-6 [*Laurentianus* Lexikon], where *pubertati* [or *pubertatos*] is translated as ἔφηβος.

37   Ibid., 307, H-6 (*Laurentianus* Lexikon; according to the app. font. based on Theophilos, 1.22 pr.), here also a Latin counterpart is lacking.

38   B. H. Stolte, "Lexikon Μαγκίπιουν," *FM* 8 (1990): 357, M 27.

39   For the regulations in his novels that concern children and juveniles, see van der Wal, *Manuale* (above, n. 16), especially nos. 492–514, and cf. index, s.v. *mineur*.

40   Whereby group 1, it would seem, consists of two subgroups, namely infants and children up to approximately 10 years of age on the one hand, and juveniles and those of marriageable age on the other: the subgroups are not always clearly differentiated in the sources.

but neglect them under the pretext of asceticism, are anathematized.[41] Canon 14 of the second council of Nicaea (787) stipulates that only ordained clerics should deliver the readings from the ambo. This regulation would exclude those who had already received the tonsure in early childhood (νηπιόθεν) without having been ordained by the bishop, but who nevertheless delivered the readings.[42] In special cases, however, the possibility of allowing a child to deliver the readings could be at least discussed, as can be seen from canon 54 of the synod of Carthage (419), which rules on the dispute between Bishop Epigonos and Bishop Julian with regard to a needy child who had been baptized and brought up by Epigonos from early childhood (ἀπὸ νηπίας ἡλικίας) before becoming lector at a provincial church for two years.[43]

Another text, the first *erotapokrisis* (question and answer) in the collection attributed to Timotheos of Alexandria (end of the fourth century), cites regulations reflecting the significance of the seventh year in the development of a young person's faith, conscience, and responsibility. Timotheos was asked: "If a child catechumen of approximately 7 years of age (παιδίον κατηχούμενον ὡς ἐτῶν ἑπτά), or also an adult catechumen, by chance comes to a Eucharist taking place somewhere and unwittingly participates in it, what must one do with him? *Answer:* He must be enlightened (baptized), because he has been summoned by God."[44] In other words, Timotheos seems to assume that a 7-year-old child would already have been baptized.

For our purposes, the importance of this erotapokrisis lies in its implications for children's liability to punishment, for which there are separate legal provisions. Children in Byzantium were not generally excluded from the "circle of delinquent persons," as might initially appear to be the case. In practice, any such exclusion applied only to the group of *infantes,* those under the age of 7, although even for them there was no "concrete, generally valid legal provision granting them a priori immunity from criminal punishment."[45] Raising the question of liability to punishment inevitably brings up the further question of whether the delinquent committed the punishable offense willfully and know-

---

41   P. P. Joannou, *Discipline générale antique (IVe–IXe s.),* vol. 1, part 2: *Les canons des synodes particuliers* (Grottaferrata, 1962), 95. See also below on canon 16 of the same synod.

42   P. P. Joannou, *Discipline générale antique (IIe–IXe s.),* part 1, 1: *Les canons des conciles oecuméniques* (Grottaferrata, 1962), 269–71.

43   Joannou, *Les canons des synodes particuliers,* 277–79.

44   P. P. Joannou, *Discipline générale antique (IVe–IXe s.),* part 2: *Les canons des Pères grecs* (Grottaferrata, 1963), 240–41.

45   Troianos, "Die Strafen" (above, n. 28), 58–59. Both quotations are from 59.

ingly; thus, when assessing the punishment to be imposed, jurists took into account both the minor's age and maturity and the circumstances of each individual case. This approach is clearly shown by the provisions on murder as well as those on sexual offenses.

Turning to secular law, while the *Ecloga* 17.45 (promulgated 741) still stipulated the penalty for premeditated murder as death for everyone, regardless of age,[46] the *Eisagoge* (*Epanagoge*), the first law book of the Macedonian dynasty, promulgated under Basil I in order to replace the *Ecloga,* stated in 40.85 that, as Troianos put it, "the punishment by the sword shall be permissible only if the offender has reached the age of seven."[47] Consequently, the following rule, 40.86 of the same law book (based on CIC *Dig* 48.8.12), stipulated with respect to younger children that "neither an *infant,* that is, a child up to the age of 7, nor the insane who has committed murder shall be punished by death."[48]

According to Troianos, who reminds us of the "notorious contradictory wording of the Roman legal sources with respect to the criminal capacity of the *infantes* in case of willful murder," there is a lack of clarity here, because "the wording of these laws allows the conclusion to be drawn" that even being under the age of seven "does not represent a general reason for exemption from punishment."[49] Despite this, Troianos notes that it was the legislation of the Macedonian dynasty (beginning with the *Eisagoge*) that clarified matters in this field with enduring regulations.[50] Therefore it is no surprise to find in the greatest law book of the Macedonian era, the *Basilika,* a rule (60.39.8 = CIC *Dig* 48.8.12) worded very similarly to *Eisagoge* 40.86, which excludes from the ambit

46 *Ecloga: Das Gesetzbuch Leons III. und Konstantinos' V,* ed. L. Burgmann (Frankfurt, 1983), 242–43 (taken over, inter alia, into the *Procheiros Nomos* 39.79 and into Κωνσταντίνου Ἁρμενοπούλου Πρόχειρον, ed. Pitsakes [above, n. 24], 6.6.3 [= p. 353]). Cf. Troianos, "Die Strafen," 59, with the restricting remark: "Angesichts der bekannten Widersprüchlichkeit der römischen Rechtsquellen in Bezug auf die Schuldunfähigkeit der *infantes* bei vorsätzlicher Tötung [with reference (n. 25) to CIC *CI* 9.16.5 and CIC *Dig* 48.8.12, G.P.] kann der Formulierung der Ecloga nicht eindeutig entnommen werden, ob hier auch die erste Altersstufe einbezogen ist," and Tourtoglou, "Οἱ ἀνήλικοι" (above, n. 25), 368.

47 Troianos, "Die Strafen," 59–60, cf. also Tourtoglou, "Οἱ ἀνήλικοι," 368, n. 21 (with further references). For the text of the law itself, see Zepos and Zepos, *Jus graecoromanum* (above, n. 2), 2:367: Ὁ φονεύων ἑκουσίως οὐκ ἐν μάχῃ, οἱασἂν εἴη ἡλικίας τὴν ἑπταετίαν παρελθούσης, ξίφει τιμωρείσθω. On the *Eisagoge,* see A. Schminck, "Epanagoge," *ODB* 1:793–94.

48 Zepos and Zepos, *Jus graecoromanum,* 2:367: Οὔτε ἴνφανς, τουτέστιν ἑπταέτης, οὔτε μαινόμενος φονεύων ὑπόκειται τῷ θανάτῳ. See Troianos, "Die Strafen" (above, n. 28), 60.

49 Troianos, "Die Strafen," 60.

50 Ibid., 59 (cf. also his statement quoted in n. 46). Cf. Tourtoglou, "Οἱ ἀνήλικοι," 368, n. 21 (with further references).

of criminal law those who have not reached the age of 7.[51] An especially interesting comment by a scholiast of this rule states that the ἴμφας (clearly the very young child, certainly under 7) will be exempt from punishment, as such a child does not intend or want to commit any unlawful act.[52] This statement indicates that Byzantine society wanted to protect young children (that is, those under 7) in general. This concern is also reflected in the fact that the killing or abandonment of nurslings (whether or not it resulted in death) incurred severe punishment, even death.[53]

The possibility of special provision for older children, too, is indicated by a passage of the *Basilika* that stated that no one was to go unpunished because of his or her age, which applied in the case of "someone approaching puberty" (πλησιάζων τῇ ἥβῃ τις)—that is, a minor aged about 11 to 14, old enough to be conscious of sin.[54] This issue was taken up by several later law books (even some from the post-Byzantine era).[55] It is echoed in a *scholion* to Bas. 60.51.46, which declares that a child who has committed a criminal act cannot expect any leniency, if the child was of an age to be capable of a malicious act.[56] Again there is no doubt about the importance of the seventh year, as a scholiast defines the minor mentioned above as ὁ ἐπέκεινα τῶν ἑπτὰ ἐτῶν, that is, "the one who is over 7."[57] Nevertheless, several other rules in the *Basilika* allude to the "minor approaching puberty" as being capable of fraud or of planning criminal acts.[58]

A short glance at the ecclesiastical source material shows that early on the

---

51   Bas. 60.39.8: Οὔτε ὁ μὴ ὢν ἑπταέτης οὔτε ὁ μαινόμενος φονεύων ὑπόκειται τῷ περὶ ἀνδροφόνων νόμῳ (above, n. 2). Cf. Tourtoglou, "Οἱ ἀνήλικοι," 368 with n. 21. On the *Basilika* in general, see A. Schminck and A. Kazhdan, "Basilika," *ODB* 1:265–66.

52   Schol. 2 ad Bas. 60.39.8: Τὸν μὲν γὰρ ἴμφαντα τὸ μὴ ἔχειν σκοπὸν ἢ βουλὴν τοῦ ἀδικῆσαι ὑπεξαιρεῖ τῆς τιμωρίας. Cf. Tourtoglou, "Οἱ ἀνήλικοι," 368.

53   Cf. Antoniadis-Bibicou, "Quelques notes" (above, n. 2), 79, mentioning *Epanagoge (Eisagoge),* 47.1 (*recte* 40.14) and Syn. Bas. N.3.1 (add:-2) (above, n. 2), but cf. also *Ecloga,* ed. Burgmann (above, n. 46), 243 (17.54, based on CIC *CI* 9.16.7), where the nursling is called νήπιον.

54   Bas. 60.51.46 (= CIC *CI* 9, 47, 8): Οὐδέποτε διὰ τὴν ἡλικίαν συγχωρεῖται ἡ τιμωρία τοῦ ἁμαρτήματος, μόνον ἐάν ἐστι πλησιάζων τῇ ἥβῃ τις, ὅτε καὶ αἰσθάνεται τῶν παρ' αὐτοῦ ἁμαρτανομένων. Cf. also Syn. Bas. Π.18.9.

55   See Tourtoglou, "Οἱ ἀνήλικοι," 368–69, with n. 23 (with further references, but read Bas. 60.51.46 instead of 45). Cf. also Troianos, "Die Strafen" (above, n. 28), 59–60.

56   Schol. 2 ad Bas. 60.51.46: Μήτε παιδίῳ συγχωρεῖται πλημμέλημα, ἐὰν γέγονεν ἡλικίας δεκτικῆς ἁμαρτήματος.

57   Schol. 22* ad Bas. 60.3.5; cf. Tourtoglou, "Οἱ ἀνήλικοι," 368–69.

58   See, e.g., Bas. 51.4.4. (= p. 2408, line 23 = CIC *Dig* 44.4.4): Καὶ ὁ πλησιάζων γὰρ τῇ ἥβῃ ἄνηβος δεκτικός ἐστι δόλου. Cf. Tourtoglou, "Οἱ ἀνήλικοι," 368, with n. 18, and—with respect to Roman law—Klijwegt and Amedick, "Kind" (above, n. 6), 890. Also Bas. 2.3.111 (= CIC *Dig* 50, 17,111) and 10.3.13 (= CIC *Dig* 4.3.13).

church had similarly taken into consideration children's mental development by trying to define more precisely the age at which a child could be held responsible for a breach of the law. In the *Erotapokrisis* 18*, falsely attributed to Timotheos of Alexandria, the author answered the question about the age from which (ἀπὸ ποίας κείρας) God passes judgment for sins by stating that there were many distinctions, because each individual would be judged according to his knowledge and his discernment or wisdom: some from the age of ten, but others when they were older (μείζονες).[59] However, with regard to this question, the twelfth-century canonist Balsamon emphasized in his commentary that the diversity of human nature did not allow the fixing of such age limits.[60]

Returning to secular matters, considerations of this kind were being applied in concrete terms in criminal law already in the *Ecloga* (17.38), which, with regard to homosexuals, quite contrary to the earlier legislation of Justinian's time, stipulates that the under-12-year-old partner of those having homosexual intercourse (which was in itself subject to the death penalty), "if he is the passive partner, shall gain forgiveness: because his age shows that he did not know what was happening to him."[61] According to Troianos, the age limit is set higher here (compared to the age of 7), presumably on account of the type of offense, which presupposes the partner's sexual maturity.[62] And Tourtoglou emphasizes that this regulation remained unchanged up to the time of later compilations of laws.[63] The age limit and punishment varied, however, because the *Eklogadion* (early ninth century) stipulates that the special treatment of the juvenile passive homosexual shall be extended up to the age of 15 (17.6). The *Eklogadion* replaces exemption from punishment (stipulated by the *Ecloga*) by corporal punishment combined with compulsory committal to a monastery—a reform *in peius,* as Troianos, the coeditor of the *Eklogadion,* called this regulation.[64] The

---

59   Joannou, *Les canons des Pères grecs* (above, n. 44), 252. Cf. Troianos, "Die Strafen," 59 n. 23.

60   G. Rhalles and M. Potles, eds., Σύνταγμα τῶν θείων καὶ ἱερῶν κανόνων, 4 (repr. Athens, 1966), 341; cf. Troianos, "Die Strafen," 59 n. 23, where, in addition, he comments that the same canonist Balsamon, in contrast to the correct remark he made here, had argued then in his canonical response no. 50 for the reduction of the age limit to the age of 6.

61   *Ecloga*, ed. Burgmann (above, n. 46), 238: Οἱ ἀσελγεῖς, ὅ τε ποιῶν καὶ ὁ ὑπομένων, ξίφει τιμωρείσθωσαν· εἰ δὲ ὁ ὑπομένων ἥττων τῶν δώδεκα ἐτῶν εὑρέθη, συγχωρείσθω ὡς τῆς ἡλικίας δηλούσης μὴ εἰδέναι αὐτόν, τί ὑπέμεινεν.

62   Troianos, "Die Strafen," 61. Cf. also the remarks of Patlagean, "L'enfant" (above, n. 6), 88, concerning *Ecloga* 17.38.

63   Tourtoglou, "Οἱ ἀνήλικοι," 370–71 (where Justinian's harsher regulations are also mentioned).

64   Troianos, "Die Strafen," 61, Text: D. Simon and S. Troianos, "Eklogadion and Ecloga privata

fact that otherwise a milder punishment is envisaged for persons who have not yet reached the age of 12 (for girls) or 14 (for boys) is to be seen from Bas. 35.16.1 (= CIC *Dig* 29.5.1.33), a passage which is preserved only in Cod. Sinait. gr. 1117 (fol. 16r). It stipulated: "Minors [ἄνηβοι] shall be neither punished nor tortured, but filled with fear, and beaten with a leather belt or cane."[65]

Rules on betrothal and marriage form by far the largest category of regulations. The basic principle is found in Syn. Bas. M. 15. 7, with reference to Bas. 28.1.12 (= CIC *Dig* 23.1.14): "He who understands what it is about, becomes well betrothed, i.e., [he] who is not younger than seven years of age."[66] Already Leo VI (886–912) in his novel 109 declared that betrothals of children younger than 7 were in general invalid, and only the emperor could make exceptions. At the same time he forbade, as also in novel 74, in confirmation of older legislation, the blessing by the church of betrothals of girls younger than 12 and boys younger than 14.[67] Here it can be seen for the first time that the church in particular was endeavoring to promote the convergence of betrothal and marriage.[68]

The regulations of Leo VI were modified by the legislation of Alexios I Komnenos (1081–1118). The latter's novel from June 1084[69] stipulated, among other things, that there is only a betrothal in the strict sense after a church blessing, and provided the betrothed are at least 12 (for girls) and 14 (for boys). On the other hand, provisional betrothals were marriage agreements concluded before the betrothed couple reached the stipulated ages: for these the older imperial law

aucta," *FM* 2 (1977): 71: Ὁ ἀσελγὴς ὅ τε ποιῶν καὶ ὁ ὑπομένων ξίφει τιμωρείσθω· ὁ δὲ ἥττων τῶν δεκαπέντε ἐτῶν τυπτέσθω καὶ ἐν μοναστηρίῳ εἰσαγέσθω, ὡς τῆς ἡλικίας δηλούσης τοῦτο ἀκουσίως πεπονθέναι αὐτόν.

65   Troianos, "Die Strafen," 60 n. 29, quoting there also the Sinaiticus (fol. 16r): οἱ ἄνηβοι οὐ κολάζονται, οὔτε βασανίζονται, φοβερίζονται δὲ καὶ λώρῳ ἢ νάρθηξι τύπτονται. Concerning the prohibition on torturing minors under 14, cf. Antoniadis-Bibicou, "Quelques notes" (above, n. 2), 78.

66   Zepos and Zepos, *Jus graecoromanum* (above, n. 2), 5:425: Ὁ τὸ γινόμενον νοῶν καλῶς μνηστεύεται, τουτέστιν ὁ μὴ ὢν ἥττων τῶν ἑπτὰ ἐτῶν. See Patlagean, "L'entrée" (above, n. 6), 265.

67   Noailles and Dain, *Les Novelles de Léon VI* (above, n. 17), 354–57, 262–65.

68   See Patlagean, "L'enfant" (above, n. 6), 88–89; A. Schminck, "Zur Entwicklung des Eherechts in der Komnenenepoche," in *Byzantium in the 12th Century: Canon Law, State and Society,* ed. N. Oikonomides (Athens, 1991), 557. Two synodal decrees of Patriarch John VIII Xiphilinos, issued 26 April 1066 and 19 March 1067, have made this tendency clear for the first time (V. Grumel and J. Darrouzès, *Les regestes des Actes du patriarcat de Constantinople,* vol. 1, *Les Actes des patriarches,* fasc. 2 and 3, *Les Actes de 715 à 1206,* 2nd rev. ed. [Paris, 1989], nos. 896 and 897). Emperor Nikephoros III Botaneiates confirmed the decrees at the synod's demand in 1080 (= *Regesten der Kaiserurkunden des Oströmischen Reiches von 565–1453,* ed. F. Dölger, part 2: *Regesten von 1025–1204,* 2nd rev. ed., ed. P. Wirth [Munich, 1995], no. 1048).

69   With respect to the decree of Nikephoros III Botaneiates from 1080.

applied. Therefore, the existing custom "of giving the blessings already after the children reached the age of 7 and then allowing the betrothed couple to associate freely with one another" was forbidden so long as they had not yet reached the legal age.[70] A later novel of Alexios I, issued in 1092, confirms the indissolubility of "proper" betrothals and the provisions of the previous novel, but emphasizes in addition, with reference to novel 109 of Leo VI, that the emperor had the right (κατ᾽ οἰκονομίαν) to grant a dispensation with respect to the age regulations.[71] Very often, however, these regulations were contravened in practice, even without an imperial dispensation, and betrothals were concluded before the age of seven at the parents' instigation. Several such marriages or betrothals were successfully contested later in court.[72] In any case, the regulations about the minimum age (12/14 years) for "proper" betrothal or marriage remained continuously in force. Finally, the consent (or assent) of both partners was a basic prerequisite for marriage—or, if one or both parties to a marriage were still of minority age, the assent of the fathers or guardians.[73]

To conclude this section, I cite a provision on the minimum age of entry for male juveniles into a monastery, in canon 40 issued by the council in Trullo (691): "We must not admit too soon nor without probation those who choose the monastic life, but must observe the decree passed down to us in this matter by the Fathers. Thus we ought to admit to the profession of the life according to God only those who have attained the age of reason and who have confirmed their choice by sure knowledge and judgment. Therefore, the one who takes upon himself the monastic yoke shall not be younger than ten years."[74] Founders

70 See Dölger and Wirth, *Regesten*, no. 1116 (with further references). The quote is from the regest.

71 See Dölger and Wirth, *Regesten*, no. 1167 (with further references). Add to the bibliography given there Patlagean, "L'enfant," 89. On *oikonomia*, see A. Papadakis, "Oikonomia," *ODB* 3:1516–17, and G. Prinzing, "Oikonomia," *LMA* 6:1381.

72 Patlagean, "L'enfant," 91–92, and eadem, "L'entrée," 266–67.

73 Cf. already canon 42 of Basil the Great, Joannou, *Les canons des Pères grecs* (above, n. 44), 135, l. 5–13, which stipulated that the marriage contracts of *hypexousioi* were valid only with the father's or curator's consent. See in addition Zhishman, *Das Eherecht* (above, n. 2), 616–31 (concerning the father's rights), 632–33 (concerning the mother's rights); Beaucamp, "La christianisation" (above, n. 15), 939–41. See also n. 16 above.

74 See G. Nedungatt and M. Featherstone, eds., *The Council in Trullo Revisited*, Kanonika 6 (Rome, 1995), 119–20: χρὴ μὴ ἀνεξετάστως ἡμᾶς παρὰ τὸν καιρὸν τοὺς τὸν μονήρη βίον αἱρουμένους προσίεσθαι, ἀλλὰ τὸν παραδοθέντα ἡμῖν παρὰ τῶν πατέρων καὶ ἐν αὐτοῖς φυλάττειν ὅρον· ὥστε τὴν ὁμολογίαν τοῦ κατὰ θεὸν βίου τότε προσίεσθαι δεῖ, ὡς ἤδη βεβαίαν καὶ ἀπὸ γνώσεως καὶ κρίσεως γινομένην, μετὰ τὴν τοῦ λόγου συμπλήρωσιν.Ἔστω τοίνυν ὁ μέλλων τὸν μοναχικὸν ὑπέρχεσθαι ζυγὸν οὐχ ἥττων ἢ δεκαετής.

of monasteries were, of course, absolutely free to demand in their *typika* a higher minimum age of admittance. Leo VI confirmed the regulation of the Trullan canon by novel 6, but with the restriction that the applicant should wait until he had reached the age of sixteen or seventeen, when he could dispose of his property.[75]

Minors in the Sense of Young People, ἔφηβοι or ἀφήλικες, Ages 12–14 to 25

Let us now turn to the older group of minors. I begin with a quotation from an early ecclesiastical source, the canons of the synod of Gangra, one of which (canon 16) stipulated as follows: "If children (τέκνα) of pious parents withdraw from worldly life under the pretext of worship of God and do not show their parents the due honor, because they give preference to the worship of God, may anathema be imposed upon them."[76] The synod of Gangra was directed against Eustathios and his followers, who preached a radical break with society and its norms based on some of the injunctions found in the gospels, a movement that pushed the "mainstream" church to make explicit its acceptance of the prevailing social order. This canon is very clear on the importance for the church of the principle of filial piety and obligations toward one's parents.

The principle formulated by the church was in line with Roman secular legislation and was consistently repeated in Byzantine secular law from Justinian onwards. Justinian's novel 115, for instance, lists fifteen reasons to disinherit children because of their ingratitude toward their parents, a passage that was later

75 Noailles and Dain, *Les Novelles de Léon VI* (above, n. 17), 32–35. See Antoniadis-Bibicou, "Quelques notes" (above, n. 2), 78; Patlagean, "L'entrée"(above, n. 6), 265, points to the fact that Nikephoros Blemmydes (thirteenth century) decreed in his typikon not only that the minimum age of admittance to his own monastic foundation should be at least 10, but that the novices had to pass two further stages of preliminary training: first a period of three years, until they reached the age of 12, then another period of at least seven years, after which, provided they had reached the age of 20, they could adopt the full monastic habit. See *Byzantine Monastic Foundation Documents*, ed. J. Thomas and A. Constantinides Hero (Washington, D.C., 2000), 3:1202–3 (trans. J. Munitiz). This regulation provides just one example of the fact that founders of monasteries were to a certain degree free to decide about the stages of the novitiate. Thus, a certain variation in practice is evident in this regard. See also below on the minimum age for girls for admission to a convent.
76 Joannou, *Les canons des synodes particuliers* (above, n. 41), 96. Cf. Zhishman, *Das Eherecht* (above, n. 2), 722.

incorporated into the *Basilika*.[77] Novel 155.1 deals with the respect and concern children should have for their parents.[78] However, all the above regulations, including the one from the synod of Gangra, likely applied not only to the children we are discussing here but also to adult offspring who still had one or both of their parents.[79]

Several other provisions regulate parent-child relationships, an important part of which deal with questions of property. *Ecloga* 2.5.1 stipulates that when the father dies before the mother, "Her children cannot confront her or demand paternal property from her, but must, on the contrary, show her every honor and obedience as their mother in accordance with God's commandment; of course, the mother must, as is fitting for parents, educate her children, give them in marriage and provide them with a marriage portion, as she considers correct. However, if she enters into a new marriage, her children may separate from her and accept their entire paternal heritage undiminished."[80]

Ecloga 2.5.2 deals with the case of the mother's predeceasing the father, and its provisions are in part analogous. It also stresses, quoting the Bible, that children shall honor their fathers and mothers.[81] However, the parents are also reminded of their duty, as the next section (2.5.3) says: "If one of the spouses, either the husband or the wife, wants to separate from their children (τέκνα) without entering into a second marriage, then he may not do so as long as the

---

77 Bas. 35.8.41 (= Syn. Bas. A.71.1, pp. 118–121 [above, n. 2]). On the novel, see T. Lounghis, B. Blysidu, and S. Lampakes, eds., *Regesten der Kaiserurkunden des oströmischen Reiches von 476 bis 565* (Nicosia, 2005), 309 no. 1261; cf. van der Wal, ed., *Manuale* (above, n. 16), 142–43. Concrete reference was also made to this in later Byzantine administration of justice, as shown, e.g., by Archbishop Demetrios Chomatenos, record no. 99; see *Demetrii Chomateni Ponemata diaphora*, ed. G. Prinzing, CFHB 38 (Berlin, 2002), 325, l. 66–70, but note that the text should be corrected in line 69: instead of καθὰ περὶ τούτων ὁ λη΄ τίτλ. τοῦ λε΄ βιβλίου, read καθὰ περὶ τούτων ὁ λη΄ < κεφ. τοῦ η΄ > τίτλ. τοῦ λε΄ βιβλίου. The record says nothing about the age of the children mentioned here, but they must have been without exception of adolescent age.

78 Cf. Beaucamp, *Le statut de la femme* (above, n. 15), 1:311. On the gratitude expected from children toward their parents, see also in general Zhishman, *Das Eherecht,* 723.

79 I thank Dr. Ludwig Burgmann, Frankfurt am Main, for drawing my attention to this.

80 *Ecloga,* ed. Burgmann (above, n. 46), 174, l. 185–92.

81 *Ecloga,* ed. Burgmann, 174–77. The text quotes Ex. 20:12; Deut. 5:16; Sirac. 3:8–9; 7.28; Eph. 6:1, 4. To my knowledge this is the only passage of an official legal text concerning children that is explicitly based on the Old Testament. Here I disregard the so-called *Nomos Mosaikos,* a collection of excerpts from books 2–5 of the Pentateuch, which never formed part of the official Byzantine imperial or ecclesiastical legislation. See L. Burgmann and S. Troianos, eds., "Nomos Mosaikos," *FM* 3 (1979): 126–67, text 140–67, and, most recently, A. Schminck, "Bemerkungen zum sog. *Nomos Mosaikos,*" *FM* 11 (2005): 249–68 (with further references).

children are still in their minority (ἀνηλίκων αὐτῶν τυγχανόντων), but must safeguard them and their property," in accordance with Saint Paul's First Epistle to Timothy 5:4.[82]

Among the general legal provisions that should also be mentioned here are all those that characterize the status of free persons subject to authority (ὑπεξούσιοι), such as the general ban on concluding contracts independently. Basil the Great also stresses this in his canon 40, with the observation that the contracts made by individuals who could not act freely would not be certain to endure and were thus invalid.[83]

With regard to the punishment of juveniles (ἀφήλικες), the general regulation from Bas. 60.59.2 (= CIC *CI* 9.15.1), which is repeated in Syn. Bas. Π.2.1, stipulates that relatives can also discipline a juvenile who gets out of hand (ἀτακτοῦντα). If the offenses (πταίσματα) are more serious and require a more severe punishment, then coercive measures by state authorities can be used. And if minors under 20 (ὅσοι πρὶν εἰκοσαετεῖς γενέσθαι) commit an act of bestiality (illicit sexual practices with animals), canon 16 of the synod of Ankyra (314) stipulates that they be excommunicated for fifteen years; after that they may come to prayers but may not attend the presentation of the Eucharist (προσφορά).[84]

The capacity to make a will was not granted until the fourteenth year for males and the twelfth year for females (Bas. 35.1.6 = Syn. Bas. Δ.13.4 = CIC *Dig* 28.1.5; cf. also *Ecloga* 5.1). Children who had been cheated of their property as minors aged under 14/12 (ἄνηβοι) could prosecute the matter within thirty years calculated from the time of their restricted majority (ἥβη, thus the age of 14/12); if they were older (thus no longer ἄνηβοι), they could prosecute their case within ten or twenty years after having reached the age of 25. (This last regulation was first formulated as a general principle in *Peira* 8.13.)[85]

---

82   Ibid., 176, lines 212–15 (quote).

83   Cf. Joannou, *Les canons des Pères grecs* (above, n. 44), 134, lines 17–18 (admittedly, the canon refers to secret marriage contracts of slaves: however, the closing passage is generally formulated).

84   Joannou, *Les canons des synodes particuliers* (above, n. 41), 67; canon 16 of Ankyra is not mentioned in J. Herrin, "Bestiality," *ODB* 1:286.

85   D. Simon, "Byzantinische Provinzialjustiz," *BZ* 79 (1986): 313 (read *Peira* 8.13 instead of 13.8), with reference to Demetrios Chomatenos, *Ponemata diaphora* (above, n. 77), no. 42, 157, lines 120–124 [= J.-B. Pitra, ed., *Analecta sacra et classica Spicilegio Solesmensi parata, iuris ecclesiastici graecorum selecta paralipomena,* vol. 6 (Paris, 1891; repr. Farnborough, 1967), 190.5–13], no. 59, 211, lines 61–67 [= Pitra, 264, 6–10]), and no. 85, 295, lines 100–106 [=Pitra, 381, 6–382,4]); cf. also S. Perentidis, "Trois notes sur la tradition de la Peira," Ἐπετηρίς τοῦ Κέντρου Ἐρεύνης Ἱστορίας Ἑλληνικοῦ Δικαίου Ἀκαδημίας Ἀθηνῶν 27–28 (1985): 650–51. According to Simon, the regulation in the *Peira* was developed from N.22.24 and Bas. 28.14.1 (p. 1417, lines 17–22) (above, n. 2). Con-

For girls and virgins, who, instead of marrying, wanted to dedicate themselves voluntarily to the service of the Lord by entering a convent, Basil the Great
stipulated in canon 18 that they could do so only at an *age when wisdom is fully
formed* (ἀφ᾽ οὗπερ ἂν ἡ ἡλικία τὴν τοῦ λόγου συμπλήρωσιν ἔχῃ). It did not befit
childish voices to make these decisions, he emphasized, but a girl who was older
than sixteen or seventeen was the mistress of her thoughts.[86]

Canon 35 of the synod of Carthage stipulates that bishops and the clergy
should not let their children (τὰ τέκνα αὐτῶν) become independent through the
act of emancipation without having informed themselves carefully beforehand
about their habits and their maturity and age, as otherwise the children's sins
would fall back upon them.[87]

A guardian could apply to the emperor for conferral of advance majority for
men and women aged between 20 (or 18 for women) and 25. They would then
receive the so-called *venia aetatis* (συγγνώμη ἡλικίας), in order to be able to administer their property independently, as can be seen in Bas. 10.4. 26–27 (cf. Syn. Bas.
A.70. 45–46) and novel 28 of Leo VI.[88] The same emperor confirmed the reduction of the minimum age for subdeacons from 25 (fixed by Justinian's novel 123)
to 20 (fixed by canon 15 of the council in Trullo) in his novels 16 and 75.[89]

Finally, age became a factor in the transmission of dignities and offices under
Alexios I Komnenos, who ruled in a novel of 1092 (or January 1107) that nobody
might assign to a person aged under 20 an ἀξίωμα or ὀφφίκιον that was conferred
on him in return for information to the tax authorities or as a special imperial
gift. However, if the emperor made such an assignment directly, and without
special cause, to juveniles under the age of 20, then the assignment held good
and was valid and was also entered in the list of ranks.[90]

---

cerning no. 42 of the *Ponemata diaphora,* I would like to emphasize that the plaintiff Melias mentioned here is identical with the semiorphan Melias Basilikos, mentioned in no. 29. Hence the
closing remark of my summary of no. 42 (see p. 116* of my edition) should be corrected: because
Melias of no. 42 was aged 33 in 1230, he was 25 in 1222. Now, because no. 29 deals with Melias
shortly after he reached the age of 25, that fits well with my dating of no. 29: "before 1225" (cf. p.
96* of my edition).

86 Joannou, *Les canons de Pères grecs* (above, n. 44), 118–21, quote: 120.23–121.1.

87 Joannou, *Les canons des synodes particuliers* (above, n. 41), 67.

88 See Zachariä von Lingenthal, *Geschichte* (above, n. 1), 122, and Antoniadis-Bibicou, "Quelques
notes" (above, n. 2), 77, speaking here erroneously of nov. 38; Noailles and Dain, *Les Novelles de
Léon VI* (above, n. 17), 110–15.

89 Noailles and Dain, *Les Novelles de Léon VI,* 60–63, 264–65. Cf. Antoniadis-Bibicou,
"Quelques notes," 78.

90 See Dölger and Wirth, *Regesten*, no. 1165 (with further references, but add Antioniadis-
Bibicou, "Quelques notes," 77).

Conclusion

To sum up, a number of important points can be noted. All children and juveniles up to the age of 25 were ὑπεξούσιοι (subject to parental authority), so long as their father or grandfather was alive and did not perform an act of emancipation; as such, they could not, for example, conclude contracts independently. The *venia aetatis,* leading to emancipation at the age of 18 or 20, was granted by the emperor only as the result of a special application.

The twenty-five-year span of youth was divided into several different stages. These were determined by both physical and intellectual development.

The first important transition was at the age of seven. In criminal law, from the age of seven, children were liable to the death penalty for murder, whereas younger children were in general exempt from punishment. In civil law, only children over seven received permission for betrothal.

A relatively minor transition was the age of ten or eleven, at which boys could enter monasteries.

The second important transition happened at 12 for girls and 14 for boys. At this age, children became entitled to marry and to make a will. They also acquired the ability to prosecute within thirty years from this age for loss of property incurred while they were still legally impaired by age.

Another less important transition came at around 18 to 20, when young people could benefit from the emperor's issuing of the *venia aetatis.* The ecclesiastical punishment for illicit sexual practices with animals was no longer the one for "young people" (i.e., fifteen years' excommunication). The minimum age for an ἀναγνώστης (reader) or subdeacon was 20 years.

In conclusion, I would like to underline the statement of Alexander Kazhdan, Judith Herrin, and Anthony Cutler at the end of the *ODB* article on childhood: "Legally adulthood began at 25, but in fact the borderline between childhood and maturity was not sharply defined. . . . In reality it occurred about the age of 16 or 18."[91]

Johannes Gutenberg-Universität, Mainz

---

91 See Kazhdan, Herrin, and Cutler, "Childhood" (above, n. 6).

GÜNTER PRINZING

LES VARIATIONS DU DÉSIR
D'ENFANT À BYZANCE

Marie-Hélène Congourdeau

ARLER DU DÉSIR D'ENFANT à Byzance représente une double gageure. La première gageure est chronologique. Le sujet abordé est par excellence l'un de ceux qui concernent la longue durée. L'attitude vis-à-vis de la procréation (avoir ou ne pas avoir d'enfants) fait partie de ces tendances longues de l'humanité, qui n'évoluent pas au même rythme que les événements de l'histoire. Il faut de profonds changements de civilisation, s'imposant euxmêmes lentement (comme, par exemple, la christianisation de l'empire romain) pour que les mentalités et les comportements se modifient, avec d'énormes résistances et des retours en arrière. C'est pourquoi les sources consultées seront parfois des textes bien datés (comme les vies de saints), mais très souvent il s'agira de très anciens textes véhiculés au long des siècles par les copistes, remaniés, modifiés, recomposés (ainsi, les recettes médicales), ou insérés dans de nouveaux recueils (comme les lois et les canons). La pertinence de ces vieux textes est ravivée dans les derniers siècles de Byzance par le mouvement humaniste qui donne une nouvelle jeunesse aux textes antiques, savants (la médecine) ou irrationnels (l'astrologie, les sciences occultes).

Une seconde gageure est que notre sujet, l'enfant désiré ou non désiré, ne peut être atteint qu'à travers celle qui, au premier chef, le désire ou ne le désire pas, c'est-à-dire la femme. Or, cette femme elle-même a rarement la parole (notre seul auteur féminin, Mètrodôra, ne parle pas ici en tant que femme, mais en tant que médecin),[1] et nous l'atteignons le plus souvent par l'intermédiaire d'hommes: le médecin, le législateur, le prêtre.

---

1 Tout ce que l'on peut dire de Mètrodôra est qu'elle exerça probablement entre le 2e et le 3e siècle de notre ère; toute tentative de datation précise ne peut être qu'hypothétique. Voir M.-H.

C'est à travers ces médiations que nous essaierons néanmoins d'appréhender le désir d'enfant à Byzance, en nous situant tout d'abord du point de vue de la femme, aux prises avec ses désirs et ses refus, puis en analysant le regard que la société byzantine porte sur ces vicissitudes du désir. Peut-être cette enquête nous en apprendra-t-elle autant sur les auteurs consultés que sur le sujet qu'ils abordent.

Du côté de la femme
Avoir un enfant

Lorsque les conditions s'y prêtent, la plupart des femmes désirent être mères. Dans les cas où le désir naturel n'est pas assez fort, la pression extérieure, qui dans les sociétés traditionnelles valorise la mère, vient en aide au désir défaillant. L'opinion courante sur la femme stérile est celle que l'évangéliste Luc place dans la bouche d'Élisabeth lorsqu'elle a conçu Jean-Baptiste: "Le Seigneur ... a daigné mettre fin à ce qui faisait ma honte [τὸ ὄνειδός μου] aux yeux des hommes" (Lc 1:25). Élisabeth n'est ici que la dernière d'une longue lignée de femmes stériles délivrées de cette honte, depuis Sarah, la femme d'Abraham.

Si, aux premiers siècles chrétiens, dans le contexte d'attente eschatologique et d'exaltation de la virginité, la procréation est peu valorisée, et si l'on voit apparaître un nouveau modèle de femme, celui de la moniale qui renonce à la maternité,[2] pour le commun des mortels la stérilité reste une malédiction. Mieux que dans les discours des Pères de l'Église, cette malédiction transparaît dans une question posée, au 7e siècle, au moine-médecin Anastase le Sinaïte: "D'où vient que souvent ... certains ont beaucoup d'enfants alors qu'ils sont mauvais, tandis que d'autres, alors qu'ils sont bons, sont sans enfants?"[3] Au 12e siècle encore, l'épopée de Digenis Akritas rend compte de la souffrance que cause à un couple "la flamme inextinguible et tout à fait terrible de la stérilité, dont seuls ont fait l'expérience les gens privés d'enfants, et qui cause aux vivants le plus grand des malheurs."[4]

Congourdeau, "Mètrodôra et son oeuvre," dans *Maladie et société à Byzance,* éd. É. Patlagean (Spoleto, 1993), 57–96.

2   Voir É. Patlagean, "Sur la limitation de la fécondité dans la haute époque byzantine," *Annales: Economie, sociétés, civilisations* 6 (nov.–déc. 1969): 1353–69.

3   Anastase le Sinaïte, *Erôtapokriseis,* éd. M. Richard et J. A. Munitiz, *Anastasii Sinaitae Quaestiones et responsiones,* CCSG 59 (Turnhout, 2006), q. 28.

4   Digenis Akritas, VII, trad. C. Jouanno, *Digénis Akritas, le héros des frontières: Une épopée byzantine* (Turnhout, 1998), 294.

MARIE-HÉLÈNE CONGOURDEAU

De ce malheur, la femme est doublement victime. Dans les sociétés traditionnelles, c'est elle en effet qui est rendue responsable de ce qui fait son malheur. Dans une homélie sur Hannah, la mère du prophète Samuel, qui se plaignait à Dieu du mépris que lui valait son ventre stérile (1 Sm 1:9–11), Jean Chrysostome fustige les hommes qui font retomber sur la femme seule le poids de la stérilité: "Vous savez tous que la stérilité est insupportable pour les femmes surtout à cause de leurs époux. Car beaucoup d'hommes sont insensés au point d'accuser leurs femmes quand elles n'enfantent pas, ignorant que la fécondité tient son origine du ciel, de la providence de Dieu, et que ni la nature de la femme ni l'union conjugale ni aucune autre cause n'y suffit. Et cependant, même s'ils savent que c'est injustement qu'ils les accusent, souvent ils les insultent, se détournent d'elles et ne trouvent pas leur plaisir en elles."[5] Le prédicateur semble ici suggérer que pour certains hommes, la stérilité de leur femme fournit un prétexte commode pour justifier leur propre infidélité. Il va plus loin dans une autre homélie où il fait porter aux maris la responsabilité du refus d'enfant: par cupidité, certains d'entre eux "supportent mal la longévité de leur père, et même ce qui est doux et chéri de tous, avoir des enfants, leur paraît lourd et insupportable. C'est ainsi que beaucoup, pour cette raison, achètent des drogues de stérilité et mutilent la nature, ne se contentant pas de supprimer leurs enfants une fois nés, mais ne permettant pas même qu'en croissent les prémisses."[6]

De ces quelques notations de Jean Chrysostome on ne saurait tirer de règles générales. Elles sont cependant des indices de ce que l'ambivalence envers la procréation ne touche pas que les femmes. Les plaidoyers de Jean Chrysostome, comme les réquisitoires des sources juridiques (qui ne sanctionnent un refus d'enfant que quand il est le fait de la mère, non du père), sont autant d'indicateurs de la situation inférieure de la femme, sommée d'être féconde, mise en accusation quand l'enfant ne vient pas, laissée seule avec son fardeau quand il arrive sans être attendu, et accusée à nouveau si elle vient à s'en débarrasser.

Il n'en est que plus intéressant d'essayer de lui donner la parole, en commençant par laisser parler son désir d'être mère.

Ce désir d'enfant se décline en trois actes: concevoir, garder l'enfant conçu, et le mettre au monde. A ces objectifs correspondent plusieurs sortes de recours.

5   Jean Chrysostome, *Hom. 1 de Anna,* 5 (PG 54:639).
6   Jean Chrysostome, *Hom. 28 in Mt* (PG 57:357).

L'hagiographie nous donne accès à un premier type de recours: la prière. Dieu qui a exaucé la prière d'Hannah, mère de Samuel, peut "ôter la honte" de la femme qui le supplie. Un grand nombre de saints byzantins ont été conçus à la suite d'une prière de leurs parents. Cette prière peut s'adresser à Dieu lui-même (Paraskeva, Michel le Synkellos, Alexis).[7] Mais elle peut aussi passer par l'intercession d'un saint. La Mère de Dieu, dont la conception et la maternité furent de l'ordre du miracle, est particulièrement sollicitée. La mère d'Étienne le Jeune (8e s.) la prie en son église des Blakhernes;[8] celle de Michel Maleinos (10e s.), dans son sanctuaire de Kouka.[9] Saint Jean-Baptiste, lui-même enfant d'une mère stérile, peut aussi jouer ce rôle: c'est au sanctuaire du Précurseur que va prier la future mère de Syméon Stylite le Jeune (6e s.).[10] Il est à noter que dans ces trois cas, c'est en songe que la mère reçoit l'annonce du miracle, selon un procédé qui rappelle l'incubation (dans les sanctuaires à incubation, le patient dort dans le sanctuaire et le dieu guérisseur—plus tard le saint guérisseur—le guérit durant son sommeil, parfois en lui apparaissant dans un songe).

La prière peut aussi s'adresser à un saint homme qui sert d'intermédiaire entre Dieu et des femmes stériles qui viennent le supplier de les rendre fécondes: citons Syméon Stylite le Jeune et Théodore de Sykéon (7e s.).[11] L'intermédiaire peut aussi bien être mort (invocation d'Ignace le patriarche dans un accouchement difficile)[12] que vivant (intervention du patriarche Germain pour faire concevoir la mère d'Étienne le Jeune).[13] Il est à noter que ces deux saints protecteurs de la procréation partagent, outre le fait d'être patriarches de Constantinople, la particularité d'avoir été castrés dans leur jeunesse, contre leur volonté. On peut

---

7   Passion de sainte Paraskeva par Jean d'Eubée (*BHG* 1420p), c. 2, éd. F. Halkin, *Recherches et documents d'hagiographie byzantine* (Bruxelles, 1971), 231. Vie de Michel le Synkellos (*BHG* 1296), c. 1, éd. M. Cunningham, *The Life of Michael the Synkellos* (Belfast, 1991), 44–46. Vie de saint Alexis (*BHG* 51), cc. 1–2, éd. F. M. Esteves Pereira, *AB* 19 (1900): 243–45; légende grecque de saint Alexis (*BHG* 56d), c. 1, éd. F. Halkin, *AB* 98 (1980): 7. Ces Vies furent écrites entre le 8e et le 10e siècle.
8   Vie d'Étienne le Jeune (*BHG* 1666), éd. et trad. M.-F. Auzépy, *La vie d'Étienne le Jeune par Étienne le Diacre,* Birmingham Byzantine and Ottoman Monographs 3 (Birmingham, 1997), 92.
9   Vie de Michel Maleinos (*BHG* 1295), éd. L. Petit, *ROC* 7 (1902): 551.
10   Vie de Syméon Stylite le Jeune (*BHG* 1689), c. 2, éd. P. van den Ven, *La Vie ancienne de S. Syméon Stylite le Jeune* (Bruxelles, 1962), 3–4.
11   Vie de Syméon Stylite le Jeune, c. 140, p. 130; dans le chapitre précédent, Syméon vient en aide aux femmes qui souffrent d'une grossesse pathologique. Vie de Théodore de Sykéon (*BHG* 1748), c. 93, c. 140, c. 145, éd. et trad. A.-J. Festugière, *Vie de Théodore de Sykéôn,* tome 1: *Texte grec,* tome 2: *Traduction, commentaire et appendice* (Bruxelles, 1970), 11–12, 110–11, 113–15.
12   Vie d'Ignace de Constantinople (PG 105:564B).
13   Vie d'Etienne le Jeune, 5.

y voir l'affirmation d'une fécondité différente, par le miracle, chez ces hommes privés de fécondité naturelle.[14]

Concevoir ne suffit pas: il faut aussi porter le fruit jusqu'à son terme. La mère de Théodoret de Cyr (5e s.), au cinquième mois, est menacée par une fausse-couche (ἀμβλώσεως κίνδυνος). Elle envoie un serviteur à Macédonios, qui lui avait prédit sa maternité; le saint homme lui fait boire une eau qui "met en fuite le risque d'avortement."[15] Syméon Stylite le Jeune est également efficace dans ces cas.[16]

L'accouchement est source d'angoisse, car la mortalité péri-natale est élevée. L'*Historia Lausiaca* (5e s.) nous montre ainsi un futur père de Bethléem (lieu de naissance prestigieux) supplier l'ascète Poseidonios de Thèbes de secourir sa femme qui ne parvient pas à accoucher.[17] Parfois, quand la présentation du foetus est mauvaise, les médecins impuissants vont se résoudre à sacrifier l'enfant, cet objet du désir, en recourant à l'embryotomie, lorsque l'intervention du saint (Porphyre de Gaza, 5e s.),[18] voire d'un morceau de son manteau (Ignatios de Constantinople, 9e s.),[19] permet une naissance heureuse.[20]

DROGUES ET AMULETTES

Les Vies de saints nous donnent à connaître ce que leurs rédacteurs, et sans doute aussi leurs lecteurs, pensaient du désir d'enfant. Mais elles ne nous donnent pas accès à la réalité vécue par la majorité des femmes byzantines. Il nous faut donc recourir à d'autres sources.

La médecine byzantine est l'héritière des deux grands courants de l'Antiquité: la médecine savante, qui recherche les causes des anomalies pour pouvoir y

14   Cf. Ch. Messis, "La construction sociale, les réalités rhétoriques et les représentations de l'identité masculine à Byzance" (thèse dactylographiée, École des Hautes Etudes en Sciences Sociales, 2006), 934.

15   Théodoret de Cyr, *Histoire Philothée*, 13.17, éd. P. Canivet et A. Leroy-Molinghen, *Histoire des moines de Syrie*, "Histoire Philothée" I, SC 234 (Paris, 1979), 506: ὁ τῆς ἀμβλώσεως ἐδραπέτευσε κίνδυνος (notons que le terme δραπετεύω est employé dans les exorcismes).

16   Vie de Syméon Stylite le Jeune, c. 139, p. 129.

17   *Historia Lausiaca*, 36, éd. G. M. J. Bartelink, *Palladio: La storia lausiaca*, Vite dei santi 2 (Milano, 1990), 178–82.

18   Vie de Porphyre de Gaza (*BHG* 1570), 28–30, éd. et trad. H. Grégoire et M.-A. Kugener (Paris, 1930), 24–26.

19   Vie d'Ignatios de Constantinople par Niketas Paphlagôn (*BHG* 817) (PG 105:564B).

20   Je laisse de côté le cas particulier de la femme qui ne peut pas accoucher à cause d'un péché, par exemple, lorsqu'elle accuse un saint d'être le géniteur; il faut l'intervention du saint accusé pour que l'accouchement aboutisse: *Historia Lausiaca*, c. 70, pp. 284–87; Vie de Syméon Salos (*BHG* 1677), c. 39 (PG 93:1717).

remédier, et la médecine populaire, qui fournit des recettes "éprouvées" sans s'attacher à comprendre pourquoi elles sont efficaces. Si, dans l'Antiquité, la distinction entre ces deux sortes de médecines était assez floue (on trouve dans le corpus hippocratique de nombreux éléments de médecine populaire), à Byzance elle l'est encore davantage. Tout au plus distingue-t-on entre des auteurs médicaux (Aetios d'Amida au 6e s., Théophane Chrysobalantès au 10e, Jean Zacharias au 14e) et des recueils de recettes anonymes (les *iatrosophia,* ces manuels de thérapeutique dont beaucoup furent copiés et utilisés dans les xénons byzantins jusqu'à l'époque des Paléologues et au-delà). Les recettes que fournissent ces manuels nous rapprochent davantage du "vécu" de la femme byzantine. Enfin, quand ni l'homme de Dieu ni l'homme de l'art ne sont efficaces, la femme a encore la ressource de se tourner vers des personnages moins "orthodoxes": c'est à dire, les astrologues et les magiciens. Sur ce point encore, la frontière entre médecine et procédés irrationnels s'avère poreuse.

Concevoir. La première question qui se pose est de savoir si la femme est féconde. Une méthode éprouvée, puisqu'on la trouve déjà chez Hippocrate et Aristote,[21] se retrouve dans les manuels d'époque plus tardive, Soranos (2e s.) ou Mètrodôra (dont l'unique manuscrit conservé fut copié au 12e s.);[22] il s'agit de faire brûler au-dessous de la femme des résines ou encens divers; si l'odeur s'échappe par la bouche, la femme est féconde; si l'odeur ne s'exhale pas, c'est que la matrice est fermée et ne pourra concevoir.

La femme peut aussi aller consulter un astrologue qui trouvera dans ses grimoires que "si le maître de maison du cinquième lieu, la Lune, et leur maître se trouvent sur l'horoscope ou sur la culmination supérieure, la femme concevra, et surtout si eux et leurs lieux sont vus par les [astres] bienveillants."[23] Pour celle qui s'interroge sur son état, l'astrologue connaît plusieurs méthodes "pour savoir par l'observation des astres si la femme est enceinte ou non."[24]

21   Hippocrate, *Aphorisme* 5.59 (Littré 4:554); *De la nature des femmes,* 2.214 (Littré 8:424); Aristote, *Génération des animaux,* 747a.
22   Soranos, *Maladies des femmes,* 1.11, éd. P. Burguière, D. Gourevitch, et Y. Malinas, *Soranos, Maladies des femmes,* tome 1 (Paris, 1988), 32; Mètrodôra, Περὶ τῶν γυναικείων παθῶν τῆς μήτρας, 1.32, éd. A. P. Kouzis, "Metrodora's Work 'On the Feminine Diseases of the Womb,' according to the Greek Codex 75.3 of the Laurentian Library," Πρακτικὰ τῆς Ἀκαδημίας 20 (1945): 55; trad. Congourdeau, "Mètrodôra et son oeuvre," 73.
23   Pseudo-Palchos, pseudonyme d'un astronome du 14e siècle: Barocc. 216, f. 446 = *CCAG* 9 (Bruxelles, 1951), 172.
24   Paris. gr. 2194 (15e s.), f. 461v.

MARIE-HÉLÈNE CONGOURDEAU

La médecine, savante et populaire, fournit de nombreuses drogues pour faire concevoir une femme (beaucoup plus que de drogues contraceptives, ce qui suggère que la stérilité angoissait davantage la femme que la grossesse non désirée). Aetios d'Amida décrit la préparation de potions, pessaires, et fumigations "sulleptiques" à base de plantes. Il indique aussi, sans garantie, une "amulette naturelle" à base d'os trouvés dans le coeur d'une biche, que "l'on croit propre à faire concevoir naturellement" si on l'attache au bras gauche.[25] Mètrodôra indique aussi plusieurs pessaires ou onguents à base de plantes ou de substances animales. En voici un: "Plonge de la vraie pourpre dans de la bile de chèvre et applique sur le nombril de la femme pendant sept jours. Et qu'elle s'unisse à l'homme quand la lune est croissante."[26] Syméon Seth (11e s.) conseille des aliments qui favorisent la procréation (testicules de jars, asperges, baumier).[27] Selon un iatrosophion du 15e siècle, utilisé dans les hôpitaux de Constantinople, la gelée de coing, connue pour ses propriétés antidiarrhéiques, est aussi apte à retenir le sperme.[28] Certaines pierres, comme l'aétite[29] ou l'orite,[30] passent aussi pour faire concevoir les femmes qui les portent contre leur ventre.

Les *Koiranides,* ce recueil médico-magique, d'origine hermétique, dont l'audience s'étend jusqu'à la fin de l'empire, fournit le moyen de concevoir ou de ne pas concevoir, à la demande: "Éteins des charbons ardents dans les menstrues d'une femme, elle ne concevra pas. Alors enlève convenablement le charbon, et garde-le, et lorsque tu voudras qu'elle conçoive, allume-le au feu et elle concevra."[31]

25   Aetios d'Amida, *Tetrabiblos,* c. 16.34, éd. S. Zervos, *Aetii Sermo sextidecimus et ultimus* (Leipzig, 1901), 47–50. Aétios ne précise pas comment l'on pouvait trouver des os dans le coeur d'une biche. Peut-être le mot *cœur* (καρδία) désigne-t-il ici simplement les entrailles.

26   Mètrodôra, 1.26, p. 54 (traduction, 71). Il est difficile de savoir ce que Mètrodôra entend par "vraie pourpre [πορφύρα]." Étant donné le contexte, il peut s'agir d'un tissu de pourpre que l'on utilise comme une ceinture. Le *Calendrier d'Hiérophile* recommande l'automne et l'hiver pour des unions fécondes: éd. A. Delatte, *Anecdota atheniensia et alia* (Liège, 1939), 2:457–66.

27   Syméon Seth, éd. B. Langkavel, *Simeonis Sethi Syntagma de alimentorum facultatibus* (Leipzig, 1868), alpha, lin. 174; bèta, lin. 74–78; chi, lin. 57–59.

28   Paris. gr. 2194, f. 445.

29   *Geoponica sive Cassiani Bassi scholastici De re rustica eclogae,* 15.1.30, éd. H. Beckh (Stuttgart, 1895; réimpr. 1994), 437–38.

30   *Lapidaire orphique,* vv. 457–60, éd. R. Halleux et J. Schamp, *Les Lapidaires grecs* (Paris, 1985), 106.

31   *Koiranides,* Gamma, 7, dans F. De Mely et C.-E. Ruelle, *Les Lapidaires de l'Antiquité et du Moyen Âge,* tome 2: *Les Lapidaires grecs* (Paris, 1898–1902). Ce recueil à la réputation sulfureuse était encore copié au 15e siècle dans le xénon de Pétra. Voir A. Rigo, "Da Costantinopoli alla Biblioteca di Venezia: I libri ermetici di medici, astrologi e maghi dell'ultima Bisanzio," dans *Magia, alchimia, scienza dal '400 al '700: L'influsso di Ermete Trismegisto / Magic, Alchemy and Science 15th–*

Médecins et astrologues donnent aussi des conseils aux femmes qui souhaitent concevoir des garçons (ce qui est fréquent) ou des filles (ce qui est plus rare).[32] Michel Psellos (11e s.) rapporte à ce propos cet avis de Julien l'Africain: "La génération relève de l'art [τεχνική ἐστι γέννησις] et l'on peut engendrer en ayant recours à l'art [τεχνικῶς], si l'homme sur le point de s'unir à la femme enduit son membre de sang de lièvre ou de graisse d'oie. Avec la première méthode, il concevra un mâle, et avec la seconde une femelle."[33]

L'emploi de ces méthodes ne se limite pas aux couches populaires, comme le montrent deux exemples impériaux des 10e et 11e siècles. Zoé Karbonopsina, la concubine de Léon VI, obtient un enfant en portant autour des reins un écheveau de soie de la taille d'une icône de la Vierge qui se trouve au sanctuaire de Pègè.[34] L'empereur Romain III et sa femme, prénommée aussi Zoé, dans leur désir d'avoir un héritier, usent d'onctions et de potions (ἀλείμμασι καὶ τρίμμασι); Zoé applique contre son ventre des pierres (sans doute l'aétite ou la sardoine) et des amulettes, elle s'entoure de bandelettes, avant de finir par renoncer. Il faut dire qu'elle avait dépassé cinquante ans.[35]

Garder l'enfant. Une fois la conception assurée, il faut garder l'enfant. Les fausses couches sont fréquentes dans les conditions d'alimentation et d'hygiène des sociétés traditionnelles. Aux "femmes qui accouchent prématurément, qui ne portent pas à terme leurs enfants et qui perdent les embryons," Mètrodôra conseille de faire boire "de l'herbe d'armoise hachée avec du vin odoriférant."[36]

Mais ce sont surtout les vertus des pierres qui sont invoquées pour garder l'enfant.[37] L'aétite, ou pierre d'aigle, dont on dit que l'aigle la met dans son nid

---

18th Centuries: The Influence of Hermes Trismegistus, éd. Carlos Gilly et Cis van Heertum (Firenze, 2002).

32 Mètrodôra, 1.33, p. 55 (traduction, 73).

33 Michel Psellos, Περὶ παραδόξων, éd. J. M. Duffy, *Michaelis Pselli Philosophica minora* (Stuttgart, 1992), op. 32, 110.

34 *De sacris aedibus deque miraculis Deiparae in fontem,* c. 26, *AASS* nov. 3, 885e; cité par H. Maguire, "Magic and the Christian Image," dans *Byzantine Magic,* éd. H. Maguire (Washington, D.C., 1995), 70. Voir A.-M. Talbot, "Two Accounts of Miracles at the Pege Shrine in Constantinople," *TM* 14 (2002): 608.

35 Michel Psellos, *Chronographie, Romain III,* 5, éd. et trad. E. Renauld (Paris, 1926), 34–35.

36 Mètrodôra, 1.30, pp. 54–55 (traduction, 72). D'autres drogues pour empêcher les avortements ou les accouchements avant terme se trouvent dans les manuscrits suivants: Paris. gr. 2151, f. 65; Paris. gr. 2181, f. 15 (Dioscoride et Stéphanos); Paris. gr. 2236, f. 43v.

37 Les lapidaires, souvent compilés dès l'Antiquité, furent copiés sans interruption pendant toute la période byzantine. Ils étaient donc probablement utilisés, comme les recettes médicinales ou magiques qui relèvent de la même logique.

pour protéger ses oeufs, est une pierre creuse contenant une autre pierre: par "sympathie," cette pierre "enceinte" est donc "utile aux femmes enceintes."[38] Aetios d'Amida, qui consacre un chapitre aux femmes qui perdent leur fruit au deuxième ou au troisième mois, la recommande en amulette portée contre le ventre,[39] tandis que le *Lapidaire Damigéron-Evax* conseille de la lier au bras gauche.[40] Par analogie, d'autres objets évoquant la grossesse peuvent aussi servir d'amulettes, comme un grain de blé trouvé dans le pain ou une pierre trouvée dans la matrice ou le coeur d'une biche.[41] Très populaire aussi est la pierre de Sardes, connue sous deux formes, la sardoine et la sardonyx (composé de sardoine et d'onyx). Aetios conseille à la femme sujette aux avortements de porter sur le bas-ventre une sardoine enveloppée dans un linge, et de l'ôter aux premières douleurs.[42] Psellos rapporte que "la sardonyx monochrome nouée à la ceinture retient les embryons glissants."[43] Enfin, l'hématite, qui peut avoir la couleur de sang, arrête les flux de sang et peut donc aussi être efficace contre les avortements.[44]

Accoucher. L'accouchement, épreuve redoutée, est le moment de tous les dangers.[45] Pour secourir la femme en travail, tous les moyens sont bienvenus.

Lorsque l'heure d'accoucher est venue, si la femme souffre et ne parvient pas à faire sortir l'enfant, Mètrodôra recommande d'oindre le col de l'utérus avec des amandes cuites dans de l'huile ou une peau de hérisson de terre broyée dans de l'eau.[46]

Ici encore les pierres sont utiles: une aétite broyée dans de l'eau et appliquée sur les reins de la parturiente peut accélérer l'accouchement;[47] une galactite liée autour de la cuisse gauche avec un fil de laine d'une brebis féconde promet un accouchement rapide et sans douleurs.[48] A partir de ces pierres bienfaisantes de par leur nature, sont confectionnées des amulettes spécifiques: les *okytokia*, qui assurent un accouchement rapide conformément à leur appellation, sont

38   *Lapidaire Damigéron-Evax,* ed. Halleux et Schamp, *Les Lapidaires grecs,* 234, 336–37 n. 4.
39   Aetios d'Amida, 16.21, pp. 25–26.
40   *Damigéron-Evax,* 235–36.
41   Aetios, 16.21, pp. 25–26.
42   Aetios, 16.21, p. 26.
43   Michel Psellos, Περὶ λίθων δυνάμεων, ed. Duffy, op. 34.118.
44   Voir A. A. Barb, "Bois du sang, Tantale," *Syria* 19 (1952): 271.
45   Meurent en couches: Galla, femme de Théodose Ier; Eudokia, femme de Léon VI; la soeur de Michel Psellos. Meurt des suites d'une fausse couche: Eudoxia, femme d'Arcadius.
46   Mètrodôra, 1.29.31, pp. 54–55 (traduction, 72–73).
47   *Damigéron-Evax,* 236.
48   *Damigéron-Evax,* 275–76.

des pierres souvent de couleur rouge (rappelant le sang) où se trouve gravée une inscription enjoignant à l'enfant de sortir.[49]

En désespoir de cause, il reste les antiques incantations sommairement christianisées, pour obliger l'enfant à sortir: "Femme, le Christ t'appelle. Sarra, Sarra, et toi, bébé, tombe parce que le Christ t'appelle et la terre t'attend";[50] ou encore celle-ci, gravée sur un tesson de poterie à placer sur le flanc droit de la parturiente: "Sors de ton tombeau, le Christ t'appelle."[51]

La femme n'est pas seulement victime d'un utérus rebelle ou d'un enfant récalcitrant. Elle est aussi la proie de la jalousie des démons, telle cette démone connue sous les noms d'Obizouth, de Lilith, ou de Gello, qui peut faire avorter les embryons et qui guette les nouveau-nés pour les étouffer.[52] Pour lui faire barrage, le *Testament de Salomon,* texte de démonologie à la longue destinée, conseille d'écrire le nom de l'archange Raphael sur la femme qui accouche.[53] A ces procédés, on pourrait ajouter toutes les amulettes utérines où sont gravés les noms et les images de Salomon ou de Sisinnios,[54] et qui ont fait l'objet de nombreuses études.

Je voudrais, en terminant cette évocation des procédés au service du désir d'enfant, souligner la parenté entre ces différentes méthodes, une parenté qui trahit l'antiquité de ces pratiques. Je prendrai l'exemple de la ceinture, que l'on retrouve aussi bien dans l'hagiographie que dans les recettes médico-magiques.

La ceinture est tout d'abord associée à la conception. Théodore de Sykéon bénit les ceintures des couples stériles qui viennent le supplier.[55] Un de ces couples

---

49   Sur ces *okytokia,* déjà évoquées dans le corpus hippocratique et dont on retrouve des exemplaires jusqu'à l'époque néo-grecque, cf. A. E. Hanson, "The Gradualist View of Fetal Development," dans *L'embryon: Formation et Animation; Antiquité grecque et latine, tradition hébraïque, chrétienne et islamique,* éd. L. Brisson, M.-H. Congourdeau et J.-L. Solère (Paris, 2008).

50   A. Vasiliev, *Anecdota Graecobyzantina,* Pars Prior (Moscou, 1893), 339–40.

51   Papyrus graecus magicus 123.a.50, cité par J. J. Aubert, "Threatened Wombs: Aspects of Ancient Uterine Magic," *GRBS* 30, no. 3 (1989): 421–49.

52   Ce n'est pas ici le lieu de développer les croyances autour de la démone Gello, tueuse de nouveau-nés. Sur ce sujet, à l'article fondateur d'I. Sorlin, "Striges et Géloudes: Histoire d'une croyance et d'une tradition," *TM* 11 (1991): 411–36, il faut ajouter désormais K. Hartnup, *On the Beliefs of the Greeks: Leo Allatios and Popular Orthodoxy* (Leiden, 2004); et M. Patera, "Gylou, démon et sorcière, du monde byzantin au monde néo-grec," *REB* 64–65 (2006–7): 311–27. Sur Gello, voir aussi les essais de Brigitte Pitarakis et Alice-Mary Talbot, *infra* dans ce volume.

53   *Testament de Salomon* (PG 122:1335).

54   Voir G. Vikan, "Art, Medicine, and Magic in Early Byzantium," *DOP* 38 (1984): 65–86; A. D. Bakaloudi, "The Kinds and the Special Function of the Epôdai (Epodes) in Apotropaic Amulets of the First Byzantine Period," *BSl* 59 (1998): 222–38; eadem, "*Deisidaimonia* and the Role of the Apotropaic Magic Amulets in the Early Byzantine Empire," *Byzantion* 70 (2000): 182–210.

55   Vie de Théodore de Sykéon, c. 145, pp. 113–15.

bénéficie d'un rituel particulier: Théodore "leur prit leurs ceintures à tous deux, les plaça l'une à sa droite, l'autre à sa gauche, et s'étant agenouillé au milieu, fit pour eux une prière, puis leur rendit leurs ceintures pour qu'ils s'en ceignissent; et par la grâce du Christ, il leur naquit au bout de neuf mois un petit garçon."[56] Les deux Zoé impériales s'entourent le ventre de bandes de tissu qui font office de ceintures. D'autre part, un iatrosophion du 16e siècle rapporte que pour concevoir, "certaines femmes font une ceinture avec sept teintures et la portent. Voici ces teintures ou couleurs: rouge, bleu-noir, androsème, vert, cuivre, noir.[57] Pose sur chaque partie de la ceinture des écailles: trois sur le rouge, et de même pour les autres couleurs. La ceinture doit venir d'un linge de lin, et tu écris sur un papier, que tu mets à l'intérieur, les caractères suivants: α, φ, ω, στ, ξ, β, δ (etc.)."[58] Les *Koiranides* également évoquent un "linge de lin teint des sept couleurs" que la femme doit porter autour du bas-ventre, en y nouant une graine de pivoine.[59]

Ensuite, selon les lapidaires, pour éviter les fausses couches, la femme doit porter, nouée à la ceinture, une pierre polyzone[60]—ce nom est un symbole à lui seul—ou une sardoine.[61] Enfin, la ceinture est encore présente au moment de la délivrance: Mélanie la Jeune (5e s.) détache sa ceinture, qu'elle tient d'un saint homme, pour faire accoucher une parturiente en détresse;[62] Théophano (9e s.) parvient à naître grâce à une ceinture que son père va détacher d'une colonne dans l'église de la Théotokos tou Bassou et qu'il attache autour des reins de son épouse.[63] La ceinture est donc un objet chargé de symboles, où sainteté et magie se côtoient pour faire advenir la vie.[64]

Ne pas avoir un enfant

Si la stérilité est un handicap, la survenue d'un enfant non désiré peut être un malheur. Soit la femme est sans mari (elle n'en a pas, ou elle est veuve, ou son mari est absent, à la guerre, par exemple) et sa grossesse dénonce son "inconduite," soit

---

56 Vie de Théodore de Sykéon, c. 93, pp. 76–77.
57 Le manuscrit évoque sept couleurs et en nomme six.
58 Paris. gr. 2181, f. 14v.
59 *Koiranides,* Gamma, 7.
60 *Damigéron-Evax,* 284.
61 Psellos, Περὶ λιθῶν δυνάμεων, 118.
62 Vie de Mélanie la Jeune, c. 61, éd. D. Gorce, SC 90 (Paris, 1962), 248–50.
63 Vie de Théophano (*BHG* 1794), c. 3, éd. E. Kurtz, *Zwei griechische Texte über die Hl. Theophano die Gemahlin Kaisers Leo VI* (St. Petersburg, 1898), 2–3.
64 Voir également la Vie d'Antoine le Jeune (*BHG* 142), éd. A. Papadopoulos-Kerameus, Συλλογὴ παλαιστινῆς καὶ συριακῆς ἁγιολογίας 1.196, cité par Messis, "L'identité masculine," 224–25.

elle est déjà chargée d'enfants et ne peut les élever tous, soit son âge ou sa santé ne lui permettent pas de mener sans danger une grossesse à son terme. La femme peut donc rechercher un moyen de devenir stérile, de ne pas concevoir, d'expulser l'embryon imprévu, ou d'éliminer le nouveau-né importun. Je laisse de côté cette dernière éventualité qui demanderait une étude particulière.

Il est inutile de préciser que dans tous ces cas, la prière est mal venue. Je n'ai pas trouvé, dans les sources hagiographiques, de saint qui accepte d'intercéder pour un refus d'enfant. Tout juste peut-on mentionner saint Nicolas (4e s.), qui rend stérile sa mère après sa propre naissance—son hagiographe nous fait savoir que, à l'imitation inversée de Jean-Baptiste qui en naissant délia la stérilité du ventre de sa mère, Nicolas, en naissant, clôt la matrice de la sienne[65]—ou Cyrille le Philéote (12e s.) qui, une fois devenu père, espace ses relations conjugales.[66]

C'est donc vers des moyens plus profanes que se tourne la femme qui ne souhaite pas d'enfants.

DROGUES DE STÉRILITÉ

Parmi les nombreuses substances et recettes fournies par les iatrosophia et autres recueils, figurent des drogues qui rendent stérile. Aetios d'Amida en cite quelques-unes.[67] Psellos rapporte que, selon (Julien) l'Africain, on rend une femme stérile en lui attachant une chose stérile, comme un cerveau de grenouille enveloppé dans un chiffon de lin.[68] Étant donné qu'une femme souhaite rarement la stérilité définitive, ces procédés sont parfois utilisés à son insu, pour de sordides histoires d'héritage, par exemple. Un iatrosophion du 16e siècle nous informe que pour rendre une femme stérile, il suffit de lui donner à boire en secret la cire de l'oreille d'une mule avec du vin, ou une potion à base de testicules de castor.[69]

Rappelons que d'après l'historien Jean Kinnamos (12e s.), Alexis Axouch, gendre du frère de Manuel Ier, fut accusé d'avoir cherché à rendre Manuel stérile, au moyen de drogues fournies par un sorcier latin,[70] afin sans doute de prévenir la naissance d'un héritier mâle.

---

65   PG 116:320A.

66   Vie de Cyrille le Philéote (*BHG* 468), c. 3.1, éd. et trad. E. Sargologos, *La Vie de saint Cyrille le Philéote, moine byzantin († 1110)* (Bruxelles, 1964), 48–49. Depuis les débuts de l'ère chrétienne, la méthode préconisée par le discours d'Église pour éviter des naissances est l'abstention ou, plus drastique, la séparation: voir Patlagean, "Sur la limitation de la fécondité."

67   Aetios d'Amida, 16.17, p. 18.

68   Psellos, Περὶ παραδόξων ἀκουσμάτων, 110.

69   Paris. gr. 1603, f. 277v.

70   Jean Kinnamos, *Epitome rerum ab Ioanne et Alexio* [sic] *Comnenis gestarum,* ed. A. Meineke

CONTRACEPTIFS

Nos sources fournissent aussi toute une gamme de contraceptifs. Ceux-ci peuvent être à usage interne: Aetios d'Amida offre des recettes à base de grenade ou d'autres substances végétales à absorber une fois par mois ou au moment de l'union.[71] Syméon Seth conseille le chou ou l'estomac du lièvre,[72] un iatrosophion préfère des pommes de cyprès broyées dans du vin pur,[73] tandis que les *Koiranides* préconisent du mouton avec de l'orge souillé dans ses menstrues.[74]

D'autres recettes sont à usage externe: onctions de miel, de baume, ou d'huile de cèdre sur le col de la matrice; moelle d'aigle ou poivre après les rapports sexuels; pessaires divers.

Ici encore, nous retrouvons les amulettes, à porter sur le bras ou sur le ventre, telle la première dent d'un enfant, tombée sans toucher terre (Aetios); la pierre d'orite, sulleptique pour le *Lapidaire orphique,* mais contraceptive pour celui de *Damigéron-Evax;* ou de la graine de pivoine ouverte avec la cire d'oreille de mulet (*Koiranides*).[75] La graine de pivoine apparaît comme une figure de la matrice: nouée dans une ceinture, elle favorise la conception; ouverte, elle laisse s'écouler la semence.[76]

ABORTIFS

Lorsque les moyens contraceptifs échouent, la femme se voit forcée d'affronter les risques de l'avortement. Tous les médecins mettent en garde contre les dangers que celui-ci comporte. Mais celle qui veut à tout prix interrompre une grossesse intempestive trouvera toujours les moyens de le faire, parfois au prix de sa vie.

Dans le meilleur des cas, s'il y a une indication médicale sérieuse, elle aura recours au médecin. Celui-ci dispose, depuis Hippocrate et Dioscoride, d'une multitude de recettes. Mais on peut penser que la médecine populaire est ici très présente. Les *Ephodia,* un manuel de thérapeutique traduit de l'arabe au

---

(Bonn, 1836), 267. Voir C. M. Brand, "The Turkish Element in Byzantium, Eleventh–Twelfth Centuries," *DOP* 43 (1989): 8.

71   Aetios d'Amida, 16.16–17, pp. 17–20.

72   Syméon Seth, kappa, lin. 88; lambda, lin. 12.

73   *Iatrosophion dit de Staphidakis:* Paris. gr. 2316, f. 337.

74   *Koiranides,* Gamma, 7.

75   Aetios d'Amida, 16.17, p. 19; *Lapidaire orphique,* vv. 459–60; *Damigéron-Evax,* 253; *Koiranides,* Gamma, 8.

76   Sur l'utilisation de la pivoine en gynécologie et la recrudescence de copies des manuscrits sur ce sujet à Byzance aux 14e et 15e siècles, voir A. Gribomont, "La pivoine dans les herbiers astrologiques grecs: Entre magie et médecine," *Bulletin de l'Institut Historique Belge de Rome* 74 (2004): 5–74.

10e siècle et qui eut une grande fortune à Byzance, comporte un chapitre sur les substances abortives et expulsives, dont la plupart trouvent leur origine chez les médecins antérieurs (Soranos, Galien, Oribase, Dioscoride, mais aussi Aetios, Paul d'Égine, ou Syméon Seth). On y trouve, seuls ou en composition, en potion, pessaire, ou cataplasmes: la résine de cèdre (qui a aussi des vertus contraceptives), le cyclamen, la gentiane, l'aristoloche, l'absinthe, etc.[77]

Mais la femme qui cherche à se débarrasser d'un fardeau encombrant ne souhaite pas toujours avoir recours au médecin, ne serait-ce que parce que ses motivations ne sont pas forcément médicales. De la simple misère au fruit d'amours illicites, les motifs sont nombreux qui peuvent pousser une femme à "se débrouiller seule" ou avec l'aide d'une "vieille femme" compatissante. On peut supposer que les listes d'abortifs qui nous sont parvenues sous la plume d'auteurs médicaux ne sont que la partie émergée, officialisée en quelque sorte, d'un savoir empirique beaucoup plus vaste. Lorsque Dioscoride nous apprend que "l'on rapporte que la fiente de vautour en fumigation fait tomber les embryons" ou que "l'on dit que la femme enceinte qui enjambe la racine du cyclamen avorte,"[78] il ne fait que mettre par écrit une tradition orale ancienne et largement répandue dans les campagnes, dont rien n'indique qu'elle avait disparu à l'époque byzantine.

Les pratiques abortives ne se limitent sans doute pas à l'absorption de drogues. En dehors même des instruments chirurgicaux qui seront abordés plus bas, il est légitime de supposer que les "aiguilles à tricoter" évoquées pour des époques plus proches de nous avaient leurs équivalents en des temps plus éloignés. Deux vers d'Ovide suggèrent les deux sortes de méthodes employées pour expulser un enfant importun:

Pourquoi creuser vos entrailles en y introduisant des armes
Et en donnant aux enfants non nés des poisons funestes?

vestra quid effoditis subiectis viscera telis,
et nondum natis dira venena datis?[79]

---

77   Voir M.-H. Congourdeau, "A propos d'un chapitre des *Ephodia:* L'avortement chez les médecins grecs," *REB* 55 (1997): 260–78. Des études ont été menées sur les diverses substances contraceptives et abortives présentes dans les manuels médicaux antiques et médiévaux. Les analyses récentes concluent généralement à une certaine efficacité de ces substances: voir J. Riddle, *Contraception and Abortion from the Ancient World to the Renaissance* (Cambridge, Mass., 1992).
78   Dioscoride, *Euporiston,* II.80, II.164.
79   Ovide, *Amores,* II.14.27–28. L'exemple est latin et antique, mais il est légitime en ce domaine de présumer une permanence des pratiques.

Les deux extrémités de l'échelle sociale nous offrent des exemples de motifs "non médicaux" pour supprimer un enfant avant sa naissance, ainsi que de la vaste diffusion des savoirs en ce domaine, même en milieu non rural. Dans les cercles du pouvoir, on peut citer l'exemple d'Eusébia, femme de Constance II, qui fit boire un *venenum* à sa belle-soeur Hélène, pour "la faire avorter toutes les fois qu'elle concevrait."[80] Deux siècles plus tard, Théodora, aux dires de Procope, mettait régulièrement fin à ses grossesses;[81] mais dans ce cas précis, nous avons affaire à l'autre bout de l'échelle sociale, car c'est durant sa vie de courtisane, avant sa rencontre avec Justinien, que la future impératrice pratiquait ainsi des avortements répétés.

Il existe en effet une catégorie de femmes pour lesquelles l'avortement peut relever de motifs "professionnels": les prostituées.[82] Jean Chrysostome évoque ces femmes qui interrompent une grossesse "pour être toujours disponibles et désirables et gagner davantage d'argent."[83] Deux siècles plus tard, Théophylacte Simocates reproche à une femme de supprimer systématiquement les enfants en son sein, pour plaire à ses nombreux amants.[84] Il est légitime de penser que les lois byzantines qui évoquent le motif de "fornication" pour le crime d'avortement avaient largement en vue la prostitution.

Quand l'enfant naît quand même, ou que l'avortement, trop tardif, n'est pas possible, il reste à la femme à abandonner son enfant, refuser de le nourrir, ou tout simplement le supprimer. L'infanticide est un sujet trop vaste pour entrer dans le cadre de cette étude.[85] J'évoquerai simplement, dans la continuité du paragraphe précédent, la découverte, lors des fouilles des thermes d'Ashkelon en Israel, d'ossements d'une centaine de nouveau-nés dans un égout courant au-dessous des bains: ces thermes faisant fonction de bordel, ces ossements (qui appartiennent majoritairement à des nouveau-nés de sexe masculin) sont

---

80   Ammien Marcellin, 16.10.18, éd. E. Galletier et J. Fontaine, *Ammien Marcellin, Histoire* (Paris, 1968), 168.

81   Procope, *Histoire secrète*, 9.19, éd. O. Veh, *Prokop Anekdota,* Tusculum-Bücherei (München, 1970), 80; voir 17.16, p. 146, pour un échec de ses manoeuvres abortives.

82   Sur l'avortement chez les prostituées à Byzance, cf. S. Leontsini, *Die Prostitution im frühen Byzanz* (Wien, 1989), 109–10.

83   Jean Chrysostome, *Hom. 24 in Romanos* (PG 60:627).

84   Théophylacte Simocates, ep. 30 à Kalliope Rhodinè, éd. I. Zanetto, *Theophylacti Simocatae Epistulae* (Leipzig, 1985), 17–18.

85   Une bibliographie sur l'infanticide se trouve dans *Naissance et petite enfance dans l'Antiquité: Actes du colloque de Fribourg, 28 novembre–1er décembre 2001,* éd. V. Dasen (Fribourg, 2004), 391–92.

les témoins d'un infanticide systématique chez des prostituées de la Palestine byzantine.[86]

Du côté de la société

Quittons à présent le point de vue de la femme pour nous tourner vers le regard que la société byzantine porte sur ces pratiques. Trois regards seront ici analysés: celui du médecin, celui de l'État impérial, celui de l'Église.

Quand la femme veut un enfant

LE MÉDECIN

Le médecin, à Byzance aussi bien qu'à l'époque antique, se préoccupe avant tout de la santé de ses patientes. La première question qu'il se pose est de savoir s'il est bon pour une femme de porter un enfant. Cette question fait débat depuis l'Antiquité. Un auteur hippocratique présente la grossesse comme le seul remède à la suffocation utérine qui guette toute vierge pubère.[87] Le caractère bénéfique de la maternité est une opinion répandue, y compris de nos jours, pour cette raison que rapporte Soranos: le corps de la femme est fait pour enfanter, donc enfanter est bon pour elle. Mais Soranos est réservé vis-à-vis de cette opinion. Pour lui, la grossesse serait plutôt un mal nécessaire, qui altère la santé de la femme et la vieillit prématurément.[88] Les médecins de l'époque byzantine se partagent entre ces deux extrêmes. Aetios d'Amida met en garde contre les dangers d'une grossesse trop précoce,[89] tandis que Mètrodôra s'inscrit dans la lignée hippocratique: "Les femmes restées veuves dans leur jeunesse, ou vierges, qui ont dépassé l'âge qui convient au mariage, et qui souffrent de l'utérus à cause de leur stérilité, parce que le désir naturel est resté inactif, subissent de nombreux malaises."[90]

Peut-être cette perplexité médicale devant les effets de la grossesse sur la santé explique-t-elle la réticence de certains médecins à conseiller, pour favoriser la conception, d'autres remèdes que ceux qui soignent les causes mêmes de la stérilité.

---

86   Voir C. Dauphin, "Bordels et filles de joie: La prostitution en Palestine byzantine," in *EYΨYXIA: Mélanges offerts à Hélène Ahrweiler* (Paris, 1998), 1:177–94.

87   Hippocrate, *Sur les maladies des jeunes filles* (Littré 8:469).

88   Soranos, 1.10, pp. 28–29.

89   Aetios d'Amida, 16.16, pp. 17–18.

90   Mètrodôra, 1.2, pp. 48–49 (traduction, 62).

La stérilité étant une maladie, il faut soigner la femme pour rétablir un équilibre naturel, et non user de *sulleptika* qui forcent la nature.

Aetios est intéressant à plus d'un titre. Tout d'abord, il place la cause d'une stérilité aussi bien chez l'homme que chez la femme, alors que les sociétés traditionnelles incriminent généralement la femme seule.[91] D'autre part, il attribue une certaine forme de stérilité à la contrainte exercée sur une femme forcée de s'unir à un homme qu'elle n'aime pas. "Les unions faites avec amour sont les plus fécondes [αἱ μετ᾽ ἔρωτος μίξεις ταχυτεκνόταταί εἰσι]."[92] Les conseils qu'il donne pour favoriser la fécondité sont de bons sens: ne pas commencer trop tôt; avoir un mode de vie naturel, un régime équilibré; tirer profit de la période la plus apte à la conception, à savoir la fin des règles; soigner les matrices trop humides ou trop sèches par des traitements qui concernent le corps entier. Il s'emporte contre ceux qui appliquent des remèdes trop agressifs et déplore les dégâts de contraceptifs irritants qui provoquent des stérilités incurables.

La prudence d'Aetios n'est pas suivie par tous. Les auteurs de manuels thérapeutiques fournissent nombre de sulleptika, sans toujours en préciser les dangers. Mètrodôra, après avoir esquissé une analyse des causes de stérilité, s'empresse de donner toutes sortes de recettes, drogues sulleptiques ou aphrodisiaques, voire les deux ensemble, tel un pessaire "aphrodisiaque pour l'érection et la conception" à base de graine de satyrion, de poivre, et d'alun.[93]

LE LÉGISLATEUR

La position du législateur est très différente. Alors que le médecin a en vue le bien de la femme, accordant toute son attention tantôt à son bien-être, tantôt à son désir d'être mère, le législateur demeure méfiant envers tout ce qui relève des drogues.[94]

Un chapitre du *Digeste* de Justinien, reprenant un commentaire du jurisconsulte Marcianus, étend l'application de la *Lex Cornelia de sicariis et veneficiis* non seulement aux fabricants, vendeurs, ou détenteurs de poisons (*venena*) mais à quiconque a fabriqué, vendu, ou détenu des *mala medicamenta* susceptibles

---

91   Nous avons vu que Jean Chrysostome refusait lui aussi de faire porter à la femme le poids de la stérilité du couple.

92   Aetios d'Amida, 16.26, pp. 36–40.

93   Mètrodôra, 2.21 (90), p. 60 (traduction, 85).

94   Voir M.-H. Congourdeau, "Les abortifs dans les sources byzantines," dans *Le corps à l'épreuve: Poisons, remèdes et chirurgie; Aspects des pratiques médicales dans l'Antiquité et le Moyen Âge,* éd. F. Collard et E. Samama (Reims, 2002), 57–70.

d'entraîner la mort. Après avoir partagé les *medicamenta* entre ceux qui sont faits pour soigner (*ad sanandum*), ceux qui sont faits pour tuer (*ad occidendum*), et les philtres d'amour (*amatoria*), il ajoute à la liste des *mala medicamenta* le "médicament destiné à faire concevoir" (*medicamentum ad conceptionem*) si la femme qui l'a pris en est morte.[95] Il est curieux de constater que, pour donner un exemple de *medicamentum ad sanandum* pouvant devenir un *medicamentum malum* du fait de son résultat, le législateur choisisse justement une drogue sulleptique.

Cette disposition est reprise dans la plupart des recueils de lois d'époque byzantine.[96] L'un d'entre eux, l'*Ecloga ad Procheiron mutata* (9e–10e s.), remplace la liste classique des *medicamenta*, dans laquelle le sulleptikon peut devenir un poison, par un trio légèrement différent: *pharmaka* pour soigner, philtres d'amour (*philtra*), et sulleptika.[97] Le sulleptikon, détaché des pharmaka pour soigner, n'est plus un simple exemple de médicament pouvant entraîner la mort, mais une catégorie séparée: un médicament dangereux est forcément un sulleptikon. Si on renverse la proposition, le sulleptikon est un poison.

L'attitude méfiante, sinon hostile, du législateur à l'égard des drogues pour concevoir a une double motivation: le souci de l'ordre public, et donc la répression des "empoisonneurs," et la répression de la sorcellerie, car philtres et drogues sulleptiques relèvent souvent de ce type de pratiques illicites. Sur ce point, il est intéressant de rapprocher cette méfiance envers les drogues, même fournies dans une bonne intention (cas des sulleptika), avec celle dont témoigne la Novelle 65 de Léon VI, à la fin du 9e siècle, contre toutes les formes de magie: selon cette Novelle, la magie est répréhensible même lorsqu'elle a pour but la guérison du corps.[98]

L'HOMME DE DIEU

L'Église porte généralement un regard favorable sur le désir d'enfant, quand il s'exerce dans le cadre du mariage. Les Pères de l'Église perçoivent la stérilité comme un malheur, tout en refusant d'y voir une punition divine.[99]

---

95 CIC *Dig* 4.8.3, 852.
96 *Appendix eclogae* 6.5, éd. L. Burgmann et Sp. Troianos, "Appendix Eclogae," dans *FM* 3 (Frankfurt, 1979), 110; Basiliques 60.39.3, éd. H. J. Scheltema et N. van der Wal, *Basilicorum libri LX,* Scripta Universitatis Groninganae, sér. B, 8 (Groningen, 1983), 3744; *Epitome legum* 45.21, éd. C. E. Zachariae von Lingenthal, *Jus Graeco-romanum,* tome 4 (Athènes, 1931), 574.
97 *Ecloga ad Procheiron mutata* 35.7, *Jus Graeco-romanum,* tome 6 (Athènes, 1962), 295.
98 Léon VI, *Novelle* 65, éd. et trad. P. Noailles et A. Dain, *Les Novelles de Léon VI le Sage* (Paris, 1944), 237–39.
99 Voir Jean Chrysostome, *Hom. 49 sur la Genèse* (PG 154:445).

Les saints accèdent volontiers à la demande des femmes stériles, et les miracles récompensent la prière. La stérilité est considérée comme un "lien" démoniaque dont le saint délivre la femme ou le couple. Un cas intéressant, qui ne concerne pas directement la stérilité mais une de ses causes, est fourni par un chapitre de la Vie de Léontios de Jérusalem, au 12e siècle, dans lequel le saint guérit un cas d'impuissance sexuelle. Un diacre de Palestine, qui n'avait pu "connaître" sa femme depuis trois ans qu'ils vivaient ensemble, vient lui demander la permission de dissoudre son mariage. Au lieu de cela, Léontios bénit de l'eau, la lui donne à boire, et lui dit d'en donner à boire aussi à sa femme. Aussitôt, "le lien est dénoué," et la nuit suivante, le diacre peut connaître sa femme. On suppose qu'un enfant viendra couronner le miracle.[100] Le même terme de "lien" empêchant la conception d'un enfant est employé pour la mère d'Étienne le Jeune, au 8e siècle (là aussi, le "lien" est dénoué par de l'eau bénite), et pour celle de Michel Maléinos au 10e siècle.[101] Dans l'*Historia Lausiaca,* un "lien" empêche non la conception mais la naissance d'un enfant. Cette historiette est particulièrement intéressante parce que le lien qui empêche l'enfant de sortir de la matrice a été imposé par un ascète calomnié, accusé à tort par la femme d'être le père de son enfant; le lien n'est dénoué qu'après l'aveu de ce mensonge.[102] Il est tentant de rapprocher tous ces miracles des croyances populaires dans les "sorts" jetés par l'intermédiaire d'incantations ou d'objets envoûtés, et qu'il fallait conjurer ("dénouer") en liant à son tour le démon enrôlé par le jeteur de sort, au moyen d'autres incantations (des exorcismes) ou d'autres objets (des amulettes protectrices).[103] C'est à ce symbolisme du lien noué et dénoué qu'il faut probablement rapporter le rôle de la ceinture que nous avons évoqué plus haut.

Lorsque la femme a recours à d'autres procédés que la prière et l'imploration d'un miracle, l'attitude des gens d'Église est plus dubitative. Si le but est louable, tous les moyens ne se valent pas. Cependant, un détour par la littérature canonique conduit à nuancer ce point de vue.

---

100   Vie de Léontios de Jérusalem, c. 81 (τοῦ δεσμοῦ ἄμφω ἐλύετο), éd. et trad. D. Tsougarakis, *The Life of Leontios Patriarch of Jerusalem* (Leiden, 1993), 128.

101   Vie d'Étienne le Jeune, c. 4, p. 92: "Romps le lien qui est en moi [ῥῆξον τὸν ἐν ἐμοὶ δεσμόν], comme fut rompu celui de ta génitrice, Anne, quand tu fus engendrée." Vie de Michel Maleinos, c. 4, p. 551. Sa mère prie la Théotokos de "rompre les liens de la stérilité [τὰ δεσμὰ λυθῆναι τῆς ἀπαιδίας]."

102   *Historia Lausiaca,* c. 70, p. 286 : "Dénoue le lien que tu as noué [λῦσον ὃ ἔδησας]."

103   Sur les incantations, sorts, et pratiques magiques à Byzance, voir Bakaloudi, "*Deisidaimonia* and the Role of the Apotropaic Magic Amulets," 182–210.

Le huitième canon de Basile traite des pénitences à appliquer aux meurtriers volontaires et involontaires. Distinguant entre le but et le résultat d'un acte ayant entraîné la mort, il aborde le cas de celui qui tue en administrant un philtre d'amour ou un abortif, et le fait entrer dans la catégorie des meurtres volontaires. En effet, les philtres et les abortifs sont des produits illicites qui relèvent de la magie, et ils sont dangereux en soi. Cependant, Basile ne range pas dans cette liste les drogues sulleptiques. On peut supposer que pour lui, le sulleptikon relève de la médecine, non de la magie, et que le motif en est louable, ce qui n'est pas le cas des abortifs et des philtres d'amour.[104]

Ce n'est que tardivement, au 12e siècle, que Balsamon, et lui seul parmi les canonistes, rapprochera la législation canonique de la législation impériale, et rangera les sulleptika dans la même catégorie que les abortifs et les philtra, précisant que les posséder, les donner, ou les prendre relève de la peine du meurtre, même en l'absence de résultat fatal.[105] Dans les sources ecclésiastiques, la méfiance envers les drogues sulleptiques est donc secondaire, et introduite sous l'influence du droit profane.

Quand la femme ne veut pas d'enfant

LE MÉDECIN

Les listes de recettes que l'on trouve dans les manuels thérapeutiques permettent difficilement de se faire une idée du regard que leurs auteurs portaient sur le refus d'enfant.[106] Les seuls critères évoqués dans les recettes sont la dangerosité parfois, l'efficacité surtout.

Il n'en est pas de même des auteurs médicaux de la tradition hippocratique, qui s'expliquent plus volontiers. Les pratiques contraceptives n'entraînent de leur part aucun jugement négatif, et il ne semble pas que sur ce point, les médecins d'époque byzantine aient différé de leurs prédécesseurs antiques. A la suite d'Hippocrate et de Soranos, Aetios d'Amida l'exprime sans ambiguïté: "Certaines femmes, quand elles conçoivent, sont en danger quand elles accoucheront, à cause de l'étroitesse du col de l'utérus, ou parce que la matrice tout entière est trop petite et incapable de mener à bien son office, ou parce qu'à l'orifice de

---

104   Basile, canon 8, éd. G. A. Rallès et M. Potlès, Σύνταγμα τῶν θείων καὶ ἱερῶν κανόνων, 4 (Athènes, 1854), 112–14.

105   Balsamon, *Sur le canon 91 in Trullo,* dans Rallès-Potlès, 2 (Athènes, 1852), 519–20.

106   Sur le rôle du médecin, voir Riddle, *Abortion from the Ancient World to the Renaissance;* Congourdeau, "A propos d'un chapitre des *Ephodia.*"

la matrice se trouve un kyste ou autre chose de ce genre, qui rend impossible l'accouchement."[107] Il s'accorde avec Soranos d'Ephèse qui, au 2e siècle, expliquait que "pour éviter d'avoir à détruire le produit de la conception, il vaut bien mieux ne pas concevoir."[108] La contraception, à condition de ne pas user de produits toxiques, est, pour ces médecins, bien préférable à l'avortement. C'est pourquoi la littérature médicale est riche en procédés propres à empêcher la conception.

La réticence est plus grande à l'égard des abortifs. Outre le Serment d'Hippocrate, qui garde une légitimité constante au cours des siècles, les dangers de l'avortement, déjà dénoncés par Hippocrate,[109] sont soulignés par l'ensemble des médecins s'occupant de gynécologie.[110] Mais ce qui est regrettable en soi peut parfois se révéler souhaitable: le médecin peut avoir à expulser un embryon mort dans le sein de sa mère, ou trop faible pour se développer complètement, ou se trouver devant une femme enceinte incapable de mener sa grossesse à terme ou d'accoucher. Aetios, à la suite de Soranos, évoque l'âge trop jeune ou la matrice trop étroite (les deux allant parfois de pair),[111] et il déclare que de toute façon, "l'avortement est préférable à l'embryotomie."[112] Tertullien avait fait écho, en son temps, à cette répugnance des médecins pour le découpage de l'enfant sorti morceau par morceau de la matrice d'une parturiente.[113]

Les médecins se contentaient-ils de fournir des drogues abortives, ou avaient-ils recours également à la chirurgie pour mettre fin à une grossesse indésirable? La découverte, dans des fouilles archéologiques, d'instruments chirurgicaux— par exemple, des crochets pouvant être utilisés pour extraire un foetus—et la présence de tels outils dans des listes d'instruments figurant dans des manuscrits médicaux semblent suggérer l'emploi de procédés invasifs.[114] Mais les témoignages écrits qui nous sont parvenus semblent concerner non des avortements mais des accouchements pathologiques et en particulier l'embryotomie.[115]

107   Aetios d'Amida, 16.7, pp. 9–10.
108   Soranos, 1.20, p. 59.
109   Hippocrate, *Sur les maladies des femmes*, 1.72 (Littré 8:152–53).
110   Voir Congourdeau, "A propos d'un chapitre des *Ephodia*."
111   Aetios d'Amida, 16.26, pp. 36–40; Soranos, 1.20, p. 59.
112   Aetios d'Amida, 16.16, p. 17.
113   Tertullien, *De anima,* 25.4–5.
114   Voir L. J. Bliquez, "Two Lists of Greek Surgical Instruments and the State of Surgery in Byzantine Times," *DOP* 38 (1984): 187–204. Le Laurentianus Graecus 74.2, par exemple, fournit une liste d'instruments chirurgicaux dont une partie concerne l'extraction de foetus.
115   Voir Paul d'Égine, *Chirurgie,* Livre 6, ch. 74. Contrairement à A. L. McClanan ("Weapons to Probe the Womb: The Material Culture of Abortion and Contraception in the Early Byzantine Period," dans *The Material Culture of Sex, Procreation and Marriage in Premodern Europe,*

Même pour extraire un embryon mort, le risque couru par la femme en cas d'intervention chirurgicale aurait en effet été encore plus grand que celui induit par l'emploi d'une drogue toxique: à mon sens, seul le danger mortel occasionné par un accouchement mal engagé pouvait pousser un médecin à utiliser cet arsenal chirurgical.[116]

Nous laissons de côté l'infanticide médical des nouveau-nés malformés, nous contentant de rappeler que Soranos énumère, dans son manuel à l'usage des sages-femmes, les critères permettant de reconnaître les enfants qui valent la peine d'être mis au sein.[117] Le manque de témoignages d'époque byzantine empêche de discerner ce que deviennent ces recommandations dans l'empire chrétien.

Cette enquête permet cependant de constater que le non-désir d'enfant est parfaitement reconnu par le médecin quand le bien-être de sa patiente est en jeu.

LE LÉGISLATEUR

Ici encore, il en est tout autrement avec le législateur. L'avortement dans le droit romain et à Byzance (la contraception est absente des textes juridiques) a été largement étudié.[118] Je me contenterai de quelques remarques sur ce que ces textes, très répétitifs, nous apprennent du regard porté sur le refus d'enfant. Je laisse de côté la législation sur les abortifs, qui ne concerne pas directement le refus d'enfant mais les drogues.[119]

Ce qui frappe en premier lieu, c'est que la femme est seule en cause. S'il faut bien l'intervention d'un homme pour qu'une femme devienne enceinte, celui-ci n'est mentionné que comme plaignant, jamais comme accusé. Le cas d'une femme avortant sur la demande ou avec l'accord de son mari n'existe pas au regard de la loi byzantine.

Sur ce sujet comme sur bien d'autres, le droit romain est à la base du droit byzantin. Les principales dispositions, collationnées dans le *Digeste* de Justinien, et

---

éd. A. L. McClanan et K. Encarnacion [New York, 2002], 33–57), je pense que ce chapitre sur l'extraction de foetus ne concerne pas l'avortement mais l'embryotomie.

116   Voir, pour une analyse des sources aboutissant à une conclusion semblable, S. Dowsing, "Contraception and Abortion in the Early Roman Empire: A Critical Examination of Ancient Sources and Modern Interpretations" (thèse de maîtrise, Université d'Ottawa, 1999), www.collectionscanada.ca/obj/s4/f2/dsk2/ftp01/MQ57109.pdf.

117   Soranos, 2.5, *Maladies des femmes,* tome 2 (Paris, 1990), 16–17.

118   Voir E. Nardi, *Procurato aborto nel mondo greco romano* (Milano, 1971); Sp. Troianos, "H ἄμβλωση στο βυζαντινό δίκαιο," *Byzantiaka* 4 (1984): 169–89; E. Koch, "Der Nasciturus als Rechtsgut: Historische Lehren und Begründungen," dans *Cupido Legum* (Francfurt, 1985), 87–98.

119   Voir Congourdeau, "Les abortifs," 58–60.

que l'on retrouve de code en code dans les recueils byzantins, sont les suivantes: la femme qui avorte volontairement frustre son mari de sa postérité; la sanction en est l'exil, un exil temporaire si la femme répudiée a avorté par ressentiment envers son époux, ou la mort si la femme, étant veuve, a reçu de l'argent de la part d'héritiers voulant éliminer un concurrent.[120] Quelques évolutions apparaissent à l'époque byzantine: l'avortement, qui figure parmi les motifs de répudiation dans le Code de Justinien[121] et dans une de ses Novelles,[122] ne figure plus dans une autre Novelle de Justinien,[123] mais il est rétabli par Léon VI, qui invoque le caractère sacré de la procréation.[124] L'*Ecloga,* pour une femme qui avorte après avoir forniqué, ajoute la flagellation à l'exil,[125] mesure qui sera reprise par la suite. Des recueils tardifs (*Epitome legum,* 10e s.) rangent l'avortement parmi les meurtres, avec le refus de nourrir un nouveau-né ou l'exposition des enfants.[126] On peut voir là une influence du droit canon.

Dans le regard du législateur sur la femme qui refuse un enfant, on trouve donc beaucoup moins de compréhension que dans celui du médecin. Le médecin voyait dans ce refus une souffrance ou un danger couru par la femme. Le législateur y lit la haine envers le mari que l'on veut frustrer de sa descendance, la vénalité dans le cas de la femme soudoyée par des héritiers, ou l'inconduite dans celui de la femme qui veut cacher sa faute. L'échelle des sanctions semble établir une gradation de la culpabilité: l'exil sera temporaire pour la femme répudiée, qui semble bénéficier de circonstances atténuantes, mais aggravé par la flagellation pour celle qui a forniqué (prostituée ou femme adultère); si la femme s'est laissé corrompre par des héritiers, le droit patrimonial est en jeu, et la peine de mort est envisagée.[127]

Il est instructif d'analyser les justificatifs de la Novelle 31 de Léon VI. Celui-ci n'envisage, à l'origine d'un avortement, que la haine de la femme envers son mari, haine qui lui paraît contre-nature puisque selon la Genèse, la femme a été créée comme une "aide" pour son époux: "Quelle preuve plus claire cherchera-t-on

---

120   Voir CIC *Dig* 47.11.4, p. 836; 48.8.8, p. 853; 48.19.39, p. 869.
121   CIC *CI* 5.17.11.2, 448.
122   CIC *Nov*, 22.16.1, 157.
123   CIC *Nov*, 117.8, pp. 557–58. Justinien semble avoir voulu simplifier la législation sur le divorce.
124   Léon VI, *Nov.* 31, pp. 122–26.
125   *Ecloga* 17.36, éd. J. Zepos et P. Zepos, *Jus graecoromanum,* tome 2 (Aalen, 1962), 58.
126   *Epitome legum* 45.7, p. 573.
127   Voir CIC *Dig* 48.19.39, p. 869.

encore," écrit-il, "pour voir que la femme est hostile envers son mari? Comment ne serait-il pas évident que c'est par malveillance contre lui qu'elle prive la semence de son processus vers la vie?"[128] Léon s'en tient délibérément à la dimension de l'offense faite au mari, sans doute parce qu'il traite du divorce, et il ne porte pas de jugement sur l'éventuelle suppression d'un être humain: "J'écarte," dit-il simplement, "le fait qu'elle est aussi coupable de comploter contre la nature commune." Ce n'est que plus tard que l'avortement sera rangé parmi les meurtres.

Dans une société largement patriarcale, la femme qui ne désire pas d'enfant a peu de chances de trouver grâce aux yeux du législateur, si son époux en a décidé autrement. L'absence de toute loi réprimant un avortement avec l'accord (ou sur l'ordre) du chef de famille montre que ce qui est réprimé est l'atteinte aux droits de l'époux, non à la vie d'un être humain.

Il serait intéressant de se demander dans quelle mesure cette législation répressive a été appliquée. Les sources manquent malheureusement. Dans le seul cas, à ma connaissance, où nous ayons les actes d'un procès pour avortement, la femme est singulièrement absente. Il s'agit du cas scabreux d'une moniale enceinte des oeuvres d'un hiéromoine, qui nous est rapporté dans le cadre du procès-fleuve en sorcellerie qui eut lieu devant le tribunal patriarcal de Constantinople en 1370.[129] Si le hiéromoine est jugé (sans doute davantage pour sorcellerie que pour avortement), nous ne savons rien de la sanction subie par la femme. Il faut dire que ce cas d'une moniale qui avorte n'est pas envisagé par le droit impérial: nul mari lésé n'avait ici besoin de faire valoir ses droits. On peut imaginer que la moniale subit des peines canoniques (privation de communion, jeûnes, métanies). Au regard des peines prévues par le droit impérial pour la femme qui avorte, la simple déposition du hiéromoine fautif nous apparaît légère. Mais cette légèreté peut être attribuée au statut clérical de l'accusé, qui relève du tribunal patriarcal et n'encourt pas les peines prévues par le droit impérial.

L'HOMME DE DIEU

Qu'en est-il de l'homme de Dieu? Deux types de sources se partagent notre sujet. Aux canonistes l'avortement, aux pénitentiels la contraception.

---

128 Léon VI, *Nov.* 31, pp. 122–26.
129 Voir une analyse de ce cas dans M.-H. Congourdeau, "Un procès d'avortement à Constantinople au 14e s.," *REB* 40 (1982): 103–15.

Avortement: le droit canon.   Trois canons forment la source de la doctrine canonique sur l'avortement. Le canon 21 d'Ancyre[130] fixe à dix ans la privation de communion pour les femmes qui ont avorté ou fourni un abortif; le canon 2 de Basile assimile l'avortement à un meurtre, en précisant que l'âge de l'embryon n'a pas à intervenir, étant donné que la femme risque de mourir en avortant; le canon 91 du concile in Trullo prévoit la peine du meurtre pour la femme qui avorte et celle qui fournit l'abortif.[131] Le canon de Basile est le plus intéressant parce qu'il argumente ce qu'il prescrit. Son principal apport réside dans le fait que pour lui, le motif essentiel de la peine réside dans le danger mortel couru par la femme.

Voici le texte de ce canon, dans une traduction la plus littérale possible:

> Celle qui a détruit [son fruit] volontairement [κατ' ἐπιτήδευσιν] encourt la peine du meurtre. Il n'y a pas lieu pour nous de préciser si [l'embryon était] formé ou non configuré [ἐκμεμορφωμένου καὶ ἀνεξεικονίστου]. En effet, ici doit être défendu non seulement l'être en devenir [τὸ γενησόμενον], mais aussi celui qui a attenté à lui-même, parce que la plupart du temps les femmes meurent de telles entreprises. Et s'ajoute à cela la destruction de l'embryon, autre meurtre, du moins dans le dessein de celles qui osent ces actions. Il faut pourtant ne pas prolonger jusqu'à la mort leur pénitence, mais accepter la mesure des dix ans; et il ne faut pas définir la thérapie seulement en fonction de la durée mais en fonction du mode du repentir.

Si nous nous tournons vers les canonistes byzantins, le seul qui ne se contente pas de paraphraser ces canons mais qui fournit une argumentation personnelle est Balsamon, dans son commentaire du canon 91 in Trullo, qui rassemble toute la législation canonique sur l'avortement.

Pour Balsamon, la peine appliquée en cas d'avortement est la peine du meurtre, même si l'embryon ne meurt pas, car c'est l'intention qui compte. Il introduit

---

130   Le canon publié sous le nom de canon 21 du synode d'Ancyre (314) est en fait un canon édicté par le synode de Césarée en 315. Voir F. van de Paverd, "Die Quellen der kanonischen Briefe Basileios des Grossen," *OCP* 38 (1972): 5–63, qui contient la bibliographie antérieure sur les canons des conciles d'Ancyre et de Césarée.
131   Canon 21 "d'Ancyre": Rallès-Potlès, 3 (Athènes, 1853), 63; Canon 2 de Basile (= Lettre 188.2 à Amphiloque d'Iconion): Rallès-Potlès, 4 (Athènes, 1854), 50–51; Canon 91 in Trullo: Rallès-Potlès, 2:518–19.

ainsi une discussion sur l'acte volontaire et l'acte involontaire. D'après lui, certains canonistes, prenant prétexte de ce que Basile attribue dix ans de pénitence à la femme qui avorte, rangent l'avortement dans la catégorie des meurtres involontaires: dix ans est en effet la durée que Basile assigne aux meurtres involontaires. Balsamon réfute cet argument en affirmant qu'il s'agit en réalité d'un meurtre volontaire, auquel on applique une peine moins lourde, pour deux raisons. La première raison est que "ce qui est conçu n'existe pas par nature [μὴ εἶναι ἐν φύσει τὸ κυοφορούμενον]," et la deuxième est que la femme doit bénéficier de circonstances atténuantes. En effet, dans la majorité des cas, elle a agi non par désir de tuer, mais "par peur de ses parents ou de son maître ou d'un autre danger."[132]

Dans le cas de Balsamon comme dans celui de Basile, on constate deux différences flagrantes avec le droit profane: l'absence de prise en considération des droits du mari, exclu de son rang de victime au profit de la femme et de l'embryon, et un effort de compréhension du motif qui pousse une femme à avorter: non pas la malveillance mais la peur. La prise en considération de la femme l'emporte même sur celle de l'embryon puisque pour Basile, l'âge de ce dernier ne doit pas entrer en ligne de compte, tandis que pour Balsamon, l'embryon n'existe tout simplement pas en tant qu'être humain.

Contraception: les Pénitentiels.   En revanche, la contraception, qui ne trouble pas le législateur profane, devient la cible d'un nouveau type de sources, les Pénitentiels, ou manuels du confesseur, qui ont pour fonction d'adapter la règle à la pratique.[133] Textes de praticiens, ces manuels semblent reconnaître la distinction, opérée par d'autres praticiens, les médecins, entre contraception et avortement. Mais alors que les médecins jugent la contraception bien préférable à l'avortement (plutôt que de détruire le fruit conçu, il vaut bien mieux ne pas concevoir), les auteurs de Pénitentiels semblent poser le jugement inverse. Ce qui incite à se demander dans quelle mesure ces auteurs, qui ne connaissaient de ces pratiques que ce qu'ils entendaient en confession, de la part de femmes qui ne devaient pas non plus comprendre exactement ce qui leur arrivait, apprécient réellement la distinction entre contraception et avortement.

Parler des "auteurs de Pénitentiels" est d'ailleurs bien peu précis, car la grande majorité de ces textes dérivent en fait d'un même corpus, qui décline, sous des

132   Balsamon, Commentaire du canon 91 in Trullo, Rallès-Potlès, 2:519–20.
133   Sur les pénitentiels, voir M. Arranz, *I Penitenziali bizantini: 1. Il 'protokanonarion o Kanonarion Primitivo' di Giovanni monaco e diacono; 2. Il Deuterokanonarion o Secondo kanonarion di Basilio monaco* (Roma, 1993).

formes différentes, un noyau primitif attribué à Jean le Jeûneur (6e siècle). Sur l'avortement, ces Pénitentiels se contentent de suivre les canons. Je m'attacherai donc aux textes qui traitent de la contraception.

En regardant ces textes, on perçoit, à travers les réécritures et adaptations, une distinction entre trois sortes de refus d'enfant de la part des pénitentes. L'une consiste à "boire un *pharmakon* et ne pas concevoir," ce qui est jugé "plus grave que tout, parce que la femme ne sait pas combien d'enfants elle aurait eu"; la seconde, à procéder "par des trimmata [τὸ διὰ τριμμάτων]"; la troisième consiste à "expulser [ἀποκτείνειν dans une version, ἀποτίθεσθαι dans une autre] un embryon par mois au moyen d'une herbe," ce qui là aussi est jugé "très grave."[134]

Quelles pratiques exactes se cachent sous ces expressions? Un rapprochement avec Aetios d'Amida peut nous éclairer. Ce médecin évoque, parmi les contraceptifs, des drogues "à absorber une fois par mois." Voilà sans doute ce qui, à travers les aveux d'une femme, est parvenu jusqu'aux oreilles du rédacteur de pénitentiel, et qui, dans son esprit, est devenu "tuer [ou expulser] un embryon par mois au moyen d'une herbe." Ce meurtre d'embryon est-il à prendre au pied de la lettre, si bien que le confesseur confondrait un simple contraceptif avec un abortif, ou est-ce une figure de style, selon laquelle empêcher la venue à l'être d'un enfant équivaut à le tuer? Une seconde pratique, jugée moins grave, consiste à user de *trimmata,* terme qui désigne dans la littérature médicale des potions à base de plantes pilées, mais qui pourrait éventuellement renvoyer à des manipulations mécaniques (écrasement du ventre). Comme cette pratique est opposée à celle qui a lieu "une fois par mois," nous pouvons supposer qu'il s'agit là d'un procédé "au coup par coup," c'est-à-dire soit un contraceptif à prendre "au moment de l'union," comme on en trouve de nombreux exemples dans les iatrosophia, soit un abortif ponctuel, soit encore, nous l'avons vu, un procédé mécanique. Le pharmakon que l'on boit pour "ne pas concevoir," "plus grave que tout, parce que la femme ne sait pas combien d'enfants elle aurait eu," pourrait désigner alors une drogue de stérilité.[135] Paradoxalement, nous aboutissons à un classement dans lequel la pratique jugée la moins grave est la seule dont on puisse supposer qu'elle peut avoir une action abortive, les autres étant stérilisantes ou contraceptives.

---

134   Ἀκολουθία καὶ τάξις (PG 88:1904B–C) (ἀποτίθεσθαι); Διδασκαλία Πατέρων (PG 88:1928D) (ἀποκτείνειν).

135   A propos des "drogues de stérilité," on peut évoquer une tradition midrashique rapportée dans *Bereshit Rabbah* 23.2: à l'époque du déluge, tout homme aurait eu deux femmes, l'une pour la procréation d'enfants, l'autre pour assouvir ses désirs sexuels; cette dernière aurait bu, justement, une potion de stérilité à base de racines. Cité par Dauphin, "Bordels et filles de joie," 194.

Mais on voit que les choses ne sont pas vraiment claires, et qu'il serait imprudent d'en conclure que pour les confesseurs byzantins, la contraception est jugée plus grave que l'avortement.

Signalons enfin que, parmi les sujets à aborder en confession, figurent "le désir de stérilité [πόθου τῆς ἀτεκνίας]" et la fabrication de "plantes pour ne pas concevoir [τὰ μὴ συλλαμβάνειν ποιῆσαι βοτάνην],"[136] qui sont donc classés comme des péchés, c'est-à-dire non comme des crimes à sanctionner, puisque le confesseur n'est ni un juge séculier ni même un canoniste, mais comme des maladies à soigner. La confession à Byzance est vue essentiellement comme une thérapie.

Conclusion

Il est donc possible d'appréhender, dans le brouillard des sources indirectes, le désir et le non-désir d'enfant de la femme byzantine. Il est probable que, compte tenu de l'importance de la maternité pour le statut de la femme, et des conditions sanitaires qui rendaient cette maternité incertaine (du fait des stérilités pathologiques et de la mortalité infantile), le désir d'enfant était le plus répandu, d'où l'importance des drogues pour concevoir, plus nombreuses que les contraceptifs. Mais la suspicion dans laquelle était tenue la femme, son assujettissement au chef de la famille, et la pauvreté d'une grande partie de la population pouvaient rendre dramatique la survenue d'un enfant. Pour cacher un amour défendu, pour limiter des grossesses trop nombreuses, ou pour toute autre raison, plus d'une femme pouvait souhaiter éviter ou interrompre une grossesse. C'est sur ce point qu'il est intéressant d'analyser les différences entre les sociétés antiques et l'empire chrétien.

Du côté de la femme, on est frappé par la permanence des désirs, des croyances et des comportements, le saint homme se substituant au besoin à la divinité païenne. C'est pourquoi il est difficile de discerner une évolution chronologique dans ce domaine qui est par excellence celui de la longue durée. Tout au plus peut-on voir apparaître dans les sources chrétiennes une catégorie nouvelle de femmes sans enfants: les moniales et autres vierges consacrées.

Du côté de la société, la pesanteur des structures et des mentalités freine la mise en place de jugements et de comportements nouveaux. Le médecin, pour sa part, ne semble pas changer de rôle avec l'avènement d'une société chrétienne, et le médecin byzantin ne se démarque pas vraiment du médecin antique. Ce

---

136   PG 88:1924A.

n'est pas faire preuve de naïveté que de constater qu'il est généralement pour la femme un allié, au risque de la décevoir quand son désir n'est pas compatible avec sa santé. Le législateur, de son côté, évolue lentement, et cette évolution n'est pas favorable à la femme: il reste méfiant vis-à-vis des drogues pour concevoir, et l'on a vu que les Isauriens (avec l'*Ecloga* qui ajoute la flagellation à l'exil) et Léon VI (qui rétablit le droit pour le mari de se séparer de sa femme en cas d'avortement) durcissent au détriment de la femme la législation sur l'avortement.

Quant à l'homme de Dieu, son rôle est ambivalent. La femme qui désire un enfant trouve en lui un allié: il n'a pas envers les sulleptika la méfiance du législateur, et pour qualifier un acte, il s'intéresse prioritairement à l'intention. Il est moins bienveillant vis-à-vis du refus d'enfant, qu'il s'agisse d'absorber des herbes contraceptives ou de supprimer un embryon importun. Mais, à la suite de Basile ou de Balsamon, il peut reconnaître dans la femme non une criminelle qui offense son époux, mais une victime qui met sa vie en danger et qui agit par crainte plus que par malveillance, ou une pécheresse à guérir. C'est bien Jean Chrysostome qui, l'un des premiers, osa dire que si les prostituées avortaient, la faute en revenait à leurs clients.[137]

Centre National de la Recherche Scientifique

---

137   Jean Chrysostome, *Hom. 24 in Romanos* (PG 60:626–27).

BREASTFEEDING AND WEANING PATTERNS IN BYZANTINE TIMES

Evidence from Human Remains and Written Sources

Chryssi Bourbou and Sandra J. Garvie-Lok

B REASTFEEDING AND WEANING PATTERNS in past societies are of considerable interest, not only in their own right but also for their implications for issues such as juvenile health and attitudes toward women and children. Traditionally, these patterns have been reconstructed using documentary evidence. However, reconstruction through the stable isotope analysis of human remains provides an alternative source of information. Together, documentary and isotopic evidence can provide a detailed portrait of breastfeeding and weaning in the past. This paper presents a small set of isotopic data on weaning in Byzantine Greece, as well as a summary of the relevant documentary evidence. The available data do not yet allow firm conclusions on Byzantine weaning to be drawn. However, they are consistent with weaning patterns seen in some imperial and late Roman communities, perhaps indicating significant continuity in weaning customs in the Byzantine era.

We thank Dr. Alice-Mary Talbot for the kind encouragement and advice she gave us during the preparation of this manuscript. Thanks for permission to study skeletal material, and advice and feedback on the remains, are due to E. Barnes, M. Becker, J. Camp, L. M. Little-Georgakopoulos, S. G. Miller, N. Tsilipakou, M. Tsipopoulou, C. K. Williams II, E. H. Williams, M. Andrianakis, L. Starida, and M. Kirimi. Special thanks to M. Richards and E. Petroutsa for their valuable help in the preparation and analysis of the derived data for the Kastella sample. Funding for the research of Sandra Garvie-Lok was provided by the Wiener Laboratory of the American School of Classical Studies at Athens, the Social Sciences and Humanities Research Council of Canada, and the University of Calgary. Funding for the research of Chryssi Bourbou was provided by the Centenary Bursary of the British School of Athens (2003–4).

Stable Nitrogen Isotopes: Some Essentials

The stable nitrogen isotope analysis of archaeological skeletal remains is an established and powerful method for the reconstruction of breastfeeding and weaning behavior in past populations. However, little research has been conducted in most regions, mainly because infants are not often represented in many archaeological cemetery sites in the numbers necessary for isotopic reconstruction of feeding patterns.[1] The basis of this technique lies in the relationship between the stable nitrogen isotope ratios of the tissues and those of the diet, and in the difference in stable nitrogen isotope ratios seen between the tissues of nursing infants and of their mothers.

Nitrogen has two stable isotopes, the common ^{14}N and the much rarer ^{15}N.[2] The relative content of these two isotopes in any material is referred to as its stable nitrogen isotope ratio or $\delta^{15}N$ value. This ratio is expressed relative to an international standard, in per mil (‰), with a higher value indicating a higher proportion of ^{15}N in the sample. ^{14}N and ^{15}N are essentially identical chemically, participating in the same reactions to produce the same molecules. However, the slight difference in their weights can cause one isotope (usually the lighter ^{14}N) to participate in a reaction more readily than the other, causing the $\delta^{15}N$ value of the products of the reaction to differ from that of the reactants. This effect, called fractionation, causes variation in the $\delta^{15}N$ values of various substances. For living organisms, this variation follows a predictable pattern, allowing aspects of diet and behavior to be inferred from the $\delta^{15}N$ values of an organism's tissues.

The $\delta^{15}N$ values of most plants reflect the values of the available nitrogen in local soil nutrients and are often quite low.[3] In animals, the $\delta^{15}N$ values of the tissues are determined by the $\delta^{15}N$ values of items in the diet. Because of the

---

1   B. T. Fuller, T. I. Molleson, D. A. Harris, L. T. Gilmour, and R. E. M. Hedges, "Isotopic Evidence for Breastfeeding and Possible Adult Dietary Differences from Late/Sub-Roman Britain," *AJPA* 129 (2006): 45–54.

2   For more extensive background information on stable nitrogen isotope analysis, see M. A. Katzenberg, "Stable Isotope Analysis: A Tool for Studying Past Diet, Demography, and Life History," in *Biological Anthropology of the Human Skeleton,* ed. M. A. Katzenberg and S. R. Saunders (New York, 2000), 305–27.

3   R. A. Virginia and C. C. Delwiche, "Natural ^{15}N Abundance of Presumed N_2-fixing and Non-N_2-fixing Plants from Selected Ecosystems," *Oecologia* 54 (1982): 317–25; M. J. Schoeninger and M. J. DeNiro, "Nitrogen and Carbon Isotope Composition of Bone Collagen from Marine and Terrestrial Animals," *GCA* 48 (1984): 625–29.

CHRYSSI BOURBOU AND SANDRA J. GARVIE-LOK

tendency of ^{14}N to be concentrated and excreted in the urine, the nitrogen that remains in the body's tissues is relatively rich in ^{15}N. As a result, the δ^{15}N value of an animal's tissue proteins is elevated by 2‰ to 5‰ above the mean value of its diet. This effect is seen at each level in the food web, as herbivore consumes plant and carnivore consumes herbivore, and is referred to as the trophic level effect.[4]

Nursing, Weaning, and Stable Nitrogen Isotopes

One of the most interesting manifestations of the trophic level effect is the δ^{15}N difference seen between the tissues of mothers and of their nursing infants. A lactating mother's milk protein, like her tissue proteins, shows a δ^{15}N value roughly one trophic level above that of her diet. In turn, a nursing infant consuming this milk will show a trophic level effect between the milk and its own tissues. In effect, the infant is positioned one trophic level above its mother, with correspondingly higher tissue δ^{15}N values.[5]

Observations made on fingernail clippings of modern human mothers and their babies show how this effect leads to shifting δ^{15}N values in the tissues of infants as they are born, nurse, and are weaned.[6] At birth, an infant's fingernail δ^{15}N value is the same as that of its mother, reflecting the fact that these tissues were synthesized in utero, using the proteins of the mother's diet. However, as the fingernails grow, nail tissue synthesized after birth, on a diet of milk, moves

4   K. W. Steele and R. M. Daniel, "Fractionation of Nitrogen Isotopes by Animals: A Further Complication to the Use of Variations in the Natural Abundance of ^{15}N for Tracer Studies," *Journal of Agricultural Science* 90 (1978): 7–9; M. J. DeNiro and S. Epstein, "Influence of Diet on the Distribution of Nitrogen Isotopes in Animals," *GCA* 45 (1981): 341–51; M. Minagawa and E. Wada, "Step-wise Enrichment of ^{15}N along Food Chains: Further Evidence and the Relationship between δ^{15}N and Animal Age," *GCA* 48 (1984): 1135–40; P. E. Hare, M. L. Fogel, T. W. Stafford Jr., A. D. Mitchell, and T. C. Hoering, "The Isotopic Composition of Carbon and Nitrogen in Individual Amino Acids Isolated from Modern and Fossil Proteins," *JArS* 18 (1991): 277–92; H. Bocherens and D. Drucker, "Trophic Level Isotopic Enrichment of Carbon and Nitrogen in Bone Collagen: Case Studies from Recent and Ancient Terrestrial Ecosystems," *International Journal of Osteoarchaeology* 13 (2003): 46–53.
5   See reviews in M. A. Katzenberg, D. A. Herring, and S. R. Saunders, "Weaning and Infant Mortality: Evaluating the Skeletal Evidence," *Yearbook of Physical Anthropology* 39 (1996): 177–99; B. T. Fuller, J. L. Fuller, D. A. Harris, and R. E. M. Hedges, "Detection of Breastfeeding and Weaning in Modern Human Infants with Carbon and Nitrogen Stable Isotope Ratios," *AJPA* 129 (2006): 279–93.
6   M. L. Fogel, N. Tuross, and D. Owsley, "Nitrogen Isotope Tracers of Human Lactation in Modern and Archaeological Populations," *Carnegie Institution Year Book* 88 (1989): 111–17.

out toward the nail edge, replacing nail tissue formed in utero. This change is reflected in a rise in the $\delta^{15}N$ values of the infant's fingernails. The infant's fingernail $\delta^{15}N$ values peak at roughly one trophic level above those of the mother and remain elevated while the infant is obtaining all of its nutrition from its mother's milk. As milk begins to be supplemented with solid foods, the mean $\delta^{15}N$ value of an infant's diet begins to decrease toward that of its mother's diet. This change is reflected by a decline in the infant's fingernail $\delta^{15}N$ value. The magnitude of this decline is influenced by the amount of breast milk still consumed: initially an infant may show only a small change, as a largely milk-based diet is supplemented with limited quantities of solid food, followed by a greater change as solid food comes to constitute a major portion of the diet. After weaning is complete, the infant's fingernails show a $\delta^{15}N$ value similar to that of the mother.

Stable Nitrogen Isotopes and Weaning in Archaeological Populations

Since the effects of nursing and weaning on human $\delta^{15}N$ values were first documented, stable nitrogen isotope analysis has been used to study nursing and weaning in a number of archaeological human populations.[7] This application is possible because changes in the $\delta^{15}N$ value of an infant's diet are reflected in

7   M. A. Katzenberg, S. R. Saunders, and W. R. Fitzgerald, "Age Differences in Stable Carbon and Nitrogen Isotope Ratios in a Population of Prehistoric Maize Horticulturists," *AJPA* 90 (1993): 267–81; M. A. Katzenberg and S. Pfeiffer, "Nitrogen Isotope Evidence for Weaning Age in a Nineteenth Century Canadian Skeletal Sample," in *Bodies of Evidence,* ed. A. Grauer (New York, 1995), 221–35; M. R. Schurr, "Stable Nitrogen Isotopes as Evidence for the Age of Weaning at the Angel Site: A Comparison of Isotopic and Demographic Measures of Weaning Age," *JArS* 24 (1997): 919–27; D. A. Herring, S. R. Saunders, and M. A. Katzenberg, "Investigating the Weaning Process in Past Populations," *AJPA* 105 (1998): 425–39; T. L. Dupras, H. P. Schwarcz, and S. I. Fairgrieve, "Infant Feeding and Weaning Practices in Roman Egypt," *AJPA* 115 (2001): 204–12; M. P. Richards, S. Mays, and B. T. Fuller, "Stable Carbon and Nitrogen Isotope Values of Bone and Teeth Reflect Weaning Age at the Medieval Wharram Percy Site, Yorkshire, U.K.," *AJPA* 119 (2002): 205–10; T. Prowse, H. P. Schwarcz, S. Saunders, R. Macchiarelli, and L. Bondioli, "Isotopic Paleodiet Studies of Skeletons from the Imperial Roman-Age Cemetery of Isola Sacra, Rome, Italy," *JArS* 31 (2004): 259–72; M. R. Schurr and M. L. Powell, "The Role of Changing Childhood Diets in the Prehistoric Evolution of Food Production: An Isotopic Assessment," *AJPA* 128 (2005): 278–94; J. S. Williams, C. D. White, and F. J. Longstaffe, "Trophic Level and Macronutrient Shift Effects Associated with the Weaning Process in the Post-classic Maya," *AJPA* 128 (2005): 781–90; Fuller et al., "Isotopic Evidence for Breastfeeding" (above, n. 1); M. P. Richards, B. T. Fuller, and T. I. Molleson, "Stable Isotope Palaeodietary Study of Humans and Fauna from the Multi-period (Iron Age, Viking and Late Medieval) Site of Newark Bay, Orkney," *JArS* 33 (2006): 122–31.

CHRYSSI BOURBOU AND SANDRA J. GARVIE-LOK

its bone collagen, the structural protein of the bone tissue, through turnover, the incorporation of freshly synthesized material into the bones due to growth and regeneration. The freshly synthesized material shows a $\delta^{15}N$ value reflecting that of the current diet. Thus, after an infant's diet is changed from breast milk to solid food, turnover begins to replace bone collagen synthesized from milk with bone collagen synthesized from solid food. As more of the bone collagen is replaced, the $\delta^{15}N$ value of the skeleton as a whole reflects that of the new diet more closely, until adjustment to the new dietary $\delta^{15}N$ value is complete. Generally speaking, bone as a tissue is slow to turn over, and the bones of adults may retain the isotopic signal of an earlier diet for many years. However, bone turnover in a rapidly growing infant is considerably faster, especially in small and porous bones such as the ribs. Observations on large samples of infants from archaeological skeletal populations have led researchers such as Katzenberg et al. and Richards et al. to suggest that the lag time between weaning and a shift in infant rib $\delta^{15}N$ value is quite brief, on the order of a few months or less.[8]

The most common approach to studying weaning through archaeological remains is the study of bone samples from a number of infants and children in a burial group.[9] These are analyzed, and their $\delta^{15}N$ values are plotted by age at death and compared to the mean value for adult females in the population. Typically, such studies show $\delta^{15}N$ values for neonates that are similar to those of adult females. The values then rise fairly rapidly with age at death to roughly one trophic level above the mean adult female value as nursing incorporates ^{15}N-enriched collagen into the bones. After a given age, they begin to drop again; the point at which this drop begins is taken to indicate the age by which weaning typically began for the population in question.

Although powerful, this application of stable nitrogen isotope analysis has its limitations.[10] First, although the evidence to date suggests that the lag between the onset of weaning and a detectable change in bone $\delta^{15}N$ values is on the order

8   Katzenberg et al., "Weaning and Infant Mortality" (above, n. 5); Richards, Mays, and Fuller, "Stable Carbon and Nitrogen Isotope Values."
9   Katzenberg et al., "Age Differences"; Katzenberg and Pfeiffer, "Nitrogen Isotope Evidence for Weaning Age"; Richards, Mays, and Fuller, "Stable Carbon and Nitrogen Isotope Values"; Richards, Fuller, and Molleson, "Stable Isotope Palaeodietary Study"; Schurr and Powell, "The Role of Changing Childhood Diets"; Schurr, "Stable Nitrogen Isotopes"; Williams, White, and Longstaffe, "Trophic Level and Macronutrient Shift Effects."
10   For some discussions of these limitations, see Katzenberg et al., "Weaning and Infant Mortality"; Fuller et al., "Detection of Breastfeeding" (above, n. 5); Fuller et al., "Isotopic Evidence for Breastfeeding."

of a few months, its precise duration is unknown and likely varies according to individual factors such as health and metabolism. Thus, the onset of a drop in $\delta^{15}N$ values must be taken as the time by which weaning had typically begun for a population, rather than a precise estimate of weaning age. A second proviso is that in a severely ill or malnourished infant, growth is likely to be reduced, with the possible effect of delaying the apparent onset of weaning as reflected in skeletal $\delta^{15}N$ values. Because the infants in a burial group represent those who did not survive infancy, they may well include individuals who had been severely ill or malnourished for some time before death. The weaning age suggested by the $\delta^{15}N$ values of such individuals may be somewhat older than the age at which surviving infants—those who lived to enter the cemetery as older subadults or adults—were actually weaned. This problem may be further complicated by differences between the approach taken in weaning healthy and sickly infants, as the weaning pattern reflected in the deceased infants from the burial population is more likely to reflect the approach preferred for an unwell child.

Because of these issues, and because of a certain normal variation in weaning age expected for any population, it is preferable to examine a large number of infants from several sites before weaning practices in a given era can be confidently reconstructed. Measurements on a smaller number of infants, such as those reported in this study, should be taken as a step in that direction, and as suggestive rather than conclusive.

Perinatal Nutrition as Attested in the Written Sources

Byzantine physicians included in their works chapters on the care of the newborn and in particular on perinatal nutrition, conveying the eclectic knowledge of ancient Greek physicians, enriched with additional remarks and clarifications based on their own experience.[11] The most eminent early Byzantine physician was Oribasius from Pergamum (fourth century C.E.), whose work influenced later Byzantine physicians as well as Arabic medicine.[12] Aetius of Amida (sixth century C.E.) and Paul of Aegina (seventh century C.E.) followed Oribasius's rec-

---

11   For further discussion of infant and child nutrition, see the article by Brigitte Pitarakis in this volume.
12   I. Raeder, *Oribasii collectionum medicarum reliquiae,* vol. 4 (Amsterdam, 1964); J. Laskaratos and E. Poulakou-Rebelakou, "Oribasius (Fourth Century) and Early Byzantine Perinatal Nutrition," *Journal of Pediatric Gastroenterology and Nutrition* 36 (2003): 186–89; J. Beaucamp, "L'allaitement: Mère ou nourrice?" *JÖB* 32, no. 2 (1982): 549–58.

ommendatons on perinatal nutrition and weaning patterns, and a famous midwife of the seventh century C.E., Metrodora, followed Oribasius in her prescriptions of various milk-producing substances.[13] Oribasius gave detailed accounts of the child's nutrition immediately after birth until the age of fourteen years, focusing mainly on the period up to two years of age. He argued that immediately after birth, the newborn must be fed with clear honey of high quality, followed by drops of a lukewarm solution of honey and water (hydromel) to be given slowly over the subsequent four days. He was specific in urging that the child not be fed colostrum (the enriched milk secreted by the mother for the first few days after birth), which he felt to be harmful. After this period nursing could commence, with the infant receiving two or three feedings per day. Here Oribasius accepts the opinions of two earlier physicians on the feeding of newborns.[14] Rufus from Ephesus (first century C.E.) recommended that the infant initially be fed honey, followed by the gradual introduction of breast milk.

Oribasius further accepted some suggestions offered by Soranus from Ephesus (first century C.E.), who was also opposed to immediate breastfeeding.[15] He recommended that food be withheld from a newborn for at least two days, until its body was fully recovered from the process of birth. After this interval, the baby should be given food to lick. Soranus rejected the apparently popular choices of butter, southernwood with butter, nosesmart (a type of cress), or kneaded barley meal for this first food, feeling them to be too hard on the child's sensitive gastrointestinal system.[16] Instead, the newborn should be given hydromel or honey mixed with goat's milk. After the second day, the baby could also receive breast milk; however, this should come from a wet nurse for the first twenty days, as Soranus felt the mother's milk to be unwholesome in most cases during this period.[17]

Oribasius and Soranus both rejected the belief of some other ancient physicians who ordered mothers to give newborns breast milk immediately after birth.[18] Although Soranus argued that after the initial twenty days a baby should

---

13   Laskaratos and Poulakou-Rebelakou, "Oribasius," 189; M.-H. Congourdeau, "Mètrodôra et son oeuvre," in *Maladie et Société à Byzance,* ed. É. Patlagean (Spoleto, 1993), 57–96.
14   Laskaratos and Poulakou-Rebelakou, "Oribasius," 186, 188.
15   O. Temkin, *Soranus's Gynecology* (Baltimore, 1991), 88–89 (book 2, 11 [31]).
16   Ibid., 88 (book 2, 11 [31]); Oribasius also rejected butter, as he thought it was too heavy for the stomach of the newborn. Laskaratos and Poulakou-Rebelakou, "Oribasius," 186.
17   Temkin, *Soranus's Gynecology,* 88–90 (book 2, 11 [31]).
18   Laskaratos and Poulakou-Rebelakou, "Oribasius," 188; Temkin, *Soranus's Gynecology,* 89 (book 2, 11 [31]).

be nursed by its mother, he also commented that a wet nurse was preferable in many cases to prevent the exhaustion of the mother.[19] In fact, the attention Soranus and Oribasius devote to the proper selection of a wet nurse suggests that their employment was common.[20] Here, as in all aspects of nursing and weaning, we must be cautious in deciding how accurately the medical texts reflect the behavior of ordinary women. For example, Beaucamp's research on late antique Egyptian documents suggests that although hiring a wet nurse was considered the ideal, this was not usually possible for the poor.[21] Whether the milk an infant consumed came from its own mother or a wet nurse would make no difference to its stable isotope ratio, as the child's tissue $\delta^{15}N$ values during nursing would be elevated above the adult tissue $\delta^{15}N$ values of any woman providing the milk.

Although Oribasius and Soranus advised a considerable delay between birth and the onset of nursing, breast milk was seen as being the infant's ideal food. This is evident from the attention that both devote to milk quality and its links to a wet nurse's diet and health.[22] It is also clear from the gradual nature of the recommended weaning process. Soranus described the young infant's body as being soft, delicate, and malleable and argued that while it was in this condition, the child must be given only milk.[23] Thus he opposed the introduction of cereal food as early as forty days after birth, as he said was sometimes done.[24] Soranus believed the baby's body to become firm enough to tolerate solid food at around the age of six months. The first solid food given should be crumbs of bread softened with hydromel, milk, sweet wine, or honey wine. Later, he said, one could also give the child soup made of spelt, a very moist porridge, or an egg cooked soft enough to be sipped.[25] The recommended weaning process was gradual: Soranus advised a diet of breast milk supplemented by these soft foods for at least another year. When development of the teeth allowed more solid foods to be chewed, at around eighteen to twenty-four months, he said, gradual weaning of the infant should begin.[26]

19   Temkin, *Soranus's Gynecology*, 90 (book 2, 11 [31]).
20   Laskaratos and Poulakou-Rebelakou, "Oribasius"; Temkin, *Soranus's Gynecology*, 90–94 (book 2, 12 [32]).
21   Beaucamp, "L'allaitement" (above, n. 12), 546–59.
22   Laskaratos and Poulakou-Rebelakou, "Oribasius," 186–87; Temkin, *Soranus's Gynecology*, 90–101 (book 2, 12 [32]–14 [34]).
23   See for example book 2, 12 [29] and 16 [36], in which Soranus detailed how to swaddle and massage the neonate to shape its body into a pleasing form.
24   Temkin, *Soranus's Gynecology*, 117 (book 2, 21 [61]).
25   Ibid.
26   Soranus's precise wording is "third or fourth half year." Ibid., 118–19 (book 2, 21 [61]).

His comments that a child should not be weaned in the unhealthy autumn season and that weaning should be halted if the child sickened suggest that Soranus saw weaning as a fairly serious step, to be approached with caution. Given the age at which weaning was to commence and its gradual nature, it seems that most children fed according to Soranus's advice would not have been completely weaned until the age of two years or even later. Oribasius was in agreement with this general time frame, referring to the time before the age of two as the period during which the child was nourished by milk.[27]

Medieval writers in Western Europe also recommended the gradual cessation of breastfeeding by about two years of age.[28] Liquid or semiliquid foods, such as animal milk, gruel, or pap (a mixture of flour and bread cooked in water) might be given before the emergence of the first teeth (i.e., before about six to nine months of age), after which other foods might be introduced.[29]

Useful information about the age of weaning can be also found in the lives and miracles of saints. Tales of miraculous healing of women unable to lactate demonstrate that for new Byzantine mothers, breastfeeding was the desirable norm.[30] In the miracles of Saint Thecla (miracle 24), a child who has just been weaned is said to be old enough to walk and run, suggesting that it was at least eighteen months old.[31] In the Life of Simeon Stylites the Younger, Simeon, after his baptism at age two, refused to nurse from his mother because she had eaten meat which had been sacrificed to idols. This tale indicates that children could still be breastfeeding at age two; the hagiographer also relates that when Simeon began to eat solid food, his mother gave him honey on bread, and water to drink.[32] The Life of Saint Alypios relates that the saint was taken to church by his mother at the age of three after his father had died, and that at this point he had already been weaned.[33] In the Life of Michael Synkellos, we see a reference to a boy who had been weaned and had reached the age of three years.[34] Finally,

27   Laskaratos and Poulakou-Rebelakou, "Oribasius," 188–89.
28   S. Shahar, *Childhood in the Middle Ages* (London, 1990).
29   V. A. Fildes, *Breasts, Bottles, and Babies: A History of Infant Feeding* (Edinburgh, 1986); eadem, "The Culture and Biology of Breastfeeding: An Historical Review of Western Europe," in *Breastfeeding: Biocultural Perspectives,* ed. P. Stuart-Macadam and K. A Dettwyler (New York, 1995), 101–26.
30   Vita of Mary the Younger, *AASS* Nov. 4:698, ch. 15; Vita of Ignatios, PG 105:561C.
31   G. Dagron, *Vie et miracles de sainte Thècle* (Brussels, 1978), miracle 24, 350.
32   P. van den Ven, *La vie ancienne de s. Syméon Stylite le Jeune* (Brussels, 1962), chapters 5–6, p. 7.
33   H. Delehaye, *Les saints stylites* (Brussels, 1923), 149.
34   M. B. Cunningham, *The Life of Michael the Synkellos* (Belfast, 1991), 46.

the Life of Basil the Younger (316.37) includes a description of a woman holding in her arms a child of four who was breastfeeding.[35]

Some of the practices documented in the written sources, such as the use of honey and goat's milk in infant feeding, could have had serious consequences for infant health.[36] Honey is often contaminated with the spores of *Clostridium botulinum,* the bacterium that secretes the toxin that causes botulism, a severe and often fatal form of food poisoning.[37] Botulinum toxin blocks the transmission of chemical signals at neuromuscular junctions; left untreated, it can cause death through paralysis of the respiratory muscles.[38] In the infant, *C. botulinum* spores can colonize the intestinal tract, leading to infant botulism, an illness of varying severity whose symptoms include reduced muscle tone, difficulty suckling, and sometimes respiratory problems.[39] In modern populations, most infants recover after several weeks or several months; in antiquity, however, recovery might have been less certain.

The use of goat's milk as a dietary staple for infants can also have serious adverse effects. Although goat's milk is commonly seen as similar to human milk, it is relatively low in both cobalamine and folic acid (0.1 μg/L and 6 μg/L, respectively) compared to human milk (4μg/L and 52 μg/L, respectively). Infants who are fed goat's milk rather than human milk starting shortly after birth often develop severe megaloblastic anemia by the age of three to five months as a result of folic acid deficiency.[40] In some cases, these health consequences are visible in the osteological record. Megaloblastic anemia causes marrow hypertrophy, which can lead to cribra orbitalia, porous lesions of the roofs of the orbits. Given

---

35   S. G. Viliskij, *Žitie sv. Vasilija Novogo v russkoj literature* (Odessa, 1911), 316.37.

36   S. I. Fairgrieve and J. E. Molto, "Cribra Orbitalia in Two Temporally Disjunct Population Samples from the Dakhleh Oasis, Egypt," *AJPA* 111 (2000): 319–31.

37   M. Nevas, M. Lindström, K. Hautamäki, S. Puoskari, and H. Korkeala, "Prevalence and Diversity of *Clostridium botulinum* Types A, B, E and F in Honey Produced in the Nordic Countries," *International Journal of Food Microbiology* 105 (2005): 145–51.

38   R. Passmore and M. A. Eastwood, *Human Nutrition and Dietetics* (London, 1986); R. L. Shapiro, C. Hatheway, and D. L. Swerdlow, "Botulism in the United States: A Clinical and Epidemiologic Review," *Annals of Internal Medicine* 129 (1998): 221–28.

39   S. S. Arnon, T. F. Madura, K. Damus, B. Thompson, R. M. Wood, and J. Chin, "Honey and Other Environmental Risk Factors for Infant Botulism," *Journal of Pediatrics* 94 (1979): 331–36; G. B. Merenstein, D. W. Kaplan, and A. A. Rosenberg, *Silver, Kempe Bruyn and Fulginiti's Handbook of Pediatrics* (Norwalk, 1991); Shapiro, Hatheway, and Swerdlow, "Botulism in the United States."

40   For a thorough discussion of the recommended folic acid intake and its implications, see I. Chanarin, *The Megaloblastic Anemias,* 3rd ed. (Oxford, 1990).

Figure 1   Example of cribra orbitalia in the orbital roof of an infant from
Eleutherna, Crete (sixth to seventh centuries C.E.) aged approximately 24 ± 8
months. Source: C. Bourbou, *The People of Early Byzantine Eleutherna and Messene,
6th–7th Centuries A.D.: A Bioarchaeological Approach* (Athens, 2004).

this connection, the occurrence of active cribra orbitalia in an infant younger
than six months suggests that the diet of the child was based on or supplemented
with goat's milk (fig. 1).[41]

Materials and Methods

The present work assembles the results of a number of stable isotope studies
of Byzantine-era Greek populations. Although most of the study populations
include very few subadults and are of limited interest for weaning research when
considered individually, together they provide an interesting preliminary data set

41   Fairgrieve and Molto, "Cribra Orbitalia." The porous lesions on the orbital roof known as
cribra orbitalia have a number of potential causes, including iron deficiency anemia and megaloblastic anemia (for review, see P. Stuart-Macadam, "Nutritional Deficiency Diseases: A Survey
of Scurvy, Rickets, and Iron-Deficiency Anemia," in *Reconstruction of Life From the Skeleton,* ed.
M. Y. İşcan and K. A. R. Kennedy [New York, 1989], 201–22). Fairgrieve and Molto have argued
that in the Roman Mediterranean, where goat's milk is known to have been given to infants, the
development of cribra orbitalia in individuals younger than six months may reflect folic acid deficiency caused by a diet based on goat's milk.

on weaning in Byzantine-era populations that may be compared to the results of larger stable isotope studies on Roman and medieval European populations and used to generate hypotheses on Byzantine weaning that could be tested through the study of larger Byzantine skeletal samples.

The largest group of subadults for which values are reported here was recovered in 2003 from a middle Byzantine cemetery at the site of Kastella, in the modern city of Heraklion in central Crete. These remains date to the eleventh century C.E.[42] Analysis of subadult individuals from this burial group provided eight of the sixteen values considered here. Smaller numbers of subadults have been studied as part of work on several other Byzantine-era sites in Greece. These analyses were originally part of a wider study on dietary differences between Greek Orthodox, Frankish, and Muslim populations in medieval and early modern Greece.[43] Three middle to late Byzantine groups are considered here. The earliest of these groups was recovered from subfloor graves in the episcopal church of Kastron at Servia, Kozani. This series of burials, which likely date to the initial use of the church after its construction in the eleventh century C.E.,[44] includes three subadults whose values are reported here. A further four subadults are part of the burial group recovered from the medieval cemetery of Petras at Siteia, Crete, which dates to the late twelfth or early thirteenth century C.E.[45] The third group of burials was left by a late Byzantine farming community occupying the area in and around ancient Nemea; this group dates from the twelfth through the thirteenth centuries C.E. and yielded one individual considered here.[46]

For the subadults discussed here, age was estimated from dental eruption and development, skeletal maturity, and length of the long bones.[47] Samples of bone were collected from ribs, and collagen was purified from these for analysis. Collagen was extracted from the Kastella material following a modified Longin

42   C. Bourbou and M. P. Richards, "The Middle-Byzantine Menu: Palaeodietary Information from Isotopic Analysis of Humans and Fauna from Kastella, Crete," *International Journal of Osteoarchaeology* 17 (2007): 63–72.

43   S. J. Garvie-Lok, "Loaves and Fishes: A Stable Isotope Reconstruction of Diet in Medieval Greece" (PhD diss., University of Calgary, 2001).

44   N. Tsilipakou, personal communication, 1997.

45   M. Tsipopoulou, personal communication, 1997.

46   S. G. Miller, "Excavations at Nemea, 1980," *Hesperia* 50 (1981): 45–67; D. E. Birge, L. H. Kraynak, and S. G. Miller, *Excavations at Nemea,* vol. 1, *Topographical and Architectural Studies: The Sacred Square, the Xenon, and the Bath* (Berkeley, 1992).

47   D. H. Ubelaker, *Human Skeletal Remains* (Washington, D.C., 1989); J. E. Buikstra and D. H. Ubelaker, eds., *Standards for Data Collection from Human Skeletal Remains* (Fayetteville, 1994).

procedure, as outlined in detail elsewhere,[48] with the addition of an ultrafiltration step.[49] For the Servia, Petras, and Nemea material, the ultrafiltration step was omitted, but the material was treated with NaOH to remove contaminants.[50] Collagen preservation was assessed from sample C:N ratios, following criteria outlined by DeNiro.[51] Isotopic values for the Kastella samples were measured using a Carlo Erba elemental analyzer coupled to a ThermoFinnigan Delta Plus XL mass spectrometer at the Isotope Laboratory, Department of Archaeological Sciences, University of Bradford. Remains from the other sites were analyzed at the Stable Isotope Laboratory of the University of Calgary Department of Physics and Astronomy, using an NA 1500 elemental analyzer coupled to a Finnigan Mat TracerMat mass spectrometer.

Results

The stable nitrogen isotope data are presented in table 1. The fact that the samples represent several sites complicates the interpretation of the data, as the typical adult female stable $\delta^{15}N$ values for each site differ, reflecting local variation in diet. The data are more easily interpreted when each subadult value is considered in relation to the mean adult female value for its site. This essentially standardizes the subadult values in terms of their elevation relative to adult female values from the same site. Figure 2, which presents the data for the four sites in this format, shows a clear $\delta^{15}N$ elevation in the youngest individuals. All of the subadults aged three years or less at death show a substantial elevation (2.6‰ to 3.5‰) over the mean adult female value for their site. In contrast to the general elevation seen in the youngest individuals, the $\delta^{15}N$ values of subadults aged four years or older at death are scattered around the adult female mean, reflecting an essentially adult diet. The ±1‰ fluctuation around the adult female mean for these older subadults reflects normal individual variation within each population and is seen in adults from these sites as well.

48 M. P. Richards and R. E. M. Hedges, "Stable Isotope Evidence for Similarities in the Types of Marine Foods Used by Late Mesolithic Humans at Sites along the Atlantic Coast of Europe," *JArS* 26 (1999): 717–22.

49 T. A. Brown, D. E. Nelson, and J. R. Southon, "Improved Collagen Extraction by Modified Longin Method," *Radiocarbon* 30 (1988): 171–77.

50 See M. A. Katzenberg and A. Weber, "Stable Isotope Ecology and Palaeodiet in the Lake Baikal Region of Siberia," *JArS* 26 (1999): 651–59.

51 M. J. DeNiro, "Postmortem Preservation and Alteration of *in vivo* Bone Collagen Isotope Ratios in Relation to Palaeodietary Reconstruction," *Nature* 317 (1985): 806–9.

TABLE I
Subadult δ¹⁵N values for
Byzantine Greek burial group

Site	Age at death	$\delta^{15}N$ (‰)
Kastella	9 months	11.6
	2 years	12.1
	4 years	7.5
	5 years	8.3
	7 years	8.9
	8 years	8.5
	10 years	7.9
	12 years	8.8
Adult female mean		9.0
Petras	3 years	12.7
	4.5 years	8.6
	5 years	9.6
	6.5 years	8.9
Adult female mean		9.2
Servia	1 year	11.3
	5 years	9.5
	9.5 years	9.2
Adult female mean		8.5
Nemea	4 years	8.6
Adult female mean		8.6

Discussion

The few data available do not allow firm conclusions to be drawn about weaning behavior in Byzantine Greece. However, they allow us to make some tentative suggestions and to suggest directions for further research. The contrast between the elevated values seen in subadults aged three years or younger and the adult-like pattern seen in children aged four and older suggests that weaning was complete by the fourth year. This conclusion is consistent with the documentary evidence, which, with the exception of the reference in the Vita of Basil the Younger, does not suggest that children would normally have been nursed into

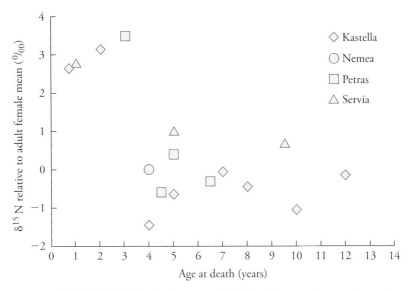

Figure 2   Subadult δ^{15}N values for Byzantine Greek burial groups, showing elevated values in children age three years or less at death.

the fourth year. These data form a contrast to the stable isotope values obtained for some non-Western archaeological populations, which indicate significant nursing well into the fourth year of life.[52]

Arriving at a more precise weaning age than "before four years of age" is not possible given the data available. The four subadults aged three years or younger at death show a substantial δ^{15}N elevation above the adult female mean for their site, suggesting that mother's milk formed a significant portion of their diet. Because of the lag between a change in diet and a shift in bone δ^{15}N value, these results do not necessarily suggest significant nursing up to the age of three, but they do indicate that breast milk formed a substantial part of some infants' diets well into the third year of life.

A comparison between these data and data for larger Roman and medieval study samples from elsewhere in Europe is instructive. Weaning practices have been reconstructed for the burial populations of Isola Sacra, near Rome (first through third centuries C.E.),[53] the Dakhleh oasis of Egypt (ca. 250–450

52   Schurr and Powell, "The Role of Changing Childhood Diets"; Williams, White, and Longstaffe, "Trophic Level and Macronutrient Shift Effects" (both above, n. 7).
53   Prowse et al., "Isotopic Palaeodiet Studies of Skeletons" (above, n. 7).

C.E.),[54] and Queenford Farm in Britain (late fourth to mid-sixth century C.E.).[55] Despite the wide geographic separation of these groups and presumed local cultural differences, all three studies suggest a similar weaning pattern, with solid foods introduced after six months of age and full weaning established in a gradual process, with some subadults nursing to the age of three years. Fuller and colleagues note a contrast between this pattern and that seen at the medieval British site of Wharram Percy (tenth through sixteenth centuries C.E.), whose stable isotope values suggest that subadults were weaned earlier, between the ages of eighteen months and two years.[56] They suggest that this contrast reflects a stronger influence of Soranus and other medical scholars in the earlier populations, with Roman and late Roman populations tending to heed the call for a gradual weaning process, whereas later medieval populations weaned their children at a younger age. Further research may confirm a significant temporal difference in weaning practices between the Roman and medieval periods. The model is of interest for the data discussed here, as this small set of values does fit reasonably well to the earlier Roman pattern proposed by Fuller and colleagues.

Some further insight is gained by comparing the Byzantine values already discussed to other values from slightly later periods in Greece. Data are available for two groups of Greek Orthodox burials from the Frankish occupation period: a slightly later group of fourteenth- to fifteenth-century C.E. burials from Nemea,[57] and the subfloor ossuaries of the church of Ayios Nikolaos in the Athenian Agora, which appear to have come into use in the thirteenth or fourteenth century C.E.[58] Although these burials are later, it can be argued that Greek populations of the period are more likely to have preserved their own traditions in weaning and other aspects of daily life than to have adopted the practices of the Frankish occupiers; this hypothesis is supported by the fact that the earlier and later Nemea groups are isotopically indistinguishable. If these later burials are considered along with the Byzantine ones, the pattern suggested by the Byzantine sample alone persists, with all six subadults below the age of three showing isotopic enrichment consistent with nursing (fig. 3).

54   Dupras, Schwarcz, and Fairgrieve, "Infant Feeding and Weaning Practices" (above, n. 7).
55   Fuller et al., "Isotopic Evidence for Breastfeeding" (above, n. 1).
56   Ibid.; Richards, Mays, and Fuller, "Stable Carbon and Nitrogen Isotope Values" (above, n. 7).
57   Miller, "Excavations at Nemea" (above, n. 46).
58   T. L. Shear Jr., "The Athenian Agora: Excavations of 1989–1993," *Hesperia* 66 (1997): 519–48.

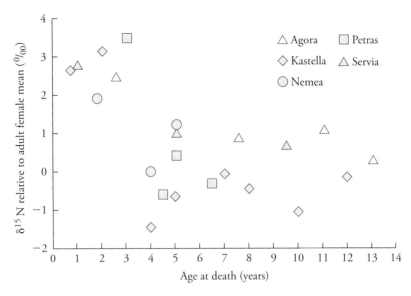

Figure 3   Subadult δ^{15}N values for Byzantine and Frankish-era Greek burial groups, showing elevated values in children age three years or less at death.

These burials may be compared as a group to the values of some possible members of the Frankish community in Greece (fig. 4). Most of these subadults were recovered from two cemeteries of Frankish-ruled Corinth; their close association with a building that appears to have been a Frankish pilgrims' hostel strongly suggests Frankish cultural affiliation.[59] Two more subadults are associated with a small burial chapel in the upper fortress of Mitilini that likely served as a resting place for the island's Gatteliusi ruling family.[60] In contrast to the Byzantine and Frankish-era Greek remains, these burials appear to reflect an earlier weaning age. Here, infants aged less than eighteen months clearly show δ^{15}N values elevated above the female mean, whereas those two years or older show values typical of adults. These data suggest a pattern for Franks that is more similar to what Fuller and colleagues feel is a medieval European pattern.[61] It may be

59   C. K. Williams, E. Barnes, and L. M. Snyder, "Frankish Corinth, 1996," *Hesperia* 66 (1997): 1–47; C. K. Williams, L. M. Snyder, E. Barnes, and O. H. Zervos, "Frankish Corinth, 1997," *Hesperia* 67 (1998): 222–81.

60   C. Williams and E. H. Williams, "Excavations at Mytilene (Lesbos), 1986," *Classical Views* 31 (1987): 247–62; C. Williams and E. H. Williams, "Excavations at Mytilene (Lesbos), 1987," *Classical Views* 32 (1988): 135–50.

61   Fuller et al., "Isotopic Evidence for Breastfeeding" (above, n. 1).

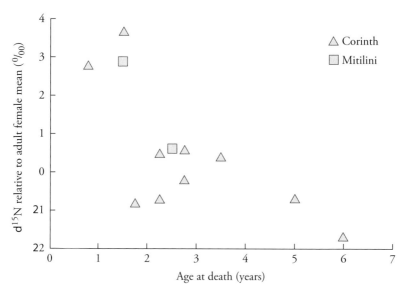

Figure 4 Subadult δ15N Values for Frankish burial groups, showing elevated values in children age eighteen months or less at death.

that Byzantine populations persisted in what might be called a Roman pattern of weaning longer than did Western European populations. If this idea could be borne out through further research on the two culture areas, it would have extremely interesting implications for comparative subadult health and child-rearing practices in the East and the West.

Conclusions

The available stable isotope data for Greek Byzantine-era populations suggest very tentatively that weaning was a gradual process for these groups, perhaps terminating around the age of three years. The data are in general agreement with the recommendations of ancient and early Byzantine physicians and are consistent with isotopic data for larger imperial and late Roman samples from Italy, Egypt, and Britain. As such, they contrast with data for some Western European medieval groups that suggest a more rapid weaning process, complete by two years of age. This hypothesis of continuity with earlier Roman practices and of a difference between Byzantine and Western practices must be tested by examining larger samples from more populations, both East and West.

CHRYSSI BOURBOU AND SANDRA J. GARVIE-LOK

Whatever the conclusions of future work, it appears that Greek Byzantine children were often not fully weaned until at least eighteen months of age and sometimes far later. Given ancient and early Byzantine physicians' suggestions that solid foods be introduced around six months of age, the data suggest a further period of a year or more during which much nutrition was still obtained from breast milk. Thus, even the earliest weaning age suggested by the data reviewed here could be said to be in agreement with the medical writers' caution that weaning be done gradually. In fact, it seems that Byzantine-era infants enjoyed a far more gradual weaning process than many European or American infants receive today, despite current medical understanding of the benefits of breastfeeding to the child.

Hellenic Ministry of Culture / University of the Aegean (Bourbou)
University of Alberta (Garvie-Lok)

EMPERORS AND PATRIARCHS AS IDEAL CHILDREN AND ADOLESCENTS
Literary Conventions and Cultural Expectations

Dimiter G. Angelov

A MUTE AND MARGINAL GROUP, children make rare appearances in Byzantine literary and historical texts. The large corpus of biographical literature devoted to holy men and women is a fortunate exception, as this volume shows.[1] The focus of this article lies in a limited, homogeneous, and elite category of biographical subjects: the future leaders of the Byzantine state and church, namely the emperors and patriarchs of Constantinople. The lives of these politically powerful men were treated in various biographies, hagiographical as well as encomiastic and, in rare cases, historical. For convenience's sake, and to restrict the evidential base to a workable and clearly defined quantity, we do not deal here with biographical accounts of other politically powerful figures, such as imperial dignitaries or provincial bishops. The discussion of empresses is subsumed into that of emperors, for the biographical sources on the childhoods of imperial women are too few and patchy to afford a separate treatment. Of interest to the present article is the entire early life of the future great individuals, from the time of birth through teenage years: that is, what we call today—and what was called in Byzantium—childhood and adolescence. They are identified by the mention of a specific age or by the usage of terms such as "infant" (βρέφος), "child" (παῖς or παιδίον), or "adolescent" (μεῖραξ or μειράκιον).

As children and adolescents, rulers and patriarchs may seem an unusual group to study. Neither their childhoods nor their relationships with their parents were representative of the experiences of common people. Yet the imperial and patriarchal biographies present us with a particularly intriguing subset of

---

1   On the childhood of saints, see the article by Béatrice Caseau in this volume.

ideal children. As long as we remain aware of the distinct profile of the examined children and the nature of the biographical texts, we can wrest from them historically meaningful insights. Two considerations warrant the choice of subject matter and frame our subsequent analysis.

First, these ideal children enable us to investigate the expectations that the educated literary classes in Byzantium held about the early phases of life of their rulers. We pose various historical questions regarding these childhood expectations: the role of adult ideals of power in formulating conceptions of childhood, the differences between the childhoods of future emperors and those of future patriarchs, and issues of continuity and change. Second, this set of ideal children permits us to test the validity of modern theories about medieval childhood. One important problem to consider is the notion of childhood as a distinct period of life. Ever since the surge of interest in medieval childhood during the 1970s and 1980s, scholars have found it necessary to discuss, and defend, the autonomy of medieval ideas of childhood. The problem was first formulated in a path-opening, although highly controversial, study by Philippe Ariès. In his sweeping cultural survey of family life during the medieval, but mostly the early modern period, published in 1960, Ariès argued that "in medieval society the idea of childhood did not exist." According to Ariès, medieval art depicted children as little adults and medieval society treated them as such, forcing them to behave and dress like grown-up individuals.[2] As a distinct period of life, he asserts, childhood was "discovered" gradually in the West between the fifteenth and the eighteenth century.

The Ariès thesis has been subjected to severe criticism. Medievalists have pointed out that Ariès's opinions rested on scant and one-sided evidence.[3] His notion of a medieval period of ignorance followed by an age of "discovery" has been deemed simplistic, ignoring historical categories such as class and demography.[4] Moreover, his negative view of childhood in the Middle Ages has been dismissed as resting on Whiggish presumptions of historical progress.[5] Most

<hr>

2 P. Ariès, *L'enfant et la vie familiale sous l'Ancien Régime* (Paris, 1960); English translation, *Centuries of Childhood: A Social History of Family Life,* trans. R. Baldick (New York, 1962), esp. 33–49, 128–33.

3 U. T. Holmes, "Medieval Children," *Journal of Social History* 2 (1968): 164–72 (a review of Ariès's book).

4 D. Herlihy, "Medieval Children," in *Essays on Medieval Civilization,* ed. B. K. Lackner and K. R. Phelp (Austin, 1978), 155–73.

5 B. Hanawalt, "The Child in the Middle Ages and the Renaissance," in *Beyond the Century*

important, in the past twenty-five years medievalists have undertaken comprehensive studies of texts and material culture, bringing to light plentiful evidence of the special and loving treatment of children. Today we know that medieval children played games, possessed toys, listened to lullabies and stories, and had parents capable of displaying affection and caring for them in ways not fundamentally different from those in our own times.[6] Medievalists no longer need to go on proving that childhood was "discovered" earlier than Ariès postulated. Nonetheless, as the study of Byzantine childhood is still at its inception, we may be justified in retracing the steps of our Western colleagues and testing the relevance of the Ariès thesis to the limited body of Byzantine biographical literature examined here.

The episodes of childhood and adolescence in the biographical texts present an intricate tangle of literary motifs and representations grounded in historical reality and embody cultural values associated with childhood as well as adulthood. Fact and fiction were amalgamated to varying degrees in different texts, often inextricably. It is not our task to investigate systematically those realistic representations that provide snippets of historical information about genuine experiences (such as orphanhood). Our sole focus is on the construction of the image of ideal childhood and the literary and cultural values this image reflected, pointing only when it is possible and relevant to likely echoes from the realities of childhood.

The literary motifs that shape the representation of childhood in our texts derive partly from the requirements of Byzantine rhetorical theory and partly from general medieval stereotypes of children. Two stereotypes were literary topoi of childhood.[7] The topos of the *puer senex* (literally "the boy old man") was ubiquitous in medieval literature and hagiography, including Byzantine hagiography. Ernst Curtius, who coined the phrase *puer senex,* traced the origins of the

---

of the Child: Cultural History and Developmental Psychology, ed. W. Koops and M. Zuckerman (Philadelphia, 2003), 21–42, esp. 39–42.

6   The scholarship challenging Ariès's interpretations has been surveyed in Hanawalt, "The Child." Important monograph-length studies on medieval childhood include S. Shahar, *Children in the Middle Ages* (London, 1990); B. Hanawalt, *Growing Up in Medieval London: The Experience of Childhood in History* (Oxford, 1993); P. Riché and D. Alexandre-Bidon, *L'enfance au Moyen Age* (Paris, 1994); R. Finucane, *The Rescue of the Innocents: Endangered Children in Medieval Miracles* (New York, 1997); N. Orme, *Medieval Children* (New Haven, 2001).

7   Aspects of the conventional images of childhood in medieval literature and imagination are examined in Shahar, *Children,* 9–20.

motif to Roman literature and observed parallels with non-Western cultures.[8] In this sense, *puer senex* offers a universal way of representing childhood across various civilizations and time periods. The other stereotypical image of children in the Middle Ages is specifically Christian. In the Middle Ages, children were commonly seen as innocent and pure creatures, full of faith and uncorrupted by the sins of adults.[9] At the root of this perception was Christ's exhortation (Matt. 18:3–5) that the faithful should acquire the purity and humility of children in order to enter the kingdom of God. Early Greek church fathers, such as Clement of Alexandria and Origen, elaborated on the pure nature of the child and discussed other common characteristics and behaviors of children, such as laughter and crying.[10] In contrast to the topos of the *puer senex,* that of innocence confers on childhood a sense of intrinsic worth.

Our discussion begins by considering the characteristics and limitations of our sources, focusing especially on issues of genre and time distribution during the Byzantine millennium. Then we analyze separately the accounts of the childhoods of future emperors and future patriarchs so as not to lose track of their different political roles. Our analysis aims to obtain a comprehensive picture of the literary and cultural attitudes to childhood reflected in our texts. To this end, we isolate distinct themes in the representation of childhood while keeping in mind that each biographical text functioned as an organic whole. This thematic approach enables us to trace important patterns and illuminating tensions in the representation of childhood over the centuries.

Sources on the Ideals of Imperial and Patriarchal Childhood

The biographies of emperors and patriarchs belong to two main genres: encomia (called also panegyrics or laudatory orations) and hagiographical Vitae. A third, much rarer biographical genre is that of the historical Vita of an emperor.

8   E. Curtius, *European Literature in the Latin Middle Ages,* trans. W. R. Trask (New York, 1952), 98–105, esp. 100. For Byzantine hagiography, see T. Pratsch, *Der hagiographische Topos: Griechische Heiligenviten in mittelbyzantinischer Zeit* (Berlin, 2005), 88ff. The expression "gray-haired since childhood" or "gray-haired in intelligence" (πολιὸς ἐκ νεότητος or πολιὸς τὴν σύνεσιν) is often encountered in reference to children, as in the epitaph on Basil the Great by Gregory of Nyssa and in the Vita of Patriarch Athanasios I by Joseph Kalothetos. See PG 46:789B; Ἰωσὴφ Καλοθέτου συγγράμματα, ed. D. Tsames (Thessalonike, 1980), 457.132 (ch. 4).
9   Shahar, *Children,* 17–19.
10   N. Kalogeras, "What Do They Think about Children? Perceptions of Childhood in Early Byzantine Literature," *BMGS* 25 (2001): 5–6.

DIMITER G. ANGELOV

Beyond the biographies, two other genres contribute to the study of the idealized image of childhood of our great men: autobiographies and the so-called mirrors of princes.

The encomia of interest to us are mostly imperial. More than one hundred specimens have been preserved from the millennium of Byzantine history.[11] Doubtless more were written but have been lost. In theory, and most often also in practice, the imperial and patriarchal encomia were composed for oral declamation. As high-style oral literature, imperial panegyrics added luster to the public image of the ruler projected to the political elite. They accompanied occasional celebrations at the court, such as weddings and coronations. The overwhelming majority of the surviving imperial encomia date to late antiquity and thereafter cluster in the period from the eleventh through the fifteenth century.[12] A large number come from the middle and the second half of the twelfth century, as well as from the second half of the thirteenth century (post-1261), periods when the performance of imperial panegyrics in prose formed part of the annual ceremonial cycle of the court.[13]

In spite of their impressive numbers, relatively few imperial panegyrics follow a full biographical scheme that traces imperial lives from birth and childhood.[14] Almost all encomia that contain episodes of childhood and adolescence date to between the late eleventh and the late thirteenth century. As a consequence, imperial orations alone do not enable us to compare the representation of imperial childhood over the centuries of Byzantine history, although,

---

11   For a survey, see H. Hunger, *Die hochsprachliche profane Literatur der Byzantiner,* vol. 1 (Munich, 1978), 120–32.

12   This imbalance reflects shifts in popularity of court recitations and the higher likelihood of survival of pieces composed by well-known Byzantine literati, such as Themistius (fourth century), Arethas of Caesarea (ninth–tenth century), and Michael Psellos (eleventh century).

13   In the mid- and late twelfth century, Epiphany Day (6 January) was the annual occasion for the recitation of a series of panegyrics of the emperor. After the Byzantine reconquest of Constantinople in 1261, Christmas Day was briefly established as the annual occasion. See P. Magdalino, *Empire of Manuel I Komnenos, 1143–1180* (Cambridge, 1993), 248; D. Angelov, *Imperial Ideology and Political Thought in Byzantium, 1204–1330* (Cambridge, 2007), 44–47.

14   The reasons for the omission of childhood episodes in imperial encomia were several. Among them, Menander's guidelines for the imperial encomium gave orators the choice to skip the episodes of family origins and birth when the orator judged the omission to be appropriate. In addition, Menander envisaged the possibility of a shorter laudatory speech addressed to the emperor (*prosphonematikos logos*). See *Menander Rhetor,* ed. D. Russell and N. Wilson (Oxford, 1981), 165–71. Further, the practice of Byzantine court oratory was not limited to the guidelines of the rhetorical manuals: some authors (such as Dio Chrysostom and Themistius in late antiquity) cultivated their own abstract and at times didactic styles of court oratory.

fortunately, hagiographical works, mirrors of princes, and historical biography permit us to broaden the temporal scope of the investigation. In contrast to the imperial orations, the encomia on patriarchs of Constantinople are much fewer in number, all of them dating between the twelfth and the early fourteenth century.[15] The great majority of the patriarchal encomia, and all of those valuable for the study of images of youth, date to the twelfth century, when the recitation of these works was an annual event on the Saturday of Lazarus, during Lent.[16]

Saints' Lives, the second type of biographical accounts examined here, feature episodes of childhood and youth more frequently than do imperial and patriarchal encomia. The patriarchs of Constantinople—some of them important church fathers—were the main subjects of saints' Lives. Fourteen patriarchs spread out throughout Byzantine history, from late antiquity to the fourteenth century, were the theme of hagiographical Vitae.[17] A notable lacuna in patriarchal hagiography between the tenth and the thirteenth century is partly filled by the twelfth-century panegyrics of patriarchs. Much rarer than the saints' Lives of patriarchs are the hagiographical Vitae of empresses, the only type of biographical text on imperial consorts. Five empresses were subjects of Vitae, and only the Vitae of the ninth-century empress Theophano, the first wife of Leo VI the Wise (886–912), are of value for our study.[18]

15   The substantial body of evidence from the twelfth century—sixteen *logoi* in praise of patriarchs and a few laudatory *didaskaliai*—has been surveyed by M. Loukaki, "Ο ιδανικός πατριάρχης μέσα από τα ρητορικά κείμενα του 12ου αιώνα," in *Byzantium in the Twelfth Century,* ed. N. Oikonomides (Athens, 1990), 301–19. The evidence from the thirteenth century is scanter and offers nothing of interest: a *didaskalia* in praise of Patriarch Michael IV Autoreianos (1208–1214) (ed. M. Loukaki, *REB* 52 [1994]: 151–73), an encomium associated with the inauguration of Patriarch Germanos II (1223–1240) (ed. A. Karpozilos, *Byzantina* 6 [1974]: 227–49), and Thomas Magistros's panegyric of Patriarch Niphon (1310–1314) (PG 145:389–96).

16   See Marina Loukaki's observations in *Discours annuels en l'honneur du patriarche Georges Xiphilin,* ed. M. Loukaki, trans. C. Jouanno (Paris, 2005), 65–67.

17   The fourteen patriarchs, along with the relevant entries in F. Halkin, *Bibliotheca hagiographica graeca,* 3rd ed., 3 vols. (Brussels, 1957), are as follows: Gregory I (Gregory of Nazianzos) (380–381) (*BHG* 723–30); John I Chrysostom (398–404) (*BHG* 870–76); Eutychios (552–565, 577–582) (*BHG* 657); John IV the Faster (582–595) (*BHG* 893, fragmentary Vita); Germanos I (715–730) (*BHG* 697); Tarasios (784–806) (*BHG* 1698); Nikephoros I (806–815) (*BHG* 1335); Methodios I (843–847) (*BHG* 1278); Ignatios (847–858, 867–877) (*BHG* 817); Anthony II Kauleas (893–901) (*BHG* 139); Euthymios (ca. 907–ca. 912) (*BHG* 651, fragmentary Vita); Arsenios Autoreianos (1254–1260, 1261–1264) (*BHG* entry missing); Athanasios I (1289–1293, 1303–1309) (*BHG* 194, 194c); and Isidore I (1347–1350) (*BHG* 962).

18   The five empresses with Vitae are as follows: Irene (797–802) (*BHG, supplementum,* 2205) (the Vita is mostly excerpts from chronicles); Theodora (*BHG* 962), wife of Theophilos (829–842); Theophano (*BHG* 1794–1795), wife of Leo VI; Irene-Xene (*BHG supplementum* 2206), wife of

Saints' Lives of emperors are exceptional, with only two emperors taken as subjects of hagiographic Vitae: the Nicaean emperor John III Vatatzes (1221–1254), whose fourteenth-century Life (mixing freely the genres of encomium, history, and saint's Life) features no childhood episodes;[19] and the emperor Constantine I (d. 337), Byzantium's saintly founding father, whose numerous hagiographical Vitae are a valuable source for our investigation. The Vitae of Constantine that refer to the emperor's childhood were written between the ninth and the fifteenth century. They present illuminating variations. The earliest Lives of Constantine to contain episodes of the emperor's childhood are the so-called Guidi Vita, Opitz Vita, and Patmos Vita, all composed after the final victory over Iconoclasm.[20] The most popular among them, in terms of both manuscript transmission and subsequent influence, is the Guidi Vita, which dates to the ninth century.[21] Another hagiographical Life of Constantine, which is important for tracing the evolution of the presentation of Constantine's childhood, was composed during the eleventh or the twelfth century.[22] The late Byzantine period saw the preparation of three new redactions with interesting variations authored by the scholars Constantine Akropolites, Nikephoros Gregoras, and John Chortasmenos.[23]

John II Komnenos (1118–1143); and Theodora of Arta (*BHG* 1736), wife of Michael II Komnenos Doukas of Epiros (ca. 1230–1266/68).

19   A. Heisenberg, "Kaiser Johannes Batatzes der Barmherzige," *BZ* 14 (1905): 160–233 (*BHG* 933). On its authorship and context, see G. Moravcsik, "Der Verfasser der mittelgriechischen Legende von Johannes dem Barmherzigen," *BZ* 27 (1927): 36–39; Angelov, *Imperial Ideology* (above, n. 13), 263–67, 282–85.

20   The three earliest post-Iconoclastic Vitae have been published by M. Guidi, "Un Βίος di Costantino," *Rendiconti della Reale Accademia dei Lincei: Classe di scienze morali, storiche e filologiche,* Serie Quinta, 16 (1907): 304–40, 637–55 (*BHG* 364); H. G. Opitz, "Die Vita Constantini des Codex Angelicus 22," *Byzantion* 9 (1934): 535–93 (*BHG* 365); F. Halkin, "Une nouvelle vie de Constantin dans un légendier de Patmos," *AB* 77 (1959), 63–107 (*BHG* 365n). These Vitae have been surveyed in A. Kazhdan, "'Constantin Imaginaire': Byzantine Legends of the Ninth Century about Constantine the Great," *Byzantion* 57 (1987): 196–250.

21   On the date of this Vita preserved in more than forty manuscripts, see F. Winkelmann, "Die vormetaphrastischen griechischen hagiographischen *Vitae* Constantini Magni," in *Actes du XIIe Congrès International des Études Byzantines,* vol. 2 (Belgrade, 1964), 405–14, esp. 406ff. Kazhdan, "Constantin Imaginaire," 201.

22   M. I. Gedeon, "Δύο παλαιὰ κείμενα περὶ τοῦ μεγάλου Κωνσταντίνου," Ἐκκλ. Ἀλήθ. 20 (1900): 253–54, 262–63, 279–80, 303–4 (*BHG* 363).

23   C. Simonides, *The Panegyric of that Holy, Apostolic, and Heaven-Crowned King Constantine the Great, Composed by His [sic] Head Logothetes Constantine Acropoliti* (London, 1853) (*BHG* 368). (The edition is faulty, and its credibility is further compromised by the notoriety of Constantine Simonides as one of the most versatile forgers of the nineteenth century.) *Nicephori Gregorae*

There are two unique examples of historical biographies of emperors. The *Life of Constantine* by Eusebius of Caesarea offers nothing of interest for our examination. More valuable is the *Historical Account* (*Historike Diegesis*) of the life of the emperor Basil I (867–886), the founder of the Macedonian dynasty, a historical text commonly known as the *Vita Basilii*. The title of the *Vita Basilii* attributes its authorship to the learned emperor Constantine VII Porphyrogennetos (913–959), Basil I's grandson, but this attribution has been challenged and remains uncertain.[24] We will make ample use here of the *Vita Basilii*. The work presents a remarkably detailed account of an imperial childhood, which is also unique in that the emperor was born into a peasant family. Many of the episodes of Basil I's childhood belong to a common pool of legendary and propagandist material and appear also in other historical works of the rich pro-Macedonian historiography.[25]

The three biographical genres share similar sequences of early-life episodes, which tend to follow the rules for composing encomia set by rhetorical schoolbooks. Two early and influential textbooks, the *Preparatory Exercises* (*Progymnasmata*) of Hermogenes (second century) and Aphthonios (fourth century), prescribe that an encomium should begin by extolling the city of birth of the subject before going on to praise parents, birth, nurture, and upbringing.[26] Menander Rhetor's influential chapter on the imperial encomium (third–fourth century) advocates nearly the same sequence of early-life episodes.[27] Court orators were to speak about the ethnic origin, city of birth, and parents of the emperor, and were to continue with the theme of birth. They were to look for divine signs and omens at the time of birth, such as the dream of Cyrus's mother reported by Herodotus or the suckling of Romulus by the she-wolf.[28] Menander

---

Vita Constantini, ed. P. Leone (Catania, 1994) (*BHG* 369); *Mnemeia Hagiologica,* ed. T. Ioannou (Venice, 1884; repr. Leipzig, 1973), 164–229 (*BHG* 362) On the attribution to John Chortasmenos of the last work, published by Ioannou as anonymous, see H. Hunger, *Johannes Chortasmenos (ca. 1370–ca. 1436/37): Briefe, Gedichte und kleine Schriften* (Vienna, 1969), 8. On the rewriting of saints' Lives in late Byzantium, see A.-M. Talbot, "Old Wine in New Bottles: The Re-writing of Saints' Lives in the Palaiologan Period," in *The Twilight of Byzantium,* ed. S. Ćurčić and D. Mouriki (Princeton, N.J., 1991), 15–26.

24   See I. Ševčenko, "Re-reading Constantine Porphyrogenitus," in *Byzantine Diplomacy,* ed. J. Shepard and S. Franklin (London, 1992), 167–95, esp. 184–85.

25   See G. Moravcsik, "Sagen und Legenden über Kaiser Basileios," *DOP* 15 (1961): 59–126.

26   *Hermogenis Opera,* ed. H. Rabe (Leipzig, 1913), 14–18; *Aphthonii Progymnasmata,* ed. H. Rabe (Leipzig, 1926), 21–27.

27   *Menander Rhetor* (above, n. 14), 76–96, esp. 79–83.

28   The same insistence on the importance of divine omens is found in the *progymnasmata* on the genre of encomium. The *progymnasmata* of Hermogenes speak of divine signs in general, while

notes that the orator was fully entitled to invent stories of birth, "because the audience has no choice but to accept the encomium without an examination."[29] An encomiastic account of nurture and education, in terms of both schooling and exercise in arms, was to follow and bring to an end the description of the early years of the emperor's biography. Even though the instructions of the rhetorical manuals pertain to composing encomia, they influenced all biographical genres by providing a standard scheme of narration. Encomium, hagiography, and historical biography were sister genres related by origin.[30] Saints' Lives frequently bear the title of *encomium*. The main example of a historical biography, the *Vita Basilii,* has obvious similarities with an imperial encomium.[31] Thus the distinction among the three types of biography was never rigid and absolute: they exhibit prominent cases of borrowing and cross-fertilization.[32]

Autobiography provides supplementary material for the study of images of the childhoods of emperors and patriarchs.[33] More autobiographical accounts were written by patriarchs than by emperors, although not all of these texts mention the childhood of the author. For example, the testaments of Patriarchs Arsenios Autoreianos (1254–1260, 1261–1264) and Isidore I (1347–1350) offer nothing of interest—in sharp contrast to the saints' Lives of the two patriarchs,

---

the *progymnasmata* of Nicholas of Myra (fifth century) adduce as examples the dream visions of Cyrus's and Pericles' mothers. See *Rhetores Graeci*, ed. L. Spengel, vol. 2 (Leipzig, 1854), 12; vol. 3 (Leipzig, 1856), 480–81.

29   *Menander Rhetor,* 82.12–14.

30   H. Delehaye, "L'Ancienne Hagiographie byzantine: Origine, sources d'inspiration, formation des genres," *Byzantion* 10 (1935): 379–80; Hunger, *Die hochsprachliche profane Literatur* (above, n. 11), 1:121–22; C. Mango, *Byzantium: The Empire of New Rome* (London, 1980), 247–48.

31   P. Alexander, "Secular Biography at Byzantium," *Speculum* 15 (1940): 194–209, esp. 198ff.; P. Agapitos, "Ἡ εἰκόνα τοῦ αὐτοκράτορα Βασιλείου Α' στὴ φιλομακεδονικὴ γραμματεία, 867–959," *Hellenika* 40 (1989): 285–322, esp. 308ff.

32   A number of saints' Vitae of eighth- and ninth-century patriarchs are mostly secular in spirit and historical in content. See Alexander, "Secular Biography at Byzantium"; S. Paschalides, "From Hagiography to History: The Case of the *Vita Ignatii* (*BHG* 817) by Nicetas David the Paphlagonian," in *Les vies des saints à Byzance: Genre littéraire ou biographie historique? Actes du IIe Colloque International Philologique, Paris, 6–8 juin 2002,* ed. P. Odorico and P. A. Agapitos (Paris, 2004), 161–73. The hagiographical output of Nikephoros Gregoras during the fourteenth century is replete with historical digressions and comments. See M. Hinterberger, "Les *Vies des saints* du XIVe siècle en tant que biographie historique: l'oeuvre de Nicéphore Grégoras," in Odorico and Agapitos, *Les vies des saints à Byzance*, 281–301. The late fourteenth-century Vita of the emperor John III Vatatzes was also a mixture of the three genres. See the bibliography above in n. 19.

33   On autobiography in Byzantium, see M. Angold, "The Autobiographical Impulse in Byzantium," *DOP* 52 (1998): 225–57; M. Hinterberger, *Autobiographische Traditionen in Byzanz* (Vienna, 1999).

which are replete with references to their upbringing and education. Other auto-biographies, however, are rich sources for our investigation: those of Gregory of Cyprus, who served as Patriarch Gregory II (1283–1289), and Patriarch Matthew I (1397–1410). Informative, too, are the two autobiographical accounts of the emperor Michael VIII Palaiologos, the only emperor who described events of his own adolescence. These texts were not immune to influences from other bio-graphical genres, and each has been classed in a different tradition of Byzantine autobiographical writing.[34]

Another group of sources which we need to consider are the so-called mir-rors of princes, or books of advice to rulers.[35] *Mirrors of princes* is a rather decep-tive description for the court-advice literature of the Byzantines. The expres-sion was coined during the twelfth century in Italy, but even in the West it was rarely used to refer to the numerous specimens of court-advice literature com-posed during the high and late Middle Ages.[36] Furthermore, many of the Byz-antine mirrors address reigning emperors during their mature years rather than adolescent princes. For example, the most frequently copied Byzantine mirror of princes—the *Ekthesis* of Agapetos the Deacon—addresses, as its acrostic makes clear, the reigning emperor Justinian (b. ca. 482, r. 527–565) who acceded to the throne at the age of about forty-five. Another influential late antique mirror of princes, Synesius of Cyrene's *On Kingship,* was addressed to the emperor Arka-dios (b. 377/78, r. 395–408), a young man who was between twenty-one and twenty-five years of age.[37]

A teenage princely audience seems probable for two of the three mirrors of princes composed in the form of counsel given by emperors to their sons.[38] It has been argued that Emperor Basil I's *Hortatory Chapters* (Κεφάλαια

---

34   That is, the autobiography of a literary man (Gregory of Cyprus) as well as of a monk (Patri-arch Matthew I) and a layman (Michael VIII) within monastic *typika*. See Hinterberger, *Auto-biographische Traditionen,* 208–28, 256–98, 345–66. For parallels between Patriarch Matthew I's testament and hagiography with regard to the presentation of childhood, see ibid., 216, and below.

35   For a survey of the self-contained works, see Hunger, *Die hochsprachliche profane Literatur* (above, n. 11), 1:157–65.

36   P. Hadot, "Fürstenspiegel," *RAC* (Stuttgart, 1972), 8:556.

37   Synesius's *On Kingship* has been dated to 399–402. See A. Cameron and J. Long, *Barbarians and Politics at the Court of Arcadius* (Berkeley, 1993), 91–142.

38   These works are the *Hortatory Chapters,* attributed to Emperor Basil I and addressed to his son Leo VI; the *Muses* of Emperor Alexios I Komnenos, addressed to his son John II Komnenos; and the *Foundations of Imperial Conduct* of Emperor Manuel II Palaiologos, addressed to his son John VIII Palaiologos.

DIMITER G. ANGELOV

παραινετικά) was in reality a work by the learned patriarch Photios, composed between 880 and 883. If so, the addressee, Basil I's son and successor, Leo VI (b. 866, r. 886–912), was at the time an adolescent prince aged between fourteen and seventeen.[39] In the early fourteenth century, Emperor Manuel II's *Foundations of Imperial Conduct* (Ὑποθῆκαι βασιλικῆς ἀγωγῆς) also addresses a prince and heir to the throne, the future emperor John VIII Palaiologos (b. 1392, r. 1425–1448), who was at the time most probably a teenager.[40] We should add to these two works the oration, itself a mixture of an imperial panegyric and a mirror of princes, composed by Theophylaktos of Ohrid and addressed to his princely pupil, the *porphyrogennetos* and heir presumptive Constantine Doukas (b. 1074), a boy between the ages of ten and twelve.[41]

The youth of the princely addressees of these three texts did not provoke specifically pedagogical discussion, although it certainly makes them valuable for tracing ideals of imperial upbringing and education. All Byzantine mirrors (whether addressed to adults or adolescents) are imbued with the lofty spirit of the imperial office and are dissociated from the trivia of childhood: they expound the principles of just and legitimate kingship, give theoretical and specific advice on government, and feature moral philosophy appropriate for the conduct of an emperor in the tradition of classical and Christian Greek paraenetic literature.

This situation contrasts with the Western medieval tradition of mirrors of princes as it evolved from the thirteenth century onward. The influential works of Vincent of Beauvais (d. 1264) and Giles of Rome (ca. 1243–1316), both addressed to adult members of the French royal house, include substantial pedagogical sections on the upbringing and education of both boys and girls.[42] Giles

---

39   The edition of the *Hortatory Chapters* used here is that of K. Emminger, *Studien zu den griechischen Fürstenspiegeln*, vol. 3: *Βασιλείου κεφάλαια παραινετικά* (Munich, 1913). For authorship and dating of the *Hortatory Chapters*, see A. Markopoulos, "Autour des *Chapîtres parénétiques* de Basile Ier," in *EΥΨΥΧΙΑ: Mélanges offerts à Hélène Ahrweiler*, ed. A. Laiou, vol. 2 (Paris, 1998), 469–79.

40   The *Foundation of Imperial Conduct* is found in PG 156:319–84. The dedicatory letter by Manuel II mentions that his son was a μειράκιον at the time of composition of this instructive work (PG 156:313A). The terminus post quem for its composition has been set to 1406, when John VIII was fourteen. See John W. Barker, *Manuel II Palaeologus (1391–1425): A Study in Late Byzantine Statesmanship* (New Brunswick, 1969), xxx, 344–45, 494 n. 84.

41   According to Paul Gautier, the work was composed between 1081 and 1087, and most probably ca. 1085–86. See *Théophylacte d'Achrida: Discours, traités, poésies,* ed. P. Gautier, vol. 1 (Thessalonike, 1980), 67.

42   Vincent of Beauvais's *De eruditione filiorum nobilium* was a pedagogical work on the education of royal children composed in 1249–50 at the request of Queen Marguerite, the wife of King Louis IX. It was conceived as the fourth book of a large opus on "the status of the prince

of Rome's *De regimine principum* was particularly popular in the late medieval West, undergoing successive translation into Europe's vernacular languages and influencing later works.[43] It is not surprising, therefore, that scholars have already made use of this court literature for studying ideals of childhood upbringing of the elite and conceptions of medieval childhood in general.[44] Those interested in Byzantine court education do not, unfortunately, have similar sources at their disposal.

The circulation and audience of the examined body of literature is an important issue to consider, for knowing this would allow us to identify the segment of Byzantine society whose ideals of childhood the literature reflects. A great many of our texts (the laudatory orations on emperors and patriarchs, and the mirrors of princes) circulated in the imperial court, often disseminating a propagandist version of the biography of the powerful men of the day. The authors of these texts tended to serve as spokesmen of the official line, and even when they made individual interpretations, they still voiced images and concepts current among the imperial literary elite. Similar propagandist and legitimizing concerns can be detected in the *Vita Basilii* and in the universally positive portrayal of the emperor-usurper Basil I in pro-Macedonian historiography. The autobiographies of Michael VIII Palaiologos, who was also an emperor-usurper and the founder of a new dynasty, show similarities with the portrait of the emperor flaunted in court rhetoric.[45]

By contrast, hagiography circulated among less elite audiences and reflects

---

and the entire royal court." See R. Schneider, "Vincent of Beauvais' *Opus universale de statu principis*: A Reconstruction of Its History and Contents," in *Vincent de Beauvais: Intentions et réceptions d'une oeuvre encyclopédique*, ed. S. Lusignan, M. Paulmier-Foucart, and A. Nadeau (Saint-Laurent, 1990), 285–99. Giles of Rome (Aegidius Romanus or Aegidius Colonna) devoted a large part of his *De regimine principum* to the nature of children and the upbringing of princes. See *Li livres du gouvernement des rois: A XIIIth Century French Version of Egidio Colonna's Treatise*, ed. S. P. Molenaer (London, 1899), 180–233. The work was composed in the 1280s, when the author was tutor to the future King Philip IV the Fair (1285–1314).

43   For the translation of this work into French, English, Italian, German, Venetian, Castilian, Catalan, Dutch, Portuguese, Swedish, and Hebrew, see W. Berges, *Die Fürstenspiegel des hohen und späten Mittelalters* (Leipzig, 1938), 320–28. For similar pedagogical advice given to adult rulers in subsequent Western mirrors of princes, see L. K. Born, "The Perfect Prince: A Study of Thirteenth and Fourteenth Century Ideals," *Speculum* 3 (1928): 484 n. 2, 493–94; Berges, *Die Fürstenspiegel*, 340–41.

44   Shahar, *Children* (above, n. 6), 16 nn. 32–33, 113 n. 189.

45   For example, the close connection between John III Vatatzes and Michael VIII described in the biographies is similar to that referred to in panegyrics. See Angelov, *Imperial Ideology* (above, n. 13), 124–25, and n. 80 below.

DIMITER G. ANGELOV

to a greater extent popular beliefs and imagination. Even so, it portrays exceptional and exemplary children, the chosen few who grew up to attain the status of sainthood (and in our cases attained also political power). Scholars have already pointed out that the ideal children depicted in hagiography could serve the didactic purpose of providing paragons of good behavior to a youthful audience.[46] Notably, we find one example of this use of hagiography in the Vita of a patriarch. In his *Encomiastic Oration* on John Chrysostom, the emperor Leo VI the Wise rehearsed a familiar story of how the saint behaved humbly when going to school with other children, declining to ride a horse and to be escorted by servants. The author then added his own exhortation: "Listen, you children, who can boast the fame, wealth, and arrogance of your parents, and imitate."[47] The interpolated comment is meant to suggest an elite audience of youths. We can plausibly conclude that both the subject matter and the circulation of most of the examined texts point to ideals of childhood that were promoted by, or were at least current among, elite Constantinople audiences.

The Childhood of Emperors

Common motifs and themes run through the idealized representations of imperial childhood. They are distinguishable mostly in terms of the thematic typology of the episodes: divine signs for the royal future of the child; the precocious maturity of the child (the topos of the *puer senex*); upbringing and education; and unique childhood characteristics, such as mischief, innocence, and playfulness. The first two of the mentioned themes deserve to be discussed together, for they both treat childhood as a literary backdrop for the early manifestation of adulthood and imperial authority.

Divine Signs of Imperial Future

The divine omens auguring greatness—a motif recommended by the rhetorical manuals—vary widely and appear at different times during the emperor's early life, from his conception and birth through his infancy, and throughout his childhood in the form of dream visions. On the night when the first Christian

---

46   See Kalogeras, "What Do They Think about Children?" (above, n. 10), 13, with a reference to the Vita of the seventh-century saint Theodore of Sykeon.

47   PG 107:229C (*BHG* 880).

emperor, Constantine, was conceived, the sun reversed its course and miraculously illuminated the inn in Bithynia where the emperor Constantius met Helena, the innkeeper's daughter.[48] Tremors of the earth and the appearance of comets are said to have greeted the birth of new emperors.[49] The symbols of royalty sometimes miraculously appear around the newborn baby, signifying God's plans for the future. Thus, a purple nimbus is reported to have been seen during the first growth of hair on the head of the infant Basil I.[50]

A common omen at the birth of an emperor or an empress was the appearance of an eagle, an ancient symbol of royalty.[51] An eagle is said to have attempted to enter through the window of the house where the newborn Theophano, the future wife of Leo the Wise, lay in her cradle.[52] According to the *Vita Basilii,* an eagle once appeared when the child Basil was resting from work in the fields: to shield him from the scorching sun, it hovered long above his head with outstretched wings.[53] In 1169, after the long-awaited birth of a male heir to the emperor Manuel I Komnenos (1143–80), a similar story is reported in an instructive oration (*didaskalia*) composed for the occasion by a certain Skizenos, *oikoumenikos didaskalos* at the patriarchate. Skizenos relates how a young eagle desired to witness the birth of the imperial child. Just as the star in heaven guided the three wise men to Christ's manger, so the eagle flew on its quest until it hovered above the *porphyra* (porphyry chamber) of the palace. Then the eagle is said to have flown to the area of the church of Saint Sophia, where youths at play hunted

48   Guidi, "Un Βίος di Costantinto" (above, n. 20), 308. "Annunciation" omens were a common hagiographical topos. See Pratsch, *Der hagiographische Topos* (above, n. 8), 74–77, and below.

49   The entire river Rhine and the wild forests of the Caucasus trembled to greet the birth of the future Western emperor Honorius (b. 384; r. 393–423). See Claudian, *Panegyricus de tertio consulatu Honorii augusti,* vv. 16–18, and *Panegyricus de quarto consulatu Honorii augusti,* vv. 139–50, in J.-L. Charlet, ed., *Oeuvres complètes de Claudien: Poèmes politiques (395–398),* vol. 2 (Paris, 2000), part 1, 35; part 2, 15–16. The appearance of a bright star or comet marked the moment when the future emperor Manuel I Komnenos (1143–1180) came out of his mother's womb. See P. Gautier, ed., *Michel Italikos: Lettres et discours* (Paris, 1972), 281.

50   *Theophanes Continuatus, Ioannes Cameniata, Symeon Magister, Georgius Monachus,* ed. I. Bekker, CSHB (Bonn, 1838), 216.

51   On the classical literary association of the eagle with royalty, which persisted in Byzantium, see Moravcsik, "Sagen und Legenden" (above, n. 25), 83–88. Imperial panegyrists in late Byzantium were fond of comparing emperors to eagles. See Angelov, *Imperial Ideology* (above, n. 13), 85 and n. 41.

52   E. Kurtz, *Zwei griechische Texte über die Hl. Theophano, die Gemahlin Kaisers Leo VI.* (St. Petersburg, 1898), 3.

53   Bekker, *Theophanes Continuatus,* 218–19; *Ioannis Scylitzae synopsis historiarum,* ed. I. Thurn, CFHB (Berlin, 1973), 118–19.

it down. The Great Church donated the trophy to the newly born emperor Alexios II, for the eagle had inaugurated his birth.[54]

Another kind of divine sign was the dream vision, which could appear either to the parents or to the future emperor or empress.[55] The symbols of imperial authority are prominent in dream visions. When the Virgin appeared to the twelve-year-old future emperor Manuel I in his dreams, she placed the imperial purple buskins on his feet. Manuel is reported to have cried out once he awakened, "My boots! Where are they, and who took them away?" The meaning of this divine sign is said to have been understood by everyone who witnessed it, even though Manuel was not the eldest son in the imperial family.[56]

Some of the omens that appeared during imperial childhood were more down-to-earth, though still with a legitimizing purpose. Between 1296 and 1303, the court orator Nicholas Lampenos praised the emperor Andronikos II (b. 1259, r. 1282–1328) for smiling as a baby during his baptism. This story seems to have pursued an agenda beyond the obvious (namely, praise of the uncanny wisdom of the infant emperor). The unnamed patriarch who baptized the child is said to have marveled at the baby Andronikos and to have prophesied his imperial accession. The reference is clearly to Patriarch Arsenios (1254–1260, 1261–1264), a political dissident and a holy man who caused a schism in the Byzantine church. His partisans, the Arsenites, did not recognize the legitimacy of the Palaiologan dynasty until 1310, despite Andronikos II's attempts at reconciliation. By including the saintly Arsenios in the narrative, the orator created the propagandist illusion that Arsenios favored the Palaiologan emperor even during his infancy.[57]

54 *Fontes rerum byzantinarum: Rhetorum saeculi XII orationes politicae*, ed. V. Regel and N. Novosadskii (St. Petersburg, 1892–1917; repr. Leipzig, 1982), 366–67. On the year of birth of Alexios II, see Charles Brand and Anthony Cutler, "Alexios II Komnenos," *ODB* 1:64.

55 Basil I's mother dreamed before her adolescent son's imminent departure for Constantinople that a golden tree grew out of her and blossomed in such a way as to adorn her entire house, an allusion to her son's imperial elevation and the foundation of a dynasty. The *Vita Basilii* and Genesios compared this dream to that of Cyrus's mother, reported by Herodotus, and Menander's example of a divine sign at birth; see Bekker, *Theophanes Continuatus,* 221–222; *Iosephi Genesii Regum libri quattuor*, ed. A. Lesmueller-Werner and I. Thurn, CFHB (Berlin, 1978), 76.74–80. When the future empress Theophano was a child older than six, the Virgin appeared in her dreams and anointed her entire body with holy oil: Kurtz, *Zwei griechische Texte*, 6.

56 Gautier, *Michel Italikos* (above, n. 49), 279–80. Like the empress Theophano, Manuel I is said to have identified the Virgin from her icons.

57 I. Polemis, Ὁ λόγιος Νικόλαος Λαμπηνὸς καὶ τὸ ἐγκώμιον αὐτοῦ εἰς τὸν Ἀνδρόνικον Β΄ Παλαιολόγον (Athens, 1992), 41, esp. 41.32–36 (ch. 22). This passage suggests that patriarchs were

Twelfth- and thirteenth-century court oratory shows an interesting pecu-liarity. Panegyrics of this period tend to assign birthdays of emperors to impor-tant feast days: Emperor Alexios II is said to have been born on the day of the Elevation of the Cross (14 September 1169);[58] Andronikos II on the day of the Annunciation of the Virgin (25 March 1259);[59] and Michael IX on Easter day (17 April 1278).[60] There are two more thirteenth-century attributions of imperial birthdays to major feast days.[61] One need not necessarily cast these happy coin-cidences into doubt, for the Byzantine liturgical calendar was replete with feasts. Still, these five examples in less than 130 years raise the question of whether some of the reported birthdays were merely an approximation to the closest important Christian feast. The orator Skizenos, who makes much of Alexios II's birthday on the day of the Elevation of the Cross, refers to the proximity of the birth-day, almost as an additional omen, to the feast of the Nativity of the Virgin (9 September).[62] An illuminating similarity is seen in the reported dates of the bap-tism of princes in an earlier period. Between the fifth and the ninth century, the baptism of imperial princes is often said to have been conducted on major feast days.[63] Nothing is known about the preferred days of baptism of the emperor's children in the later Byzantine period, but the incentive to fit imperial biogra-

still responsible for baptizing the children of emperors in the thirteenth century, as the case had been in the tenth. See *De cerimoniis aulae byzantinae libri duo*, ed. I. Reiske (Bonn, 1829), 2:619–20 (ch. 22). On the likely day of Andronikos II's birth in the spring of 1259, see n. 59 below. A smiling rather than crying baby seems to have been interpreted as a divine sign. The empress Theophano is said to have been born with a smile on her face and without bringing any pain to her mother dur-ing a particularly difficult birth. See Kurtz, *Zwei griechische Texte*, 3. This episode was omitted by Nikephoras Gregoras in his fourteenth-century version of the Vita (*BHG* 1795).

58   Bekker, *Theophanes Continuatus*, 218–19; Thurn, *Ioannis Scylitzae synopsis historiarum* (above, n. 53), 118–19.

59   Polemis, Ὁ λόγιος Νικόλαος Λαμπηνός, 39 (ch. 19). Cf. I. Ševčenko, *Études sur la polémique entre Théodore Métochite et Nicéphore Choumnos* (Brussels, 1962), 137 n. 6 (a marginal note by Gregoras in Marcianus gr. 235 reports the same date of birth and the year 1259).

60   S. Kourouses, "Νέος κῶδιξ τοῦ 'βασιλικοῦ' Μαξίμου τοῦ Πλανούδη," Ἀθηνᾶ 73–74 (1972–73): 432.

61   A poem by Nikephoros Blemmydes celebrates the birth of an emperor, traditionally identi-fied as John IV Laskaris (b. 1250), at Christmas. See *Nicephori Blemmydae curriculum vitae et car-mina*, ed. A. Heisenberg (Leipzig, 1896), 110–11. Ruth Macrides, in *George Akropolites: The His-tory* (Oxford, 2007), 276, has suggested the possibility that the poem might refer to the birth of Emperor Theodore II Laskaris. An anonymous short chronicle reports that the emperor Androni-kos III was born on the day of the Annunciation of the Virgin (25 March 1297 or 1298), just like his grandfather Andronikos II. See P. Schreiner, *Die byzantinischen Kleinchroniken*, vol. 2 (Vienna, 1977), 215; vol. 3 (Vienna, 1979), 174–75. Cf. A.-M. Talbot, "Andronikos III," *ODB* 1:95.

62   Regel and Novosadskii, *Fontes rerum byzantinarum* (above, n. 54), 367.18–23.

63   G. Dagron, "Nés dans la pourpre," *TM* 10 (1994): 125–26.

DIMITER G. ANGELOV

phies into a providential Christian scheme must have remained. It is interesting that the emperor Manuel I Komnenos, Alexios II's father, repealed by legislation the practice of celebrating of imperial birthdays as official public holidays.[64] The lapse of the public holiday ought to have led to a degree of ignorance about the day the emperor was born that court rhetoric could have exploited. Therefore, we should be cautious in accepting at face value the birthdays reported in panegyrics and should seek corroborating evidence where possible.

Another peculiar characteristic of twelfth- and thirteenth-century court oratory is the search for historical omens around the birth of the emperor at the expense of miraculous or supernatural ones. Emperors Manuel I Komnenos and Andronikos II Palaiologos were said to be born at the time when their fathers acceded to the throne. The panegyrists of Andronikos II called attention also to important victories: the battle of Pelagonia (autumn 1259) and the Byzantine recapture of Constantinople (summer 1261).[65] During the thirteenth century, fantastic omens and dreams drop out of the laudatory accounts of imperial childhood. Instead, interestingly, we are confronted by pessimism about the credibility of dream visions around the time of birth. Commenting on the birth of Michael IX Palaiologos, Maximos Planoudes mentioned the vision of Cyrus's mother (Menander's example of a miracle at birth) and exclaimed, "I do not know whether one should believe in these stories or not."[66] The orator chose instead to focus on a purportedly real event: the birth of the emperor on Easter day. The express reluctance to speak of miraculous signs in front of the court seems to underlie a new, more rationalistic and practical attitude toward the early phase of the imperial biography, seen also in the emphasis on military training and war games during the later Byzantine period (see below).

64   R. Macrides, "Justice under Manuel I Komnenos: Four Novels on Court Business and Murder," *FM* 6 (1984): 154. Cf. P. Koukoules, *Βυζαντινῶν βίος καὶ πολιτισμός,* vol. 2, fascicle 1 (Athens, 1948), 35–36. In the tenth century, Constantine VII Porphyrogennetos' *Book of Ceremonies* describes the court festivities in detail. Cf. A. Moffatt, "Celebrating a Byzantine Imperial Birthday," in *ΦΙΛΕΛΛΗΝ: Studies in Honour of Robert Browning,* ed. C. Constantinides et al. (Venice, 1996), 244–66. Nothing is known about such a celebration from the fourteenth-century ceremonial book of Pseudo-Kodinos.

65   On Manuel I, see Gautier, *Michel Italikos* (above, n. 49), 279. On Andronikos II, see Gregory of Cyprus, PG 142:393C; Nikephoros Choumnos, in J. Boissonade, ed., *Anecdota graeca e codicibus regiis,* vol. 2 (Paris, 1830; repr. Hildesheim, 1962), 12–13; Polemis, *Ὁ λόγιος Νικόλαος Λαμπηνός* (above, n. 57), 39–40 (ch. 20).

66   S. Kourouses, "Νέος κῶδιξ" (above, n. 60), 431.4–5: οὐκ οἶδ᾽ εἴτε χρὴ τοιαῦτα πιστεύειν, εἴτε μή.

Imperial Princes as Pueri Senes

Imperial princes and children destined to become emperors are commonly represented as possessing the traits of adults. We find various propagandist comments revolving around the topos of the *puer senex*. Court orators made general observations regarding the extraordinary maturity of imperial children. For example, as a child, Michael VIII Palaiologos (1259–1282) is said to have rivaled adults with his sharp mind.[67] Michael VIII's son, Constantine the Porphyrogennetos, aged between six and eleven, was praised for his "adult mind (πρεσβευτικὸν φρόνημα) shining forth in his soul during a puerile age (ἡλικία παιδική)."[68] As children, future rulers were praised for already possessing the virtues of adult emperors, such as bravery,[69] intelligence,[70] and piety.[71] Finally, court orators could play on the theme of the *puer senex* by commenting rhetorically that the child-emperor passed rapidly into the adult world because the empire needed effective military leadership. In his speech delivered at the wedding in 1180 of the ten-year-old Alexios II to Agnes of France, Eustathios of Thessalonike wrote: "You left the swaddling clothes soon, for nature did not wish to confine in them the one who holds out steady hopes of extending the Roman boundaries."[72] As

---

67   *Manuelis Holoboli orationes*, ed. M. Treu (Potsdam, 1906–7), 33. In the same spirit the orator Themistius declared to the seventeen- or eighteen-year-old Gratian, emperor of the Western Empire (375–383): "Your youth will be counted along with the old age of Cyrus, and your adolescence along with the maturity of Marcus Aurelius." See *Themistii orationes quae supersunt*, vol. 1, ed. H. Schenkl and G. Downey (Leipzig, 1965), 244.25–245.2. The oration was given in Rome in the autumn of 376 or 377. Gratian was born in 359. See T. Gregory, "Gratian," *ODB* 2:867.

68   Treu, *Manuelis Holoboli orationes*, 91. The reference is to the third Christmas oration, which Holobolos delivered between 1267 and 1272, probably closer to the former date; see R. Macrides, "The New Constantine and the New Constantinople—1261?" *BMGS* 6 (1980): 19, 37 n. 137. Constantine the Porphyrogennetos was born in 1261, shortly after the Byzantine recapture of Constantinople from the Latins.

69   In the panegyrical preface to his *History,* Michael Attaleiates praised his patron, the emperor Nikephoros III Botaneiates (1078–1081), for his great bravery "since childhood" (ἐκ παίδων). See *Miguel Ataliates: Historia*, ed. I. Pérez Martín (Madrid, 2002), 2.16–17.

70   An encomium on Isaac II Angelos (1185–1195) lauded the emperor for possessing "since childhood" (ἐκ παίδων) the two cardinal imperial virtues of intelligence and bravery. See Μιχαὴλ Ἀχομινάτου τοῦ Χωνιάτου τὰ σωζόμενα, vol. 1, ed. S. Lampros (Athens, 1879; repr. Groningen, 1968), 213.

71   Both Michael VIII and his son, the emperor Andronikos II (1282–1328), were praised for being pious from the time when they were in their swaddling clothes. See Gregory of Cyprus, in PG 142:357BC; Maximos Planoudes, in L. G. Westerink, "Le basilikos de Maxime Planude," *BSl* 29 (1968): 37.901.

72   Regel and Novosadskii, *Fontes rerum byzantinarum* (above, n. 54), 89. The marriage took place on 2 March 1180; Alexios II was born in 1169.

for King Louis VII's daughter Agnes, who was seven or eight years old, he noted that she "had shown the wisdom of an old person at a young age."[73] The hunting exploits of Andronikos II, aged between eight and thirteen, were presented in an imperial encomium as "heralding to the barbarians the kind of people who protect the Romans and the kind of God-mightiest, most invincible and strong fighter they are about to experience in a little while."[74] There was an element of wishful thinking in these comments. A court poet celebrated the birth in 1332 of the future emperor John V Palaiologos (1341–1391) by wishing: "May the Graces applaud a baby larger than the world . . . and may they swathe him with weapons infused with might."[75]

The topos of the *puer senex* manifested itself also in the years of entry into adulthood. Imperial princes are sometimes presented, rather unbelievably, as having begun their military careers in their early teenage years. One of the post-Iconoclastic Lives of Constantine narrates how his father Constantius appointed the ten-year-old boy as *komes* (low-ranking commander) of fifteen *noumera* (regiments in the Byzantine army).[76] The future patriarch Ignatios, son of Emperor Michael I (811–813), is said to have been appointed at the age of ten to the newly established cadet corps of the *hikanatoi* by his grandfather, the emperor Nikephoros I (802–811).[77]

Assumption of military command by ten-year-old boys is not only implausible but also contradicts the harder evidence of contemporary chronicles and histories. An anonymous ninth-century chronicle reports that when founding the new corps of the *hikanatoi,* Nikephoros I enrolled children of officials who were fifteen years of age or older.[78] Anna Komnena mentions in the *Alexiad* how her father, the emperor Alexios I, eagerly wanted to enter battle when he was fourteen years of age, but his mother did not permit him to do so.[79] A propagandist desire to assign the assumption of military command to an early age, in contradiction to the realities, is also seen in the two autobiographies of Michael

73   Ibid., 88.

74   Treu, *Manuelis Holoboli orationes,* 94.4–6. On the date of this oration and the birth of Andronikos II, see nn. 59, 68 above.

75   C. von Holzinger, "Ein Panegyrikus des Manuel Philes," *BZ* 20 (1911): 385, vv. 1–3.

76   Halkin, "Une nouvelle vie de Constantin" (above, n. 20), 75.24, 76.

77   Niketas David the Paphlagonian, Life of Patriarch Ignatios, PG 105:492B. The hagiographer's use of reported speech ("so they say") when mentioning Ignatios's appointment at the age of ten may suggest doubts as to the reported age.

78   I. Dujčev, "La chronique byzantine de l'an 811," *TM* 1 (1965): 210.1–8. For the corps of the *hikanatoi*, see J. Haldon, *Byzantine Praetorians* (Bonn, 1984), 245–46.

79   *Annae Comnenae Alexias,* ed. D. Reinsch and A. Kambylis, CFHB (Berlin, 2001), 11 (1.1).

VIII Palaiologos. Whereas in one of them the emperor reports his appointment as general at eighteen, in the other he writes that the Nicaean ruler John III Vatatzes chose him as a military commander as an adolescent (μεῖραξ), as soon as he was able to bear arms. The term μεῖραξ is conveniently imprecise and casts Michael in a more heroic light by implying that he might have begun to command troops before the age of eighteen.[80] The precocious age of assumption of military posts touted in the imperial biographies seems to be related to a literary tendency observable in several Byzantine romances, according to which the hero enters adulthood during his early teens. Digenis Akritas, Paris in the Byzantine *Iliad,* and Achilles in the *Achilleid* accomplish their first manly feats between the ages of ten and thirteen.[81]

The common themes traced thus far in the imperial biographies can hardly be called realistic images of childhood. They relegate childhood to a subaltern period of life, when adult power is first legitimized and when future emperors begin to display skills and characteristics associated with their office. One might, therefore, be inclined to adopt Ariès's thesis that medieval Byzantium did not view childhood as an autonomous stage of life. To do so, however, would mean falling into a trap laid by the biographical sources. Numerous descriptions point to an alternative conception of imperial childhood, one firmly grounded in the realities, which often coexists alongside the literary clichés. This alternative conception is seen primarily in the strong emphasis on childhood and adolescent education of future emperors.

---

80   A. Dmitrievskii, *Opisanie liturgicheskikh rukopisei*, vol. 1: *Typika*, part 1 (Kiev, 1895), 790; H. Grégoire, "Imperatoris Michaelis Palaeologi de *Vita* Sua," *Byzantion* 29–30 (1959–60): 451 (ch. IV): ἐγὼ δὲ ὡς εἰς μείρακας ἤδη πρώτως παρήγγελλον καὶ ὅπλα φέρειν ἦν ἱκανός, ὑπ᾽ αὐτοῦ δὴ ἐκείνου στρατηγεῖν ἐκρινόμην. Cf. the translation by G. Dennis in *Byzantine Monastic Foundation Documents*, ed. J. Thomas and A. C. Hero (Washington, D.C., 2000), 3:1230, 1245. The term μειράκιον could cover a wide span of years. According to the Hippocratic text *De hebdomadibus,* the age of μειράκιον is between 14 and 21. See W. H. Roscher, ed., *Die hippokratische Schrift von der Siebenzahl* (Paderborn, 1913; repr., New York, 1967), ch. 5. The span of years of a μειράκιον could, however, cover the ages six to fourteen. See the article by G. Prinzing in this volume.

81   See the observations by O. Smith, *The Byzantine Achilleid: The Naples Version* (Vienna, 1999), 88–89. Achilles accomplishes his first feat at the age of 13, Paris in the Byzantine *Iliad* at 10, and Digenis Akritas at 12 (Grottaferrata version, 4, 85ff.). Cf. C. Jouanno, "Récits d'enfances dans la littérature byzantine d'imagination," *Pris-ma: Bulletin de liaison de l'Équipe de recherche sur la littérature d'imagination au moyen âge* 12 (1996): 39–56, esp. 47–49.

Mental and Physical Education of Princes

The ideal of the well-educated prince runs throughout Byzantine history. The representations of imperial education went beyond literary conventions, some of which are shared with hagiography, such as the theme of the self-taught man (*autodidaktos*).[82] Education tends to be presented realistically, as an integral part of imperial childhood and adolescence. There are frequent hints at the youthful age of the prince receiving instruction. Some of these hints are mere rhetorical allusions, such as the comparison of the prince studying the Holy Scriptures with a well-watered young sapling.[83] In other cases, terms such as *child* (παῖς), *adolescent* (μεῖραξ), and "youth" (νέος) refer to the age when future emperors or princes born to the purple were educated.[84] These terms evoke the image of a princely youngster, not an adult.

Our information on the subjects in which future emperors received instruction is not as rich as one would hope to find; yet a few subjects stand out, and they seem to reflect the realities of princely education. As with every child, education began with the study of reading and writing (the so-called *hiera grammata*).[85] Subsequent education was geared toward the practicalities of rulership and was carried out by special tutors; it is never referred to by the general term for secondary

82 Nikephoros Choumnos, in Boissonade, *Anecdota graeca* (above, n. 65), 2:14–15, 34, 36 (μόνος αὐτοδιδάκτως θεοσόφως ἐξεπιστάμενος). On the panegyrical portrait of Andronikos II, including the emperor's education, see N. Radošević, "Pohvalna slova caru Androniku II Paleologu," *ZRVI* 21 (1982): 61–83. On the topos of the saint-*autodidaktos*, see Pratsch, *Der hagiographische Topos* (above, n. 8), 103–5.

83 See the *Hortatory Chapters* of Pseudo-Basil, in Emminger, *Studien* (above, n. 39), 55 (ch. 17). Note especially the expression τὰ νεοθαλῆ τῶν φυτῶν.

84 In his address to Constantine Doukas during the late eleventh century, Theophylaktos used the words *child* (παῖς) and *youth* (νέος). See Gautier, *Théophylacte d'Achrida* (above, n. 41), 1:191.27–29. In the twelfth century, Michael Italikos called Manuel I Komnenos a "youth" (νέος) during his education. See Gautier, *Michel Italikos* (above, n. 49), 283, 1–2. In the second half of the thirteenth century, Nikephoros Choumnos referred to Andronikos's perusal of religious texts when he was "an adolescent" (μεῖραξ). See Nikephoros Choumnos, in Boissonade, *Anecdota graeca*, 2:18. In the early fifteenth century, Manuel II Palaiologos referred to the applicability of his advice to "children" (παῖδες) and "youths" (νέοι, νεώτεροι, νεότης). See PG 156:344D, 353A, 365D, 375D, 380B.

85 According to the Guidi Vita, Constantine began his elementary education (*hiera grammata*) when Constantius arranged for the transfer of his adolescent son to the West. The empress Theophano, the only empress whose educational experience is described in a Vita, is said to have started her primary education at the age of six. See Guidi, "Un Βίος di Costantino" (above, n. 20), 311.21–22; Kurtz, *Zwei griechische Texte* (above, n. 52), 5.

education, *enkyklios paideia*.[86] History, especially the study of past examples of good and bad kings, was emphasized. Thus, in his versified panegyric of the Western emperor Honorius (395–423), the orator Claudian relates how the emperor's father Theodosius I (379–395) counseled his child to peruse the historical biographies of great leaders from Greek and Roman antiquity.[87] Pseudo-Basil similarly exhorts the young Leo the Wise to read history, from which he could readily learn about the importance of virtue and the fragility of royal power.[88] During the late eleventh century, the mother of Constantine Doukas, heir to the throne, is praised for having appointed tutors who taught him history and rhetoric.[89]

The reading of moralistic and paraenetic texts was a part of both the practice and the ideal of princely education. The mirrors of princes—some of which, as we saw, address teenage princes—are not the sole examples of such educational literature. The *Hortatory Chapters* of Pseudo-Basil advises the young Leo to read the Wisdom and Proverbs of Solomon, the Book of Ecclesiasticus (the Wisdom of Sirach), and the works of Isocrates, the author of the most popular ancient Greek mirror of princes.[90] According to a twelfth-century author and court orator, the body of knowledge appropriate for princes was in a class of its own, distinct from the learning needed by their subjects. The orator praised the emperor Manuel I Komnenos for being educated during his youth in "imperial science" (βασιλικὴ ἐπιστήμη), that is, the skill of kingship, which included knowledge of military strategy and rhetoric.[91]

A special part of the education of future emperors was physical and military training. Here we find some interesting variations in the ideal of imperial childhood over time. Generally speaking, physical and military education became an integral part of the cultural and literary ideal of imperial childhood and adolescence only from the second half of the eleventh century. This evolution is seen in a large array of sources that paint idealized portraits of child and adolescent emperors. It is true that late antique court oratory (a problematic source, as we noted, because it does not include childhood in the imperial biography) did not

86   On *enkyklios paideia*, see G. Buckler, "Byzantine Education," in N. H. Baynes and H. St. L. B. Moss, *Byzantium: An Introduction to East Roman Civilization* (Oxford, 1948), 204–7; P. Lemerle, *Le premier humanisme byzantin* (Paris, 1971), 101–3.
87   Charlet, ed., *Panegyricus de quarto consulatu Honorii augusti* (above, n. 49), vv. 397–418, vol. 2.2, 32–34.
88   Emminger, *Studien* (above, n. 39), 69–70 (ch. 56).
89   Gautier, *Théophylacte d'Achrida*, 1:191.27–29.
90   Emminger, *Studien*, 73 (ch. 66).
91   Gautier, *Michel Italikos,* 283.14–21.

ignore the importance of military education of the young heir to the throne. Claudian's panegyrics of the Western emperor Honorius make much of this component of education, especially in a reported speech by the emperor Theodosius I to his son, who was in his early teens.[92] A lengthy lacuna, however, follows after this example from the late antique West: no mention of physical training appears in imperial biographies and mirrors of princes between the fifth and the eleventh century. This lacuna appears to me to be not simply a matter of the survival of sources but rather symptomatic of changes in the princely ideal. In this respect, tracing the evolution of the hagiographical Vitae of Constantine the Great is especially illuminating.

The three earliest Vitae of the emperor Constantine that feature episodes of childhood, all of them dating to the period between the ninth and the eleventh centuries, relate the story of how Constantius, Constantine's father, had a casual, one-night affair in an inn in Drepanon in Bithynia with Helena, the innkeeper's daughter. The child Constantine grew up with his mother in the inn without knowing his father. Only much later did an embassy sent by Constantius to the East chance upon the emperor's bastard son, and Constantius arranged for his transfer to the West, showering him with attention and honors. Of the three Vitae, only the Patmos Vita (ninth or tenth century) reports the military abilities of the prince, stating that Constantius appointed his son commander (*komes* of the *noumera*) at the age of ten. The Vita does not, however, elaborate on any military or physical education of the child. The late Byzantine versions of Constantine's Life present his childhood differently. First of all, most of these versions make Helena a daughter of noble senators and a wife of Constantius.[93] Constantine was thus conceived within wedlock, even though his parents' marriage was later dissolved at the insistence of Diocletian. According to the hagiographer Gregoras, Constantius still interested himself in his son's upbringing and arranged for his education in Bithynia, which included military training,

92 Charlet, ed., *Panegyricus de quarto consulatu Honorii augusti*, vv. 321–51, vol. 2.2, 27–29. Cf. *Panegyricus de tertio consulatu Honori augustii*, vv. 40–62, vol. 2.1, 36–37 (above, n. 49). See also L. K. Born, "The Perfect Prince According to the Latin Panegyrists," *American Journal of Philology* 55 (1934): 20–35, esp. 27–28.
93 Already the anonymous eleventh- or twelfth-century Vita (*BHG* 363) omits the story of Helena's disreputable origin. See Gedeon, "Δύο παλαιὰ κείμενα," 253. Gregoras and Chortasmenos make Helena the daughter of noble senators and the wife of Constantius. See Leone, *Nicephori Gregorae Vita Constantini* (above, n. 23), 16; Ioannou, *Mnemeia Hagiologica*, 165–66. According to Constantine Akropolites, Helena was not married to Constantius when Constantine was conceived, even though the author sanitized the lewd story. See Simonides, *Panegyric* (above, n. 23), 6–8.

wrestling, and chariot and horseback riding. Constantine Akropolites' *Vita* speaks of gymnastic exercises and wrestling, while that of Chortasmenos refers to military exercises and stamina-building training.[94] Thus, late Byzantine hagiography brought Constantine's childhood and adolescence in line with Christian norms of propriety and in accordance with the contemporary ideal of the military education of an imperial prince.

The evolution of the ideal of imperial youth with regard to physical and military training is clearly seen in the mirrors of princes. The ninth-century *Hortatory Chapters* of Pseudo-Basil displays both a curious neglect of and an ambiguous attitude toward the acquisition of physical virtues by the adolescent prince. Leo the Wise is urged to "adorn his youth not with gymnastic exercises, but with a virtuous character," and is advised to "honor and be content with the strength of the body only if it is adorned with intelligence." The beauty and nobility of the soul are said to be worthier than those of the body.[95] In a similar fashion, earlier mirrors of princes addressed to adult rulers, such as those of Synesius and Agapetos the Deacon, do not recommend any bodily or military exercises. The later period of Byzantine history saw a new emphasis on physical and military training. In an oration addressed during the 1080s to the heir to the throne, Constantine Doukas, who was in his early teens, his tutor, Theophylaktos of Ohrid, praised the prince for taking part in a hunting expedition on which he killed, while riding on horseback, a beast his peers would not have dared to look upon even when it was dead. In the admonitory part of the same oration, Theophylaktos recommended that his tutee take part in military training and heed the advice of old and experienced soldiers.[96] Similarly, in his *Foundations of Imperial Conduct,* composed in the early fifteenth century, the emperor Manuel II Palaiologos advised his adolescent son, the future emperor John VIII, to exercise himself in preparation for war and to go hunting in order to ease his mind.[97] Post–eleventh century mirrors of princes addressed to adult emperors also pay attention to imperial physical and military virtues. Thus, in his *Imperial Statue,* composed in the late 1240s and addressed to the Nicaean rulers John III Vatatzes and Theodore II Laskaris (1254–1258), the scholar Nikephoros Blemmydes gave

---

94   Leone, *Nicephori Gregorae Vita Constantini*, 17; Ioannou, *Mnemeia Hagiologica* (above, n. 23), 169–70; Simonides, *Panegyric*, 9.

95   Emminger, *Studien*, 67 (ch. 49), 55 (ch. 13), 69 (ch. 53), 70 (ch. 58).

96   Gautier, *Théophylacte d'Achrida*, 1:183, 207.

97   PG 156:356C, 369D–370A. In the dedicatory letter of the work, Manuel mentions that the prince had already acquired skills in hunting and the use of weapons. See ibid., col. 313A.

specific advice on military exercises: he favored racing, jumping in full armor, wrestling, and javelin throwing.[98] In his work *On Kingship,* composed in the early fourteenth century, the Thessalonican scholar Thomas Magistros recommends to his adult royal addressee the study of tactics as well as physical activities in the form of military exercises and hunting.[99]

Imperial panegyrics from the twelfth century onward refer to the physical education of princes, military exercises as well as sports and games. In the twelfth-century Komnenian court, rhetoric emphasized the role of the emperor in providing military education to his son and heir to the throne. Thus, John II Komnenos (1118–1143) was said to have taught his son Manuel I the use of weapons and military strategy.[100] Manuel I in turn was described as having provided military training to his young son Alexios II, who was then no older than eleven.[101] In the thirteenth century, Andronikos II is said to have put his sixteen-year-old son Michael IX through the same rigorous military training that he had undergone at the same age, without, however, actually supervising him.[102]

Court oratory between the late eleventh and the late thirteenth century notes various princely games and physical activities. Among these, hunting was the main sport. As we have seen, Constantine Doukas was praised for hunting on horseback. In the second half of the thirteenth century, panegyrics of Michael VIII and Andronikos II presented hunting as an integral part of the upbringing of a prince. In his third Christmas panegyric of Michael VIII, delivered when his son Andronikos (the future Andronikos II) was between the ages of eight and thirteen, Holobolos describes the prince as leading the hounds and hunting

---

98   H. Hunger and I. Ševčenko, *Des Nikephoros Blemmydes Βασιλικὸς Ἀνδριάς und dessen Metaphrase von Georgios Galesiotes und Georgios Oinaiotes* (Vienna, 1986), 86–87 (ch. 131). The work dates to the 1240s, postdating John III's scandalous love affair. See I. Ševčenko, "A New Manuscript of Nicephorus Blemmydes' 'Imperial Statue,' and of Some Patriarchal Letters," *Byzantine Studies/Études Byzantines* 5 (1978): 225 and n. 20. For further discussion of the context of this work, see now Angelov, *Imperial Ideology* (above, n. 13), 188.

99   P. Cacciatore, ed., *Toma Magistro: La regalità* (Naples, 1997), 41–43, esp. 42.318–23 (ch. 8). On the likely date and context of this work, see A. Laiou, "Le débat sur les droits du fisc et les droits régaliens au début du 14e siècle," *REB* 58 (2000): 97–122, esp. 98–99.

100   Gautier, *Michel Italikos,* 282–84; Eustathios of Thessalonike, in Regel and Novosadskii, *Fontes rerum byzantinarum* (above, n. 54), 121 (= P. Wirth, ed., *Eustathii Thessalonicensis opera minora,* CSHB [Berlin, 2000], 285).

101   Eustathios of Thessalonike, in Regel and Novosadskii, *Fontes rerum byzantinarum,* 11 (= Wirth, *Eustathii Thessalonicensis opera minora,* 190).

102   L. G. Westerink, "Le basilikos de Maxime Planude," *BSl* 28 (1967): 54.145–48.

down hares and birds.[103] Mastery of horsemanship was greatly praised in panegyrical accounts of the upbringing of the early Palaiologan emperors.[104] The orator Nikephoros Choumnos mentions that he had witnessed how Andronikos II excelled at discus throwing, jumping, and horse riding.[105]

One game that tested princes' horsemanship was polo. In the twelfth century, John Kinnamos, Manuel I's official historiographer, describes polo as a perilous game loved by emperors and the sons of emperors.[106] Andronikos II was lauded for the skill at polo he displayed during the period of his education. Nikephoros Choumnos noted that he himself had witnessed the agility with which Andronikos played the game. The adolescent prince masterfully hit the ball in midair or on the ground, and was not afraid of the swiftness of his horse; nor was he impaired by other players riding around him.[107] Polo did not, however, meet with universal approval. In his *Imperial Statue,* Blemmydes disapproved of polo because it did not develop practical military skills. Instead he recommended exercises that simulated real battlefield experience.[108] Yet this piece of educational advice seems not to have been entirely heeded, as in the later thirteenth century Andronikos II was lauded for his skill at polo.

The incorporation of physical and military skills into the ideals of princely education after the eleventh century does not necessarily reflect a change in educational practices at the court. Hunting, for example, was a traditional pastime

103 Treu, *Manuelis Holoboli orationes* (above, n. 67), 93.35–94.2: "[The prince] gives orders to the hunting dogs and makes sounds in answer to them, and intercepts running hares and deftly stretches the bow tipped with horns and releases successfully arrows drawn by the string, and pulls down from the sky birds who dance but to the sound of death, bringing them to earth." On the date of this panegyric and the age of Andronikos, see nn. 59, 68 above.

104 For Andronikos II, see Gregory of Cyprus, PG 142:400A (on horsemanship and hunting). For Michael IX, see Westerink, "Le basilikos de Maxime Planude," *BSl* 28 (1967): 54.139–44 (on horsemanship and military arts).

105 Boissonade, *Anecdota graeca* (above, n. 65), 2:17.

106 A. Meineke, ed., *Epitome rerum ab Ioanne et Alexio Comnenis gestarum*, CSHB (Bonn, 1836), 264–65.

107 Nikephoros Choumnos, in Boissonade, *Anecdota graeca*, 2:17. This work seems to date to about 1284–85. See J. Verpeaux, *Nicéphore Choumnos, homme d'état et humaniste byzantin, ca. 1250/1255–1327* (Paris, 1959), 35, no. 4. The description of the racket which was used to hit the ball in the Byzantine polo game (the equivalent of the mallet in modern polo) is fully identical in Kinnamos's account and Choumnos's panegyric. A versified imperial panegyric, most probably addressed to Andronikos II or his son or grandson, composed by the court poet Manuel Philes in the early fourteenth century, also associates polo with the youth of an emperor. See E. Miller, ed., *Manuelis Philae carmina*, vol. 1 (Paris, 1855; repr. Amsterdam, 1967), 272–73.

108 Hunger and Ševčenko, *Des Nikephoros Blemmydes Βασιλικὸς Ἀνδριάς* (above, n. 98), 84–87 (chs. 127–31).

of the Byzantine social elite.[109] Polo, too, had been known in Byzantium since the fifth century.[110] The reasons for the changed representation of princely education should, in my view, be sought in the new cultural trends and literary fashions that emerged in Byzantium during the eleventh and twelfth centuries. As Alexander Kazhdan has demonstrated, this period saw the opening up of Byzantine high culture to aristocratic and chivalric values associated with military valor. This cultural tendency manifested itself in the increased militarization of the imperial portrait.[111] The evidence on imperial childhood is consistent with Kazhdan's thesis about the development of a chivalric imperial ideal after the eleventh century. We can expand his conclusions by noting that this chivalric ideal was not simply projected onto the image of adult emperors but also incorporated into the upbringing and education of princes.

A Background of Childhood Mischief and Playfulness

The subjects of princely education are not the sole signs of the Byzantine appreciation of unique childhood and adolescent experiences. Just as mischief and playfulness are characteristics commonly associated nowadays with childhood, they were occasionally attributed in Byzantium to future emperors in a neutral and descriptive fashion. The three earliest Vitae of Constantine that describe his childhood relate that Constantine grew up with his mother without ever knowing his father, and they all present in a similar way the recognition episode that reveals Constantine as Emperor Constantius's son. According to the vivid description in the Patmos Vita, one day Constantius's envoys, who were seeking a son for adoption by the emperor, called at the inn in Bithynia where Constantine was conceived and raised. While the envoys rested, Constantine, who was about ten years old, played with the horses tethered outside, "enjoying himself like a child" (τερπόμενος οἷα παῖς). One of the envoys noticed him and struck Constantine, saying: "Do not misbehave! You have not been enlisted in the army." Then, rushing to protect her son, Helena revealed his identity by

---

109   The ninth-century Vita of Constantine the Philosopher (Saint Cyril, the apostle to the Slavs) mentions as an aside that "it was customary among the sons of the wealthy to take sport in the hunt." See *Medieval Slavic Lives of Saints and Princes*, comp. and trans. M. Kantor (Ann Arbor, 1983), 29.

110   Cf. A. Karpozilos and A. Cutler, "Sports," *ODB* 3:1939.

111   A. Kazhdan, "The Aristocracy and the Imperial Ideal," in *The Byzantine Aristocracy, IX to XIII Centuries*, ed. M. Angold (Oxford, 1984), 43–57; A. Kazhdan and A. W. Epstein, *Change in Byzantine Culture in the Eleventh and Twelfth Centuries* (Berkeley, 1985), 110–16.

bringing forward as evidence a purple garment given to her by Constantius.[112] According to the ninth-century Guidi Vita, when Constantius's envoys witnessed a guest staying at the inn angrily beating the adolescent (μειράκιον), Helena revealed the child's identity in the same manner.[113] The fourteenth-century *Ecclesiastical History* of Nikephoros Kallistos Xanthopoulos borrows the episodes of Constantine's conception and recognition in the inn from the Guidi Vita, although again with a modification: one of Constantius's envoys hazed the playing child (παίζων δ᾽ ὁ παῖς). When Constantine began to cry and rushed back to seek solace with his mother, she revealed his true identity.[114] Noticeable in all these versions is the realistic representation of childhood playfulness and of the attachment between mother and child. If the post-Iconoclastic Vitae of Constantine rested on orally transmitted stories recorded around the year 800, as Alexander Kazhdan has argued, then the images of childhood are remarkable not only for their realism but also for their reflection of popular cultural sensibilities.[115]

The stories of the childhood of the emperor Basil I also refer to his playfulness, although here it is the setting for divine omens. The *Vita Basilii* relates how the child Basil and his family fell captive to the pagan Bulgars. As they were being released, the khan of the Bulgars, Omurtag (814/815–ca. 831), spotted the handsome child Basil, who was said to be smiling and playfully "skipping about" [περισκαίροντα]. The Bulgar ruler drew the child toward himself and in

112 Halkin, "Une nouvelle vie de Constantin," 74–75. On its likely time of composition, see Kazhdan, "Constantin Imaginaire," 202 (both above, n. 20). According to the Vita of Eusignios (which reports the same version of Constantine's origins as the Patmos Vita), Constantine was twelve years old at the time. See P. Devos, "Une recension nouvelle de la Passion grecque *BHG* 639 de S. Eusignios," *AB* 100 (1982): 220.

113 Guidi, "Un Βίος di Costantino" (above, n. 20), 308–10. The Opitz Vita, of whose opening only a fragment survives, seems to present the episode identically, with the difference that Constantine is said to be an infant (βρέφος) at the time when his identity was made known. See F. Halkin, "L'empereur Constantin converti par Euphratas," *AB* 78 (1960): 11–12 (additions to the fragmentary Vita published earlier by H. G. Opitz, *Byzantion* 9 [1934]: 535–93). The Vita itself has been dated to between the late ninth and the eleventh centuries. See Kazhdan, "Constantin Imaginaire," 201–2, with further bibliography.

114 Nikephoros Kallistos Xanthopoulos, *Ecclesiastical History*, PG 146:13A–B.

115 The question of the existence of a pre-Iconoclastic *Vorvita*, against which Kazhdan has argued, remains open. See Kazhdan, "Constantin Imaginaire," 247–48; F. Winkelmann, "Die älteste erhaltene griechische hagiographische *Vita* Konstantins und Helenas (*BHG* Br. 365z, 366, 366a)," in *Texte und Textkritik*, ed. J. Dummer (Berlin, 1987), 623–38; R. Scott, "The Image of Constantine in Malalas and Theophanes," in *New Constantines: The Rhythm of Imperial Renewal in Byzantium, 4th–13th Centuries*, ed. P. Magdalino (Aldershot, 1994), 57–71, esp. 69–70; C. Mango, "Empress Helena, Helenopolis, Pylae," *TM* 12 (1994): 147–48 and n. 26.

a portentous act handed to him an apple of enormous size, a symbol of the orb of universal rule.[116] The child Basil is said to have leaned "guilelessly [ἀκακῶς] and boldly [θαρραλέως] onto his knees," thus revealing his noble disposition.[117] Noteworthy here is the attribution of childlike playfulness and innocence to the future emperor. Basil I appears as a playful child also in the *History* of Genesios, where he is portrayed playing a game with other children near a lake when an eagle, a symbol of his future royalty, appears and hovers with outstretched wings above him.[118]

Not only could childhood characteristics serve as backdrops to traditionally conceived omens, they could also be superimposed on literary clichés of premature adulthood. The topos of the *puer senex* and a realistically portrayed child coexist in an imperial oration in which the panegyrist Manuel Holobolos engages in a physical description of the emperor Michael VIII's son Constantine the Porphyrogennetos, a child between the age of six and eleven.[119] Indeed, the praise of the external appearance of emperors is common to twelfth- and thirteenth-century court oratory, usually introduced immediately prior to the praise of their education. The descriptions tend to be highly rhetorical and seem to refer to young adults rather than children or adolescents.[120] In this case, Holobolos rehearses a standard rhetorical topos about the imperial prince,

---

116   On the symbolism of the apple, see Moravcsik, "Sagen und Legenden" (above, n. 25), 78–81; P. E. Schramm, *Sphaira, Globus, Reichsapfel* (Stuttgart, 1958); A. R. Littlewood, "The Symbolism of the Apple in Byzantine Literature," *JÖB* 23 (1974): 33–59, esp. 55–57.

117   Bekker, *Theophanes Continuatus* (above, n. 50), 217. The episode is also reported by the chronicler Skylitzes in the eleventh century and is illustrated in the famous illuminated Skylitzes manuscript in Madrid. See V. Tsamakda, *The Illustrated Chronicle of Ioannes Skylitzes in Madrid* (Leiden, 2002), 125 and fig. 200. Noteworthy is the depiction of Basil's father with outstretched hands, most probably signifying that he was beseeching Omurtag to release his son; this detail is missing from the chronicle.

118   Lesmueller-Werner and Thurn, eds., *Iosephi Genesii Regum libri quattuor* (above, n. 55) 76.80–77.83.

119   On the date of this speech and the age of Constantine the Porphyrogennetos, see n. 68 above.

120   Thus, Michael Italikos (Gautier, *Michel Italikos* [above, n. 49], 281.21–282.7) praised Manuel I for, among other things, his large stature, which suggests that he was not describing someone in the early years of his childhood. The descriptions, unfortunately, are mostly not age-specific: they emphasize the harmony of the limbs or the color of the skin and the eyes. Gregory of Cyprus mentioned that the harmony and bodily beauty of Andronikos II (a young adult in his early twenties at the time of delivery of his speech) were characteristic of him from "the very outset." See PG 142:395C–D. On Michael VIII, see again Gregory of Cyprus in PG 142:356C–D. Planoudes, curiously, thought that such descriptions of the physical appearance were not appropriate for men (*andrasin*) and remarked that he would cover this element of the encomium succinctly and only in order to avoid reproach. See Westerink, "Le basilikos de Maxime Planude," *BSl* 27 (1966): 102.113–103.120.

marveling how the child possesses "an adult mind" (πρεσβευτικὸν φρόνημα) at a "puerile age" (ἡλικία παιδική). In the passage that immediately follows, however, Holobolos describes lovingly, and remarkably realistically, the external appearance of the child. His face is sunny, and his brows arch like bows above his eyes. His eyes are said to emit joy and to glitter with the color of the sea. The orator marvels at the healthy complexion of his cheeks and likens the smile of his perfectly shaped lips to a rose blossoming in the sun.[121] The playfulness of the smile is suggestive of a child, yet it is a child already possessing an adult mind.

These realistic depictions of childhood characteristics are hardly autonomous or self-contained; they do not stand in the texts on their own terms and for their own sakes. Even so, they demonstrate that authors who often wrote with propagandist and legitimizing agendas were willing to incorporate realistic childhood traits into the imperial portrait, whether as simple passing images or as rhetorical digressions.

The Childhood of the Patriarchs of Constantinople

The idealized representation of the childhood of future patriarchs features themes similar to those in imperial biographies and betrays the familiar dichotomy. On the one hand, literary clichés (which, in this case, are very often hagiographic) describe the childhood of patriarchs as a period of precocious manifestation of adult characteristics. On the other hand, childhood education is again an important part of the idealized portrait. The biographies and autobiographies of patriarchs make explicit references to the affectionate bond between children and parents, even though often the authors set a higher value on childhood experiences mandating separation from the family, such as entry into ascetic life or education.

Divine Omens and Precocious Adulthood

The omens described in patriarchal biographies differ from those found in imperial Vitae in the absence of symbols of royalty, even though the general structure

---

121 Treu, *Manuelis Holoboli orationes* (above, n. 67), 91, especially 91.24–30: ὀφρὺς τοῦ μετώπου προβεβλημένη τόξου δίκην ὑπερτεινομένη τοὺς ὀφθαλμούς· τῶν ὀφθαλμῶν ἡ χάρις ὁποία κἂν ἀποστίλβῃ ἄν τις εἴποι θαλάττης χροιάν· ἡ ῥὶς ἀμφοτέροις ὁμολογεῖ μεσιτεύουσα γεωμετρικῶς ἀπεξεσμένη πρὸς τὴν ἰσότητα· τὸ τῆς παρειᾶς ἄνθος ἐξαίσιον· τὸ στόμα σύμμετρον πρὸς τῆς φύσεως ἐκτετόρνευται· τὰ χείλη ῥόδον ἄρτι τοῦ φυτικοῦ κελύφους ἐξανασχὸν καὶ τῷ ἡλίῳ προσμειδιάσαν βραχύ.

of the omens is similar. Thus, supernatural signs begin at the time the future patriarch is conceived[122] and appear in dream visions during his childhood.[123] As in imperial biographies, down-to-earth events could serve as omens. For example, the birth of a twin brother was the sole omen reported dramatically in the panegyric of Patriarch Basil II Kamateros (1183–1186). In addition to being a rare and noteworthy event in itself, the birth of twins enabled the orator to compare the patriarch to famous Old Testament examples, such as Rebecca's and Tamar's twins.[124] The saint's Life of Patriarch Eutychios (552–565, 577–582) recounts an ominous occurrence during an ordinary children's game (just as in the stories of the childhood of Emperor Basil I). When playing games with other children in which they mimicked adult professions, such as officials and priests, Eutychios chose for himself the role of patriarch.[125] This positive representation of the episode is exceptional for hagiography, for this genre tended to look down on childhood games as worthless pursuits.

Future patriarchs acquired early on the characteristics and virtues expected from the holders of the highest office in the Byzantine church. In this respect the patriarchal biographies parallel again the imperial ones, even though some of the virtues displayed differed from those manifested by future emperors. Naturally, piety and devotion to God are particularly important virtues. The first words of Patriarch Anthony II Kauleas (893–901) are said to have been in praise of the Lord.[126] Patriarch Isidore I (1347–1350), who was born into a family of priests, is said to have learned by heart the Psalms and liturgical chants during his early childhood. When he fell gravely ill at the age of three, he was miraculously cured after rushing to the church and singing a hymn.[127] Humility was another important Christian virtue that future patriarchs displayed precociously. Patriarch Tarasios (784–806) is said to have possessed "the humility and meekness

---

122   C. Laga, ed., *Eustratii presbyteri Vita Eutychii patriarchae Constantinopolitani* (Turnhout, 1992), 9.164–75. The pregnant mother of the sixth-century patriarch Eutychios was miraculously illuminated at night in her bed, just like Constantius and Helena in the Guidi Vita.

123   P. Nikolopoulos, "Ἀνέκδοτος λόγος εἰς Ἀρσένιον Αὐτωρειανὸν πατριάρχην Κωνσταντινουπόλεως," Ἐπετηρὶς Ἑταιρείας Βυζαντινῶν Σπουδῶν 45 (1981–1982): 452.69–72. The father of the infant patriarch Arsenios dreamed of Christ's predicting the great career of his son.

124   M. Loukaki, ed., *Grégoire Antiochos: Éloge du patriarche Basile Kamatèros* (Paris, 1996), 53. See Genesis 25:19–26, 38:27–30.

125   Laga, *Eustratii presbyteri Vita Eutychii*, 11.237–48.

126   P. Leone, "L' 'Encomium in patriarcham Antonium II Cauleam' del filosofo e retore Niceforo," *Orpheus*, n.s. 10, fascicle 2 (1989): 414.70–77 (ch. 3).

127   Φιλοθέου Κωνσταντινουπόλεως τοῦ Κοκκίνου ἁγιολογικὰ ἔργα, vol. 1, Θεσσαλονικεῖς ἅγιοι, ed. D. Tsames (Thessalonike, 1985), 334–35 (chs. 3–4).

of Christ" from the age of an infant (βρέφος) until his old age.[128] Patriarch John Chrysostom (398–404) is presented as a humble child born into a well-off family, who preferred not to ride on horseback to school and instead went on foot like most of his classmates.[129]

Hagiographic motifs enrich the image of the precocity of future patriarchs. One example is the avoidance of games and the company of other children, found already in the influential Life of Saint Anthony by Athanasios, which served as a model for Byzantine hagiography. The motif of the child as loner appears mostly in the Lives of patriarchs who were monks for significant portions of their lives, such as Gregory of Nazianzos (380–381), Anthony II Kauleas, Athanasios I (1289–1293, 1303–1309), and Isidore I (1347–1350).[130] The Vita of Isidore, for example, describes the future patriarch as an aloof child who shunned toys, games, foul language, and vulgar laughter; his only "game" was singing in the church and imagining that he was a priest.[131] The hagiographical topos of the self-taught (*autodidaktos*) saint, too, left a trace in patriarchal biographies. As gifted and wise children, some patriarchs acquired knowledge directly from God and outclassed their teachers.[132] Finally, and again in accordance with a hagiographical motif, some patriarchs who pursued monastic careers, such as Athanasios I and Matthew I (1397–1410), are said to have received God's call

---

128   *The Life of the Patriarch Tarasios by Ignatios the Deacon*, ed. S. Efthymiadis (Aldershot, 1998), 71.1–3.

129   See the episode in the lengthy Vita by George of Alexandria (seventh century), in F. Halkin, ed., *Douze récits byzantins sur Saint Jean Chrysostome* (Brussels, 1977), 73–76 (ch. 2) (*BHG Auct* 873b–d). Cf. ibid., 304–5 (*BHG* 874d), 386 (*BHG* 875d), and Symeon Metaphrastes, in PG 114:229A–232A (*BHG* 875).

130   See the Vitae of Gregory of Nazianzos by Gregory the Priest (late sixth or early seventh century) in *Gregorii Presbyteri Vita Sancti Gregorii Theologi*, ed. X. Lequeux (Turnhout, 2001), 124 (ch. 2), and by Thomas Magistros (early fourteenth century), in PG 145:229D–232B. On Anthony II, see Leone, "L' 'Encomium'," 414.76–77 (ch. 3). On Patriarch Athanasios I, see A. Papadopoulos-Kerameus, "Zhitiia dvukh Vselenskikh patriarkhov XIV v., svv. Afanasiia I i Isidora I," *Zapiski istoriko-filol. fakul'teta Imperatorskago S.-Peterburgskago Universiteta* 76 (1905): 3 (ch. 2); Tsames, Ἰωσὴφ Καλοθέτου συγγράμματα, 457 (ch. 4). On Isidore I, see the following note. For other examples of this motif in hagiography see Pratsch, *Der hagiographische Topos* (above, n. 8), 89–90.

131   Φιλοθέου Κωνσταντινουπόλεως τοῦ Κοκκίνου ἁγιολογικὰ ἔργα, vol. 1, ed. Tsames, 334.22–34 (ch. 3).

132   On this motif, see Pratsch, *Der hagiographische Topos*, 103–5. Patriarch Anthony II Kauleas is said to have learned his letters at the age of five directly from the Holy Spirit, not from teachers. Patriarch Michael III of Anchialos (1170–1178) is reported to have put his teachers to shame with his outstanding intellectual abilities. See Leone, "L' 'Encomium'," ch. 3, 414.70–71; Wirth, *Eustathii Thessalonicensis opera minora*, 81.

during childhood and to have left their families in order to enter a monastery (see below).

Childhood Education of Patriarchs: Secular Rather than Religious

As with emperors, the ideal of the well-educated patriarch runs throughout Byzantine history. With the patriarchs, however, the emphasis is entirely on the intellectual formation and not the physical training of the future leaders of the church. References to the beginning and duration of the education of future patriarchs convey beyond any doubt the idea of childhood preparation for their future roles. John Chrysostom and Patriarch Methodios I (843–847), for example, are said to have been children (παῖδες) when they went to school. Eutychios (552–565, 577–582) studied in his native Phrygia until the age of twelve, under the guidance of his grandfather, a priest, and was then sent to Constantinople to acquire the full gamut of education.[133] Anthony II Kauleas was twelve when he is reported to have entered a monastery and begun his religious studies. In his autobiography Gregory of Cyprus, the future Patriarch Gregory II (1283–89), mentions that before the age of fifteen he attended classes in grammar and Aristotelian logic, both taught in Latin.[134] These classes were not to his taste, however, and eventually he left his native Cyprus to further his education in the empire of Nicaea.

These accounts of the education of the patriarchs vary in length, content, and level of detail, doubtless partly because of the diverse social and educational profiles of the individuals who led the Byzantine church. Some interesting patterns are distinguishable, however. Among the patriarchs whose education is described in hagiography, the great majority studied the usual secular subjects of Byzantine school curricula. The Vitae of only three patriarchs—Ignatios (847–858, 867–877), Anthony II Kauleas, and Athanasios I—portray clerics steeped in religious knowledge without referring to any formal schooling. Even so, one can assume that the three patriarchs went through elementary education, for they are reported to have been capable of reading during their early youth the holy scriptures, the works of the church fathers, and saints' Lives.[135] Most patriarchs

133   Laga, *Eustratii presbyteri Vita Eutychii*, 12.286–13.297.
134   *La tradition manuscrite de la correspondance de Grégoire de Chypre Patriarche de Constantinople (1283–1289)*, ed. W. Lameere (Brussels, 1937), 177–79.
135   When he entered the monastery under compulsion at the age of fourteen, the future patriarch Ignatios was able to read the Bible and the works of the holy fathers. See PG 105:496A–C.

acquired secular learning at least to the level of secondary education. They studied some or all the subjects sometimes grouped under the rubric *enkyklios paideia*—grammar, rhetoric, philosophy (or at least dialectic), and the quadrivium (arithmetic, geometry, music, and astronomy). As scholars have shown, the usual age for the study of *enkyklios paideia* was the early and middle teenage years.[136]

Examples from specific Vitae are illustrative of the trend noted above. Gregory of Nazianzos was said to have been educated until an adolescent (*ephebos*) in his native city, which he left to further his education in Cappadocian Caesarea, Palestine, Alexandria, and eventually at the highest level in Athens.[137] George of Alexandria's lengthy Vita of John Chrysostom, composed in the seventh century, mentions that the saint pursued his initial and some of his higher studies in his native Antioch and asserts fictitiously that he studied in the Athenian Academy (just like his earlier contemporary, Gregory of Nazianzos).[138] Notably, later versions of the Vitae of Gregory of Nazianzos and John Chrysostom refer to their secondary education in greater detail, using the term *enkyklios paideia* and referring to specific subjects.[139] The education of Patriarch Nikephoros I (806–815) is described in different portions of his Vita generally as *enkyklios paideia* and specifically as grammar, rhetoric, philosophy, and the quadrivium.[140]

Patriarch Anthony II is said to have intentionally avoided school, as he was afraid of encountering bad children there. When he entered a monastery at the age of twelve, his superior taught him *enkyklios paideia,* consisting solely of religious readings. See Leone, "L' 'Encomium'," 414.75–77 (ch. 3), 415.106–13 (ch. 5). As a child, Athanasios is said to have read only religious texts, including the holy scriptures and the Vita of the stylite saint Alypios, which inspired him to leave his family and enter a monastery at an early age. No formal schooling is reported. See Papadopoulos-Kerameus, "Zhitiia dvukh Vselenskikh patriarkhov" (above, n. 130), 3.25–4.10.

136   Lemerle, *Le premier humanisme* (above, n. 86), 101–2, refers to examples within the age group ten to eighteen.

137   Lequeux, *Gregorii Presbyteri vita Sancti Gregorii Theologi* (above, n. 130), 126–38 (chs. 3–5). Gregory of Nazianzos is even said to have declined a proposal to remain at the Athenian Academy as a professor on completing his higher education at the age of thirty.

138   Halkin, *Douze récits byzantins* (above, n. 129), 73–77. On the fiction of John Chrysostom's studies in Athens, see C. Baur, *John Chrysostom and His Time*, vol. 1, trans. M. Gonzaga (London, 1959), 25–26.

139   Thus, the Metaphrastic Vita of John Chrysostom specifies his secondary education as grammar, *enkyklios paideia*, rhetoric, and philosophy. See PG 114:1049C–D. Cf. Halkin, *Douze récits byzantins,* 387. In the fourteenth century, Thomas Magistros refers to the education Gregory of Nazianzos received in his native city as *enkyklios paideia,* a term not used in the lengthy Vita by Gregory the Priest composed in the sixth or the seventh century. See PG 145:233B ff. Pratsch, *Der hagiographische Topos* (above, n. 8), 92–93 and n. 50, observes that later redactions of hagiographical Vitae tend to provide more detail on education, in line with the usual school curricula at the time of composition of these later works.

140   C. de Boor, ed., *Nicephori archiepiscopi Constantinopolitani opuscula historica* (Leipzig,

The childhood education of Methodios I (843–847) in his native Sicily is said to have consisted of grammar, history, orthography, and tachygraphy.[141] Arsenios (1254–1260, 1261–1264) attended classes described as *enkyklios paideia* and outshone his fellow students, although he disliked reading ancient pagan literature and eventually abandoned school for the monastery.[142] Isidore I had the opportunity, as the child of a priest, to study the holy scriptures and church music at a young age, but he was able to attend classes in grammar and rhetoric only after the age of sixteen. This is said to have been a late age for beginning these subjects and a cause of anxiety for Isidore. Nonetheless, he managed to excel during his formal education, which lasted for three years.[143]

The importance accorded to education in the idealized portrait of patriarchs is seen also outside hagiography. The numerous twelfth-century encomia on patriarchs of Constantinople portray the leaders of the Byzantine church as highly learned men. The encomia tend to praise patriarchs for their excellence in studying grammar, rhetoric, and philosophy as well as for their inner learning in matters of religion.[144] Indeed, in the texts we have examined, the number of highly learned patriarchs (some of them important church fathers) praised for continuing their studies beyond their adolescent years, at the level of higher or specialized education, exceeds the number of high churchmen steeped solely in religious learning.[145]

The predominantly secular education of the leaders of the Byzantine church

---

1880), 144, 149–52. P. Alexander, *The Patriarch Nicephorus of Constantinople* (Oxford, 1958), 57–58, considers the description a topos that does not take into account Nikephoros's personal experience. Cf. Elizabeth Fisher's remarks in *Byzantine Defenders of Images*, ed. A.-M. Talbot (Washington, D.C., 1998), 53 n. 105, 54 n. 109.

141   Vita of Patriarch Methodios I, in PG 100:1245B.

142   The Nicaean patriarch Germanos II (1223–1240) is reported to have assigned a teacher to Arsenios. See Nikolopoulos, "Ἀνέκδοτος λόγος εἰς Ἀρσένιον Αὐτωρειανόν," 452–53.

143   Tsames, Φιλοθέου Κωνσταντινουπόλεως τοῦ Κοκκίνου ἁγιολογικὰ ἔργα, 1:335–37 (chs. 5–6).

144   See the discussion and examples given by M. Loukaki, "Ο ιδανικός πατριάρχης" (above, n. 15), 305–6 n. 15.

145   On John Chrysostom and Gregory of Nazianzos, see nn. 137, 138 above. George II Xiphilinos (1191–1198) is said to have learned law as well as grammar and rhetoric. See Loukaki, *Discours annuels* (above, n. 16) 141, cf. 28. Patriarch John X Kamateros (1198–1206) is said to have familiarized himself thoroughly during his education with the doctrines of Plato, Aristotle, and the Stoics, which may suggest higher education. See R. Browning, "An Unpublished Address of Nicephorus Chrysoberges to Patriarch John X Kamateros of 1202," *Byzantine Studies/Études Byzantines* 5 (1978): 53. In his autobiography, Gregory of Cyprus devotes much attention to his higher education in Constantinople under the mentorship of George Akropolites, which lasted from the age of twenty-six to thirty-three. See Lameere, *La tradition manuscrite* (above, n. 134), 185–87.

presents a curious pattern. The fact that some of the future patriarchs of Constantinople were originally destined for secular careers is not sufficient to explain the phenomenon.[146] It is true that the patriarchal biographies register the traditional division of learning in Byzantium into "inner" and "outer" and note the superiority of religious, "inner" learning. For example, according to the fictitious story in the Vita composed by George of Alexandria, during his studies in Athens John Chrysostom ridiculed the myths of the Hellenes, culled only the useful learning, and worked a miracle by converting a pagan scholar.[147] In addition, it is sometimes observed that the study of secular subjects improved the patriarch's pastoral and polemical abilities. Living in two different eras, patriarchs Nikephoros I (806–815) and Basil II Kamateros (1183–1186) are said to have used their rhetorical education for developing their skills as preachers or polemicists.[148] Yet it is interesting that the secular education of patriarchs could be praised in our texts without any references to its role and utility in an ecclesiastical career, and indeed without any mention of accompanying religious studies or learning.[149]

Some conclusions on the ideal of the education of patriarchs may be drawn at this point. Throughout Byzantine history, it was presumed that the future leaders of the church would attend school during their childhood and adolescence, in most cases through the secondary level. Secular education was more common than religious learning and could be extended well beyond the years of adolescence. The emphasis on secular learning could be explained to a large degree by the perceived duties of the patriarchal office. The ideal patriarch, at least as described in twelfth-century encomia, was a teacher of his flock and a defender

146   For the social profile of the individuals who served as patriarchs of Constantinople, see L. Bréhier, *Les institutions de l'empire byzantin* (Paris, 1949, repr. Paris, 1970), 384–88.

147   Halkin, *Douze récits byzantins* (above, n. 129), 78–88. Theology, of course, was considered by some to be the highest form of philosophy. For this notion, see the encomium on Patriarch John X Kamateros in Browning, "Unpublished Address," 53. Cf. J. Duffy, "Hellenic Philosophy in Byzantium and the Lonely Mission of Michael Psellos," in *Byzantine Philosophy and Its Ancient Sources*, ed. K. Ierodiakonou (Oxford, 2002), 139–56.

148   Patriarch Nikephoros's zeal as a teacher and polemicist is said to have moved him to acquire secular learning. See de Boor, *Nicephori archiepiscopi Constantinopolitani opuscula historica* (above, n. 140), 149. The example given of the superb rhetorical education of Patriarch Basil II Kamateros is a sermon witnessed by the encomiast. See Loukaki, *Grégoire Antiochos* (above, n. 124), 53.126–54.150.

149   This was the case with Patriarch Methodios I in the ninth century and Gregory of Cyprus during the thirteenth. Interestingly, Michael Psellos's epitaphs on three eleventh-century patriarchs—Michael I Keroularios (1043–1058), Constantine III Leichoudes (1059–1063), and John VIII Xiphilinos (1064–1075)—report solely their classical learning, sometimes at great length. See Μεσαιωνικὴ βιβλιοθήκη, vol. 4, ed. K. Sathas (Venice, 1874), 310–12, 391–96, 426–27.

of church doctrine.[150] Therefore, the knowledge of subjects such as rhetoric and logic was seen as enabling the leaders of the Byzantine church to fulfill their responsibilities.

It may be illuminating to compare the educational background of patriarchs with that of the Byzantine saints in general. Scholars have observed that in Byzantine hagiography, just as in our patriarchal biographies, the reported formal education of saints is mainly secular, and experiences of religious instruction are exceptional.[151] One important difference, however, distinguishes the patriarchs from the larger and more diverse body of the saints. Although there is a subset of uncultivated and unlettered saints, education (even in a relatively minimal form) was an integral part of the ideal of the childhood of patriarchs.[152]

Parental Affection and Separation from the Family

The body of literature on imperial princes has already shown us cases of mothers and fathers guarding their children and attending to their education. The evidence from patriarchal biographies in no way differs.[153] What distinguishes patriarchal biographies and autobiographies from the imperial ones are the frequent episodes of separation of children from their families, episodes that tend to feature explicit and powerful descriptions of parental affection. One reason for the child to leave the family was his desire to enter a monastery as a novice. The early spiritual call of the saint and the resistance he faced from his family are common topoi of hagiography.[154] Yet it is interesting that the loving bond between parents and children is often highlighted as a reason for the child to remain in the family. Thus, the mother of Athanasios I appealed to his "filial

150 See Loukaki, "Ο ιδανικός πατριάρχης" (above, n. 15), 308–10.

151 See the observation of Pratsch, *Der hagiographische Topos* (above, n. 8), 93.

152 See the discussion and examples given by E. Malamut, *Sur la route des saints byzantins* (Paris, 1993), 75–76.

153 Thus the widowed mother of John Chrysostom wished that no child in her native Antioch should surpass her son in "wisdom, intelligence and demeanor" (μὴ εἶναί τινα ἐν τῇ πόλει ἐκείνῃ ὑπερβάλλοντα αὐτὸν ἐν τε συνέσει καὶ σοφίᾳ καὶ διαγωγῇ) and succeeded in postponing his adoption of the monastic habit by pleading with him to remain living with her. See Halkin, *Douze récits byzantins,* 77, 88–91. The mother of Patriarch Tarasios (784–806) is described as being closely involved in her son's upbringing, ensuring that he kept away from the harmful company of knavish children and befriended only virtuous ones. See Efthymiadis, *Life of the Patriarch Tarasios*, 74–75, ch. 6.1–7.

154 On early spiritual calls, see Pratsch, *Der hagiographische Topos*, 109–16. On the resistance of parents to their child's becoming a novice, see A. Kiousopoulou, *Χρόνος καὶ ἡλικίες στὴ βυζαντινὴ κοινωνία* (Athens, 1997), 101–4.

affection" when he announced his decision to leave his family and enter the novitiate, just like his model Saint Alypios.[155] In his autobiography, Patriarch Matthew I (1397–1410) describes his decision to enter a monastery when he was not yet twelve years old. "Overcome by their natural affection," his parents prevented him from doing so, although two years later they consented.[156]

Education could also be a reason for the separation of the child from his family and thus a context for expression of parental affection. When the parents of Gregory of Nazianzos saw in a dream vision their son being endangered during his sea voyage to from Alexandria to Athens, they beseeched God with prayers and tears, just "as parents do—what should one say further?"[157] When, sometime after the age of fifteen, Gregory of Cyprus told his parents of his desire to go to the empire of Nicaea to further his education, they are said to have resisted, "being attached to the child by nature and on account of strong need."[158] They were more ready to give their own lives than to agree that he be sent abroad at such a young age. The dispute is said to have dragged on for two years until the young Gregory realized that the only way to leave Cyprus was without the knowledge of his parents.

The attachment between children and parents performed a literary function in our texts, highlighting the resolve and religious dedication of the young individual, which sufficed to overcome his strong bond with his parents. What was idealized here was not the affectionate relationship between parents and children but rather the strength of character of the child. Yet there can be no doubt

155   Joseph Kalothetos, in Tsames, Ἰωσὴφ Καλοθέτου συγγράμματα, 458.152 (ch. 5): τὸ υἱικὸν ἐκκαλεῖται φίλτρον. Cf. Papadopoulos-Kerameus, "Zhitiia dvukh Vselenskikh patriarkhov," 4.12–13. The affection of children for their parents is called "natural" in the eleventh-century Life of Symeon the New Theologian, who managed to overcome it through his love of God. See I. Hausherr, Un grand mystique byzantin: Vie de Syméon le Nouveau Théologien par Nicétas Stéthatos (Rome, 1928), 16, ch. 9.7–9: οὕτω δριμύτερός ἐστι παντὸς ἄλλου πράγματος καὶ αὐτῆς τῆς φυσικῆς στοργῆς πρὸς τοὺς τεκόντας ὁ διακαὴς ἔρως τοῦ οὐρανίου πατρός.

156   M. Konidares and K. A. Manaphes, "Ἐπιτελεύτιος βούλησις καὶ διδασκαλία τοῦ οἰκουμενικοῦ πατριάρχου Ματθαίου Αʹ (1397–1410)," Ἐπετηρὶς Ἑταιρείας Βυζαντινῶν Σπουδῶν 45 (1981–82): 473.55–56: ἥκιστα τοὺς ἐμοὺς παρεδέχοντο λόγους ὑπὸ τοῦ τῆς φύσεως ἡττώμενοι φίλτρου. See also the English translation by A.-M. Talbot in Thomas and Hero, Byzantine Monastic Foundation Documents (above, n. 80), 4:1634. Cf. Hinterberger, Autobiographische Traditionen (above, n. 33), 213–17.

157   Lequeux, Gregorii Presbyteri Vita Sancti Gregorii Theologi (above, n. 130), 128.35–40 (ch. 3), esp. 128.36–37: καὶ οἷα πατέρες—τί γὰρ δεῖ πλέον εἰπεῖν;—εὐχαῖς τε καὶ δάκρυσι τὸν Θεὸν ἐλιπάρουν βοηθῆσαι.

158   Lameere, La tradition manuscrite (above, n. 134), 179, esp. 179.28–29: οἱ δὲ φύσεώς τε καὶ ἰσχυροτέρας ἀνάγκης δεσμοῖς ἐχόμενοι τοῦ παιδός. The strong need seems to have been economic, for Gregory was not born into a wealthy family.

that the affectionate and caring nature of parents reported in patriarchal biographies and autobiographies was a common social ideal. It could be reported in a matter-of-fact manner, but it could also be suppressed or pushed to the background when it conflicted with ideals perceived to be of greater value, such as the desire to devote oneself to God and education.

Conclusion

As a means of addressing the Ariès thesis on medieval childhood, the evidence about ideal children that we have traced in the imperial and the patriarchal biographies points in different and contradictory directions. The dominant impression is clearly of a childhood reduced to a canvas on which adult characteristics and values are painted. The childhood of emperors and patriarchs was a time for precocious display of their virtues and for demonstration of a divine charisma that qualified the child to attain later the supreme post in the empire or the church. The authors of the biographical texts were highly selective in the images of childhood included in their accounts. The infancy of future great men tended to be omitted unless omens or signs occurred. The focus of the biographers moves from a portentous birth directly to episodes of education and passage into adulthood.

This reductionist representation of childhood arose from a combination of factors, among which literary conventions and legitimizing and practical concerns were the most important. Literary conventions played a pivotal role by providing both a rigid narrative scheme and a series of childhood-related topoi. Propagandist goals of legitimating power are inherent in most imperial biographies; hence the emphasis on divine signs symbolizing royalty and on the precocious maturity of the future emperor. Interestingly, the late Byzantine period saw a soberer attitude toward signs and omens in the imperial biographies. The fantastic stories of the childhood of earlier emperors, such as Basil I and Manuel I, gave way to historical episodes serving as divine omens in Palaiologan court oratory. Finally, practical concerns about effective leadership also mandated a shortening of the childhood of future great men. In Byzantium, just as nowadays, common sense dictated that the best leaders were the ones who grew up fast.

Adult characteristics and preoccupations are not the only themes and motifs in the representation of childhood of emperors and patriarchs. The authors of idealized biographies of great men sometimes looked with remarkably positive eyes at distinctive characteristics of children and childhood, such as playfulness (predominantly of emperors) and educational experience and schooling (of both emperors and patriarchs). Parental care and affection were universally recognized as cultural values, even if some ideal children were praised for overcoming the strong bond with their parents in the name of future greatness. To what extent do the genuine images of childhood presuppose the existence of the "idea of childhood" or at least suggest a fascination with childhood as a separate stage of life? Clearly, many of the realistic representations—images of childhood games, of playfulness and innocence, of crying and smiling—do not appear in the texts on their own terms or for their own sakes, but are only passing images in traditionally conceived biographical episodes and themes. Nonetheless, it is still instructive that authors found it acceptable to portray great men behaving as children in some ways and adults in others, just like Christ in the apocryphal Gospel of Thomas.

An appreciation of childhood on its own terms is evident, in my opinion, in the representation of schooling and education. Education is a self-contained component in the biographical texts explicitly set in the years of childhood and adolescence. Illuminating differences distinguish the description of education of emperors from that of patriarchs. Imperial princes are said to have studied subjects geared to the practicalities of government, such as history and advisory literature, rather than the usual subjects of secondary education. The period from the twelfth to the fifteenth century saw a new and strong emphasis on the physical and military training of adolescent princes, which manifested itself in all biographical and courtly genres. Physical training prepared princes for military combat and included sports such as hunting and polo.

By contrast, patriarchal biographies tend to adopt the traditional hagiographical ideal eschewing physical training and games. Thus, it was possible for a late Byzantine Vita of an early Byzantine patriarch to include among the "likely joys of youth" shunned by the saint some of the elements of princely upbringing, such as hunting, gymnastic exercises, and ball games.[159] In contrast to emperors, patriarchs were normally represented as mastering the usual secular subjects of Byzantine secondary education and sometimes as continuing their studies after adolescence. Much rarer are cases of patriarchs who avoided formal schooling (again in accordance with a saintly ideal) and were versed solely in Christian

159   Thomas Magistros, *Life of Gregory of Nazianzos (Λόγος εἰς Γρηγόριον Θεολόγον)*, PG 145:229D–232A, refers to the saint's avoiding in his childhood the "likely joys of youth" (ποιεῖν οἷς εἰκὸς τοὺς ἐν νεότητι χαίρειν), such as strolls in gardens and groves, gymnastic training, bathing, attendance at horse races and theatrical shows, hunting, archery, and ball games.

learning. To a large extent, the differences in the represented educational experiences of emperors and patriarchs stem from the differences in their perceived responsibilities as adult leaders.

On the basis of the preceding observations, we can hardly accept the Ariès thesis that the "idea of childhood" is lacking in the examined body of literature. This would mean using as evidence only a one-sided group of images of childhood, largely belonging to literary tradition and pursuing propagandist goals, and ignoring representations embodying alternative values. These, to be sure, were rarer, although equally persistent over the centuries. As ideal children, emperors and patriarchs were as much reflections of adult values as they were real children who played games, learned from their tutors, and were loved by their parents. Alternative and even competing attitudes toward children existed in the texts and therefore, we may add, ought to have existed in real life in Byzantium.

University of Birmingham

CHILDHOOD IN BYZANTINE SAINTS' LIVES

Béatrice Chevallier Caseau

I N T H E *Life of Our Saintly Father and Hieromartyr Euthymios,* written by Methodius around 831, the author declines to write about the childhood of the iconodule saint on the grounds that he knows nothing about it and feels no need to describe it.[1] He adds that he did not make the effort to inquire about the period of Euthymios's life preceding adulthood because it would be useless for readers, who cannot imitate being the parents of a saint. He writes impatiently that the saint, like everyone else, "had parents, received nourishment as a little child, and moral upbringing." Methodius justifies his approach by arguing that he writes about a martyr, whose courage in dying for his faith is the main subject for praise. Still, even with this warning, Methodius starts his tale with some discourse on parents and childhood. He acknowledges that some children display qualities leading to holiness, such as purity of thought, a disposition for learning, a taste for devotions, demure deportment, and a placid character, all virtues indicating spiritual progress.

If we leave aside passion accounts, which focus on the final episodes of a saint's life, the narration of a life is normally organized chronologically, from birth to death, and usually includes some information on the geographic origin[2] and

---

I thank Alice-Mary Talbot for her comments on this paper, and Brigitte Pitarakis and Jean-Claude Cheynet for lively conversations on this topic.

1   *Life of Euthymios of Sardis* (*BHG* 2145), 2, ed. J. Gouillard, "La Vie d'Euthyme de Sardes (†831): Une oeuvre du patriarche Méthode," *TM* 10 (1987): 20–23.

2   B. Flusin calls this geographical indication, when it is the only detail provided, "le passé minimum"; see "Le serviteur caché ou le saint sans existence," in *Les Vies de saints à Byzance: Genre littéraire ou biographie historique? Actes du IIe colloque international philologique, Paris, 6–8 juin 2002,* ed. P. Odorico and P. A. Agapitos (Paris, 2004), 63.

social background of the parents and on the saint's childhood behavior and education. Not unlike the "death scene,"[3] this description of the saint's milieu and origin was important to writers and readers alike and constitutes a "narrative situation."[4] Childhood was perceived as a time for gathering and reading signs of the future saint's greatness.[5] The Byzantines believed that the future of their children was partly inscribed in their first few years. Childhood was a time of promise: thus, when death took a child away, the loss was expressed in terms of unfulfilled expectations.[6] Reading signs and finding holy men who could foretell the future was very common among the Byzantines. So, unsurprisingly, parents wished to know what would become of their children. Paying attention to signs in early childhood was tantamount to foretelling their future as adults.[7]

Medieval hagiographers, perfectly aware of this convention, adapted the narrative of saints' childhood to fit their subsequent careers and particular forms of holiness. As Lennart Rydén wrote, hagiographers rarely had the ambition to paint a complete and true portrait of the saint; rather, they wanted to show how a particular person conformed to the saintly ideal.[8] Naturally, Byzantine hagiographers followed their society's expectations concerning holiness.[9]

The depiction of holy childhood in saints' Lives of the medieval period is often extremely stereotyped.[10] Contemporary scholars often deplore the absence of reliable and original information, as hagiographers felt compelled to follow rhetori-

3   P. A. Agapitos, "Mortuary Typology in the Lives of Saints: Michael Synkellos and Stephen the Younger," in Odorico and Agapitos, *Les Vies de saints à Byzance,* 106.

4   G. Prince, *A Dictionary of Narratology* (London, 2003).

5   P. Cox, *Biography in Late Antiquity: A Quest for the Holy Man* (Berkeley, 1983); A.-J. Festugière, "Lieux communs littéraires et thèmes du folk-lore dans l'hagiographie primitive,"*Wiener Studien* 73 (1960): 123–52; T. Wiedemann, *Adults and Children in the Roman Empire* (London, 1989).

6   M. Alexiou, *The Ritual Lament in Greek Tradition* (Cambridge, 1974). Psellos mourns his very promising daughter: C. Jouanno, "Michel Psellos, *Epitaphios logos:* A sa fille Stylianè, morte avant l'heure du mariage," *Kentron* 10 (1994): 95–107; M. J. Kyriakis, "Medieval European Society as seen in Two Eleventh-Century Texts by Michael Psellos," part 1, *Byzantine Studies* 3 (1976): 77–100; part 2, *Byzantine Studies* 4 (1977): 67–80; A. Kaldellis, *Mothers and Sons, Fathers and Daughters: The Byzantine Family of Michael Psellus* (Notre Dame, Ind., 2006), 111–38.

7   See, for example, G. Dagron, *Décrire et peindre: Essai sur le portrait iconique* (Paris, 2007), 142.

8   L. Rydén, "Literariness in Byzantine Saints' Lives," in Odorico and Agapitos, *Les Vies de saints à Byzance,* 49–58.

9   S. Hackel, *The Byzantine Saint* (London, 1981); H. Maguire, *The Icons of their Bodies: Saints and their Images in Byzantium* (Princeton, 1996); S. Efthymiadis, "The Byzantine Hagiographer and His Audience in the Ninth and Tenth Centuries," in *Metaphrasis, Redaction and Audiences in Middle Byzantine Hagiography,* ed. C. Høgel (Oslo, 1996), 59–80.

10   T. Pratsch, *Der hagiographische Topos: Griechische Heiligenviten in mittelbyzantinischer Zeit* (Berlin, 2005).

cal guidelines.[11] Alice-Mary Talbot writes that in their descriptions of childhood, writers "often confine themselves to a single paragraph containing such commonplaces as the child's learning of his first letters and his refusal to join his playmates in games."[12] It is true that middle Byzantine writers or rewriters of saints' Lives had a tendency to stick to a standard account of wellborn parents piously raising a talented and ascetic child. Yet, rather than blame this stock description on lack of imagination, one should understand it as a conscious appeal to readers' expectations. An unwritten pact existed between writers and readers concerning what to expect in a saint. Readers of a saint's Life wanted to know the signs of holiness which, like signposts, marked the road to Heaven. It was in fact extremely reassuring that these signs were so stable from one Life to another.

This paper studies the narration of childhood in Byzantine hagiography as a literary phenomenon, starting with the late antique period and ending with the Palaiologan period.[13] It examines the difference between many ancient and medieval Lives of saints in the importance granted to childhood and offers hypotheses on the reasons for such a discrepancy. It then turns to the contrasts between a future saint and an ordinary child that are pointed out in accounts of a saint's early years, and asks whether writers and readers believed that parents could create a saint. It concludes with the difficult question of how to account for the differences in the amount of attention devoted to childhood in various saints' Lives.

The Narration of Childhood

In a study of 631 saints' Lives and martyr stories written before 600, Pascal Boulhol notes that more than one-third of them make no mention of the saint's family.[14] The main reason for this silence about familial origins is that many

11   A. Moffatt, "The Byzantine Child," *Social Research* 53 (1986): 705–23. Our wish for diversity, like our taste for an artist's expression of originality, goes against the culture studied here, although "considerable room for maneuver did exist within an outwardly conventional literary genre." M. B. Cunningham has applied this approach to sermons, but it is also true for saints' Lives; see M. B. Cunningham, "Innovation or Mimesis in Byzantine Sermons," in *Originality in Byzantine Literature, Art and Music: A Collection of Essays,* ed. A. R. Littlewood (Oxford, 1995), 71.

12   A.-M. Talbot, "Children, Healing Miracles, Holy Fools: Highlights from the Hagiographical Works of Philotheos Kokkinos (1300–ca. 1379)," *Bysantinska Sällskapet Bulletin* 24 (2006): 52. I thank Dr. Talbot for sending me this very interesting article.

13   It is based on the study of fifty-six Lives of saints, from the fourth until the fifteenth century.

14   P. Boulhol, "Le complexe de Melchisedech: Famille et sainteté dans l'hagiographie antique des origines au Ve siècle" (PhD diss., University of Paris IV–Sorbonne, 1990).

saints are known only because of their martyrdom. Martyr stories often start with the trial of the saint and have nothing to say about the individual's early life. These saints are celebrated because they were arrested, tortured, and led to their deaths while remaining faithful to Christ. In many saints' Lives written during the fourth and fifth centuries, however, little or nothing is said concerning the childhood of the saints or their social and geographic origin.

This silence is particularly notable in the *Historia monachorum in Aegypto*. The author's purpose is to comment on the lifestyle of holy monks and ascetic priests. He devotes twenty-five chapters to different holy men but mentions the social origin of only one: Amoun was born to a noble and rich family.[15] The author provides no information on the geographic origins of these saints. The childhood of only two monks is mentioned: Apollo and Helle, who practiced asceticism as children.[16] Family members appear only in two cases: the rich parents of Amoun insist on his marrying, and Apollo has a brother who is also a monk in the desert. Although children appear in the text, they are mentioned as the beneficiaries of miracles performed by the saints. Their spiritual progress is irrelevant and not mentioned. The author admires many of the saints for the length of time they have spent in a very ascetic lifestyle, living in harsh conditions in the desert, and his main fascination is with elderly men. Childhood is not valued as a step toward holiness. The author contrasts childhood with manhood and its virtues, writing: "We must not always remain children and infants."[17] His biographies of saints begin with adulthood.

This practice is far from uncommon in many early saints' Lives. The *Life of Abba Aaron* starts with Aaron's parents buying him a commission in the army and his refusal to eat all the bread the army gave him.[18] The *Life of Syncletica* jumps from her birth to the time of her arranged wedding.[19] The *Life of Melania the Younger* mentions her love for Christ since her youth, but her story starts with her marriage at the age of fourteen.[20] The *Life of Simeon the Fool* starts when

---

15   *Historia monachorum in Aegypto,* ed. A.-J. Festugière (Brussels, 1961), 128.

16   Ibid., 47 (Apollo), 92 (Helle).

17   Ibid., 101: οὐ γὰρ παῖδες, φησί, καὶ νήπιοι τὸν πάντα χρόνον ὀφείλομεν διαμένειν.

18   Life of Abba Aaron, in Paphnutius, *History of the Monks of the Egyptian Desert,* ed. E. A. Wallis Budge, *Miscellaneous Coptic Texts* (London, 1915): Coptic, 471; trans., 986 and also translated in T. Vivian, *Journeying into God: Seven Early Monastic Lives* (Minneapolis, 1996), 113.

19   *Life of Syncletica,* 5, ed. B. Flusin and P. Paramelle, "*De Syncletica in deserto Jordanis* (BHG 1318w)," *AB* 100 (1982): 309; trans. Vivian, *Journeying into God,* 48.

20   *Life of Melania the Younger,* 1, ed. D. Gorce, *Vie de sainte Mélanie* (Paris, 1962), 130.

he is a young adult.[21] Leontios of Neapolis has Menas tell the life of the deceased bishop of Alexandria, John the Almsgiver, from the time of his priestly ordination, although a flashback takes us back to the time when he was fifteen.[22]

These examples are deliberately taken from Lives of different types of saints—men and women, monks and bishops—written before the eighth century. Holiness is not seen as a feature of childhood unless the child is a future martyr and the Holy Ghost speaks through the child's mouth. Children can be God's messengers, but that role is not the same as being holy. In the *Life of Porphyry of Gaza,* a seven-year-old boy starts speaking in Syriac, a language totally unknown to him, and miraculously reveals the means to destroy the temple of Marnas.[23] But a veil is drawn over his later life: there is no indication that he becomes a saint. With the exception of the baby Jesus in the apocryphal literature,[24] children generally do not perform miracles; if they do, the miracles are considered a proof of God's action through them, not evidence of their own holy powers.[25]

Drawing on the views of ancient philosophers, late antique writers believed that children, as incomplete adults, were not to be taken seriously or trusted in their judgments. Basil of Caesarea, for example, considered that maturity was a prerequisite for entering religious life and seeking holiness. He recommended that a girl wait until she was mature (ἡ ἡλικία τοῦ λόγου) enough to promise to remain a virgin and to take the veil, and that she should be held responsible for failing to keep her promise to remain a virgin only if she were adult: "For it is not proper to consider children's words entirely final in such matters, but she who is above sixteen or seventeen years, and is mistress of her faculties, who has been examined carefully and has remained constant and has persisted in her petitions for admittance, should then be enrolled among the virgins, and we should ratify

---

21   *Life of Simeon the Fool,* ed. A.-J. Festugière and L. Rydén, *Léontios de Néapolis, Vie de Syméon le Fou et Vie de Jean de Chypre* (Paris, 1974), 58.

22   Life of John the Almsgiver, in Festugière and Rydén, *Léontios de Néapolis,* 347, 351.

23   Mark the Deacon, *Life of Porphyry of Gaza,* 66, ed. H. Grégoire and M. A. Kugener (Paris, 1930), 52. On miraculous learning, see N. Kalogeras, "Education Envisioned, or the Miracle of Learning in Byzantium," *BSl* 64 (2006): 111–24.

24   On infancy gospels, see, for example, *Évangiles apocryphes,* vol. 2, *L'évangile de l'enfance, rédactions syriaques, arabe, et arméniennes,* traduites et annotées par P. Peeters (Paris, 1914).

25   This is true also for adults: miracles are performed through faith, and they are God's actions in the world. However, with children, such action is considered more direct, because a child cannot completely understand. In a way, children are more transparent to God's actions than adults, and have less merit: see O. M. Bakke, *When Children Became People: The Birth of Childhood in Early Christianity* (Minneapolis, 2005).

the profession of said virgin, and inexorably punish her violation of it."[26] He wanted such decisions to be made by adults, not children.

Many writers of saints' Lives had internalized this notion and therefore felt no need to demonstrate the holiness of their heroes during the childhood years. Theodoret of Cyrrhus, for example, presents a collection of vignettes of thirty-two saints in the *Historia religiosa*. He provides some details on geographic origin for fourteen, on childhood for eight, and on the social background of the family for only seven (see table 1).

Theodoret does not completely avoid tales of childhood. He provides some details for Simeon Stylite the Elder, for example.[27] Although, as a bishop who went to visit many of these monks, he had the opportunity to ask questions about their origins and parentage, he did not choose to provide such details in his writings, and he often starts a Vita by describing his subject's ascetic practices. He records these different lifestyles to provide models for imitation. Because there is nothing to emulate in the childhood of a saint, he finds it superfluous to describe this part of their lives. "It is impossible to tell everything," writes Theodoret, and it would be useless.

Palladius's *Lausiac History* is also mainly concerned with adult holy men and women, although this collection of edifying tales also includes sinners.[28] Very few of these spiritually enlightening stories include details on the childhood of a particular saint. Age is seldom mentioned, except to give a sense of time. We learn that Didymus became blind when he was four years old, and we marvel that he was so learned even though he could not learn to read. Some of the saintly men had practiced asceticism since their youth. Palladius is interested in the length of time they spent in the desert and in their severe ascetic practices, but not in their childhood, which is not a time when the ground for holiness is laid.

The brevity of these vignettes may partly account for their silence on the early lives of the saints, but it is also clear from these examples that in late antiquity, the childhood of saints was often considered unimportant and irrelevant to a tale dealing with ascetic feats. There is, however, yet another reason for omitting childhood and social origins from saints' Lives. These were elements deemed

26 Basil of Caesarea, canon 18, ed. P. Joannou, *Discipline générale antique,* vol. 2, *Les canons des Pères grecs* (Grottaferrata, 1963), 120–21. On the recommendation that orphans and children be welcomed in the clergy but not tonsured until they have reached the age of reason, see *Regulae fusius tractatae,* 15.4 (PG 31:956).

27 Theodoret of Cyrrhus, *Historia religiosa,* 26.2, ed. P. Canivet and A. Leroy-Molinghen, *Histoire des moines de Syrie* (Paris, 1977), 1:160–62.

28 Palladius, *Lausiac History 6,* ed. G. J. M. Bartelink (Verona, 1974), 30–36.

TABLE I
Information on background of saints mentioned
in Theodoret, *Historia religiosa*

Name	Geographic origin	Childhood details	Social background
Iakobos	Nisibis		
Ioulianos			
Markianos	Cyrrhus		ἐξ εὐπατριδῶν
Eusebios			Uncle (a monk), brother
Poublios	Zeugma		Senatorial family
Simeon the Elder			
Palladius			
Aphraates	Persia	Raised in the religion of the Magi	Good family
Peter	Galatia	Raised by his parents for seven years	
Theodosios	Antioch		
Romanos	Rhosos of Cilicia	Early education	
Zenon	Pontus		Was himself in imperial service
Makedonios			
Maesymas	Cyrrhus	Rustic education, Syriac speaker	
Askepsimas			
Maron			
Abraham	Cyrrhus	Growing up in Cyrrhus	
Eusebios			
Salamanes	Kapersana on the Euphrates		

(*continued next page*)

TABLE I (*continued*)

Name	Geographic origin	Childhood details	Social background
Maris		Beautiful voice, sings during the liturgy	
Iakobos			
Thalassios and Limnaios			
John			
Zebinas			
Asklepios			
Simeon (Stylite)	Sisa	Tends the sheep for his parents, goes to church with them	
Baradatos			
Thalelaios	Cilicia		
Marana and Cyra	Berroia	Good education	Prominent family
Domnina			

necessary in secular biographies and more generally in encomiastic literature, and Christian writers of the first three centuries were often critical toward the Second Sophistic.[29]

Latin and Greek authors more or less agreed on the list of topoi expected in a good panegyric.[30] Quintilian explained that one should start with the parents and the ancestors, then praise the qualities of the person, including physical strength, beauty, and virtues (*laus animae*), starting with inherited traits and learning.[31] Menander Rhetor, who taught the art of panegyric during the third

29   A. Momigliano, *The Development of Greek Biography* (Cambridge, 1971); L. Pernot, *La rhétorique de l'éloge dans le monde gréco-romain* (Paris, 1983), 1:137, 2:775.
30   Pernot, *Rhétorique*, 1:137–43, 1:153–78.
31   Quintilian, *Institutio Oratoria*, 3.7.10, ed. J. Cousin, *Institution oratoire* (Paris, 1976), 2:191–93.

century and who commented on Hermogenes' works, made a list of topics to be tackled: πατρίς, πόλις, ἔθνος, γένος, τὰ περὶ τῆς γενέσεως, τὰ περὶ τῆς φύσεως, ἀνατροφή, παιδεία.[32]

Menander applied similar rules to imperial praise (*logos basilikos*).[33] Imperial panegyrics praised the emperor for showing signs of greatness from infancy and gave their due along the way to his ancestors, his parents, his place of birth, and his personal talents, such as an early display of authority, courage, and intelligence.[34] Thomas Wiedemann notes that "the existence of child-emperors from the third century on also makes its presence felt in surviving panegyrics, both prose and verse. As in biography, the themes—birth miracles, childhood omens, excellence in literary and rhetorical studies—were generally traditional; what was new was a much greater emphasis on these themes."[35] These rhetorical compositions were models known to writers of saints' Lives and martyr stories, especially when they had received a classical education.[36] Yet their relationship to classical rhetoric was often complex: Christian writers criticized this formal approach to a biography, although many eventually adopted it.[37] As Averil Cameron notes, "It remained convenient to be able to decry classical rhetoric even while drawing heavily on it."[38]

Gregory of Nyssa explains his opposition, as a Christian, to this style of literature: "No one who has been trained in divine wisdom should seek to praise someone who is spiritually renowned by using the artificial devices of the encomium, in the manner of those outside," by which term he means pagan writers.[39]

32   *Menander Rhetor,* edited with translation and commentary by D. A. Russell and N. G. Wilson (Oxford, 1981). On the persistence of rhetoric and the proliferation of commentaries on Hermogenes in the third and fourth century, see M. Heath, *Menander: A Rhetor in Context* (Oxford, 2004), 295.

33   *In Praise of Later Roman Emperors: The Panegyrici Latini,* ed. R. A. B. Mynors, trans. C. E. V. Nixon and B. Saylor Rodgers (Berkeley, 1994).

34   R. Rees, *Layers of Loyalty in Latin Panegyric, A.D. 289–307* (Oxford, 2002); Wiedemann, *Adults and Children* (above, n. 5).

35   Wiedemann, *Adults and Children,* 63.

36   H. Delehaye, *Les Passions des martyrs et les genres littéraires* (Brussels, 1921; 2nd ed., 1966), 143.

37   G. J. M. Bartelink, "Adoption et rejet des topiques profanes chez les panégyristes et biographes chrétiens de langue grecque," *SicGymn* 39 (1986): 25–40; F. Heim, "Les panégyriques des martyrs ou l'impossible conversion d'un genre littéraire," *Revue des sciences religieuses* 61 (1987): 105–28.

38   A. Cameron, *Christianity and the Rhetoric of Empire: The Development of Christian Discourse* (Berkeley, 1991), 85. On the development of Christian rhetoric, see G. A. Kennedy, *Greek Rhetoric under Christian Emperors* (Princeton, N.J., 1983).

39   Gregory of Nyssa, *Life of Gregory Thaumaturgus,* 4, trans. M. Slusser, *Saint Gregory Thaumaturgus: Life and Works* (Washington, D.C., 1998), 42.

Gregory shuns "what seems great and worthy of attention . . . wealth, pedigree, glory, worldly powers, the founding stories of their homeland." He continues:

> To our mentality, just one native land deserves honor, paradise, the first home of the human race, one city, the heavenly one, fashioned of living stones, with God for its creator and builder; just one excellence of lineage, kinship to God—which no one gets automatically (like a good pedigree in the natural order of things, which often flows even to the wicked through this automatic succession) but which one acquires only by free choice. "For as many as received him," says the voice of God, "to them he gave the power to become children of God"; What could be more excellent than such a pedigree?[40]

With such a program, Gregory decides to depart from the usual rules of rhetoric when he writes the *Life of Gregory Thaumaturgus:* "Refraining from such considerations, we will not begin the praises of the great Gregory with his lineage, nor summon his ancestors to help with the encomia, knowing that no praise is true unless it is proper to those who are being praised."[41] Because a Christian encomium should be concerned with personal dispositions toward holiness, Gregory omits comments on the saint's native land and forebears.[42] "While we pass over his origins and the city where he first lived, as furnishing us with nothing relevant to our present narrative, we shall however begin our tribute here where he made the beginning of his life of virtue."[43]

Basil of Caesarea, Gregory's elder brother, expresses similar concerns. First he reminds his audience that Christian encomiums should praise the specific qualities of each martyr, rather than reproduce standard compliments.[44] "Whereas the encomia of other human beings are composed out of the multiplication of words, the truth of the exploits performed by the just is enough to demonstrate the superiority of their virtue. . . . Divine teaching, therefore, does not recognize

---

40   Gregory of Nyssa, *Life of Gregory Thaumaturgus,* 5, trans. Slusser, *Saint Gregory Thaumaturgus,* 43.

41   Gregory of Nyssa, *Life of Gregory Thaumaturgus,* 7, trans. Slusser, *Saint Gregory Thaumaturgus,* 44.

42   Gregory knew well the technical aspects of rhetorical writing: see L. Méridier, *L'influence de la seconde sophistique sur l'oeuvre de Grégoire de Nysse* (Rennes, 1906).

43   Gregory of Nyssa, *Life of Gregory Thaumaturgus,* 11, trans. Slusser, *Saint Gregory Thaumaturgus,* 45.

44   Basil of Caesarea, *In Mamantem martyrem* 2 (PG 31:589D–592A).

the rule of encomia. . . . For the rule of encomia is to examine the fatherland, and investigate pedigree, and discourse of education, but our rule, silencing mention of the people around them, fills the witness of each from their individual deeds."[45] Hippolyte Delehaye noted that Basil did not completely stick to his principle that "the city of martyrs is the city of God."[46] Although he criticized those who praised an individual and the city which witnessed that individual's birth, in the next paragraph, writing about Gordius, Basil praised his city indirectly: "He was born in this city, which is why we love him more, because he is our ornament."[47]

Like Basil, other Christian writers did not entirely abjure classical rhetoric, even when they agreed in principle with its rejection. When he wrote the *Life of Porphyry of Gaza,* Mark the Deacon devoted one line to the noble social origin of the saint. Yet when it came to Porphyry's geographic origin, he opted for a middle ground between Gregory of Nyssa's refusal to mention a saint's hometown and classical panegyrists, who considered it a necessary topos. He started with heavenly citizenship before descending to geographic details: "For his country indeed he has in heaven Jerusalem (for therein was his name written) and on earth Thessalonica."[48]

Even Gregory of Nyssa did not fully comply with his own rule when he wrote the Life of his eldest sister, Macrina. He did not praise her native land or mention the pride she could feel in her ancestors, yet he wrote about her parents and her childhood. He certainly knew her well and wrote memorable pages about her upbringing. In his narration, he chose some elements of praise that later became very common in later saints' Lives: a sign of divine election, a talent for studying, familiarity with the Book of Psalms, obedience to her parents, and a wish for a life of virginity, stubbornly maintained in spite of pressure from her family.

Gregory of Nyssa started his story with an explanation of her name. Macrina was named after her paternal grandmother. Her mother had received a vision in

45   Basil of Caesarea, *Panegyric of Gordius* (PG 31:492), trans. P. Allen, "A Homily on the Martyr Gordius," in *"Let Us Die That We May Live": Greek Homilies on Christian Martyrs from Asia Minor, Palestine and Syria (c. AD 350–AD 450)* (London, 2003), 58–59.

46   Basil of Caesarea, "A Homily on the Forty Martyrs of Sebaste" (PG 31:509), trans. Allen, *"Let Us Die that we May Live,"* 69: Πόλις τοίνυν μαρτύρων ἡ πόλις ἐστὶν τοῦ Θεοῦ.

47   Delehaye, *Les Passions des martyrs,* 191–93; Basil of Caesarea, *Panegyric of Gordius* (PG 31:493): Οὗτος ἔφυ μὲν ἀπὸ τῆς πόλεως ταύτης ὅθεν καὶ μᾶλλον αὐτὸν ἀγαπῶμεν διότι οἰκεῖος ἡμῖν ὁ κόσμος ἐστίν, trans. Allen, "A Homily on the Martyr Gordius," 60.

48   Mark the Deacon, *Life of Porphyry of Gaza,* 4, trans. E. F. Hill, *The Life of Porphyry of Gaza by Mark the Deacon* (Oxford, 1913), 7.

which the baby was named Thecla, after the great virgin saint buried at Meryem-lik on the southern coast of Anatolia. The vision was not enough to alter aristo-cratic traditions of naming children after their grandparents,[49] but it was inter-preted as the first sign of her future life as a holy virgin: "The visionary being seemed to me to proclaim this name not so much to guide the mother in the choice of name as to foretell what the life of the virgin would be and to show, through the identical character of the name, that she would choose the same way of life as Thecla did."[50]

The name *Thecla* remained secret because the girl's future life as a nun was still to unfold. Before her dramatic gesture of refusing marriage, she had to grow up and to show talent in learning, which would affirm her own personal virtues as well as those of her family. "When she had passed the age of infancy, she easily learned the things which children are usually taught and shone at whatever sub-ject her parents decided she should study."[51] She learned to read the Bible and to recite the Psalms at different times of day. Finally, when she reached the end of childhood, that is, her twelfth birthday, her father found her a suitable fiancé. A girl was considered an adult at age twelve, especially if she married.[52] Her fiancé died before the marriage took place, however, and her life took a different direc-tion. She decided to remain faithful to his memory and not to seek another hus-band, although her parents entreated her to do so. She remained close to her mother and helped take care of her numerous siblings.

Gregory of Nyssa used the topoi of classical rhetoric in the *Life of Macrina,* which he structured with episodes. The omen before birth, parents, and *paideia* were all elements of the encomiastic tradition, as Pierre Maraval has noted.[53] In

---

49   John Chrysostom, *De inani gloria,* 46–49, ed. A.-M. Malingrey, *Sur la vaine gloire et l'éducation des enfants* (Paris, 1972), 146–48. On the continuing practice, see J.-C. Cheynet, "L'anthroponymie aristocratique à Byzance," in *L'anthroponymie, document de l'histoire sociale des mondes méditerranéens médiévaux,* ed. M. Bourin, J.-M. Martin, and F. Menant (Rome, 1996), 282.

50   Gregory of Nyssa, *Life of Macrina,* 2, ed. P. Maraval, in *Grégoire de Nysse, Vie de sainte Macrine* (Paris, 1971), 148; trans. J. M. Petersen, *Handmaids of the Lord: Contemporary Descrip-tions of Feminine Asceticism in the First Six Centuries* (Kalamazoo, Mich., 1996), 53.

51   Gregory of Nyssa, *Life of Macrina,* 3, in Maraval, *Grégoire de Nysse,* 148, trans. Petersen, *Handmaids of the Lord,* 53.

52   J. Hopkins, "The Age of Roman Girls at Marriage," *Population Studies* 18 (1964–65): 309–27.

53   P. Maraval, "Une oeuvre littéraire," in *Grégoire de Nysse, Vie de sainte Macrine,* 105–13: idem, "La Vie de sainte Macrine de Grégoire de Nysse: Continuité et nouveauté d'un genre littéraire," in *Du héros païen au saint chrétien,* ed. G. Freyburger and L. Pernot (Paris, 1997), 133–38; A. Momigli-ano, "The Life of Macrina by Gregory of Nyssa," in *On Pagans, Jews, and Christians* (Middletown, Conn., 1989), 206–21.

this text, written around 380–83, childhood is treated as a particular and significant episode that lasts from birth until a prospective marriage.

This structure, with episodes specifically devoted to childhood, was systematically adopted in saints' Lives written from at least the sixth century onward. It is already very clear in the writings of Cyril of Scythopolis, who systematically mentions the names of the saint's parents and their geographic and social origin.[54] Medieval saints' Lives, edifying tales, miracle stories, and, to a certain extent, encomia were also composed of such episodes.[55] Gregory of Nyssa's professed reluctance to write in accordance with the rules of encomiastic literature certainly disappears. Gregory of Nazianzos, his friend and contemporary, wrote funeral orations strictly following the rules of rhetoric.[56]

Mentioning one's reluctance to include such details simply becomes a rhetorical device, added precisely to introduce them, as in this example taken from the tenth-century *Life of Saint Nikon:* "And so this blessed one's fatherland, the first and more divine to speak properly, was the Jerusalem above, where he was molded even in his earthly form, as David says. . . . Now it is petty and really contemptible to characterize those above in reference to those below. But if it is necessary to mention his earthly home in the narrative and to bring into the discussion the land of his body (I mean the land here below, the visible one) it was the Polemoniakian area situated near the Armenian theme."[57]

By the middle Byzantine period it had indeed become necessary to mention, albeit very briefly, the origins of a saint, including the names of parents, their social status, their birthplace and place of residence, and something of the child's education. Childhood and family details were of great interest to a medieval reader. A saint without a family might be given parents in the medieval rewriting of his or her Life.[58] The rules of rhetoric were applied in later saints' Lives,

54   B. Flusin, *Miracle et histoire dans l'oeuvre de Cyrille de Scythopolis* (Paris, 1983), 88–103.
55   P. A. Agapitos, "Mortuary Typology in the Lives of Saints: Michael Synkellos and Stephen the Younger," in Odorico and Agapitos, *Les Vies de saints à Byzance* (above, n. 2), 109: "To a substantial extent most medieval literary or visual narratives are composed out of such clearly defined narrative situations in an almost paratactic and additive progression of independent episodes."
56   T. Hägg, "Playing with Expectations: Gregory's Funeral Orations on his Brother, Sister and Father," in *Gregory Nazianzus: Images and Reflections,* ed. J. Bortnes and T. Hägg (Copenhagen, 2006), 133–51; D. Konstan, "How to Praise a Friend: St. Gregory of Nazianzus's Funeral Oration for St. Basil the Great," in *Greek Biography and Panegyric in Late Antiquity,* ed. T. Hägg and P. Rousseau (Berkeley, 2000), 160–79.
57   *Life of Nikon,* 2, ed. D. F. Sullivan, *The Life of Saint Nikon* (Brookline, Mass., 1987), 30–32.
58   Such is the case for the martyr Prokopios of Caesarea (d. 303): Eusebius of Caesarea, *Martyrs of Palestine,* 1.1–2 does not mention parents, nor do the Latin (*BHL* 6949) and Syriac (*BHO*

which were organized almost formulaically from birth to death. Interest in the first years of the saint and his or her environment varied, but it was manifest. A study based on medieval saints offers a catalogue of the most frequent common-places, also called topoi. The saints' common features owe a lot to the evolution of society during the middle Byzantine period and to the aristocratization of monasticism.

The Traits of Medieval Saints:
Stereotypical Topoi
Eugeneia, *Noble Birth*

Saints' Lives insist that holiness is a gift from God.[59] The place granted to the family in the making of a saint is difficult to establish.[60] Yet it seems clear that families make a comeback in medieval Christian biographies, following the rules of the encomium, and share in the saints' merits. To the question of whether God is alone responsible for creating a saint or whether parents can help in the process, Simeon Metaphrastes gives an inclusive answer in the *Life of Saint Nicholas of Myra:* "And so he grew, the model of good behavior—in part reflecting the habits of his parents, but also in part developing a goodness from within."[61]

The social prejudices of Byzantine society in favor of the wellborn emerge in saints' Lives. The elevated social status of many medieval saints is mentioned with pride by hagiographers, who often belonged to the same social group.[62] Cyril of Scythopolis, for example, had an aristocratic mentality, and when he praises the family of the saints, he mentions their social position. In the *Life of John the Hesychast*, he wrote:

1002) lives. The *Life and Passion of Prokopios* (*BHG* 1577), however, creates a noble family for the saint and provides the names of both parents, Theodosia and Christophoros: *Life and Passion of Prokopios,* ed. Papadopoulos-Kerameus, Ἀνάλεκτα Ἱεροσολυμιτικῆς Σταχυολογίας, vol. 5 (St. Petersburg, 1888; repr. Brussels, 1963): §2, 2–3. The son even converts his widowed mother, (ibid., §3, 4); H. Delehaye offered a date before the eighth century for the redaction of this Life in *Les légendes grecques des saints militaires* (Paris, 1909), 84.

59   Pratsch, *Der hagiographische Topos* (above, n. 10). See also A. Kiousopoulou, Χρόνος καὶ ἡλικίες στη βυζαντινή κοινωνία (Athens, 1997), 61–75.

60   R. Morris, *Monks and Laymen in Byzantium, 843–1118* (Cambridge, 1995).

61   Simeon Metaphrastes, *Life of Saint Nicholas,* 2, ed. G. Anrich, in *Hagios Nikolaos: Der heilige Nikolaos in der griechischen Kirche,* vol. 1, *Die Texte* (Leipzig, 1913), 236, and PG 116:320.

62   É. Patlagean, "Sainteté et pouvoir," in Hackel, *Byzantine Saint* (above, n. 9), 88–105.

First in my account I place abba John, solitary of the laura of blessed Sabas, as preceding all the others both in birth and in luster of life. Originating from Nicopolis in Armenia, our illuminated father John was born of parents named Encratius and Euphemia, who were of flourishing wealth and eminent family and had won distinction in many public offices, both military and civil, including posts at the imperial court; numerous stories of their achievements are recounted by the people of Byzantium and Armenia. Lest I make my story tedious from the beginning, I shall willingly omit them. . . . Being of Christian parents, he received a Christian upbringing along with his brothers.[63]

In his study on Cyril of Scythopolis, Bernard Flusin noted the harmony between the writer, the saints, and the audience of these texts. They were all relatively wellborn, Greek-speaking urban dwellers.[64] An aristocratic or prosperous background became a motif of praise.[65]

Some of the saints themselves, apparently aware of the good stock they came from, refused the milk of a wet nurse. In the *Life of Saint Nicholas of Bounaina* (d. 903) the baby, fed by the pure milk of his mother, receives the Holy Spirit.[66] His mother's virtues are transmitted through her milk, and he becomes wise and brave. In the *Life of Cyril/Constantine,* the apostle of the Slavs, the baby refuses to take the milk of the wet nurse and drinks only his mother's milk. A psychiatrist might have interesting things to say on this preference, but so does the hagiographer: this was a providential sign, ensuring that the child was fed only with pure milk from an excellent stock.[67] Nikephoros Blemmydes (1197–ca. 1269) also reportedly refused as improper milk that did not come from his mother.[68]

We owe details on childhood in medieval saints' Lives to the reemergence of

63   Cyril of Scythopolis, *Life of John the Hesychast,* ed. E. Schwartz, *Kyrillos of Skythopolis* (Leipzig, 1939), 201; trans. R. M. Price, *Lives of the Monks of Palestine by Cyril of Scythopolis* (Kalamazoo, 1991), 221.
64   Flusin, *Miracle et histoire* (above, n. 54).
65   D. J. Chitty, *The Desert a City: An Introduction to the Study of Egyptian and Palestinian Monasticism under the Christian Empire* (Oxford, 1966), 88.
66   *Life of Saint Nicholas of Bounaina* (d. 903), ed D. Sophianos, Ἅγιος Νικόλαος ὁ ἐν Βουναίνῃ: Ἀνέκδοτα ἁγιολογικὰ κείμενα: Ἱστορικαὶ εἰδήσεις περὶ τῆς μεσαιωνικῆς Θεσσαλίας (100ς αἰών) (Athens, 1972), 140.
67   F. Dvornik, *Les légendes de Constantin et Méthode vues de Byzance* (Prague, 1933), 350.
68   Nikephoros Blemmydes, *Autographia sive curriculum vitae,* ed. J. A. Munitiz (Turnhout, 1984); J. Munitiz, "Self-Canonisation: 'The partial account' of Nikephoros Blemmydes," in Hackel, *Byzantine Saint,* 164–68.

emphasis on the family. Hagiographers combine personal merit with social pride. Families were often absent or inconspicuous in late antique saints' Lives because the hagiographers wanted to show the saints as being as detached from the world as possible, as the sons and daughters of God. "My true father is Christ," says Justin, "my mother is my faith in him."[69] Those who died for their faith had often renounced their families, as the moving story of Saint Perpetua makes plain.[70] They were citizens of heaven. An individualist streak appears in these narratives, centered on the merits of one person. Medieval writers also mention how important it is to prefer no one to Christ, but they also value obedience to parents and respect for the family.

Out of obedience, a child might even renounce wishes for a celibate life devoted to God. John the Almsgiver (d. 616), raised by noble and pious parents, consented to take a wife to obey his father, although he did not wish to marry. He agreed to procreate children when threatened by the anger of his father-in-law.[71] Melania the Younger (ca. 383–439) did the same. The heiress of a great Roman family, she was forced to marry at age fourteen. Although she wished to remain a virgin, her husband agreed to live in continence only if she first provided him with two heirs.[72]

Medieval saints often had family duties to perform before they could take monastic vows. Saint Euthymios the Younger (ca. 823–898) was enrolled in the army at the age of seven because his family owed military service to the state. He abandoned his wife and child for the monastic life when he was eighteen.[73] The eleventh-century Cyril the Phileotes, by contrast, built a cell in his own house in order not to abandon his wife and children as so many earlier saints had done.[74]

Although God takes precedence, family members make an appearance and often play a role in medieval saints' Lives. In the *Life of Saint Auxentios* by Michael Psellos, a combination of traditions comes into play. On the one hand,

69   *Acta Iustini et sociorum,* 4, ed. D. R. Bueno, *Actas de los martires* (Madrid, 1962), 314.

70   *Passion of Perpetua,* ed. J. Amat, *Passion de Perpétue et Félicité* (Paris, 1996).

71   *The Anonymous Life of John the Almsgiver,* 3, ed. P. Delehaye, "Une vie inédite de saint Jean l'aumônier," *AB* 45 (1927): 20; trans. Festugière, in Festugière and Rydén, *Léontios de Néapolis* (above, n. 21), 322.

72   Life of Melania the Younger, 1–3, ed. Gorce, *Vie de sainte Mélanie* (above, n. 20), 130–32.

73   Life of Euthymios the Younger, ed. L. Petit, "Vie et office de saint Euthyme le Jeune," *ROC* 8 (1903): 155–205, 503–36 (repr., Bibliothèque hagiographique orientale 5 [1904]: 14–51).

74   The Life of Cyril the Phileotes, ed. E. Sargologos, *La vie de Cyrille le Philéote moine byzantin (†1110)* (Brussels, 1964); M. E. Mullett, "Literary Biography and Historical Genre in the Life of Cyril Phileotes by Nicholas Kataskepenos," in Odorico and Agapitos, *Les vies de saints à Byzance* (above, n. 2), 387–409.

Psellos, a very learned scholar, no doubt acquainted with the Cappadocian fathers, claims that he should leave aside rhetorical topoi: "I shall not praise this man based on his family, nor state that his native land was prosperous, or that his ancestors were very distinguished. It suffices to center the discourse on him."[75] Yet he also mentions the brilliant careers the saint's family members were pursuing in the army. Auxentios benefited from the familiarity of a paternal uncle with the emperor Theodosios. Michael Psellos does not provide details on the childhood of the saint but does depict him as having shown since infancy qualities that would flourish in adulthood.

Miraculous Children

All children were believed to be gifts from God, especially those long-awaited children born to couples affected by sterility. Many saints' Lives reveal that these parents had prayed for a child and felt indebted to God and to the saint whose intercession was powerful enough to grant their wish. This debt was usually repaid by offering the child to God's service, either as a cleric or as a monk. Examples are numerous from the fifth century onward. Theodoret of Cyrrhus was born after his parents pleaded with Makedonios for his intercession. He agreed to intercede if they would dedicate the child to God's service. The holy man reminded Theodoret that it had been difficult for his parents to conceive him and that he should honor their offering.[76] In the *Life of Saint Stephen the Younger* (d. 764), the mother of the saint offered her child to the Theotokos, to whom she felt indebted because she had prayed in the church of Blachernai to have a son.[77] Many narratives allude to the biblical model of Hannah, who is barren, and the birth of her son Samuel, who is offered to the temple.[78] Cyril of Scythopolis mentions that Dionysia, the mother of Saint Euthymios, had prayed in the shrine of Saint Polyeuktos for a child. When he was about three years old and had lost his father, she "fulfilled her promise, by offering him as an acceptable

---

75   Life of Auxentios, 2, ed. P. P. Joannou, *Démonologie populaire—démonologie critique au XIe siècle: La vie inédite de S. Auxence par M. Psellos* (Wiesbaden, 1971), 66.

76   Theodoret of Cyrrhus, *Historia religiosa,* 13, 16–17, ed. Canivet and Leroy-Molinghen, *Histoire des moines de Syrie* (above, n. 27), 502–6.

77   *Life of Saint Stephen the* Younger, 4, 6, ed. M.-F. Auzépy, *La vie d'Étienne le Jeune par Étienne le Diacre* (Aldershot, 1997), 92, 95.

78   This allusion has been thoroughly studied for Latin hagiography in M. de Jong, *In Samuel's Image: Child Oblation in the Early Medieval West* (Leiden, 1996).

sacrifice to God just as the celebrated Hannah had done with Samuel."[79] Her brother was in the service of the bishop of Melitene, to whom she entrusted the child. The mother of Saint Peter of Atroa (d. 837) asked the Lord for a child, yet suffered many years of sterility. She gave birth to a boy named Theophylaktos, and when the child was weaned, she offered him to the bishop "as another Samuel."[80] In the same vein, the mother of Michael the Synkellos (d. 846) softened God's heart with her lamentations: God "heard her prayer and granted to her according to her request a male child; and when he was weaned, she offered him up to Him as an acceptable gift."[81]

Once a child was born, the problem was to keep it alive, as the rate of infant mortality was very high. Peter of Atroa is said to have interceded for a family that had lost thirteen children. The last son survived and was offered to God in Peter's monastic community.[82] Some parents believed that placing the child in God's service would protect it. That gift did not make a saint out of the child, although it could be a preliminary step. In many saints' Lives, the saint is chosen by God and set apart.

Chosen in the Womb

God often provided signs concerning the exceptional destiny of the saints whom he watched over from the time of their conception, following the model of Jeremiah: "Before I formed you in the womb, I knew you, before you were born, I set you apart" (Jer. 1:4–5). The comparison to Jeremiah is made explicit in the Life of the ninth-century Saint David of Lesbos: "As soon as [this baby] had just poked his head out from his mother's womb, he was dedicated to the Lord as a holy person, just like the great and wondrous Samuel, having been consecrated even before birth, just like a second Jeremiah."[83] One can read a similar com-

79 Cyril of Scythopolis, *Life of Euthymius*, 3, in Schwartz, *Kyrillos von Scythopolis* (above, n. 63), 10, trans. Price, *Lives of the Monks of Palestine*, 6.
80 *Life of Peter of Atroa*, 2, in V. Laurent, *La Vie merveilleuse de saint Pierre d'Atroa († 837)* (Brussels, 1956), 69–71.
81 *Life of Michael the Synkellos*, 1, ed. and trans. M. B. Cunningham, *The Life of Michael the Synkellos* (Belfast, 1991), 46.
82 *Life of Peter of Atroa*, 59, in Laurent, *La Vie merveilleuse*, 181.
83 *Life of David, Symeon, and George of Lesbos*, 4, ed. J. van den Gheyn, "Acta graeca ss. Davidis, Symeonis et Georgii Mitylenae in insula Lesbo," *AB* 18 (1899): 214, trans. D. Domingo-Forasté, "The Life and Conduct of and Narrative about our Thrice Blessed and Inspired Fathers David, Symeon and George, those Lights Shining in Ancient and Terrible Times," in *Byzantine Defenders of Images: Eight Saints' Lives in English Translation*, ed. A.-M. Talbot (Washington, D.C., 1998), 154.

parison in the *Life of Saint Sabas* by Cyril of Scythopolis: "Sabas, being predestined by God from the womb and foreknown before his creation like the great prophet Jeremiah."[84] Divine election in the womb is also clearly alluded to in the *Life of Saint Nicholas of Sion:* "There is a child here, by name of Nicholas, son of Epiphanios, his mother being Nonna, who will dwell in this place, and glorify our Father which is in Heaven. For from his mother's womb was he chosen by God."[85]

Visions of light sent to the mother of a future saint were an indication of future sanctity.[86] The mother of Daniel the Stylite[87] saw two lights coming from heaven, and the mother of Theodore of Sykeon observed "a very large and brilliant star descending from heaven into her womb."[88] The father of this illegitimate child politely but hesitantly concluded: "Perchance God will watch over you and give you a son who will be deemed worthy to become a bishop."[89] The mother, who was an innkeeper, was not satisfied with this answer and asked the opinion of a holy man and a bishop. They predicted that the child would be great, but what she wanted was success in the imperial service. Other signs, such as sickness, forced her to change her mind. Ascetic holiness was not in her plans for her son, and the star was an ambiguous sign. Some visions contained a theological allusion: the mother of Saint Alypios saw a lamb carrying tapers, a reference to Christ.[90] Some visions simply reflected God's special attention to a child: the mother of Nikephoros Blemmydes saw angels clothing her baby.[91]

The *Life of Saint Paul of Latros,* dated to the tenth century, states the interest God has invested in Paul "from the beginning."[92] Because little Paul remained

---

84   Cyril of Scythopolis, *Life of Saint Sabas,* 2, in Schwartz, *Kyrillos von Scythopolis,* 87, trans. Price, *Lives of the Monks of Palestine,* 95.

85   *The Life of Saint Nicholas of Sion,* 3, text and translation by I. Ševčenko and N. Patterson-Ševčenko (Brookline, Mass., 1984), 32–34, trans. 33–35.

86   F. Lanzoni, "Il sogno presago della madre incinta nella letteratura medievale e antica," *AB* 45 (1927): 225–61.

87   *Life of Daniel the Stylite,* 2, ed. H. Delehaye, *Les saints stylites* (Brussels, 1923), 2.

88   *Life of Theodore of Sykeon,* 3, ed. A.-J. Festugière, *Vie de Théodore de Sykéôn* (Brussels, 1970), 1:3, trans. E. Dawes and N. Baynes, *Three Byzantine Saints: Contemporary Biographies* (Oxford, 1948), 88.

89   Life of Theodore of Sykeon, 3, in Festugière, *Vie de Théodore de Sykéôn,* 1:3, trans. Dawes and Baynes, *Three Byzantine Saints,* 88.

90   Life of Alypios, 2, ed. H. Delehaye, *Les saints stylites,* 148.

91   Nikephoros Blemmydes, *Autographia sive curriculum vitae,* ed. J. A. Munitiz (Turnhout, 1984); J. Munitiz, "Self-Canonisation" (above, n. 68), 164–68.

92   Life of Paul of Latros, 1, ed. H. Delehaye, "Vita S. Pauli Iunioris in Monte Latro cum interpretatione latina Iacobi Sirmondi," 3, *AB* 11 (1892): 22; H. Delehaye, "La Vie de Saint Paul le Jeune

with his mother and herded the village pigs, it seemed unlikely that he would become a saint, but God sent three warnings to his elder brother Basil, who himself had run away from home to avoid marriage and was a monk at Mount Olympus. Basil sent for his brother and entrusted him to Peter, *hegoumenos* of the monastery of Karya on Mount Latros. The responsibility for this whole process was ascribed to God.

Wondrous Signs after Birth

Wondrous signs were also given to parents after the birth of a child.[93] "When Lazaros emerged from his mother's womb, a light at once shone forth miraculously from heaven and filled the whole interior of the house with an indescribable flash of lightning. Indeed, the people who were there could not stand its brilliance. Leaving the mother with the baby, they rushed out of the house and stood somewhere nearby in great fear and trembling. They waited for a little while and then, after the terrible light had gone away, went back into the house. When the midwife approached the new mother, she found the baby standing upright; he was facing east and had his hands pressed tightly in the form of the cross."[94] Although quite clear in this case, these signs often needed to be explicitly interpreted. Lazaros's uncle, a monk, had heard about the miraculous events surrounding his nephew's birth. He sent word that "it had certainly not happened without God's aid, and for this reason he urged the boy's parents to let him receive the proper attention for instruction in the holy letters."[95] Eventually, Lazaros became a stylite monk and spent his life standing in prayer.

For a pillar saint, such a sign was easy to interpret, yet signs may have more than one meaning. The precociously standing baby is mentioned in the *Life of Saint Nicholas of Sion,* who did not become a pillar saint: "For at the time of his birth, while he was still in the washbasin, by the power of God he stood upright

---

(† 956) et la chronologie de Métaphraste," *Revue des questions historiques* (1893): 3–31; D. Papachryssanthou, "La vie monastique dans les campagnes byzantines du VIIIe au XIe siècle," *Byzantion* 43 (1973): 158–80; O. Kresten, "Das Kloster des Heiligen Paulos am Berge Latros," *JÖB* 50 (2000): 457–77.

93 For similar phenomena at the birth of imperial children, see the essay by Dimiter Angelov in this volume.

94 *The Life of Lazaros of Mt. Galesion,* 3, ed. R. P. H. Greenfield, *The Life of Lazaros of Mt. Galesion: An Eleventh Century Pillar Saint* (Washington, D.C., 2000), 78–79.

95 *Life of Lazaros of Mt. Galesion,* 3, in Greenfield, *Life of Lazaros,* 79.

on his feet for about two hours. And awestruck, his parents praised God."[96] Parents indulging in admiration of their offspring's achievements, even a feat like standing in the tub, might not surprise us, but in the case of a saint, the event had to be interpreted. The baby was named for his uncle Nicholas, the founder of the shrine of Holy Sion. The uncle immediately interpreted the event as a sign from God. He explained to the proud parents: "A servant of God has been born to us."[97]

Every childhood gesture could also be interpreted. A regurgitating baby would not attract particular attention—unless it was Pachomius who spat up. We are told that Pachomius gave signs of his destiny from the time he was in his mother's arms.[98] He was born into a pagan family, but he had been given power over demons since birth. When his parents brought him to a temple of the gods, he vomited up the libation that his parents had made him drink, and the local priests chased him away as an "enemy of the gods."[99]

Food and Fasting

Many future saints revealed at an early age what kind of saints they would become. A child inclined toward ascetic practices indicated a future monk. Even a baby could offer such signs. In the *Life of Saint Simeon Stylite the Younger,* the baby refused to take milk from the left breast and fed only from the right one.[100] Future monks were not the only ascetic figures who fasted. Theodore of Sykeon skipped lunch after school in order to pray.[101] Saint Nicholas of Myra, who had started fasting during infancy, dutifully abstained from food in accordance with the ecclesiastical calendar, a proper sign for a future bishop. Simeon Metaphrastes' *Life of Nicholas of Myra* emphasizes his religiously motivated

---

96 *Life of Nicholas of Sion,* 2, in Ševčenko and Patterson-Ševčenko (above, n. 85), 22–23: ἅμα γὰρ τῷ κυηθῆναι αὐτόν, ὄντα ἔτι ἐν τῇ σκάφῃ, τῇ τοῦ θεοῦ δυνάμει ἔστη ἐπὶ τοὺς πόδας αὐτοῦ ὀρθὸς ὡς ὥρας δύο. καὶ ἔμφοβοι γενάμενοι οἱ γονεῖς αὐτοῦ ἐδόξασαν τὸν θεόν.

97 Ibid., 23: ἐγεννήθη ἡμῖν ἄνθρωπος δοῦλος τοῦ θεοῦ.

98 *Life of Pachomius* (codex Patmensis 736, saec. 14), 1, ed. F. Halkin, "La Vie abrégée de saint Pachôme dans le ménologe impérial (BHG 1401b)," *AB* 96 (1978): 368.

99 *Life of Pachomius* (BHG 1396a), 3, ed. F. Halkin, *Le corpus athénien de saint Pachôme* (Geneva, 1982), 12: Τὸν ἐχθρὸν τῶν θεῶν ἐντεῦθεν ἀποδιώξατε.

100 *La Vie ancienne de S. Syméon Stylite le Jeune (521–592),* 4, ed. P. van den Ven (Brussels, 1962), 1:6. I have argued that there are traces of anorexia in Simeon's behavior: see B. Caseau, "Syméon Stylite le Jeune (521–92): Un Cas de Sainte Anorexie?" *Kentron* 19 (2003): 179–203.

101 *Life of Theodore of Sykeon,* 7–8, in Festugière, *Vie de Théodore de Sykéôn* (above, n. 89), 1:6–9.

abstinence: "When it came time to nurse the infant and he was placed at the maternal breast, God signified to all what kind of man Nicholas was to be when he should come to the age of discretion. For it is a fact that though throughout the rest of the week he would nurse at the breast like any infant, when Wednesday and Friday came he would take milk but once on each of them. Thus from the earliest moment, self-disciplined by rigid rule even before boyhood and from the very beginning, Nicholas showed how abstinence was a familiar token."[102]

Fastidiousness in eating has always been a feature of monastic literature.[103] In the Lives of monks who became saints, details on youthful asceticism may include precise information on the eating habits of the holy child and a comparison with those of other children. The *Life of Saint Luke of Steiris,* for example, lists the foods the saint renounced:

> He did not eat fruit, not to mention other pleasant things, which some might disbelieve, knowing that for children fruit is the most delightful food. But he was so unusual and extreme a lover of self-control that even from childhood he abstained not only from meat but from cheese and eggs and everything else that provides pleasure. He lived on barley bread, water, and vegetables, and whatever kind of legume was at hand. On Wednesday and Friday he did not eat until sunset. Most astonishing is that he did not use a teacher or guide, but waged war of his own accord against everything that gratifies the belly, welcoming from the depths of his soul toils and fasting and everything that grieves the flesh.[104]

102   Simeon Metaphrastes, *Life of Saint Nicholas of Myra,* 2, in Anrich, *Hagios Nikolaos* (above, n. 61), 1:236 (PG 116:320), trans. C. W. Jones, *Saint Nicholas of Myra, Bari, and Manhattan: Biography of a Legend* (Chicago, 1978), 51.

103   É. Patlagean, *Pauvreté économique et pauvreté sociale à Byzance, 4e–7e siècles* (Paris, 1977), 36–53; P. Devos, "Règles et pratiques alimentaires selon les textes," in *Le site monastique copte des Kellia, sources historiques et explorations archéologiques: Actes du colloque de Genève, 13–15 août 1984* (Geneva, 1986), 73–84; Y. Hirschfeld, "The Importance of Bread in the Diet of Monks in the Judaean Desert," *Byzantion* 66 (1996): 143–55; J. Patrich, *Sabas, Leader of Palestinian Monasticism: A Comparative Study in Eastern Monasticism, Fourth to Seventh Centuries* (Washington, D.C., 1995), 207–8; B. Layton, "Social Structure and Food Consumption in an Early Christian Monastery: The Evidence of Shenoute's Canons and the White Monastery Federation, A.D. 385–465," *Le Muséon* 115 (2002):25–55; A.-M. Talbot, "Mealtime in Monasteries: The Culture of the Byzantine Refectory," in *Eat, Drink and be Merry (Luke 12:19): Food and Wine in Byzantium in Honour of Professor A. M. Bryer,* ed. L. Brubaker and K. Linardou (Aldershot, 2007), 109–25.

104   *Life of Luke of Steiris,* 3, in *The Life and Miracles of Saint Luke of Steiris: A Translation and Commentary,* ed. and trans. C. L. Connor and W. R. Connor (Brookline, Mass., 1994), 8–11.

BÉATRICE CHEVALLIER CASEAU

A child's rejection of food highlights the difficulty of the sacrifice, because one of the recognized features of childhood is the inability to control the appetite. In the *Life of Saint Marinos,* the baby boy allegedly fathered by Marinos (who is in fact a woman disguised as a monk) constantly cried for food and gave Marinos a lot of trouble. This child was not destined to become a saint, and there is no romanticism in the depiction of his behavior. Rather one detects a sense of annoyance: "He [Marinos] undertook to procure milk from some shepherds, and so nursed the child as a father. But the distress that overwhelmed him was not all, for the child, whimpering and wailing, continually soiled Marinos' garments." Accepted in the monastic enclosure, "the child was forever following him about, crying and saying, 'Dada, dada,' and such things as children say when they wish to eat. Thus, in addition to the [usual] trials and temptations that beset a monk, Marinos was continually anxious about procuring and providing sustenance for the child."[105]

By contrast, Saint Anthony the Great never bothered his parents for food and ate only what he was given.[106] Future saints do not have the flaws associated with ordinary children. On the contrary, they show signs of wisdom, particularly during play with young friends.

Prophetic Games and Wisdom

The Byzantines were well aware of children's love of playacting and games, which were depicted in both art and literature.[107] Miracle stories and edifying spiritual tales often include descriptions of children at play. Especially popular was the διήγησις ψυχωφελής or "story beneficial for the soul," a genre close to the *apophthegma.* Such stories were usually short and easy to memorize. Unlike *apophthegmata,* however, which circulated mainly in monastic circles, spiritual tales

---

105   *Life of Marinos,* 14, 17, ed. M. Richard, "La Vie ancienne de sainte Marie surnommée Marinos," in *Corona Gratiarum: Miscellanea patristica, historica et liturgica Eligio Dekkers O.S.B. XII Lustra complenti oblata* (Brugge, 1975), 1:83–94, trans. N. Constas, in *Holy Women of Byzantium: Ten Saints' Lives in English Translation,* ed. A.-M. Talbot (Washington, D.C., 1996), 10.

106   *Life of Anthony,* 1.4, ed. G. J. M. Bartelink, *Athanase d'Alexandrie, Vie d'Antoine* (Paris, 1994), 130.

107   C. B. Horn, "Children's Play as Social Ritual," in *A People's History of Christianity,* vol. 2, *Late Ancient Christianity,* ed. V. Burrus (Minneapolis, 2005), 95–116. For scenes with children playing, see J. Huskinson, *Roman Children's Sarcophagi* (Oxford, 1996); the mosaics at the Great Palace of Constantinople, F. Cimak, *Mosaics in Istanbul* (Istanbul, 1997); and C. Hennessy, *Images of Children in Byzantium* (Aldershot, 2008). See also the extensive discussion in the article by Brigitte Pitarakis in this volume.

had a large audience. Theodoret of Cyrrhus mentions that they could entertain as well as edify.[108] John Moschos wrote a collection of such tales, borrowing from different sources.[109] In one of them, children are described playing: "Some children were pasturing animals about a mile from the property. As is usually the case, these children wanted to play games the way children do."[110]

Saints' Lives sometimes acknowledge the high spirits of fun-loving children. In the *Life of Saint Simeon the Holy Fool,* little girls play in the streets of Emesa, dancing and singing satirical songs. In a funny scene, after he has made them miraculously squinty-eyed, they run after him asking to be kissed and freed from the spell.[111] Children were not perfect beings. In church, their behavior sometimes lacked decorum. A preacher whose sermon was attributed to John Chrysostom expressed indignation that children brought marbles to church, played with nuts, and wrote graffiti on the walls.[112] As catechumens, children were allowed to leave the church and play outside after the sermon. Some of their already-baptized friends, who were tempted to go and play with them, were reluctant to stay in church. Their disruptive behavior was so common that boys were apparently often placed close to the ambo, under the surveillance of a deacon.[113] Little girls stayed close to their mothers, who were also in charge of the very young children, who tended to be noisy. Mothers were encouraged to supervise their children so that they would not run around the church, especially during the most sacred moments of the liturgy, the oblation and consecration.[114]

Saintly children, however, behaved well in church and exerted self-control.

108   Theodoret of Cyrrhus, *Historia religiosa,* Prologos, 1–2, in Canivet and Leroy-Molinghen, *Histoire des moines de Syrie* (above, n. 27), 1:124–26.

109   H. Chadwick, "John Moschus and His Friend Sophronius the Sophist," *JTS* 25 (1974): 41–74.

110   John Moschos, *The Spiritual Meadow,* 196, trans. J. Wortley (Kalamazoo, Mich., 1992), 172–73; ed. in PG 87.3:3081: ἀπὸ μιλίου ἑνὸς παιδία ἔβοσκον θρέμματα. Καὶ οἷα συμβαίνει, καὶ ὀφείλει γίνεσθαι παιδίοις, ἠθέλησαν παῖξαι κατὰ τὴν τῶν παίδιων συνήθειαν.

111   *Life of Simeon the Holy Fool,* 26, in Festugière and Rydén, *Léontios de Néapolis* (above, n. 21), 91–92.

112   F. Rilliet-Maillard, "Une homélie sur le début du jeûne attribuée à Mar Jean," in *ΑΝΤΙΔΩΡΟΝ: Hommage à M. Geerard pour célébrer l'achèvement de la Clavis Patrum Graecorum* (Wetteren, 1984), 70–71.

113   *Canons of the Apostles,* 1, 52, ed. J. and A. Périer, "Les '127 canons des apôtres,' texte arabe, en partie inédit, publ. et trad. en français d'après les manuscrits de Paris, de Rome et de Londres," *Patrologia Orientalis,* 8, fasc. 4 (Paris, 1912), 635.

114   B. Caseau, "La place des enfants dans les églises d'Orient (IIIe–Xe siècle)," in *Famille, violence et christianisation au Moyen Âge: Mélanges offerts à Michel Rouche,* ed. M. Aurell and T. Deswarte (Paris, 2005), 15–27.

They chose only same-sex friends with spiritual aspirations akin to theirs. Nicholas of Myra "avoided immoderate companions and consorting and conversing with women."[115] The future patriarch Tarasios, reminded by his mother not to associate with bad boys, happily complied. The young saints were sensible and well-behaved children who avoided bad influences. From saints' Lives one can understand implicitly the behavior expected from ordinary children, which is contrasted with the mature behavior of future saints. As Ann Moffatt has shown, "it is a commonplace of hagiography to describe how the young saint did not participate in jesting and spectacles which so delighted ordinary youth. Nor, according to the biographers, did he associate with his contemporaries except with like-minded children also aspiring to a life of virtue."[116]

Unlike his or her little friends, the saint had a childhood as free of childishness as possible. Of Saint Anthony, the *Coptic Life* says: "He would join his parents in church, and he was never recklessly playful like a child, nor was he contemptuous while growing up."[117] The saint prays more than his friends and refuses to indulge in silly games or idle talk. Saint Theodore of Sykeon does not swear, nor does he utter a blasphemous word or an indecent one. He leaves a game if a quarrel starts.[118] A simple and frequent comparison between the future saint and his or her companions reveals the differences between them, as, for example, in the *Life of Saint Luke of Steiris:* "The third child was Luke, the most divine in every way, who, from earliest infancy and while still considered a child, did nothing in childish fashion. Most children enjoy and delight in toys, jokes, games, lively activity, and running; but for Luke there was none of this, but rather calmness, tranquility, a steady character, and maturity in all things."[119]

The more the child's behavior resembles that of an adult, the better. This idea is an ancient one and not specifically Christian. We read, for example, in Plutarch's *Life of Themistocles* that when the boy had free time, he did not play or relax, but instead composed discourses.[120] Children with a brilliant future

115   Simeon Metaphrastes, *Life of Nicholas of Myra,* 2, in Anrich, *Hagios Nikolaos* (above, n. 61), 1:236–37.
116   Moffatt, "The Byzantine Child" (above, n. 11), 706.
117   *Coptic Life of Saint Anthony,* 1, ed. G. Garitte, *S. Antonii Vitae Versio Sahidica* (Paris, 1949), trans. Vivian, *Journeying into God* (above, n. 18), 12.
118   *Life of Theodore of Sykeon,* 5, in Festugière, *Vie de Théodore de Sykéôn* (above, n. 89), 1:4–5.
119   *Life of Luke of Steiris,* 3, in Connor and Connor, *Life and Miracles of St. Luke of Steiris,* (above, n. 104), 9.
120   Plutarch, *Life of Themistokles,* 2.1–2, ed. and trans. B. Perrin, *Plutarch's Lives* (London, 1968), 2:4–5: "However lowly his birth, it is agreed on all hands that while yet a boy he was impetuous, by nature sagacious, and by election enterprising and prone to public life. In times of relaxation and

should show signs of their ability to overcome the natural defects of childhood and resemble wise adults, even old men. The concept of the *puer senex,* the elderly child, continues in Christian hagiography: the ideal is for the child to closely resemble the mature adult.[121] Makarios the Egyptian is called παιδαριογέρων by Palladius in the *Lausiac History.*[122] Athanasios of Lavra "did not play like a child, if he sometimes had to play, but like a wise old man."[123] In the eleventh century, the same praise is directed at Saint Nikon:

> For he alone beyond his other peers, while still of an early age and being counted among children, did not have the mind of a child. Nor did he devote himself to toys and sports and races and horses and the other things desirable and beloved by the young. But immediately, as it were from the starting line, he fought against all desire of the flesh. He was glad to spend his time in churches and holy places; he was always completely eager to look on the fairest of habits and to direct himself to a life dear to God and blessed. And in that immature and early age he displayed the wisdom of an old man. To speak briefly, it was clear from his very birth, as it is with noble plants, what sort of person he would turn out to be with respect to virtue.[124]

If a future saint is described as playing, it is at some kind of prophetic game that reflects his destiny: Athanasios of Alexandria plays at baptizing his friends on the beach;[125] Athanasios of Lavra plays at being a monastic leader, a *hegoumenos.*[126] Both later adopted these respective roles in adult life. Role-playing is a

---

leisure, when absolved from his lessons, he would not play nor indulge his ease, as the rest of the boys did, but would be found composing and rehearsing to himself mock speeches."

121 Festugière, "Lieux communs littéraires" (above, n. 5), 137–39.

122 Palladius, *Histoire lausiaque* (above, n. 28), 106.

123 *Life of Athanasius of Lavra,* vita A, 8, ed. J. Noret, *Vitae duae antiquae sancti Athanasii Athonitae,* 6 (Turnhout, 1982): οὐχ ὡς παῖς, εἴ ποτε καὶ παίζειν ἔδει ἀλλὰ σωφρόνως ὡς γέρων ἔπαιζεν.

124 *The Life of Saint Nikon,* 2, text, translation, and commentary by D. F. Sullivan, 32–33; H. A. Théologitis, "Histoire et littérature dans l'hagiographie byzantine: Le cas de saint Nikôn dit le 'Metanoeite'," in Odorico and Agapitos, *Les Vies de saints à Byzance* (above, n. 2), 201–31.

125 John Moschos, *The Spiritual Meadow,* 197, trans. Wortley, 174–76 (above, n. 110; PG 87:3084). John Moschos borrows the story from Rufinus, *Historia ecclesiastica,* 1. 15, ed. T. Mommsen, *Eusebius Caesariensis secundum translationem quam fecit Rufinus, Historia ecclesiastica,* Corpus Berolinense, 9:1–2 (Berlin, 1903–8), 980–81.

126 *Life of Athanasius of Lavra,* vita A, 8, ed. Noret, 6.

natural feature in children's games: it helps them work out and internalize the rules and roles of the adult world. Because both clerics and monks were familiar figures to children, religious role-playing was an important part of Byzantine children's games.[127] However, the Byzantines were so intent on finding portents that they identified the children's choices of roles during playtime with revelations concerning the children's destiny. John Moschos (ca. 540–ca. 634), in the *Spiritual Meadow,* explains how some children were sent to a monastery by the bishop for having pretended to celebrate the liturgy: "While they were playing, they said to each other: 'Let us have a service and offer the holy sacrifice.' They thought this was a good idea, so they chose one of their members to serve as priest and two others to be deacons. They came to a flat rock and began their game." A fire that descended from heaven burned up their eucharistic offerings, and they were struck dumb for a day. Finally, the bishop came to the spot: "He saw the evidence of the fire from heaven. He sent the children to a monastery and converted the place where the event happened into a distinguished monastery."[128]

The same reaction is noted in the story concerning Athanasios of Alexandria and his little friends. Alexander, patriarch of Alexandria, "saw some children playing on the shore as children usually do. They were imitating a bishop and all the ceremonies which are customary in church." He asked the children what game they were playing. "Being children, they were frightened, [and at first] they denied everything. But they told him every detail of their game: how they had baptized some catechumens by the hand of Athanasios—whom the children had appointed as their bishop." Finally, he summoned the parents of Athanasios and of the other children, and, "with God as witness, handed them over to the church to be nourished therein." Soon after, he consecrated Athanasios as a member of his clergy.[129] This story proved very popular. It was reused in the Life of Eutychios, future patriarch of Constantinople (mid-sixth century), who played a similar role in a game with friends.[130]

127 J. Duffy, "Playing at Ritual: Variations on a Theme in Byzantine Religious Tales," in *Greek Ritual Poetics,* ed. D. Yatromanolakis and P. Roilos (Washington, D.C., 2004), 199–209.

128 John Moschos, *The Spiritual Meadow,* 196, trans. Wortley, 174 (PG 87:3081, 3084).

129 Ibid., 174–76 (PG 87:3085).

130 Eustratios, *Life of Eutychios,* 9 (PG 86:2884C–D).

Little children with a talent for learning were singled out and encouraged to pursue their education, if we are to believe the saints' Lives. Andrew of Crete, born in Syria of pious parents, did not learn to speak until age seven, yet when he started to learn his letters, he was revealed to be a brilliant student.[131] He was made a cleric at Jerusalem. Peter of Atroa was also a quiet and clever child. His bishop, recognizing these qualities, and made Peter a member of his clergy.[132]

The intelligence of the saints and their ability to learn the Psalms by heart and to study the holy scriptures were frequently noted in Byzantine hagiography. A taste for letters and for theology was naturally appropriate for boys destined to become bishops, but it was also found in future monastic saints and even holy fools. The *Life of Saint Andrew the Fool* reports that his master had bought him when he was still a child and rejoiced in his handsome appearance. He sent him to school and "being intelligent, the boy quickly learnt the Psalms and the use of numbers, amazing his teacher with his receptivity."[133] Because the child had neat penmanship, his master made him his secretary. Saint Andrew "loved to read the Holy Scriptures but even more the Passions of the martyrs and the Lives of the God-bearing Fathers, so that his heart was aflame with trust in them and aroused to imitation of their good way of living."[134]

The medieval Byzantine saint sometimes appears so gifted in intellect that he can surpass even his teacher. Little Saint Nicholas of Sion learned how to read when he was seven years old and outdid his inexperienced teacher.[135] Neilos of Rossano (d. 1004) was extremely intelligent and asked clever questions of his teachers. He was described as having a quick mind and better judgment than other children of his age.[136] Neilos loved to read saints' Lives from the time of his youth.[137] Simeon the New Theologian (d. 1022) was extremely serious in his studies and did not permit childish pursuits to distract him. He managed to master shorthand, grammar, and rhetoric, although his biographer tried to min-

131   *Life of Andrew of Crete,* 2–3, ed. Papadopoulos-Kerameus, Ἀνάλεκτα Ἱεροσολυμιτικῆς Σταχυο-λογίας, vol. 5 (above, n. 58), 170–71.

132   *The Life of Saint Peter of Atroa,* 3, in Laurent, *La Vie merveilleuse* (above, n. 80), 71.

133   *The Life of St. Andrew the Fool,* ed. L. Rydén (Uppsala, 1995), 13.

134   Ibid., 14, trans. 15.

135   *Life of Saint Nicholas of Sion,* 3, in Ševčenko and Patterson-Ševčenko (above, n. 85), 22.

136   *Life of Neilos the Younger,* ed. P. G. Giovanelli, *ΝΕΙΛΟΥ ΤΟΥ ΝΕΟΥ, testo originale Greco e studio introduttivo* (Grottaferrata, 1972), 48.

137   Ibid.

imize what might appear as ambition for worldly success.[138] Saint Maximos the Kausokalybites (ca. 1270–ca. 1365) was also smarter than his teachers.[139]

Unsurprisingly, precocious wisdom is frequently associated with future saints. Little Cyril/Constantine revealed his talent for learning and his intelligence early on. When he was seven years old, he had a vision of his future marriage. He saw young girls and was asked to choose one. He selected the most beautiful, called Sophia: the name means *wisdom,* explains the hagiographer, thus foretelling the boy's career as a philosopher.[140] As soon as he was entrusted to a schoolteacher, he astonished everyone with his excellent memory and was first in his class.[141] He was later sent to Constantinople, where he learned the subjects taught in the secondary curriculum, and went on to study philosophy, thus completing his education.

A taste for letters and the importance of learning were greatly emphasized in the middle Byzantine period. Unlike Saint Anthony the Great, who refused to learn letters because he wanted to avoid the company of other children and therefore was supposedly illiterate,[142] and unlike Benedict of Nursia, who ran away from Rome and from his studies to remain *indoctus,*[143] the little Byzantines of the medieval period were often praised for studying hard and for demonstrating intelligence. It seems that in Byzantium, literacy was a prerequisite for sainthood. Compared to their fellows, saints revealed a greater aptitude for their studies. In this competitive society, such ability was interpreted as a sign of divine election.

Only a few saints do not fit this mold. In one of his Lives, little Phokas is described as preferring to gaze at the sea rather than go to school.[144] His destiny was to save seamen from shipwrecks. Ioannikios kept pigs before becoming a

---

138 *Life of Simeon the New Theologian,* 2, ed. I. Hausherr, *Vie de Syméon le Nouveau Théologien* (Rome, 1928), 2–4.

139 *Life of Maximos the Kausokalybites by Theophanes,* 2, in F. Halkin, "Deux vies de S. Maxime le Kausokalybe, ermite au Mont Athos (XIVe s.)," *AB* 54 (1936): 68.

140 *Life of Cyril/Constantine,* in Dvornik, *Les légendes de Constantin et Méthode* (above, n. 67), 350.

141 Ibid., 351.

142 *Life of Saint Anthony,* 1, 2, in Bartelink, *Athanase d'Alexandrie, Vie d'Antoine* (above, n. 106), 130. The Coptic *Life* says only that "he did not wish to continue his writing lessons, wishing to stand apart from the ordinary activities of children."

143 Gregory the Great, *Dialogues,* 2, Prol., ed. A. de Vogüé, *Grégoire le Grand, Dialogues* (Paris, 1979), 126.

144 *Life of Phokas,* ed. C. Van de Vorst, "Saint Phocas," *AB* 30 (1911): 273.

soldier.[145] These two saints, however, were unusual. The ability to learn quickly was usually considered a sign of holiness, yet an inability to learn might lead to a miracle, as in the case of Saint Theodore of Sykeon, who found it difficult to learn the Psalms. After praying in front of the icon of the Savior, on the feast of Saint Christopher, he was suddenly able to memorize with ease.[146] Saint Meletios (d. 1110) had a hard time learning his letters when he was a child, but his hagiographer, Nicholas of Methone, transformed his eventual success into a miracle.[147]

All these childhood qualities are recorded in hagiographical accounts to explain how the early years of a saint presaged his or her particular vocation. Yet it seems clear that parents or family members also played a key role in transforming these somewhat standard qualities into the fabric of a saint. The Byzantines disagreed, however, on how much the role of the family influenced the making of a saint.

A Saint in the Family: A Matter of Chance or Hard Work?

For the ninth-century patriarch Methodios, a saint is a God-given gift, not made by humans. He does not believe that the education provided by parents is the key to making a saint. Education can create pious individuals, including nuns, monks, and clerics; but it is powerless, in his eyes, to create sanctity. In his *Life of Saint Euthymios of Sardis,* Methodios does not deny that some children are more innocent than others, better suited for study, and calmer in disposition than most, or that one can follow their spiritual progress from their early years until adulthood. However, he feels it is pointless to emphasize what is a matter of chance. Nobody can imitate being the parents of a saint, because no one can choose such a gift.[148]

This idea is confirmed by the fact that in a family of many children, there is usually (with memorable exceptions) only one saint. In the *Life of Michael*

---

145 *Life of Ioannikios* (*BHG* 935) by Sabas, 2, *AASS,* Nov. 2.1 (Brussels, 1984), 333. This detail is not included in the Life by the monk Peter (*BHG* 936).

146 *Life of Theodore of Sykeon,* 13, in Festugière, *Vie de Théodore de Sykéôn* (above, n. 88), 1:11–12.

147 Nicholas of Methone, *Life of Meletios of Myoupolis* (*BHG* 1247), ed. V. G. Vasiljevskij, "Νικολάου ἐκ Μεθώνης καὶ Θεοδώρου τοῦ Προδρόμου συγγραφέων τῆς ιβ' ἑκατονταετηρίδος βίοι Μελετίου τοῦ νέου," *Pravoslavnyj Palestinskij Sbornik,* 17 (St. Petersburg, 1886), 2–3; on the author, see C. Messis, "Deux versions de la meme 'vérité': Les deux Vies d'Hosios Meletios," in Odorico and Agapitos, *Les Vies de saints à Byzance,* (above, n. 2), 316–17.

148 J. Gouillard, "La vie d'Euthyme de Sardes († 831)," *TM* 10 (1987): 21–23.

Maleinos, one can read the story of the Virgin Mary appearing to a priest and holding four *maphoria* (veils) and three *soudaria* (napkins) and then announcing that she wants one of the *soudaria* returned. This vision is interpreted as the sign of Michael's vocation for the religious life and his divine election. If the special *soudarion* represents a boy, we can deduce that the *maphoria* represent the girls. Thus this vision announces a family of seven children, four girls and three boys, with only one child destined to become a saint.[149] In the Life of the three brothers David, Simeon, and George of Lesbos, we learn that their parents had four other children. Two were married in the hope of continuing the family line; two were sent to a monastery. Thus five out of the seven children were consecrated to God, and three became saints.[150] This is an exceptional case. The family of Luke of Steiris also had seven children, a figure characterized in the Vita as "a perfect number and one especially esteemed in Scripture."[151] In this ideal family, the third, fourth, and fifth children—one girl and two boys—entered monastic life, although only Luke became a saint. The Life describes him as "divine in every way" from childhood.[152] Monastic life or a life in the service of the church was not sufficient to create a saint, yet it was still preferable to remaining in the world.

Creating a Family Saint by Providing Role Models

The presence of a saint in a family certainly boosted the family's prestige.[153] The spiritual benefits could also be great, as family members could count on the prayers of their personal intercessor. The holy man or woman could pray for the family while on earth, and later the saint could intercede for family members in heaven. As a result, some children obviously received special attention to increase their chances of achieving sainthood. Some aristocratic families dedicated one or more of their children to this purpose. Sometimes they promoted

---

149   *Life of Michael Maleinos,* ed. L. Petit, "Vie de saint Michel Maléinos," *ROC* 7 (1902): 551–552 (repr., *Bibliothèque hagiographique orientale* 4 [Paris, 1903]).

150   *Life of David, Symeon, and George of Lesbos* (above, n. 83), 2, trans. Domingo-Forasté, in *Byzantine Defenders of Images,* 152.

151   *Life of Saint Luke of Steiris,* 2, in Connor and Connor, *The Life and Miracles of St. Luke of Steiris* (above, n. 104), 8–9.

152   Ibid., 8–9: ὁ θειότατος τὰ πάντα.

153   A. Laiou, "The General and the Saint: Michael Maleinos and Nikephoros Phokas," in *ΕΥΨΥΧΙΑ: Mélanges Hélène Ahrweiler,* ed. M. Balard et al. (Paris, 1998), 399–412.

a family member's claim to holiness with such methods as the composition of a Vita.[154]

There were guidelines to follow, because the church fathers had devoted their attention to this matter and provided recommendations on how to raise a child destined for a celibate life. The preparation for holiness naturally started at home, as early as possible.

Hagiographical narratives give the impression that parents who wanted a saint in the family created conditions that enhanced the child's chance at holiness. Spiritual advisers such as Jerome and John Chrysostom recommended that a chosen child be isolated from the world and its temptations. This was particularly salient advice for a child dedicated to God by his parents. The child should grow up in angelic fashion, his or her senses completely protected from improper words and dangerously seductive images.[155]

John Chrysostom certainly believed that parents had a role to play in making saints: he compares them to painters and sculptors.[156] In the *De inani gloria*, he compares the soul of a child to a city, which needs protection against robbers and invaders.[157] He warns parents to protect the child from unholy persons, by whom he means in particular gossiping servants and slaves.[158] He tells parents to take care to lead children toward a pious life by teaching them the value of virginity and detachment from wealth and glory.[159] Such an education should start at a very early age (ἐκ πρώτης ἡλικίας).[160] He realizes that he cannot ask parents to send all their children into the desert or prepare them for monastic life, although he very much wishes to do so: "Raise an athlete for Christ. I am not telling you to refuse his marrying or to send him into the desert or to prepare him to live the life of the monks. No, I am not saying that. I want that and I pray that all embrace it, but since it seems to be a burden, I will not constrain you."[161]

---

154   A.-M. Talbot, "Family Cults in Byzantium: The Case of St. Theodora of Thessalonike," in *ΛΕΙΜΩΝ: Studies Presented to Lennart Rydén on His Sixty-fifth Birthday,* ed. J. O. Rosenqvist (Uppsala, 1996), 49–69.

155   John Chrysostom, *De inani gloria,* 54–63, ed. Malingrey, *Jean Chrysostome: Sur la vaine gloire et l'éducation des enfants* (above, n. 49), 152–64.

156   Ibid., 106.

157   Ibid., 108–10.

158   Ibid., 128.

159   Ibid., 100.

160   John Chrysostom, *Vidua eligitur* (PG 51:330).

161   John Chrysostom, *De inani gloria,* 17, in Malingrey, *Jean Chrysostome,* 102–4: Θρέψον ἀθλητὴν τῷ Χριστῷ. Οὐ τοῦτο λέγω ὅτι γάμου ἀπάγαγε καὶ τὰς ἐρημίας ἀπόστειλον καὶ τὸν τῶν

His ideal would be a monastic upbringing for all Christian children, prepared by an ascetic lifestyle at home from infancy. To prepare the child for an ascetic life and free the soul for prayer—to keep the child as a "precious vessel," to quote from the *Life of Simeon Stylite the Younger*—it was important to create en environment of sensory deprivation.[162]

The seeds of holiness should first be planted at home, where parents could choose pious servants and tutors to raise their children. Even in an unholy environment such as the inn where Theodore of Sykeon grew up, the presence of a pious person could make a difference. Theodore was introduced to ascetic practices by a manservant living in his household who went to church to pray morning and night. He gave his money to churches and used to fast all the days of Lent, eating very little and only in the evening. The child, impressed by this behavior, started emulating the manservant, in spite of his mother's worries. He became very pious, running long distances in the countryside so as not to miss a saint's festival, spending his school lunch break meditating on the scriptures in a little church, and passing his nights in vigils.[163]

Role models were also important for little girls, as the Life of Saint Theodora of Thessalonike reveals. Her father entrusted her to the care of a relative living "a pure and immaculate" life. The writer stresses how much the undeveloped mind "adapts and conforms to the habit of the guardian who converses with it."[164]

Family Mentors from Monastic and Clerical Circles

The religious training of very young Byzantines was entrusted to their pious parents or, when the child was destined to enter the clergy or a monastic community, to a surrogate parent. A monastic uncle frequently plays a major role. The

---

μοναχῶν παρασκεύασον ἐλέσθαι βίον· οὐ τοῦτο λέγω. Βούλομαι μὲν τοῦτο καὶ πάντας ηὐχόμην καταδέξασθαι ἀλλ᾽ ἐπειδὴ φορτικὸν εἶναι δοκεῖ, οὐκ ἀναγκάζω.

162 *Life of Simeon Stylite the Younger*, 3, ed. P. van den Ven, *La Vie ancienne de S. Syméon Stylite le Jeune (521–592)* (above, n. 100), 1:5: σκεῦος ἅγιον καὶ παραθήκην τιμίαν; G. Gould, "Childhood in Eastern Patristic Thought: Some Problems of Theology and Theological Anthropology," in *The Church and Childhood,* ed. D. Wood, Studies in Church History 31 (Oxford, 1994), 39–52; B. Caseau, "Christian Bodies: The Senses and Early Byzantine Christianity," in *Desire and Denial in Byzantium,* ed. L. James (Aldershot, 1999), 101–9.

163 *Life of Theodore of Sykeon,* 6–7, in Festugière, *Vie de Théodore de Sykéôn* (above, n. 88), 1:5–7.

164 *Life of Saint Theodora of Thessalonike,* 4, ed. S. Paschalides, Ὁ Βίος τῆς ὁσιομυροβλύτιδος Θεοδώρας τῆς ἐν Θεσσαλονίκῃ (Thessalonike, 1991): 72–74; trans. Talbot, *Holy Women of Byzantium* (above, n. 105), 167.

archbishop and an uncle both pushed Saint Nicholas of Sion toward the clerical and monastic life: "When the most holy archbishop saw the features of the child, which were full of grace, he recognized in spirit that the child was to become the 'chosen vessel' of the Lord, and he took and blessed him and ordained him to the rank of the readers without receiving of him anything at all for the act of ordination." On another occasion, "on his way back from the metropolis of Myra, the child came to the *martyrium* of Saint John, to his uncle. And he bowed to the ground before him and was blessed by him. And the uncle gave him the book, which contained the Divine Liturgy and other prayers, for him to study."[165]

The uncle prayed over the child: "O our God, Thou Who art faithful in promises, steadfast in Thy gifts of grace and infinite in Thy love of man, Who hast summoned Thy handiwork through [Thy] summons, and hast gathered Thy servant for this angelic and heavenly life, give him the becoming life and virtuous and blameless ways, and may he be pleasing to Thee in all his works; so that, after a life of holiness, he may become worthy of the splendor of the saints and of the Kingdom of Thy Christ." Having thus prayed for him, he said to the boy, "My child, strive to take up the struggle of the [monastic] profession, since it has pleased God that you should rule over the glorious shrine of Holy Sion in prayers; and through you many will come to believe in Him."[166] This is a clear example of the transmission of authority from uncle to nephew, which is well attested in monastic and clerical circles. Many monastic churches were private foundations, and families considered it normal to have a relative in charge.[167]

The parents of Lazaros of Mount Galesion had some ambition for him: "The child was raised devoutly and piously by his parents in a way not unworthy of their hopes for him. When he became articulate in his speech and had reached the age of six, he was handed over by his parents to the aforesaid priest Leontios at the behest of his uncle Elias, who was a monk in the monastery of Kalathai."[168] The same uncle closely supervised his nephew's education: he sent him to study with a priest for three years and then with a notary for three more years. Eventually, he admitted him as his personal attendant in his monastic

---

165 *Life of Nicholas of Sion*, 5, in Ševčenko and Patterson-Ševčenko (above, n. 85), 26–27, 24–25.

166 Ibid., 26–27.

167 J. P. Thomas, *Private Religious Foundations in the Byzantine Empire* (Washington, D.C., 1987).

168 *The Life of Lazaros of Mount Galesion*, 3, in Greenfield, *The Life of Lazaros* (above, n. 94), 78–79.

community at Kalathai, where he taught the child, then twelve years old, about church matters.[169]

Some children traveled long distances to reach an uncle. Nicholas of Stoudios, for example, was sent from Crete to Constantinople, where his uncle was a monk at the Stoudios monastery.[170] From Saint Nicholas of Sion (d. 564) to Saint Niphon (d. 1411), the monastic uncle plays an important role model in the childhood of the future saint.

Families could ease the child's journey toward holiness. Yet, except for child martyrs, holiness was only germinating during childhood. It was not enough for a child to be holy during the first years of life if he or she did not fulfill the promises of early piety, self-control, and all the other virtues as an adult.

The New Testament presents the idea that children are especially receptive to holiness: "Unless you change and become like little children, you will never enter the Kingdom of God" (Matthew 18:3). In accounts from the nineteenth and twentieth centuries, visions of the Virgin Mary appear most often to children. Saint Bernadette Soubirous, a little peasant girl from southwest France, was favored with visions of the Virgin when she was young; she later became a nun. When she was canonized, it was precisely because she had been chosen in childhood to communicate the Virgin's words and smiles. Her innocence and truthfulness had made her worthy of the Virgin's trust. In adulthood, she led an ordinary monastic life.[171]

In modern times, we can adduce many more examples of saints who were chosen as privileged messengers when they were children. Unlike adults, children are supposed to be sexually pure, innocent, unlearned, and not manipulative. They can transmit God's messages without twisting them. Moreover, childhood is seen as a privileged time for mystical thoughts. This positive vision of childhood was not completely shared by the Byzantines, who clung to the philosophical idea that children were imperfect adults.[172] In their eyes, childhood was not a time of greater receptivity to spiritual matters or particular holiness. In most Byzantine hagiography, childhood is simply seen as a reflection of a saint's future life. Childhood is merely one phase in the continuum of the saint's life, through which holiness runs like a constant ray of sunlight. The Lives of saints convey to their audience admirable features in the saints, from their birth, or "from the

---

169 Ibid., 78–82.
170 *Life of Nicholas of Stoudios* (PG 105:870).
171 T. Taylor, *Bernadette of Lourdes: Her Life, Death and Visions* (London, 2003).
172 Bakke, *When Children Became People* (above, n. 25), 15–22.

time [the child] was in swaddling clothes," to quote the *Life of Saint Theodora of Thessalonike*.[173] Saints' Lives and secular biographies shared the same interest in providing significant details, intended to presage the future and give to a person's life a sense of direction and purpose. In hagiography, information on the child was meant to reveal that he or she possessed from the beginning the qualities deemed necessary for the type of holiness attained in adulthood.

Born of Christian parents and baptized at an early age, medieval children seldom experienced the kind of dramatic conversion described by Pelagia or Mary the Egyptian, or even of Augustine. They did not taste the forbidden fruit before becoming monks, nuns, or clerics. If we consider that saints were offered as models for admiration, but not necessarily for emulation, it is logical that the depiction of their childhood should describe ideal behavior for a future saint. Divine election must reveal itself in signs offered for interpretation, so that parents and friends can nurture the child's vocation. When a writer chose to develop the description of the saint's childhood, he often contrasted the holy child's tastes and deportment with those of ordinary children.

Hagiography as a Reflection of Society?

One point remains difficult to explain. The space allotted to the description of a saint's childhood ranges from a few lines to a number of pages. Are these differences significant? Do they reflect society's different perceptions of children in different historical periods? The importance of childhood in saints' Lives can serve as a measure of a society's attention to children only if we can prove that it is a common feature of contemporary literature and art. Can we draw a history of adult attitudes toward childhood through saints' Lives? If not, we should rather conclude that a writer's interest in a subject's childhood, revealed by the wealth of details provided on play, or food, or attitudes, is a matter of personal choice. What, then, was the purpose of including details of a saint's childhood?

The varying amount of information provided in saints' Lives is often due to the circumstances surrounding the writing of them. Medieval writers were not necessarily well informed on their heroes' lives. The writer of the *Life of Michael the Synkellos*, for example, did not know much about the years Michael lived in Palestine. He writes: "I do not know who were the parents of this most nota-

---

173 *Life of Saint Theodora of Thessalonike,* 4, in Paschalides, Ὁ Βίος τῆς ὁσιομυροβλύτιδος Θεοδώρας τῆς ἐν Θεσσαλονίκῃ, 72–74; trans. Talbot, *Holy Women of Byzantium,* 167.

ble man of God and citizen of Jerusalem."[174] The author of the *Life of Leontios of Jerusalem* had nothing to say concerning the saint's childhood: he wrote only that Leontios was "loved for the virtue which was his companion since childhood."[175] Some Lives were written so long after the saint's death that precise biographical details were lost, as no eyewitness or documents remained to provide anything but the framework of the story. Authors working soon after the saint's death were more likely to have adapted the topoi to the facts, particularly as the existence of eyewitnesses made it possible to verify the portrayal, whereas authors writing much later would find the facts covered increasingly by legend and be reluctant to deviate from the topoi.[176] For example, Clement of Ohrid was an important saint of the Bulgarian church for whom two archbishops of Ohrid felt the need to write a Vita. One lived in the thirteenth century, and the other was probably Theophylaktos, who lived in the eleventh century.[177] Both wrote at such a remove from the death of Clement in 916 that neither could provide his parents' names or personal data on the saint. Even when a writer had had personal contact with the saint, the writer usually belonged to a younger generation and had no direct knowledge of the youth of his hero. Yet the frequent efforts of hagiographers to reconstruct the early years of the saint suggest a desire to fulfill the expectations of readers, sometimes with vivid vignettes. When short on facts, writers sometimes added the missing elements by copying other, similar saints' Lives, recognizing that a good story started with childhood. They usually fell back on a reassuring and familiar canvas depicting the first signs of divine election.

Yet, as Lennart Rydén has noted, saints' Lives are extremely varied in their literary form, and this diversity is reflected in the attention they devote to the subject's early years.[178] As Alice-Mary Talbot observes, Philotheos Kokkinos describes the childhood of three of his heroes "in greater detail than is customary in saint's Lives, which often confine themselves to a single paragraph containing

---

174   Cunningham, *The Life of Michael the Synkellos* (above, n. 81), 45.
175   *Life of Leontios of Jerusalem*, 3, ed. D. Tsougarakis, *The Life of Leontios, Patriarch of Jerusalem: Text, Translation, Commentary* (Leiden, 1993), 35.
176   See Pratsch, *Der hagiographische Topos* (above, n. 10), 366–67.
177   P. Devos, "L'auteur de la vie de S. Clément d'Ochrida," *AB* 112 (1994): 32; I. G. Iliev, "The Manuscript Tradition and Authorship of the Long Life of St. Clement of Ohrid," *BSl* 53 (1992): 68–73.
178   L. Rydén, "Literariness in Byzantine Saints' Lives," in Odorico and Agapitos, *Les vies de saints à Byzance* (above, n. 2), 58; M. Van Uytfanghe, "L'hagiographie: Un 'genre' chrétien ou antique tardif?" *AB* 111 (2003): 145: "Tant l'auteur que le type de saint marquent l'ouvrage de leur propre empreinte individuelle."

such commonplaces as the child's learning of his first letters and his refusal to join his playmates in games."[179] Talbot argues that this is not just an individual concern but rather the literary expression of a particular taste for scenes of playing children during the Palaiologan period. She has contrasted the humanist tendencies of the late Byzantine era (especially in Thessalonike), which show an interest in the everyday activities of children, with texts of earlier periods, which are less likely to give details on childhood.[180] She links the artistic depiction of children at play with the longer descriptions of childhood in hagiography. Painters of this period indeed include scenes from everyday life in the cycles depicting the life of Christ, of the Theotokos, or of different saints. Female servants surround Mary as she gives birth, some bathing the newborn, others bringing the new mother a strengthening broth. Such details indeed reflect real events in a contemporary wealthy home. The artists placed Christ and Mary in their own surroundings and made them a part of their lives. The Last Supper is painted as a meal, with the addition of details not cited in the New Testament, such as cutlery and vegetables. Children naturally find a place in this realistic depiction of contemporary society.

Nevertheless, contemporary writers from the same cultural milieu could differ on the importance of childhood in their narratives of a saint's life. On the upbringing of the fourteenth-century saint Maximos the Kausokalybites, for example, his disciple Niphon writes only a short paragraph,[181] whereas Theophanes, *hegoumenos* of Vatopedi and later metropolitan bishop of Peritheorion, writes two full pages.[182] Both knew the saint, but they chose to emphasize different aspects of his life. Only in the text by Theophanes do we learn that the saint was inspired with longing for monastic life in a sanctuary of the Virgin. Theophanes also gives details on the saint's family, their desire for him to marry, and more details on his charitable activities as a young boy. Niphon simply notes his geographic origin and his inclination toward asceticism from an early age: "When he had learned his letters, he fled to the desert and the caves."[183]

Other, similar examples could be provided. The two Vitae of Athanasios of Athos, probably written fifty years apart, provide differing accounts of his

179   Talbot, "Children, Healing Miracles, Holy Fools" (above, n. 12), 52.
180   Ibid., 54.
181   Niphon, *Life of Maximos the Kausokalybites,* 2, ed. F. Halkin, "Deux Vies de S. Maxime le Kausokalybe" (above, n. 139), 43.
182   Theophanes, *Life of Maximos the Kausokalybites,* 2, in ibid., 67–69.
183   Niphon, *Life of Maximos the Kausokalybites,* 2, in ibid., 43.

childhood, one more informative than the other. The difference in the two authors' interest in the childhood of the saint is dependent not on the historical periods in which they lived but on their own choices. It is impossible to distinguish clear trends, periods of greater and less attention to childhood, based on saints' Lives. The silence of sources misled Philippe Ariès in his time: we should be careful not to judge a society based on the numbers of lines written on childhood, lest we risk dehumanizing people of the past.[184] Miracle stories, especially tales of healing, reveal a continuum in the number of children healed by the saints, and therefore in the continuous interest parents had in keeping their offspring alive and well. A study of childhood stories from these sources would indicate that the Byzantines of the eighth century had feelings for their children similar to those of the fourteenth; but that is a topic for another essay.

University of Paris–Sorbonne

Appendix: Saints' Lives Studied and Cited

Life of Aaron (*BHO* 863)
Life of Alypios (*BHG* 65)
Life of Andrew of Crete (*BHG* 114)
Life of Andrew the Fool (*BHG* 115z)
Life of Anthony by Athanasios (*BHG*)
Life of Athanasia of Aegina (*BHG* 180)
Life of Auxentios by Michael Psellos (*BHG* 203)
Life of Clement of Ohrid (*BHG* 355)
Life of Cyril/Constantine
Life of Cyrillos the Phileotes by Nicholas Kataskepenos (*BHG* 468)
Life of Daniel the Stylite (*BHG* 489)
Life of David, Simeon, and George (*BHG* 494)
Life of Elias the Younger, ed. Giuseppe Rossi Taibbi, *Vita di Sant'Elia il Giovane* (Palermo, 1962) (*BHG* 580)
Life of Euthymios of Sardis by Methodios (*BHG* 2145)
Life of Euthymios by Cyril of Scythopolis (*BHG* 647)
Life of Eutychios by Eustratios (*BHG* 657)

---

184   P. Ariès, *L'enfant et la vie familiale sous l'Ancien Régime* (Paris, 1960): "L'art médiéval, jusqu'au XIIe siècle, ne connaissait pas l'enfance ou ne tentait pas de la représenter; on a peine à croire que cette absence était due à la gaucherie ou à l'impuissance. On pensera plutôt qu'il n'y avait pas de place pour l'enfance dans ce monde" (23); "On ne pouvait s'attacher à ce qu'on considérait comme un éventuel déchet" (29); "Ce sentiment d'indifférence à l'égard d'une enfance trop fragile, où le déchet est trop grand n'est pas si loin, au fond de l'insensibilité des sociétés romaines ou chinoises qui pratiquaient l'exposition des enfants" (30).

Life of Ioannikios by Sabas (*BHG* 936)
Life of Irene, Abbess of Chrysobalanton (*BHG* 952)
Life of John the Almsgiver (*BHG* 888)
Life of Lazaros of Mount Galesion (*BHG* 979)
Life of Leontios of Jerusalem (*BHG* 985)
Life of Luke of Steiris (*BHG* 994)
Life of Marinos, ed. M. Richard (above, n. 105)
Life of Mary the Egyptian (*BHG* 1042)
Life of Matrona of Perge (*BHG* 1221)
Life of Maximos the Kausokalybites by Niphon (*BHG* 1236z)
Life of Maximos the Kausokalybites by Theophanes (*BHG* 1237)
Life of Melania the Younger (*BHG* 1240z)
Life of Meletios by Nicholas of Methone (*BHG* 1247)
Life of Meletios by Theodore Prodromos (*BHG* 1248)
Life of Methodios (*BHG* 1278)
Life of Michael Maleinos (*BHG* 1295)
Life of Michael the Synkellos (*BHG* 1296)
Life of Neilos of Rossano (*BHG* 1370)
Life of Nicholas of Bounaina (*BHG* 2309)
Life of Nicholas of Myra (*BHG* 1349)
Life of Nicholas of Sion (*BHG* 1347?)
Life of Nicholas of Stoudios (*BHG* 1365)
Life of Nikon the Metanoite (*BHG* 1366)
Life of Niphon (of Egypt) (*BHG* 1371z)
Life of Niphon the Athonite (*BHG* 1371)
Life of Pachomius (*BHG* 1396)
Life of Paul the Younger of Mount Latros (*BHG* 1474)
Life of Peter of Atroa (*BHG* 2364)
Life Retracta of Peter of Atroa (*BHG* 2365)
Life of Porphyry of Gaza (*BHG* 1570)
Life and Passion of Procopios (*BHG* 1577)
Life of Sabas by Cyril of Scythopolis (*BHG* 1608)
Life of Simeon the Holy Fool by Leontios of Neapolis (*BHG* 1677)
Life of Simeon Stylite the Elder by Theodoret (*BHG* 1678)
Life of Simeon Stylite the Younger (*BHG* 1689)
Life of Stephen the Younger (*BHG* 1666)
Life of Syncletica (*BHG* 1318w)
Life of Theodora of Thessalonike (*BHG* 1737, 1739)
Life of Theodore of Sykeon (*BHG* 1748)
Life of Theodosia of Constantinople (*BHG* 1774e)
Historia monachorum in Aegypto

THE MATERIAL CULTURE
OF CHILDHOOD IN BYZANTIUM

Brigitte Pitarakis

In memory of my *giagia*

Introduction and Methodology

MATERIAL CULTURE PROVIDES invaluable insights into the lives of the Byzantines, particularly aspects specific to age and gender. This paper aims to illustrate the daily life and environment of Byzantine boys and girls from early childhood (πρώτη ἡλικία), which lasted until the age of six to eight, and the "second age" (δευτέρα ἡλικία), which ended around the age of twelve for girls and might extend until the age of fourteen for boys.[1]

I offer many thanks to Ismail Karamut (director), Gülcan Kongaz (curator), and Turhan Birgili (head of the photographic department) at the Istanbul Archaeological Museums; Anastasia Drandaki, curator at the Benaki Museum in Athens; Jan Jordan, secretary of the Agora Excavations of the American School of Classical Studies in Athens; Dominique Bénazeth, conservateur en chef, à la section Copte, département des Antiquités égyptiennes, musée du Louvre; Christian Förstel, conservateur de la section grecque, département des Manuscrits, Bibliothèque nationale de France; and Sarantis Symeonoglu, curator of the Wulfing Collection, Kemper Art Museum, Washington University in St. Louis, for providing the required permits and photographs of objects from their collections. I am also indebted to Roberta Cortopassi, Véronique Dasen, Vincent Déroche, Maximilien Durand, Michael Featherstone, Sharon Gerstel, Ivana Jevtić, Catherine Jolivet-Lévy, Georges Kiourtzian, Garo Kürkman, Frederick Lauritzen, Christos Merantzas, Pagona Papadopoulou, Maria Parani, Halûk Perk, Fabien Tessier, Antonis Tsakalos, Alicia Walker, and Marianna Yerasimos for their generous help. My deep thanks are also due to the editors of this volume, Arietta Papaconstantinou and Alice-Mary Talbot, and to two anonymous readers for offering invaluable help.

1 For the ages of childhood, see N. Kalogeras, "What Do They Think about Children? Perceptions of Childhood in Early Byzantine Literature," *BMGS* 25 (2001): 7–8; idem, "Byzantine Childhood Education and its Social Role from the Sixth Century until the End of Iconoclasm " (PhD diss., University of Chicago, 2000), 133–34; A. Kiousopoulou, *Χρόνος και ηλικίες στη Βυζαντινή κοινωνία: Η κλίμακα των ηλικιών από τα αγιολογικά κείμενα της μέσης εποχής (7ος–11ος αι)*, Ιστορικό αρχείο ελληνικής νεολαίας 30 (Athens, 1997), 48, 53–54, 61–66; É. Patlagean, *Pauvreté économique et pauvreté sociale à Byzance: 4e–7e siècles* (Paris, 1977), 145, 151; eadem, "L'entrée dans l'âge adulte à Byzance aux XIIIe–XIVe siècles," in *Historicité de l'enfance et de la jeunesse / Ιστορικότητα τῆς*

At first sight, material evidence of childhood seems scarce. Objects handled by children were often destroyed; many were made of perishable materials. Shards from such objects that have been found in domestic contexts have usually been grouped with domestic wares, perhaps because the presence of children in the daily life of the Byzantines has often been overlooked by archaeologists. One has to also bear in mind that children could handle and play with objects that belonged to adults. After reviewing the state of research on the subject, I propose a method of investigation intended to extract more evidence from available sources.

State of Research

The subject of childhood in Graeco-Roman antiquity has attracted much scholarly attention during the past few years. Some important publications have also been devoted to the archaeology of childhood in the medieval West.[2] The material culture of childhood in Byzantium, however, has been almost totally ignored. The only objects that have prompted serious scholarly discussion are amulets related to safeguarding of childbirth,[3] and dolls from Egypt.[4] Some interesting

---

παιδικῆς ἡλικίας καὶ τῆς νεότητας: Actes du colloque international, Athènes 1–5 Octobre 1984 (Athens, 1986), 261–69. See also the article by Günter Prinzing in this volume.

2   For an overview of the literature up to 2001, see V. Dasen, D. Lett, M.-F. Morel, and C. Rollet, "Bibliographie récente sur l'histoire de l'enfance," *AnnalesDH* 102 (2001–2): 46–100. Among more recent works, I should mention J. Neils and J. H. Oakley, eds., *Coming of Age in Ancient Greece: Images of Childhood from the Classical Past,* exhibition catalogue (New Haven, 2003); J. E. Baxter, *The Archaeology of Childhood: Children, Gender and Material Culture* (New York, 2005); K. Mustakallio, J. Hanska, H.-L. Sainio, and V. Vuolanto, eds., *Hoping for Continuity: Childhood, Education and Death in Antiquity and the Middle Ages,* Acta Instituti Romani Finlandiae 33 (Rome, 2005).

3   See, for example, M.-H. Congourdeau, "Regards sur l'enfant nouveau-né à Byzance," *REB* 51 (1993): 161–76; I. Sorlin, "Striges et Géloudes: Histoire d'une croyance et d'une tradition," *TM* 11 (1991): 411–36; J. Spier, "Medieval Byzantine Magical Amulets and Their Tradition," *Journal of the Warburg and Courtauld Institutes* 56 (1993): 25–62. See also I. Kalavrezou, ed., *Byzantine Women and Their World,* exhibition catalogue (New Haven, 2003), 278–93, nos. 165–74.

4   See, for example, R. M. Janssen, "Soft Toys from Egypt," in *Archaeological Research in Roman Egypt: Proceedings of the Seventeenth Classical Colloquium of the Department of Greek and Roman Antiquities, British Museum, held on 1–4 December, 1993,* ed. D. M. Bailey, JRA Supplementary Series 19 (Ann Arbor, Mich., 1996), 231–39; C. Fluck, "Ägyptische Puppen aus römischen bis frührabischer Zeit: Ein Streifzug durch die Sammlungen des Ägyptischen Museums in Berlin, des Museums für angewandte Kunst in Wien und des Benaki Museums in Athen," in *Gedenkschrift Ulrike Horak (P. Horak),* ed. H. Harrauer and R. Pintaudi, Papyrologia Florentina 34 (Florence, 2004), 383–400.

examples, including objects such as children's footwear, jewelry, and toys, are included in the exhibition catalogue *Everyday Life in Byzantium*.[5] Another exhibition, *Spiel am Nil,* accompanied by a rich catalogue, documents toys from Byzantine Egypt.[6] A wider array of child-related objects scattered throughout numerous archaeological reports, discussed below, awaits comprehensive study. A multidisciplinary approach to the world of childhood, including references to material culture, can also be found in the essays devoted to childhood in the two consecutive volumes on late antique and Byzantine Christianity from the series *A People's History of Christianity*.[7]

Fields of Investigation, Chronological and Geographical Framework

For a broader picture of the material culture of Byzantine children, I attempt a multidisciplinary approach by combining direct and indirect sources (literary, epigraphic, iconographic, and archaeological) from a wide chronological and geographical range. This approach investigates various categories of manufactured objects (garments, jewelry, amulets, and toys), materials (metal, bone, glass, clay, wood, and textiles), and animals with which a child interacts. Indeed, the world of children was centered not only on objects specifically designed for them, but also on food and elements from their surroundings, such as animals, trees, rivers, and the sea. In many instances, I venture outside the chronological boundaries of the Byzantine Empire to compare this material with elements from Graeco-Roman antiquity, Islamic Egypt, and the folk traditions of modern Greece and Turkey. The geographical range of this study extends from Greece, the Balkans, and Anatolia to Egypt, where climatic conditions have permitted

---

5   D. Papanikola-Bakirtzi, ed., *Everyday Life in Byzantium,* exhibition catalogue (Athens, 2002), 112, no. 105 (leather sandal), 209, no. 238 (knucklebone), 416–19, nos. 526, 529, 534 (bracelets), 485–488, nos. 659–488 (amulets), 493–495, nos. 674–677 (toys).

6   H. Froschauer and H. Harrauer, eds., *Spiel am Nil: Unterhaltung im Alten Ägypten,* exhibition catalogue, Nilus: Studien zur Kultur Ägyptens und des Vorderen Orients 10 (Vienna, 2004).

7   C. B. Horn, "Children's Play as Social Ritual," in *A People's History of Christianity,* vol. 2, *Late Antique Christianity,* ed. V. Burrus (Minneapolis, 2005), 95–116; P. Hatlie, "The Religious Lives of Children and Adolescents," in *A People's History of Christianity,* vol. 3, *Byzantine Christianity,* ed. D. Krueger (Minneapolis, 2006), 182–200. See also the recent bibliography on the family and the child in late antiquity by L. A. Schahner, "Social Life in Late Antiquity: A Bibliographic Essay," in *Social and Political Life in Late Antiquity,* ed. W. Bowden, A. Gutteridge, C. Machado, and L. Lavan, Late Antique Archaeology 3.1 (Leiden, 2006), 55–57.

better preservation of textiles and wooden artifacts that may be associated with childhood.

The theoretical underpinning of this approach lies in the notion of *longue durée,* in accordance with Fernand Braudel's work on the time spans of history. Braudel points out the existence of structures that are stable through many generations. He sees material culture and mentalities as parts of slowly evolving structures (which also include organized behaviors, attitudes, and conventions), as opposed to circumstances and events of the short and medium term.[8]

The conceptual framework of this approach is further enriched by the recent publication of the papers of a colloquium that brought together historians and anthropologists to discuss the theme of kinship in the Greek world from antiquity to the present day. In the introductory paper, Alain Bresson posits the concept of *longue durée* in kinship structures, the elucidation of which requires a transhistorical perspective. He stresses the potential deficiencies of an approach that considers only continuities. To explain the recurrence of similar forms of organization in different periods, he presents two diametrically opposed views. In the first, the structures of kinship are ahistorical and have no relationship with the social milieu in which they evolve. In the second view, these structures are closely related to a specific social and cultural context. The recurrence of similar forms of organization in different societies is explained by the maintenance of external structuring elements that remain identical from one society to another.[9]

This study explores the structures of *longue durée* in the world of childhood (including popular religion, magic, funerary rites, celebration of birth, and certain aspects of playthings and games) and compares them with elements that are specific to Byzantine culture in order to illustrate the coexistence of the two. Folk tradition, for instance, has an interactive relationship with official religion.[10] My method consists in drawing comparisons between objects and practices from different periods in order to consider both their similarities (conti-

8   See F. Braudel, *Écrits sur l'histoire* (Paris, 1969), 41–83; trans. S. Matthews, *On History* (London, 1980). On *longue durée* in the techniques used by craftsmen, see the example of ivory in A. Cutler, *The Hand of the Master: Craftsmanship, Ivory, and Society in Byzantium (9th–11th Centuries)* (Princeton, N.J., 1994), 120.

9   See A. Bresson, "La parenté grecque en palindrome," in *Parenté et société dans le monde grec de l'Antiquité à l'Âge Moderne, colloque international, Volos (Grèce), 19–20–21 juin 2003,* ed. A. Bresson, M.-P. Masson, S. Perentidis, and J. Wilgaux (Bordeaux, 2006), 11–23.

10   My approach has benefited from the theoretical framework provided by J.-C. Schmitt, *Le corps, les rites, les rêves, le temps: Essais d'anthropologie médiévale* (Paris, 2001), 129–52.

nuities) and their differences (discontinuities).[11] Through such comparisons one may develop a more refined system of dating objects that demonstrate stability in their shape and technique of manufacture through the ages. In this way, it may be possible to identify the hand of a Byzantine craftsman, the clay whistle of a Byzantine boy, or the doll of a girl from Byzantine or Fatimid Egypt, or to enter into the spirit of a child who takes pleasure in imitating the divine liturgy in his games.

Parental Affection as a Motive in the Production of Material Culture for Children

I also wish to introduce the idea of parental affection as a motive in the production of material culture for children. This issue has been debated since the pioneering work of Philippe Ariès, who presents an image of medieval parents as being less emotionally tied to children than modern parents are.[12] However, Ariès's point is not really that parents were indifferent or hostile to their children in the past, but that the idea of childhood is a modern invention. In the Middle Ages, he says, parents saw children as adults in the making, not as individuals with a distinct experience of life and a developing understanding of the world. Ariès still remains a major source in childhood studies, but recent literature tends to present a more positive image of Western medieval childhood.[13] Already in 1997, in their innovative synthesis on this subject, Danièle Alexandre-Bidon and Didier Lett seemed to bring an end to the debate over the disinterest of medieval parents in their children and opened new directions of research.[14] In a similar manner, Nicholas Orme, in his book on medieval children published in 2001, offers portraits of loving, cherishing parents and caregivers and of happy children absorbed in their play.[15] Recent studies devoted to the image of children in early Christian and Byzantine literature tend to portray

11   For a broad approach to continuity and discontinuity in this period, see A. Kazhdan and A. Cutler, "Continuity and Discontinuity in Byzantine History," *Byzantion* 52 (1982): 429–78.
12   P. Ariès, *L'enfant et la vie familiale sous l'Ancien Régime* (Paris, 1960).
13   See discussion in J. Clarke, "Histories of Childhood," in *Childhood Studies: An Introduction,* ed. D. Wyse (Malden, Mass., 2004), 3–7. In his lengthy preface to the 1973 reprint of his book, Ariès responded to the general criticism of his views by moderating his position. Seven years after that, he admitted that he should have been better informed about the Middle Ages, to which his book devotes relatively limited attention. See "L'enfant à travers les siècles," interview with P. Ariès by M. Winock, *L'histoire* 19 (January 1980): 86.
14   D. Alexandre-Bidon and D. Lett, *Les enfants au Moyen Âge, Ve–XVe siècles* (Paris, 1997).
15   N. Orme, *Medieval Children* (New Haven, 2001).

children as different from miniature adults and to stress the existence of close and loving family relationships.[16]

The intense emotions provoked by the desire for a child, the struggle of parents to keep their infants alive, healthy, and well-fed, and their strong involvement in their children's education are constant themes in hagiographic literature that illustrate the value of children.[17] Traces of parental affection may also be detected in a variety of sources: for instance, the use of the diminutive form "-ακις," as in Θεοδωράκις, Παυλάκις, Ῥουφινάκις, and Στεφανάκις, in Early Byzantine funerary inscriptions.[18] Patterns of gestures of parental protection are an additional type of evidence in visual material. The hand of a parent (or a saint) gently placed on the shoulder of a child is an eloquent example. It appears repeatedly in the set of dedicatory mosaics from the basilica of Saint Demetrios of Thessalonike, the suggested datings of which range between the sixth and the late seventh century.[19] It is a frequent pattern in the thirteenth- and fourteenth-century iconography of the schooling of Saint Nicholas.[20] Escorted by his mother (or less frequently by his father or both parents), who rests her hand above his shoulder or

16   A. Moffatt, "The Byzantine Child," *Social Research* 53–54 (1986): 705–23, esp. 707, 710, 718, 723; G. Clark, "The Fathers and the Children," in *The Church and Childhood,* ed. D. Wood, Studies in Church History 31 (Oxford, 1994), 1–27; Kiousopoulou, *Χρόνος καὶ ἡλικίες,* 87–95; O. M. Bakke, *When Children Became People: The Birth of Childhood in Early Christianity* (Minneapolis, 2005), 1–13; A. Kaldellis, *Mothers and Sons, Fathers and Daughters: The Byzantine Family of Michael Psellos* (Notre Dame, Ind., 2006), 19–21, 111–17, 157–61.

17   Examples from hagiographic sources depicting caring parents concerned with the well-being and education of their children are discussed in Kiousopoulou, *Χρόνος καὶ ἡλικίες,* 67–73; see also Kalogeras, "What Do They Think about Children?" (above, n. 1), 11–13. A wealth of material on the sorrow caused by a child's sickness and the fear of losing the child is found in the seventh-century Life of Saint Artemios; see *The Miracles of St. Artemios,* ed. and trans. V. S. Crisafulli and J. W. Nesbitt (Leiden, 1997), esp. 94–95 (miracle 10), 154–57 (miracle 28). On the date of the composition of the text, see the review by V. Déroche in *REB* 56 (1998): 286–89.

18   See discussion in G. Kiourtzian, *Recueil des inscriptions grecques chrétiennes des Cyclades: De la fin du IIIe au VIIe siècle après J.-C.,* Travaux et mémoires du Centre de recherche d'histoire et civilisation de Byzance. Monographies 12 (Paris, 2000), 167, no. 97.

19   See C. Hennessy, "Iconic Images of Children in the Church of St. Demetrios, Thessaloniki," in *Icon & Word: The Power of Images in Byzantium; Studies Presented to Robin Cormack,* ed. A. Eastmond and L. James (Aldershot, 2003), 157–72.

20   In the earliest-known illustration of the episode, on a late twelfth-century icon from Sinai, the young Nicholas is accompanied by his father, who follows behind without touching the child. See N. Patterson-Ševčenko, *The Life of Saint Nicholas in Byzantine Art* (Turin, 1983), 70–75. The schooling of Saint Nicholas is also shown on a thirteenth-century marble relief panel from the Church of the Dormition of the Virgin on the hill of Episkopi in Volos; see R. Lange, *Die byzantinische Reliefikone* (Recklinghausen, 1964), 115–17, fig. 44; E. Antonopoulos, "Παιδαριογέρον: ἡ ἀπεικόνιση τῆς πρώιμης σοφίας," in *Οἱ χρόνοι τῆς ἱστορίας γιὰ μιὰ ἱστορία τῆς παιδικῆς ἡλικίας καὶ τῆς νεότητας* (Athens, 1998), 224 and fig. 7.

grasps his hand in a protective gesture, the little boy waves a writing tablet in one hand. The basket holding the writing implements is either in his other hand or carried by his accompanying parent.[21] The liveliness of the scene and the precision of the details of material objects suggest inspiration by everyday reality. Another gesture with similar overtones is the maternal hand placed above the head of a child in a sign of protection. It is attested in a dedicatory panel from the thirteenth-century decoration of the church of Karşı Kilise, Gülşehir, Cappadocia (1212), showing a woman named Irene, who stands between her two little daughters, Kale and Mary.[22]

Explicit demonstrations of parental love are also attested in both literary and visual sources. One example is the well-known funerary oration by Michael Psellos to his daughter Styliane, who died at the age of nine.[23] A similar effusion of tenderness is found in his encomium to his four-month-old grandson.[24] His correspondence with his friends contains further allusions to his passionate attachment not only to his own children and grandchildren but also to those of his close relations.[25] Psellos's evocation of his own childhood in his funerary oration to his mother, Theodote, presents a more ambivalent view of displays of

21   Patterson-Ševčenko claims to identify a wicker basket that may have served for his lunch in *Life of Saint Nicholas,* 73 and n. 12.

22   C. Jolivet-Lévy, "Images et espace culturel à Byzance: L'exemple d'une église de Cappadoce (Karşı Kilise, 1212)," in *Le sacré et son inscription dans l'espace à Byzance et en Occident: Études comparées,* ed. M. Kaplan (Paris, 2001), 167–68, fig. 3, pl. 2; eadem, *La Cappadoce médiévale: Images et spiritualité* (Paris, 2001), 82.

23   *Bibliotheca graeca Medii Aevi,* vol. 5, *Pselli miscellanea,* ed. K. N. Sathas (Paris, 1876), 62–87. See discussion in C. Jouanno, "Michel Psellos: Epitaphios logos à sa fille Stylianè morte avant l'heure du mariage; Réflexion sur le cadavre défiguré et le rôle du corps dans le travail du deuil," *Kentron* 10 (1994): 95–107. See now the English translation by Kaldellis, *Mothers and Sons* (above, n. 16), 111–38. On Styliane, see also the essay by A.-M. Talbot in this volume.

24   *Michaelis Pselli Scripta Minora,* vol. 1, *Orationes et dissertationes,* ed. E. Kurtz and F. Drexl (Milan, 1936), 77–81; A. R. Littlewood, *Michaelis Pselli oratoria minora* (Leipzig, 1985), 152–55 (encomium 38); Kaldellis, *Mothers and Sons,* 162–65.

25   See Psellos's letter to Konstantinos, nephew of the patriarch Michael Keroularios, when his son Romanos was born: "Yet my character betrays me, as it is disposed in a nonphilosophical manner toward the natural affections. Thus I become excited about newborn babies, especially if they are dearest and of dearest parents, and when I am faced with their delights and charms": Sathas, *Bibliotheca graeca Medii Aevi,* 5:409–12, letter 157; A. Leroy-Molinghen, "La descendance adoptive de Psellos," *Byzantion* 39 (1969): 290–91, 302–6; Kaldellis, *Mothers and Sons,* 173. Psellos also exudes tenderness when he speaks about the little prince Constantine, son of Michael VII Doukas, in his *Chronography,* book 7, ch. 12, *Michel Psellos: Chronographie ou Histoire d'un siècle de Byzance (976–1077),* vol. 2, ed. and trans. É. Renauld (Paris, 1967), 178–79; *Michele Psello: Imperatori di Bisanzio (Cronografia),* ed. and Italian trans. S. Impellizzeri, U. Criscuolo, and S. Ronchey (Milan, 1984), 376–77.

affection. In accordance with the rules of good upbringing and in order not to spoil her son, Psellos's mother restrained her expressions of love and took the child in her arms and kissed him only when she thought he was asleep.[26]

Beyond their theological and philosophical implications and their multiple layers of meanings, these texts illustrate the use of children in depicting emotion, a favorite theme in eleventh-century literature.[27] For instance, Basil Kekaumenos, a contemporary of Psellos, created a funerary poem for his friend the vestarch Anastasios Lizix, whose son had just died.[28] In a very personal tone, the poet addresses the father of the deceased and offers an emotional picture of the loving relationship the latter will maintain with his orphaned grandchildren.

> You desire to see him, though he is dead?
> Embrace his children, do not look further.
> Even if the infants seem to you young and small,
> They will rather drive you, their grandfather,
> To pity, simply by their baby stammering.
> Perhaps they also seem to feel
> Your sensitive and kind disposition toward them.
> They crawl towards you as suppliants,
> And eagerly embrace your legs.
> Thus if you offer your hand for a bit,
> And stretch out your leg for them as a ladder,
> You will see them running up to your neck,
> So that they may offer more kisses.
> Open the breadth of your kindness to them,
> Offer them affection daily,

26 Sathas, *Bibliotheca graeca Medii Aevi*, 5:17–18; Kaldellis, *Mothers and Sons*, 65–66.

27 In a letter from Psellos to one of his closest friends, John Doukas (Sathas, *Bibliotheca graeca Medii Aevi*, 5:307–8, letter 72), he announces with great joy the birth of his grandson. To explain his emotion at the moment of birth, Psellos reveals the feminine side of himself that he depicts elsewhere as gentleness, delicacy, and softness. See discussion in E. N. Papaioannou, "Michael Psellos' Rhetorical Gender," *BMGS* 24 (2000): 133–46; F. Lauritzen, "A Courtier in the Women's Quarters: The Rise and Fall of Psellos," *Byzantion* 77 (2007): 251–66.

28 Psellos also wrote a funerary poem for Anastasios Lizix, who also appears in two of Psellos's letters. See P. Gautier, "Monodies inédites de Michel Psellos," *REB* 36 (1978): 86–91 (esp. 89), 105–12; *Michaelis Pselli Scripta Minora*, vol. 2, *Epistulae*, ed. E. Kurtz and F. Drexl (Rome, 1941), 150–51, letter 127; 230–31, letter 202.

Revealed to them now by fate, not as their grandfather, but rather as
     their father
Because of your strong love for them.[29]

The social framework of this attitude toward children is provided by the new aristocratic and intellectual trends in the Byzantine capital, which found expression in a new emphasis on lineage, family ties, and friendship.[30] Out of this context grew an increased interest in images of emotion and tenderness in religious imagery. An outstanding example is provided by the infancy cycle of the Virgin Mary, which depicts the passionate embrace of Joachim and Anna in the

29   Many thanks to Frederick Lauritzen, who drew my attention to this poem and to whom I owe the new edition and English translation (slightly modified) of this passage. See S. G. Mercati, *Collectanea Byzantina,* vol. 1 (Bari, 1970), 341. The title of the poem is: στίχοι ἐπιτάφιοι εἰς τὸν βέσταρχον Ἀναστάσιον ὕπατον καὶ κριτὴν τὸν Λίζικα τὸν διὰ τοῦ ἁγίου καὶ μεγάλου σχήματος Ἀθανάσιον μετονομασθέντα γενόμενοι παρὰ Βασιλείου πρωτοσπαθαρίου ἀσηκρῆτις καὶ κριτοῦ ἐπὶ τοῦ ἱπποδρομίου τοῦ Κεκαυμένου, ὧν ἡ ἐπιγραφή ἐστιν οὕτως.
Lines run as follows:

ποθεῖς ἐκεῖνον τὸν τεθνηκότα βλέπειν;
τοὺς παῖδας ἀγκάλιζε, μὴ ζήτει πλέον.
κἂν καὶ νεογνὰ τὰ βρέφη καὶ μικρά σοι,
πλὴν ἀλλὰ τὸν πάππον σε μᾶλλον ἑλκύσει
πρὸς οἶκτον αὐτῶν ἐκ μόνων ψελλισμάτων.
δοκοῦσιν ἴσως αἰσθάνεσθαι καὶ τόδε
τῆς σῆς πρὸς αὐτὰ συμπαθοῦς εὐσπλαγχνίας.
καὶ δὴ προσερπύζουσιν ὥσπερ ἱκέται (ἱκέτῃ in Mercati)
καὶ σοὺς περιπλέκουσιν ἐκθύμως πόδας.
ἂν οὖν ὀρέξῃς καὶ ποσῶς σου τὴν χέρα,
τούτοις ἁπλώσῃς ὡς κλίμακα τὸν πόδα (<*> in Mercati)
ἴδῃς ἀνατρέχοντας μέχρι τῆς δέρης.
ὡς ἔμπλεω δείξωσι τῶν φιλημάτων·
τούτοις ἄνοιγε χρηστότητος τὸ πλάτος,
τούτοις τὸ φίλτρον προστίθει καθ᾽ ἡμέραν,
οὐ πάππος αὐτῶν ἢ πατὴρ πρὸς τῆς τύχης
δεικνύμενος νῦν ἐκ σφοδρᾶς τῆς ἀγάπης.

The only reference to this poem is in Gautier, "Monodies inédites," 89.
30   See A. P. Kazhdan and A. Wharton Epstein, *Change in Byzantine Culture in the Eleventh and Twelfth Centuries* (Berkeley, 1985), 102–5, 130–32. See also discussion in Kiousopoulou, *Χρόνος καὶ ἡλικίες* (above, n. 1), 94–95. In this period, concern and love are also expressed through the exchange of letters. See M. Mullett, "The Classical Tradition in the Byzantine Letter," in *Byzantium and the Classical Tradition,* ed. M. Mullett and R. Scott (Birmingham, 1981), 75–93, esp. 82; M. Mullett, "Byzantium: A Friendly Society?" *Past and Present* 118 (1988): 3–25; P. Hatlie, "Redeeming Byzantine Epistolography," *BMGS* 20 (1996): 213–48. On letters as evidence of a society that valued friendship and connections, see also A. Cameron, *The Byzantines* (Oxford, 2006), esp. 135.

Figure 1   Chora Church,
Constantinople (1316/21), Caresses
of the Virgin, inner narthex, vault of
the second bay (photo: courtesy of
Dumbarton Oaks, neg. no. K87-53-53)

scene of the conception of Mary and the image of the Virgin caressed by her parents (*kolakeia*), highlighting a moment of tenderness between parents and a little child (fig. 1).[31] The motif of cheeks pressing against each other in a gesture of embrace, a beloved feature of the art of the twelfth century, reflects the continuity of the rhetorical framework of previous centuries. Indeed, although images of the Virgin caressed by her parents do not seem to be attested before the twelfth century, the precursors of this theme appear in the imperial art of the Macedonian period. For instance, the tender embrace of Mary and Jesus, with Joseph watching alongside them, is shown in the depiction of the young Christ among the doctors in the synagogue at Jerusalem, in the ninth-century illustrations of the homilies of Gregory of Nazianzos,[32] and the image of the *kolakeia* of David on the sumptuous ivory casket of the Palazzo Venezia in Rome.[33]

31   See J. Lafontaine-Dosogne, *Iconographie de l'enfance de la Vierge dans l'Empire byzantin et en Occident,* vol. 1 (Brussels, 1992), 82–89 (conception of the Virgin), 124–28 (the Virgin caressed by her parents).

32   Par. gr. 510, fol. 165r. See L. Brubaker, *Vision and Meaning in Ninth-Century Byzantium: Image as Exegesis in the Homilies of Gregory of Nazianzus* (Cambridge, 1999), fig. 21, 83–84.

33   The dating of the Palazzo Venezia casket is disputed. Depending on the identification of the scene and the emperor depicted on the lid of the casket (either Basil I [867–886] or Leo VI [886–912]), the casket has been dated to the years shortly after 867 (I. Kalavrezou, "A New Type of Icon:

The interaction between rhetorical literature and images, especially in a period of growing interest in the depiction of details from activities of everyday life and domestic interiors, may offer a closer insight into the mentality of Byzantine society and the behavioral code of the imperial court.[34] Expressions of emotion toward children in letters, poems, and images alike seem to be more than an artificial rhetorical exercise. The tender gestures illustrating Mary's interaction with her parents in the illustrations of her infancy cycle, for instance, are probably intended to emphasize her human nature, but at the same time one may view them as archetypes of family behavior in contemporary society.[35]

Hagiography, rhetorical texts, and iconography all convey the same idea of strong emotional bonds between Byzantine parents and their children. Whether explicit or implied, spontaneous or artificial, disinterested or motivated by social, economic, and practical reasons, parental affection is well attested in Byzantium. This study traces this theme in three aspects of Byzantine childhood: children's jewelry and garments, which served as adornment and protection in both this life and the afterlife; the role of food in celebrations of childbirth and in the formation of emotional ties between parents and offspring; and the toys and playthings of Byzantine children.

Adornment and Protection

Byzantine parents were profoundly concerned with the health and well-being of their progeny. Those of the upper class tended to exhibit their pride and status by adorning their offspring with jewelry and luxurious garments. This tendency was closely associated with a desire to protect the child, which cannot be

---

Ivories and Steatites," in *Constantine VII Porphyrogenitus and His Age: Second International Byzantine Conference, Delphi, 22–26 July 1987* [Athens, 1989], 387–94; H. Maguire, "The Art of Comparing in Byzantium," *ArtB* 70, no. 1 [1988]: 88–103) or to 898 or 900 (A. Cutler and N. Oikonomides, "An Imperial Byzantine Casket and Its Fate at a Humanist's Hands," *ArtB* 70, no. 1 [1988]: 77–87; Cutler, *Hand of the Master* [above, n. 8], 201–3).

34 With regard to the link between rhetorical literature and images, see H. Maguire, *Art and Eloquence in Byzantium* (Princeton, N.J., 1981); idem, *Rhetoric, Nature and Magic in Byzantine Art* (Aldershot, 1998); idem, *Image and Imagination in Byzantine Art* (Aldershot, 2007). See also H. Belting, *Bild und Kult: Eine Geschichte des Bildes vor dem Zeitalter der Kunst* (Munich, 1990), esp. 292–314; Engl. trans. by E. Jephcott, *Likeness and Presence: A History of the Image before the Era of Art* (Chicago and London, 1994), esp. 261–81; G. Dagron, *Décrire et peindre: Essai sur le portrait iconique* (Paris, 2007), esp. 83–103.

35 For a discussion on images from the infancy cycle of the Virgin as a source for the representation of ordinary people, see Kalavrezou, *Byzantine Women and their World* (above, n. 3), 15–16.

dissociated from an expression of love and affection. The tendency to adorn children with jewelry and beautiful garments was also perpetuated in rituals of death and burial.

The Dress of Byzantine Children

GARMENTS

Byzantines swaddled their newborn infants with soft woolen bandages as the Romans did, and the practice persisted in early twentieth-century Greece and Anatolia. The principal aim of swaddling the child was to shape the body and ensure straight limbs, but it also ensured that the child was warm and protected from accidents. From Michael Psellos's encomium to his grandson we see that as early as the age of four months, some children preferred other garments. Psellos writes: "Whenever your mother adorned your head or dressed you in a fancy outfit, you wriggled and turned in every direction, delighting in and preening yourself on account of your costume."[36] The passage reflects the eagerness of parents of high status, especially mothers, to dress their progeny in precious garments. In a poem devoted to Alexios, the son of the *sebastokrator* Andronikos, brother of Manuel I, Theodore Prodromos describes the infant's golden garments, studded with precious stones and pearls.[37] Unfortunately, none of these precious garments have been preserved.

Byzantine iconography offers images of holy children—among them Christ, the Virgin, and saints such as Nicholas—clad in loose-fitting, brightly colored short dresses, highlighted with blue and red borders and geometrical motifs.[38] A more precise image of everyday reality may be provided by the representations of

36 Kurtz and Drexl, *Michaelis Pselli Scripta Minora* (above, n. 24), 1:79–80; Littlewood, *Michaelis Pselli oratoria minora* (above, n. 24), 154; Kaldellis, *Mothers and Sons* (above, n. 16), 164, chap. 154. Such an interest in costume is implausibly precocious for a four-month-old infant: rather we have here a projection onto the child of the views of an adult. This device is common in Psellos and recurs in his *Chronographia*: see, for example, the transposition of Michael VII's (1071–1077) qualities to his little son Constantine (*Chronographia*, book 7, chap. 13, ed. and trans. É. Renauld, 179; ed. S. Impellizzeri, U. Criscuolo and Ital. trans. S. Ronchey, 378–79).

37 "τὰ παιδικὰ καὶ βρεφικὰ καὶ σπαργανώδη ῥάκη χρυσᾶ καὶ λιθοκόλλητα καὶ βρίθοντα μαργάροις," Theodore Prodromos, *Historische Gedichte,* ed. W. Hörandner (Vienna, 1974), 410, no. 44.151–55. On this poem, see Kazhdan and Epstein, *Change in Byzantine Culture* (above, n. 30), 107.

38 For illustrations of the schooling of Saint Nicholas, see Patterson-Ševčenko, *The Life of Saint Nicholas* (above, n. 20), 183, 199, 204, 216, 228, 242, 246, 261, 277, 296, 306, 311, 321, 336. The Virgin dressed as an infant is only found in the scene of the caresses; see, for example, the thirteenth-century painted panel in the church of Saint Clement in Ochrid. Lafontaine-Dosogne, *Iconographie de l'enfance de la Vierge* (above, n. 31), 126 and fig. 21.

Figure 2 Chora Church, Constantinople (1316/21), wrestling boys with floating mantles, outer narthex, vault of the first bay, southeastern pendentive (photo: courtesy of The Image Collections and Fieldwork Archives, Dumbarton Oaks Research Library and Collection, neg. no. K114-50-40)

ordinary children dressed in short tunics, left loose or belted at the waist (fig. 2). The tunics often have a decorated collar and decorative bands on the sleeves and the shoulders. Sometimes a mantle is draped across the front of the body.[39]

Donors' portraits in church decoration also illustrate the garments of children of higher status. One example is a painted funerary panel found in the outer narthex of the Chora church in Constantinople, dated some time after 1330.[40] The upper part of the panel has been destroyed. It depicts a family with two standing parents flanking a child. The parents' garments are adorned with the Palaiologan monogram, indicating that they were related to the imperial family. The child wears an ankle-length, tight-fitting caftan buttoned down the front; around his waist is a girdle, knotted at the front, from which a kerchief is suspended. The caftan is decorated with a diaper pattern in gold leaf on a red ground. The white kerchief has a gold border and gold fringes. This is the

---

39   The book by C. Hennessy, *Images of Children in Byzantium* (Burlington, Vt., 2008) is a valuable tool for investigating children's costume. See also D. Mouriki, "Revival Themes with Elements of Daily Life in Two Palaeologan Frescoes Depicting the Baptism," in *Okeanos: Studies Presented to Ihor Ševčenko on his Sixtieth Birthday by his Colleagues and Students,* ed. C. Mango and O. Pritsak, Harvard Ukrainian Studies 7 (Cambridge, Mass., 1983), 458–87; E. Antonopoulos, "Prolégomènes à une typologie de l'enfance et de la jeunesse dans l'iconographie byzantine," in *Historicité de l'enfance et de la jeunesse,* 271–87.

40   Tomb F at the fourth bay of the outer narthex. P. A. Underwood, *The Kariye Djami,* vol. 1, *Historical Introduction and Description of the Mosaics and Frescoes* (New York, 1966), 288–92; ibid., vol. 3, *Plates 335–553, The Frescoes,* 546–47.

traditional male garment of this period for both adults and children.[41] The layout of the panel and the representation of the child dressed in the manner of the adults follow the conventional representations of the imperial family.[42]

It is to the dry climate of Egypt that we owe the preservation of many children's garments. They may be dated between the fourth and the ninth century; more precise dating is problematic. The most frequently found garment is a miniature version of the standard long-sleeved adult tunic.[43] Made of wool or linen, the tunic was woven from sleeve to sleeve in one piece and sewn together at the sides. A slit was left for the neck. The decorative patterns do not differ much from those of adult tunics. Most common are representations of birds and animals or vegetal and floral ornaments, though more elaborate designs, such as dancing female figures, are also found. The brown or cream color of the background is usually highlighted with tapestry strips (*clavi*) on the front and the sleeves, with two round patches on the shoulders.[44] More elaborate examples have also been found with a tapestry panel around the neck.[45]

41   For a discussion of aristocratic costume in this period, see M. Parani, *Reconstructing the Reality of Images: Byzantine Material Culture and Religious Iconography (11th–15th Centuries)* (Leiden, 2003), 59–67. See also *The City of Mystras: Byzantine Hours; Works and Days in Byzantium,* exhibition catalogue (Athens, 2001), 143–47.

42   See, for example, the imperial portrait of Alexios I Komnenos, his wife Irene Doukaina, and their son John II in the Barberini psalter (Vat. Barb. Gr. 372, fol. 5v) and the portrait of Manuel II Palaiologos, his wife Helen, and their three sons, John, Theodore, and Andronikos, in the Paris manuscript of the works of Dionysios the Areopagite, dated between 1403 and 1405. See I. Spatharakis, *The Portrait in Byzantine Illuminated Manuscripts* (Leiden, 1976), 26, 140, figs. 7 and 93. For the first example, see also A. Cutler and J.-M. Spieser, *Byzance médiévale: 700–1204* (Paris, 1996), 351, fig. 278; for the second, see *Byzance: L'art byzantin dans les collections publiques françaises,* exhibition catalogue (Paris, 1992), 463, no. 356.

43   See F. Calament, *La révélation d'Antinoé par Albert Gayet: Histoire, archéologie, muséographie,* Institut Français d'Archéologie Orientale, Bibliothèque d'Études coptes 18, no. 1 (Cairo, 2005), 1:291–93.

44   Two examples made from linen and wool at the Louvre and the Musée Dobrée in Nantes, respectively, are dated between the third or fourth and the fifth centuries. The first supposedly comes from the Fayyum, while the supposed provenance of the second is Antinoe. See *L'art copte en Égypte: 2000 ans de christianisme,* exhibition catalogue (Paris, 2000), 195, no. 218; *Au fil du Nil: Couleurs de l'Égypte chrétienne,* ed. M.-H. Santrot, M.-H. Rutschowscaya, D. Bénazeth, and C. Giroire, exhibition catalogue (Paris, 2001), 63, no. 29.

45   A luxurious example dated to the seventh or eighth century is in a private collection in Jerusalem. See A. Baginski and A. Tidhar, *Textiles from Egypt: 4th–13th Centuries C.E.,* exhibition catalogue (Jerusalem, 1980), 86, no. 110. Another example dated to the sixth or seventh century is in Berlin. See *Ägypten Schätze aus dem Wüstensand: Kunst und Kultur der Christen am Nil,* exhibition catalogue (Wiesbaden, 1996), 274, no. 314. A fragmentary example dated to the sixth or seventh century is at the musée départemental des Antiquités, Rouen. See M. Durand and F.

On an elegant tunic (now in Munich) dated to the fourth or fifth century, which, judging from its size, was probably worn by a toddler between one and three years of age, five small tapestry panels with birds are arranged in a cruciform pattern on the chest, and a red cord, extending from each shoulder, is sewn above the *clavi*.[46] Besides its decorative purpose, the red cord might have had an apotropaic function, which also seems to be the case with the red fringes found on another child's tunic, dated to the seventh century, from the Bouvier Collection.[47] During the early Christian period, the garments of laypeople, including children, were also sometimes decorated with religious images, intended to protect the wearer from evil or to attract good fortune and prosperity.[48] The *clavi* of a child's tunic now in Vienna, for example, bear representations from the life of Joseph.[49] A fragmentary child's tunic from Byzantine Egypt, now in the Krannert Art Museum at the University of Illinois in Urbana-Champaign, has a tapestry roundel on the shoulder depicting the Annunciation, and a row of haloed figures with wings folded over their torso is found on the *clavi*. Technical examination has shown that the tapestries on this piece are later additions. However, the tunic's condition argues against any addition after excavation. Rather, it appears that the tapestries were sewn onto the garment either before or after the child's death. Consequently, one may assume that their purpose was to ensure heavenly protection for the child.[50]

A variant on the standard children's tunic from Byzantine Egypt has a hood

---

Saragoza, eds., *Égypte, la trame de l'histoire: Textiles pharaoniques, coptes et islamiques,* exhibition catalogue (Paris, 2002), 119–20, no. 78.

46   Archäologische Staatssammlung, Munich. Inv. no. 1985.716. Height 48 cm; width (sleeveless) 32 cm; width (with sleeves) ca. 64 cm. See L. Wamser, ed., *Die Welt von Byzanz—Europas östliches Erbe: Glanz, Krisen und Fortleben einer tausendjährigen Kultur,* exhibition catalogue (Munich, 2004), 272, no. 410.

47   A. Stauffer, *Textiles d'Égypte de la collection Bouvier: Antiquité tardive, période copte, premiers temps de l'Islam,* exhibition catalogue (Bern, 1991), 176, no. 81.

48   On the apotropaic function of Christian images on the garments of lay people, see H. Maguire, "Magic and the Christian Image," in *Byzantine Magic,* ed. H. Maguire (Washington, D.C., 1995), 51–71, esp. 54 (about children); idem, "Garments Pleasing to God," *DOP* 44 (1990): 215–24.

49   L. H. Abdel-Malek, "Joseph Tapestries and Related Coptic Textiles" (PhD diss., Boston University, 1980), 57, 216. On the popularity of the cycle of Joseph in the decoration of tunics, see Maguire, "Garments Pleasing to God," 222–24.

50   Krannert Art Museum, University of Illinois, Urbana-Champaign. Height 68 cm; length 51.5 cm. See E. Dauterman Maguire, *Weavings from Roman, Byzantine and Islamic Egypt: The Rich Life and the Dance,* exhibition catalogue (Urbana-Champaign, 1999), 168–69, no. C26.

Figure 3 Hooded child's tunic, eighth or ninth century, Egypt, Benaki Museum, Athens (inv. no. 7160) (photo: courtesy of Benaki Museum)

attached. Two closely related examples in good state of preservation, dated to the eighth or ninth century, are found in the Benaki Museum in Athens (fig. 3)[51] and the Louvre.[52] The technical features of these pieces, which may be attributed to the same workshop, attest to the high standards of Egyptian weaving in this period. The sides of the Benaki tunic are crudely sewn together with a thick thread; on the Louvre example, the body and the sleeves are not sewn together

51 Athens, Benaki Museum. Inv. no. 7160. Height (without hood) 45 cm; width (without sleeves) 45 cm; width of sleeve 20.5 cm; hood 20 by 30 cm. See E. Georgoula, ed., *Greek Treasures from the Benaki Museum in Athens,* exhibition catalogue (Sydney, 2005), 100, no. 61.
52 Paris, Musée du Louvre. Inv. no. E 26525 (formerly collection Puy-Haubert, acquired in 1960). Height (with hood) 82.5 cm; width (without sleeves) 42 cm; hood 29 by 22 cm. See Durand and Saragoza, *Égypte, la trame de l'histoire* (above, n. 45), 119, no. 77.

BRIGITTE PITARAKIS

but could be attached by small cords at the bottom and the cuffs. The pointed hoods of both tunics are decorated with fringing flanked by two tapestry roundels enclosing stylized quadrupeds, identified as lions on the Benaki example. On both examples the *clavi,* bordered by wave-crested bands, are decorated with a row of stylized creatures: birds and a fish in profile on the Benaki piece, and stylized quadrupeds on the Louvre example. The design of the sleeve bands is essentially the same as that of the *clavi.*

A third example of a hooded child's tunic is in the Metropolitan Museum of Art. Like the preceding examples, this one was probably worn by a child of seven or eight. The large tapestry *clavi* and sleeve bands are decorated with stylized frontal figures in a laurel scroll, which are among the most commonly used decorative motifs of Roman and early Christian art.[53] A fragmentary hooded tunic dated to the fourth or fifth century was retrieved in 1998–99 from a child's grave during the excavations of the Kellis 2 cemetery, north of the site of Ismant el-Kharab/Kellis, Dakhleh Oasis. On this example, the fringes are replaced by five multicolored pom-poms, and the pair of lateral roundels is decorated with a rosette motif inscribed in a circle.[54]

Most of the surviving hooded tunics are sized for children.[55] They were also used as dresses for dolls.[56] The hood may be viewed as a type of adornment, but it also protects the child's head and ears from wind and cold. Younger children used to wear caps tied with a knot below the chin: examples include the garments of two little mummified girls from Antinoe, Egypt, who were found by Albert Gayet and brought to the museum of the Département du Rhône, Lyon. The first, about one meter in height, wears an ample tunic with *clavi* and a large tapestry band and has a red cap made in sprang technique, with its braid still tied below the chin. The second wears two layers of tunics and a similar

53   New York, Metropolitan Museum of Art. Inv. No. 1912.27.239. Length 95.5 cm; width 105 cm. See A. Stauffer et al., *Textiles of Late Antiquity,* exhibition catalogue (New York, 1995), no. 37; E. Dauterman Maguire, H. P. Maguire, and M. J. Duncan-Flowers*, Art and Holy Powers in the Early Christian House,* exhibition catalogue (Urbana-Champaign, Ill., 1989), 145, no. 69.

54   G. E. Bowen, "Textiles, Basketry and Leather Goods from Ismant el-Kharab," in *Dakleh Oasis Project: Preliminary Reports on the 1994–1995 to 1998–1999 Field Seasons,* ed. C. A. Hope and G. E. Bowen (Oxford, 2002), 87, 93, pl. 10. See also G. E. Bowen, "Textiles from Ismant el-Kharab," *Bulletin of the Australian Centre for Egyptology* 10 (1999): 7–12.

55   Monks also wore hooded tunics, however. See an eleventh-century example with an inscription naming the monk Apa Kolthi from the monastery of Neklomi (Deir al-Naqlun) in the Louvre, in Durand and Saragoza, *Égypte, la trame de l'histoire,* 129–30, no. 95.

56   See the tunic of a bone doll from the Benaki Museum, Athens, in Papanikola-Bakirtzi, *Everyday Life in Byzantium* (above, n. 5), 495, no. 675a.

Figure 4 Child's cap from Antinoe, Egypt, Byzantine period, musée du Louvre, département des Antiquités égyptiennes (inv. no. E 29423) (copyright Musée du Louvre / G. Poncet)

blue cap.[57] A child's cap with ear flaps, made from brushed wool, also found in a child's grave in Antinoe during Gayet's excavations and kept in the Louvre, is decorated on both the front and the back with an applied cross made with silk strips (fig. 4).[58] Two other examples of children's caps bearing the same type of applied cross on the front were found by the same archaeologist not far from Antinoe, in Deir al-Dik and Deir al-Nasara. The cap from Deir al-Nasara was accompanied by a pair of child's socks similarly decorated with applied crosses.[59]

Another type of garment that appears to have been designed specifically for children is the flared tunic with underarm gussets to increase the freedom of movement of the arms. Such an example from Antinoe, now in the musée Dobrée in Nantes, is made of linen (fig. 5). The round opening of the neck is bordered with a blue tapestry strip decorated with white crosses. The strip continues on to the shoulder to form a rectangular panel with a lateral slit on top, intended

---

57   The sprang technique consists in plaiting on stretched threads. It produces an elastic fabric that is sometimes mistaken for knitted fabric. For the description of the finds, see Calament, *La révélation d'Antinoé* (above, n. 43), 291.

58   Paris, musée du Louvre, département des Antiquités égyptiennes. Inv. no. E 29423. Height 22 cm; width 16.5 cm. See *Au fil du Nil,* 64, no. 30; *L'art copte en Égypte,* 138, no. 126.

59   *Au fil du Nil,* 64; A. Gayet, *Le costume en Egypte du IIIe au XIIIe siècle* (Paris, 1900), 98–99, no. 19; Calament, *La révélation d'Antinoé,* 291.

BRIGITTE PITARAKIS

Figure 5 Flared child's tunic with underarm gussets, from Antinoe, Egypt, Byzantine period, musée Dobrée, Nantes, Deposit of the musée de Cluny in 1909 (inv. no. D.2001.2.1) (photo: courtesy of E. Cochard, Musée départemental Dobrée, Conseil général de Loire-Atlantique, Nantes)

to enlarge the neck opening so as to facilitate the insertion of the child's head.[60] On another tunic of the same type, in the Victoria and Albert Museum, the rectangular tapestry border appears on both shoulders.[61] A further parallel example, in the Museum für byzantinische Kunst in Berlin, has only one opening on the left shoulder; the traces of a wide vertical band can be seen at the center of the tunic.[62]

---

60   Nantes, musée Dobrée. Inv. no. D.2001.2.1. Height 45 cm; width (with sleeves) 51 cm. *Au fil du Nil,* 62, no. 28.
61   A. F. Kendrick, *Catalogue of Textiles from Burying-Grounds in Egypt,* vol. 2 (London, 1921), 275, no. 340, pl. 14.
62   Berlin, Museum für Spätantike und byzantinische Kunst. Inv. no. 9935. Height 68 cm; width (with sleeves) 113 cm. See *Ägypten Schätze aus dem Wüstensand,* 275, no. 315 (above, n. 45).

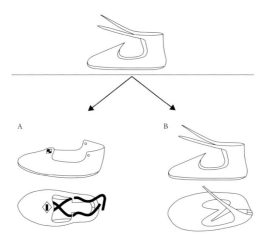

Figure 6   Children's lace-up shoes from Antinoe, Egypt, Byzantine period, classified by style of lacing (after Montembault, *Catalogue des chaussures* [see n. 63], 69, fig. 25)

One can conclude then that, like adults, children of the elite from Byzantine Egypt wore finely made garments decorated with protective devices. Besides the regular tunic, patterned on that of adults, children also wore hooded tunics for protection against bad weather and flared tunics with gussets for greater ease of movement. These devices demonstrate the special attention given to children.

FOOTWEAR

Several examples of children's footwear have also come to light through excavations in Egypt. These were often retrieved from children's burials. They include smaller versions of standard adult sandals, slippers, and boots, together with shoes lacing around the ankle, which appear to have been more commonly designed for children (fig. 6).[63] The soft leather of the closed shoes is often dyed red and highlighted with gilding.

A pair of tiny leather sandals in the Benaki Museum in Athens, dated be-

---

63   See, for example, a child's boot from Egypt, of unknown date, at the Musée Dobrée, Nantes. Inv. No. 2001.2.3. H. 15.8 cm. See *Au fil du Nil,* 66, no. 34. A group of children's footwear from Giza, including slippers, sandals, and closed shoes, is in Berlin. Their length varies between 11 and 19.8 cm. See O. Wulff, *Altchristliche und mittelalterliche, byzantinische und italienische Bildwerke,* part 1, *Altchristliche Bildwerke* (Berlin, 1909), 160–61, nos. 708–14. The length of the children's shoes from Antinoe in the Louvre varies between 10 and 24.2 cm. See V. Montembault, *Musée du Louvre, Département des Antiquités égyptiennes: Catalogue des chaussures de l'Antiquité égyptienne* (Paris, 2000), 69–70 (class V), 176–99, nos. 105–18; *Au fil du Nil,* 65, no. 33.

tween the fifth and seventh century and neatly decorated with stamped concentric circles and circles arranged in cruciform patterns, reflects the concern for the child's spiritual protection. The soles are worn, indicating that the footwear had been used, in contrast to other examples of cruder workmanship that were made exclusively for funerary purposes.[64] The discovery in Egypt of adults' woolen socks with a split toe to accommodate a sandal strap attest the practice of wearing sandals with socks.[65] In Byzantine iconography, for instance, the horizontal straps criss-crossing the calves of children, a conventional way to depict their footwear, suggest their identification as sandals worn with socks, although in some instances these may also represent the folds of calf-length boots in soft leather.

Children's Adornments and Jewelry

In discussing the duties of women in the household, John Chrysostom praises their role in raising their children, who are, he says, "the greatest of treasures."[66] He complains, however, that when a child is born, instead of striving to give it a good education, the father is mainly concerned to adorn it and envelop it in golden garments. Why, he asks, put jewelry around a child's neck? He also protests against the widespread parental practice of hanging gold ornaments from the ears of children, not only because girls start to enjoy it but also because this "evil" is also extended to boys.[67]

The practice of adorning children of both genders with jewelry remained unchanged throughout the history of the Byzantine Empire. An evocative testimony is found in the seventh-century Life of Theodore of Sykeon. As a child, Theodore spent all his time in the oratory of Saint George. The protests of his mother and grandmother, who wanted him to come back home, made him remove his gold belt, necklace, and bracelet and throw them down in front of them, thinking that their anxiety was mainly for the precious jewelry he was

---

64 Athens, Benaki Museum. Inv. No. 21859. Length 12.8 cm. See Papanikola-Bakirtzi, *Everyday Life in Byzantium* (above, n. 5), 112, no. 105; Georgoula, *Greek Treasures* (above, n. 51), 102, no. 63.
65 Two pairs from Gebel Abou Fedah are at the Musée Dobrée, Nantes. *Au fil du Nil,* 54:27.
66 *Saint John Chrysostom, On Marriage and Family Life,* trans. C. P. Roth and D. Anderson (Crestwood, N.Y., 1986), 96–97.
67 PG 58:786–88; *Jean Chrysostome: Sur la vaine gloire et l'éducation des enfants*, ed. A.-M. Malingrey (Paris, 1972), 98, chap. 16.

wearing.[68] Seven centuries later, in one of his poems to himself after the reversal of his fortune, Theodore Metochites speaks of prosperous men who devise costly adornments for themselves, their wives, and their children.[69]

The custom of putting earrings on young boys has left few traces in the sources. However, its survival in Greece into the early twentieth century is noteworthy.[70] Interesting evidence about this practice in Byzantium is found from the Komnenian era onward in the iconography of the Christ Child, and in some representations of ordinary children in the iconography of the baptism of Christ and Christ's entry into Jerusalem. In two well-known painted panels in the church of Panagia Arakiotissa in Lagoudera, Cyprus (1192)—the dedicatory panel of the Panagia Arakiotissa and that of Simeon holding the Christ Child—the child is portrayed in a three-quarter pose, wearing an earring made of a plain hoop with three drop-shaped pearl pendants.[71] The painter may have modeled his portrait on contemporary coin issues, the gold *hyperpyra* (fig. 7), *electrum trachea,* and *billon trachea* of Manuel I Komnenos (1143–1180), bearing the bust figure of Emmanuel wearing a pair of earrings with pendant pearls.[72] The same type of Christ Emmanuel was also introduced by Manuel I Komnenos on his

68   *Vie de Théodore de Sykéon,* ed. A.-J. Festugière (Brussels, 1970), 10–11, chap. 12.

69   J. M. Featherstone, *Theodore Metochites's Poems "To Himself"* (Vienna, 2000), 116–17, poem 19, lines 103–4.

70   An eloquent testimony is the portrait by Nikolaos Koutouzis of the poet Dionysios Solomos (1741–1813) as an infant enveloped in swaddling clothes. The infant wears an earring in the shape of a plain golden hoop; see N. Misirli and S. Lidakis, Θησαυροί της Νεοελληνικής τέχνης: Η συλλογή Γιάννη Περδίου (Athens, 1998), 38, no. 10. I thank Marianna Yerasimos and Petros Vergos for drawing my attention to this painting, in the collection of Iannis Perdios in Athens. In post-Byzantine local practice in Cyprus, firstborn sons wear an earring as a symbol of their birthright: see Parani, *Reconstructing the Reality of Images* (above, n. 41), 247.

71   The earring on the panel with the Panagia Arakiotissa is discussed in Parani, *Reconstructing the Reality of Images,* 225–26, 247–48, and pl. 243. For the panel of Saint Simeon with the Christ Child, see C. Baltoyanni, "Christ the Lamb and the Ενώτιον of the Law in a Wall Painting of Araka on Cyprus," Δελτ. Χριστ. Αρχ. Ετ. 17 (1993–94): 56–58. Good illustrations of both earrings are in D. Winfield and J. Winfield, *The Church of the Panaghia tou Arakos at Lagoudera, Cyprus: The Paintings and their Painterly Significance* (Washington, D.C., 2003), 248, pls. 28 and 32.

72   See M. Hendy, *Catalogue of the Byzantine Coins in the Dumbarton Oaks Collection and in the Whittemore Collection,* vol. 4, *Alexius I to Michael VIII, 1081–1261,* part 1, *Alexius I to Alexius V (1081–1204)* [hereafter *DOC* 4] (Washington, D.C., 1999), pls. 11–12. The gold and electrum coins present variants in the number of hanging pearls (one to three) that relate to the interior organization of the mint. The workshop establishes control over the production in precious metals by introducing slight changes in the types for a differentiation of the issues. I thank Pagona Papadopoulou for drawing my attention to and discussing the iconographic particularity of these coin issues.

Figure 7 *Hyperpyron nomisma,* Manuel I Komnenos (1143–
1180), obverse (left) and reverse (right), Constantinople, Wulfing
Collection, Kemper Art Museum, Washington University in St.
Louis (acc. No. WC 10998), scale 1:1.5 (photo: courtesy of Kemper
Art Museum)

seals.[73] It enjoyed great popularity and was reproduced on coin issues of subsequent emperors until 1261.[74]

Boys wearing a similar type of earring with a pendant pearl are also depicted
among the groups of children celebrating Christ's entry into Jerusalem in the
late twelfth-century decoration of the church of Saint George of Kurbinovo. The
painter has also put earrings on several male youths, including the flute-playing
shepherd from the Nativity, the personification of the Jordan in the baptism
scene, and the figure of Abel in the Anastasis.[75] The recurring use of pearl earrings in these images may allude to the symbolism of the pearl which, in Christian thought, represented the Word of God.[76] By analogy with the parable of the
merchant in the New Testament, wherein the kingdom of heaven is likened to
a precious pearl, the pearl may also stand as a pledge of the heavenly kingdom.[77]

73 G. Zacos and A. Veglery, *Byzantine Lead Seals,* vol. 1, part 1 (Basel, 1972), 96, nos. 107a–b.
74 See, for example, *DOC* 4, pls. 22, 27, 31–32, 38–39, 46.
75 L. Hadermann-Misguich, *Kurbinovo: Les fresques de Saint-Georges et la peinture byzantine du XIIe siècle* (Brussels, 1975), 130, 516, fig. 55; C. Grozdanov and L. Hadermann-Misguich,
Kurbinovo (Skopje, 1992), figs. 38–41, 43–44, 55.
76 For a discussion on the pearl symbolism in Christian theology, with an appendix on the
written sources, see R. Delbrueck, "Notes on the Wooden Doors of Santa Sabina," *ArtB* 34 (1952):
142–45. See, for example, the hymns on the pearl of Ephrem the Syrian: Fr. Graffin, "Les hymnes
sur la perle de Saint Ephrem," *OrSyr* 12 (1967): 129–49.
77 "Again the kingdom of heaven is like unto a merchant man, seeking goodly pearls: Who,
when he had found one pearl of great price, went and sold all that he had, and bought it" (Matt.
13:45–46).

Thus children wearing pearl earrings may represent those who will enter the kingdom of heaven.[78]

Besides the earrings worn by small boys, Byzantine iconography provides few depictions of children adorned with jewelry. One beautiful exception is the representation of the infant Virgin in the arms of her mother, Anna, in a seventh-century painted panel on the west wall of the presbytery of Santa Maria Antiqua. From Mary's ear hangs a large pendant with one big and one small pearl; at her neck is a piece of jewelry painted as a gold band or chain with tiny pendants.[79] But even in the absence of pictorial evidence, the survival of miniature necklaces and armbands illustrates the tendency of Byzantines of all periods to adorn their children with jewelry.

The most common type of child's bracelet throughout the Byzantine period was a plain copper hoop with open ends. More elaborate versions from the early Byzantine period sometimes include a decorated medallion on the top. A silver specimen, from the collections of the Berlin Museum, dated to the sixth or seventh century, is decorated with a miniature intaglio figure of the standing Christ in frontal view, raising his left hand in a sign of benediction while holding a staff with a cruciform top in his right.[80] This image is strikingly similar to the representations of Christ on a group of amulet gems from the fifth or sixth centuries.[81] A cheaper version with an iron hoop from Byzantine Egypt, in the collections of the musée Dobrée in Nantes, bears a copper-alloy medallion engraved with a cross.[82]

Another popular type of bracelet that continued to be manufactured from late antiquity to the middle Byzantine period is a cable made of two or more strands

---

78   "And said, Verily I say unto you, Except ye be converted, and become as little children, ye shall not enter into the kingdom of heaven" (Matt. 18:3). Or: "But Jesus said, Suffer little children, and forbid them not, to come unto me: for of such is the kingdom of heaven" (Matt. 19:14).

79   See P. J. Nordhagen, "S. Maria Antiqua: The Frescoes of the Seventh Century," in *Studies in Byzantine and Early Medieval Painting* (London, 1990), 188–89, chap. 9; J. Wilpert, *Die römischen Mosaiken und Malereien der kirchlichen Bauten vom IV. bis XIII. Jahrhundert, IV*, 2nd ed. (Freiburg im Breisgau, 1917), pls. 159–60.

80   The diameter of the bracelet is 4.5 cm. Wulff, *Altchristliche und mittelalterliche, byzantinische und italienische Bildwerke* (above, n. 63), 1:228, no. 1110.

81   J. Spier, *Late Antique and Early Christian Gems,* Spätantike–frühes Christentum–Byzanz: Kunst im Ersten Jahrtausend, Reihe B: Studien und Perspektiven, vol. 20 (Wiesbaden, 2007), 103, nos. 589–90.

82   Nantes, musée Dobrée. Inv. no. D 961.2.341. Diameter 4.6 cm. See *Au fil du Nil* (above, n. 44), 66, no. 35.

of wire twisted together and flattened at the ends, where loops are formed. A bracelet and a necklace of this type, which, judging from their small dimensions, probably belonged to a small girl, are in the Halûk Perk collection in Istanbul (figs. 8 and 9).[83] Another type of small copper bracelet, now in the Louvre, probably intended for a child, was found in Antinoe during the excavations conducted by Albert Gayet in 1903. A pair of globular bell-shaped pendants, open at the bottom, are suspended from a plain hoop with a hook-and-loop fastening system.[84] Beside serving an ornamental purpose, the pendants may have been intended to produce a rattling noise that was believed to dispel evil spirits.[85]

Byzantine parents also took pains to adorn their children in death. Coins, small ceramic pitchers and goblets, perfume flasks, dress accessories, jewelry, crosses, and amulets are among the finds in both adults' and children's graves in the early Christian period.[86] Although less numerous, artifacts like these dating from the middle Byzantine period have also been found.[87] In spite of the frequent lack of precision about the identity of the burial, it has been possible to observe that early Christian children's graves differ from those of the adults

83 Istanbul, Halûk Perk Collection. Necklace: inv. no. 1050. Diameter 11.5 cm. Bracelet: inv. no. 1032a. Diameter 4.3 cm. An adult bracelet of similar type was found in a late fourth-century context in Redina, Greece. Other examples were yielded by tenth- to twelfth-century contexts. See *Το Ελληνικό κόσμημα: 6000 χρόνια παράδοση,* exhibition catalogue (Athens, 1997), 172, nos. 172–73; 210, nos. 243–44. The style and technique of the Halûk Perk bracelet suggests a dating in the early Byzantine period.

84 Paris, Musée du Louvre, Département des Antiquités égyptiennes. Inv. no. E 12357. D. Bénazeth, *Musée du Louvre: Catalogue du département des antiquités égyptiennes; L'art du métal au début de l'ère chrétienne* (Paris, 1992), 202.

85 J. Russell, "The Archaeological Context of Magic in the Early Byzantine Period," in Maguire, *Byzantine Magic* (above, n. 48), 42–43.

86 Several recent studies are devoted to burial practices in Corinth. See E. A. Ivison, "Burial and Urbanism at Late Antique and Early Byzantine Corinth (c. A.D. 400–700)," in *Towns in Transition: Urban Evolution in Late Antiquity and the Early Middle Ages,* ed. N. Christie and S. T. Loseby (Aldershot, 1996), 112–20; G. D. R Sanders, "Problems in Interpreting Rural and Urban Settlement in Southern Greece, A.D. 375–700," in *Landscapes of Change: Rural Evolutions in Late Antiquity and the Early Middle Ages,* ed. N. Christie (Aldershot, 2004), 180–84. Sanders points out that the inclusion of liquid containers in the graves is probably connected to the burial liturgy. He says that their presence may reflect a degree of syncretism between Christian and Hellenic beliefs and burial liturgy: ibid., 184, 187. See also Papanikola-Bakirtzi, *Everyday Life in Byzantium* (above, n. 5), 536–37, 554–59, nos. 759–74; 567–71, nos. 788–800. See also the article by A.-M. Talbot in this volume.

87 See E. Ivison, "'Supplied for the Journey to Heaven': A Moment of West-East Cultural Exchange: Ceramic Chalices from Byzantine Graves," *BMGS* 24 (2000): 165–67. See also Papanikola-Bakirtzi, *Everyday Life in Byzantium,* 537, 560–62, nos. 774–79.

Figures 8 and 9   Copper-alloy necklace and bracelet, early Byzantine, Halûk Perk Collection, Istanbul, scale 1:1 (photo: courtesy of Halûk Perk)

in that they contain toys and a greater quantity of jewelry.[88] The most striking aspect of the burial of children is that jewelry continues to be found steadily in children's graves from the middle Byzantine period, whereas it is rare in adult graves of that period. Most of the well-published evidence comes from the excavations conducted in medieval cemeteries in Greece and the Balkans.[89] Details of the size and the shape of the objects and the type of metal are not always available. However, one can easily distinguish miniature pieces, originally designed for a living child's use, from those of adult size, which were used in funerary rituals for children.

For example, a group of small bracelets designed for a child's wrist was found during the excavations of children's graves dating from the tenth to the thirteenth century in the middle Byzantine settlement in Paleochora, Maroneia, Thrace. These are miniature versions of popular styles of adult bracelets. Their diameter varies from 4.0 to 4.3 centimeters. One copper bracelet is formed from a plain circular hoop with open, overlapping ends, and two others from a single grave are made of twisted copper wire with flattened, looped ends. Another child's grave from the same settlement yielded a set of five glass bracelets.[90] Some jewelry was also found during the excavations conducted in the burial area in the western sector of the ninth- or tenth-century episcopal church on the hill of Polystylon/Abdera in Thrace. This includes a pair of earrings and a ring, a twisted bracelet and a necklace, and a pearl.[91]

More detailed information on funerary rites related to early deaths can be drawn from the archaeological report of the middle Byzantine settlement of Djadovo, near Philippoupolis in Bulgaria. As in most medieval necropolises from this period, adornments were found exclusively in children's burials.[92]

---

88   For a wide range of early Christian children's burial gifts from Greece, see N. G. Laskaris, *Monuments funéraires paléochrétiens (et byzantins) de Grèce* (Athens, 2000), esp. 65–68, 130–31, 165, 171, 178, 201, 204, 219, 247, 257. Most examples of toys from children's burials of the early Christian period are yielded by the archaeology of Egypt. See Calament, *La révélation d'Antinoé* (above, n. 43), 292.

89   For a list of examples from Greece, see Laskaris, *Monuments funéraires,* 85, 92, 97, 132, 136, 248.

90   Papanikola-Bakirtzi, *Everyday Life in Byzantium,* 416, no. 526, 417, no. 529 a–b, 419, no. 534a–e.

91   S. Dadaki, "Νομός Ξάνθης, Πολύστυλον (Αβδήρα)," *Ἀρχ. Δελτ.* 46 (1991): 354; Laskaris, *Monuments funéraires,* 132.

92   *Djadovo: Bulgarian, Dutch, Japanese Expedition,* vol. 1, *Mediaeval Settlement and Necropolis (11th–12th Century),* ed. A. Fol, R. Katinčarov, J. Best, N. de Vries, K. Shoju, and H. Suzuki (Tokyo, 1989).

One of the richest graves from Djadovo belonged to a five- or six-year-old girl who was buried with eleven bracelets on her right arm: six of them were made of glass, two of bronze, and two of iron. The bracelets covered almost the entire forearm, which would have made them impossible to wear in life. A large necklace consisting of 4,456 glass beads, oversized for a child, was unearthed in the same grave.[93] Two pairs of earrings found in children's burials in Sardis should also be mentioned. The first comes from an eleventh-century context; the second belongs to the late Byzantine period. Their size corresponds to that of standard adult earrings. Both are wire hoops, the first silver, the second gold. The use of silver, which is not common in children's burials from the Balkans, reflects the higher status of the family of the deceased.[94]

The prevalence of jewelry in children's burials from the early to the middle Byzantine period illustrates the continuity of the perceptions and beliefs about premature death in ancient societies.[95] The jewelry may reflect the attachment and intense grief of the parents as well as their desire to protect their child on its journey to the realm of the dead. The authors of the Djadovo excavation report suggest that the bulk of jewelry accompanying the burials of little girls may reflect the custom of "marriage-to-death."[96] This custom alludes to the ancient Greek perception of death as a marriage to the underworld deities, especially in the case of a young, unmarried person. The journey of the soul to its last abode is likened to that of the bride to the unknown home of the bridegroom. The association between death and marriage is found in both ancient and modern Greek customs and is reflected in the burial of maiden girls in their wedding attire.[97]

93 Ibid., 1:338 (grave no. 13).
94 J. C. Waldbaum, *Metalwork from Sardis,* Archaeological Exploration of Sardis, Monograph 8 (Cambridge, Mass., 1983), 124–25, nos. 741–42 and 751.
95 See discussion in S. Martin-Kilcher, "*Mors immatura* in the Roman World: A Mirror of Society and Tradition," in *Burial, Society and Context in the Roman World,* ed. J. Pierce and M. Millet (Oxford, 2000), 63–77. The placing of grave goods in children's burials is an ancient practice in both the East and the West; see, for example, F. Laubenheimer, "La mort des tout petits dans l'Occident romain," in *Naissance et petite enfance dans l'Antiquité: Actes du colloque de Fribourg, 28 novembre–1er décembre 2001,* ed. V. Dasen (Fribourg, 2004), 293–315.
96 Fol et al., *Djadovo,* 338.
97 See R. Seaford, "The Tragic Wedding," *Journal of Hellenic Studies* 107 (1987), esp. 106–7, 110, 113; J. M. Barringer, "Europa and the Nereids: Wedding or Funeral?" *AJA* 95, no. 4 (October 1991): 657–67, esp. 662–65; M. Alexiou and P. Dronke, "The Lament of Jephtha's Daughter: Themes, Traditions, Originality," *Studi medievali* 3, 12, no. 2 (1971), esp. 825–41. For a discussion on the relationship between Greek rituals of marriage and burial, see M. Alexiou, *The Ritual Lament in Greek Tradition* (Cambridge, 1974), 120; I. Jenkins, "Is There Life after Marriage? A

This practice is also attested in late antiquity and Byzantium. For example, a passage from the fourth-century Life of Macrina refers to the "adornment of her body" as part of the preparation for her burial by her brother, Gregory of Nyssa. At the sight of the bedecked corpse of Macrina, who died a virgin, the deaconess of the monastery where she lived manifested her disapproval, declaring that "it was not fitting that she should be seen robed like a bride [νυμφικῶς ἐσταλμένην] by the eyes of the virgins." In his discussion of this passage, Pierre Maraval suggests that the bridal adornment of Macrina may have included a garland of flowers. He remarks that this very old pagan custom did not disappear with Christianity and continued to be observed for girls who died before marriage.[98] The reference to a jewelry crown from a corpse in the *Oneirocritikon* of Achmet may also be understood in relation to this custom, which appears to have been equally popular during the middle Byzantine period.[99] Pictorial testimony comes from a mid-fourteenth-century funerary icon in the Byzantine Museum in Nicosia, showing the donors, Manuel Xeros the *anagnostes* and his wife, Euphemia, presenting with tender gestures their daughter Mary, who, according to the dedicatory inscription, died a virgin in 1356. Dressed in beautiful garments, Mary wears on her head what must be her bridal wreath.[100] With regard to this icon from Gothic Cyprus, one wonders whether the diadem, consisting of an arrangement of silk cords, on the head of a young noblewoman in a fifteenth-century burial in the church of Hagia Sophia in Mistra might actually be a wedding crown, suggesting that the deceased was a virgin.[101]

Study on the Abduction Motif in Vase Paintings of the Athenian Wedding Ceremony," *Bulletin of the Institute of Classical Studies* 30 (1983): 142. See also J. C. Lawson, *Modern Greek Folklore and Ancient Greek Religion: A Study of Survivals* (Cambridge, 1910), 546–60.

98   *Vie de sainte Macrine,* ed. P. Maraval (Paris, 1971), 83, chap. 23.

99   See *The Oneirocritikon of Achmet: A Medieval Greek and Arabic Treatise on the Interpretation of Dreams,* trans. and ed. S. M. Oberhelman (Lubbock, Tex., 1991), 225, chap. 256. On the custom of crowning the bride and groom in Byzantium and its Roman antecedents, see G. Vikan, "Art and Marriage in Early Byzantium," *DOP* 44 (1990): 152–53, repr. in idem, *Sacred Images and Sacred Power in Byzantium,* Variorum Collected Studies Series (Aldershot, 2003). See also M. G. Parani, "Byzantine Bridal Costume," in *Δώρημα: A Tribute to the A. G. Leventis Foundation on the Occasion of its 20th Anniversary* (Nicosia, 2000), 185–216.

100   A. Weyl Carr, "A Palaiologan Funerary Icon from Gothic Cyprus," in *Acts of the 3rd International Congress of Cypriot Studies* (Nicosia, 2001), 599–619, esp. 601 and 603, and figs. 1–3. On the custom of dressing a maiden girl in her bridal clothes for burial in the Byzantine period, see G. K. Spyridaki, "Τὰ κατὰ τὴν τελευτὴν ἔθιμα τῶν Βυζαντινῶν ἐκ τῶν ἁγιολογικῶν πηγῶν," *Ἐπετηρὶς Ἑταιρείας Βυζαντινῶν Σπουδῶν* 20 (1950): 113–15; N. Constas, "Death and Dying in Byzantium," in Krueger, *Byzantine Christianity* (above, n. 7), 3:127.

101   *Byzantine Hours: Works and Days in Byzantium: The City of Mystras,* exhibition catalogue, Mystras, August 2001–January 2002 (Athens, 2001), 151, no. 3. For an anthropological analysis

Protective Devices and Childhood

The wide range of devices intended for enhancing fertility and protecting children are important for understanding the role of children in Byzantine society.[102] Fertility, successful pregnancies, and healthy children are universal concerns that profoundly touched the Byzantines. Miraculous births occasioned through the agency of the Mother of God or other privileged intercessors are often described in hagiographic sources.[103] From the early ninth-century Life of Saint Stephen the Younger, we learn, for example, that the saint was conceived through the fervent prayers and supplications of his mother before an icon of the Virgin and Child in the Constantinopolitan shrine of the Blachernai. The central element of the prayers she addressed to the Theotokos is the breaking of the "bond" believed to be the cause of her barrenness.[104] The intervention of holy men was also invoked to facilitate the delivery of a child. In the tenth century, the wife of John Ioubes the Illustrios, for instance, was in labor for twenty-two days. Loukas the Stylite enabled her to give birth by sending *eulogia,* bread, and blessed water.[105] In another case from the ninth century, the fetus of a pregnant woman died in the sixth month of her pregnancy, but the woman was unable to abort, and the physicians expected she would die. She finally delivered a stillborn child after she anointed herself with oil from the lamp of Peter of Atroa.[106]

Another common pious practice for combating barrenness and helping delivery was to wrap around a woman's loins a cloth girdle that had been previously applied to a miraculous icon or a specific architectural feature, such as a column in a church devoted to the Theotokos.[107] In the light of the passage from

---

pointing toward the youth of the deceased, see M. Martiniani-Reber, ed., *Parure d'une princesse byzantine: Tissus archéologiques de Sainte-Sophie de Mistra,* exh. cat. (Geneva, 2000), 31.

102   For a detailed analysis of this topic, see the article by Marie-Hélène Congourdeau in this volume.

103   Several examples are documented in J. Herrin, *The Formation of Christendom* (Princeton, N.J., 1987), 308.

104   M.-F. Auzépy, ed., *Vie d'Étienne le Jeune par Étienne le Diacre* (Aldershot, 1997), chap. 4.

105   H. Delehaye, *Les saints stylites* (Brussels, 1923, repr. 1962), 229, chap. 32, lines 24–25.

106   *La vie merveilleuse de saint Pierre d'Atroa († 837),* ed. and trans. V. Laurent (Brussels, 1956), 161, chap. 107.

107   One example is the icon of the Virgin, known as Episkepsis, in the Constantinopolitan shrine of Pege: *AASS* Nov. 3:885E (chap. 26). See also the *Life of Theophano,* in which Theophano's father had removed a belt that was hanging from a column in the Church of the Theotokos Bassou in Constantinople and tied it around the loins of his wife, Anna, who was having a difficult labor (*Zwei griechische Texte über die heilige Theophano, die Gemahlin Kaiser Leo VI* [St. Peters-

the Life of Saint Stephen the Younger alluding to barrenness as a "bond" that had to be broken, this practice may be viewed as a form of sympathetic magic. Indeed, the Greek word δεσμός, used to express the concept of *bond,* may also take on the meaning of a spell.[108] Like the well-known example of the empress Zoe described by Psellos,[109] Byzantine women suffering from infertility or concerned about safe childbirth followed the tradition of their Greek and Roman predecessors by turning to a wide range of magical practices and amulets.[110] Virtuous women who rejected such practices were exceptional. Such an example is Theoktiste of Constantinople, the mother of the ninth-century abbot Theodore of Stoudios. In his praise of his mother, Theodore stresses that she did not use omens, amulets, or spells in childbirth like other women. "On the contrary, she contented herself with the seal of the life-giving Cross alone as her armor and shield for protection."[111]

Pregnant women and young children were believed to be particularly vulnerable to the evil eye.[112] One of its manifestations was to provoke the action of a female demon, usually called Gello or Abyzou, whose aggression was principally directed against babies and mothers immediately before or after delivery.[113] The

---

burg, 1898], 2, lines 25–35). For a discussion on this subject and further bibliography, see B. Pitarakis, "Female Piety in Context: Understanding Developments in Private Devotional Practices," in *Images of the Mother of God: Perceptions of the Theotokos in Byzantium,* ed. M. Vassilaki (London, 2005), 156–57; eadem, "Objects of Devotion and Protection," 167–68; A.-M. Talbot, "The Devotional Life of Laywomen," in Krueger, *Byzantine Christianity* (above, n. 7), 3:206–7.

108   Moreover, the Greek verb καταδέω meant both to bind physically and to bind by spells. This dual meaning may explain the apotropaic use of knots and interlacements on early Christian textiles. See Maguire, "Garments Pleasing to God" (above, n. 48), 216; E. Dinkler, "Die Salomonische Knoten in der nubischen Kunst und die Geschichte des Motivs," *Études nubiennes* 77 (1978): 73–86.

109   Psellos, *Chronography* (above, n. 25), book 3, chap. 5, 34–35.

110   J.-J. Aubert, "Threatened Wombs: Aspects of Ancient Uterine Magic," *GRBS* 30, no. 3 (1989): 421–49; V. Dasen, "Les amulettes d'enfants dans le monde gréco-romain," *Latomus* 62 (2003): 274–89; eadem, "Protéger l'enfant: Amulettes et crepundia," in *Maternité et petite enfance en Gaule romaine,* ed. D. Gourevitch, A. Moirin, and N. Rouquet, exhibition catalogue (Treignes, 2005), 123–27; Congourdeau, "Regards sur l'enfant nouveau-né à Byzance" (above, n. 3), 161–76.

111   PG 99:884–85. For an English translation of this passage, see Hatlie, "Religious Lives of Children" (above, n. 7), 184. See also discussion in Pitarakis, "Objects of Devotion and Protection," in Krueger, *Byzantine Christianity,* 168.

112   Literature on the powers of the evil eye in late antiquity and Byzantium is abundant. See K. M. D. Dunbabin and M. W. Dickie, "*Invida rumpantur pectora:* The Iconography of Phthonos/ Invidia in Graeco-Roman Art," *JbAC* 26 (1983): 7–37; M. W. Dickie, "The Fathers of the Church and the Evil Eye," in Maguire, *Byzantine Magic* (above, n. 48), 9–34; J. Russell, "The Evil Eye in Early Byzantine Society: Archaeological Evidence from Anemurium in Isauria," *JÖB* 32, no. 3 (1982): 539–48; idem, "The Archaeological Context of Magic" (above, n. 85), 35–50, esp. 37.

113   See Sorlin, "Striges et Géloudes" (above, n. 3), 411–36. For a discussion on beliefs about the

fight against such demonic activity may be reflected in the decoration of a group of pendant amulets, such as a sixth- or seventh-century example in the Cabinet des Médailles, Paris. On one side it bears the image of the Holy Rider attacking a prostrate female demon; on the other side, the demoness is lying beneath the image of the "much-suffering eye," a common device against the evil eye, sometimes identified as "envy," which derives its name from the *Testament of Solomon*. The "much-suffering eye" is stabbed from above by three daggers and surrounded by attacking beasts.[114] It appears therefore that measures to deflect the power of the evil eye were also effective against the demoness who threatened to harm children.

Protective formulas accompanying the decoration of this group of amulets show that their use was extended to both genders. Protecting children was only one of the multiple facets of their function. Like the evil eye, the demoness Gello could work various kinds of evil. From the *Testament of Solomon* and the large body of exorcistic literature, we learn, for example, that Abyzou or Gello provoked eye diseases, toothaches, and other kinds of physical suffering as well as insanity and epilepsy.[115]

Another group of amulets dated to the medieval period bears on one side the distinctive motif of a face framed by radiating serpents.[116] Basing his argument on the exorcistic formulae that are paired with this motif, Jeffrey Spier has suggested that this motif is a depiction of the *hystera,* or womb, rather than the gorgon Medusa or the Egyptian Chnoubis, as has been commonly accepted.[117] One may further suggest that this motif derives from a late antique repertory of representations of *phthonos,* or envy, shown as a male figure or an evil eye surrounded by coiling serpents.[118] The group of amulets bearing invocations to the

---

female demon in relation to the decorative repertory of Byzantine amulets, see Spier, "Medieval Byzantine Magical Amulets" (above, n. 3), 33–35. On Gello, see also the articles by A.-M. Talbot and M.-H. Congourdeau in this volume.

114   T. Matantseva, "Les amulettes byzantines contre le mauvais oeil du Cabinet des Médailles," *JbAC* 37 (1994): 111, no. 2. Amulets bearing a similar decoration are discussed in H. Maguire, *The Icons of their Bodies: Saints and their Images in Byzantium* (Princeton, N.J., 1996), 120–23; Dauterman Maguire et al., *Art and Holy Powers* (above, n. 53), 216, no. 135; Kalavrezou, *Byzantine Women and their World* (above, n. 3), 286–87, no. 167; 289, no. 170.

115   Sorlin, "Striges et Géloudes," 424, 428.

116   Spier, "Medieval Byzantine Magical Amulets," 25–62. See also G. Vikan, "Art, Medicine, and Magic in Early Byzantium," *DOP* 38 (1984): 76–78, reprinted in idem, *Sacred Images* (above, n. 99).

117   Spier, "Medieval Byzantine Magical Amulets," 38–44, esp. 43.

118   The snake is seen as a symbol of the malice of the *phthoneros* turned against himself. See Dunbabin and Dickie, "*Invida rumpantur pectora*" (above, n. 112), 19, 24–26, 32.

Figure 10 Copper amulet, obverse (left) and reverse (right), twelfth or thirteenth century, Halûk Perk Collection, Istanbul (photo: courtesy of Halûk Perk)

hystera reflects a tradition of beliefs about the womb, which was viewed as an independent, animate creature roaming within the body and acting as an animal demon. The roaming of the *hystera* was thought to cause a wide range of ailments and disorders in both men and women, including bleeding, migraine, and fever.[119] In his catalogue of the *hystera* amulets, Spier distinguishes three major categories, according to the decoration on the other side of the medallion. The first category bears an exorcistic formula directed against the *hystera,* the second is devoted to the image of the Holy Rider, and the third is characterized by Christian religious iconography. The second category, including the image of the Holy Rider spearing the female demon, is considered to be more specifically connected with the protection of childbirth and nurslings.[120] To this group can be added an example in the Halûk Perk collection in Istanbul (fig. 10),[121] whose origin Spier places in medieval Constantinople.[122] But the occurrence of the

119   Spier, "Medieval Byzantine Magical Amulets," 42.
120   Ibid., 30, 33–35, 44, 51–59.
121   Istanbul, Halûk Perk Collection. Inv. no. 3819. Diameter ca. 3.5–4 cm, in E. Işın, ed., *Elemterefiş: Anadolu'da büyü ve inanışlar / Elemterefiş: Magic and Superstition in Anatolia,* exhibition catalogue (Istanbul, 2003), 111.
122   A lead medallion belonging to this category was found during the excavations of St. Polyeuktos in Istanbul, and a more luxurious enamel example in the musée du Louvre may be attributed to a Constantinopolitan workshop. See Spier, "Medieval Byzantine Magical Amulets," 50–51, 62. For the find from St. Polyeuktos, see R. M. Harrison, *Excavations at Saraçhane in Istanbul,* vol. 1, *The Excavations, Structures, Architectural Decoration, Small Finds, Coins, Bones, and Molluscs* (Princeton, N.J., 1986), 268, no. 621. The Louvre medallion is published in *Byzance,*

image of Christ healing the woman with the issue of blood, or *hemorrhoissa* in Greek (Mark 5:25–34), seldom attested on objects of private devotion, on some bronze tokens bearing the *hystera* motif on the other side, may also reflect its use in averting female menstrual problems as well as infertility or miscarriages.[123]

Gello was believed to pose a danger only in the first weeks after birth, but the evil eye was a constant threat for small children, who needed the protection of a multiplicity of practices and devices.[124] We know from the private correspondence preserved in Egyptian papyri, for instance, that both pagan and Christian letter writers, when referring to their correspondents' children, customarily added the formula "May the evil eye (or enchantment) not touch them."[125] "May the evil eye never harm you!" is also the formula used by Psellos, several centuries later, in his encomium to his four-month-old grandson.[126] From John Chrysostom's attacks on magical practices, we learn that in his time children were commonly protected by amulets, bells hanging from their hands, or scarlet threads used as armbands.[127] He also condemns the practice followed by nurses and maidservants of anointing a child's forehead with mud when they take it to the baths in order to ward off the evil eye.[128] John Chrysostom also observes that in his day, women and small children used to wear small gospel books hung around the neck for powerful protection.[129]

Archaeological evidence can offer us a contextualization of children's *phylakteria*. A protective device associated with children since antiquity is the crescent-shaped pendant, σεληνίς, or *lunula*. One example hangs from the neck of

330–31, no. 244; H. C. Evans and W. D. Wixom, eds., *The Glory of Byzantium: Art and Culture of the Middle Byzantine Era, AD 843–1261,* exhibition catalogue (New York, 1997), 166, no. 114.

123   Spier, "Medieval Byzantine Magical Amulets," 28, 56.

124   Sorlin, "Striges et Géloudes" (above, n. 3), 431–32.

125   See discussion in Dauterman Maguire et al., *Art and Holy Powers* (above, n. 53), 4, after J. R. Rea, *The Oxyrhynchus Papyri,* vol. 46 (London, 1978), 99; G. M. Browne et al., eds., *The Oxyrhynchus Papyri,* vol. 41 (London, 1972), 79; P. J. Sijpesteijn, *The Wisconsin Papyri,* vol. 2 (Zutphen, 1977), 137–38.

126   ἀλλὰ μή σε βάλοι ὀφθαλμὸς βασκανίας. Kurtz and Drexl, *Michaelis Pselli Scripta Minora* (above, n. 24), 1:80; Littlewood, *Michaelis Pselli oratoria minora* (above, n. 24), 154; Kaldellis, *Mothers and Sons* (above, n. 16), 164.

127   *Argumentum epistolae primae ad Corinthios,* homily 12, PG 61:105.

128   PG 61:106. For a discussion of this sermon, see Dickie, "Fathers of the Church" (above, n. 112), 31–32; J. Maxwell, "Lay Piety in the Sermons of John Chrysostom," in Krueger, *Byzantine Christianity* (above, n. 7), 32.

129   *Homiliae XXI de Statuis ad populum Antiochenum habitae,* homily 19, PG 49:196.

Figure 11   Terracotta bust of boy with *lunula,* rattle (?), late fourth century, Agora excavations, Athens (inv. T 2937), scale 2:5 (photo: courtesy of the American School of Classical Studies at Athens)

a late fourth-century clay figurine of a boy, perhaps a rattle, from the Athenian Agora (fig. 11).[130] Crescent-shaped good-luck charms surrounded by glass pearls are also frequently attested among the finds from children's graves dating from the sixth to the ninth century in the lower Danube area.[131] The role of the *lunulae* in protecting children is closely related to the belief that the moon influences fertility. On this basis, they were worn by women as well.[132]

Like the crescent-shaped pendants, small globular bells with a suspension loop are also among common finds from children's graves from the early to the middle Byzantine period. The practice is equally well attested in the Roman period in Palestine and is said to be maintained in modern times.[133] A bell-shaped rattle and several fragmentary bronze ornaments were among the grave goods from an early Christian child's burial excavated in the sanctuary of Demeter and Kore on

130   C. Grandjouan, *The Athenian Agora: Results of the Excavations Conducted by the American School of Classical Studies at Athens,* vol. 6, *Terracottas and Plastic Lamps of the Roman Period* (Princeton, N.J., 1961), 57, no. 458, pl. 10.

131   U. Fiedler, *Studien zu Gräbefeldern des 6. bis 9. Jahrhunderts an der unteren Donau, Teil 1–2* (Bonn, 1992), 185, pl. 105.13.

132   See Aubert, "Threatened Wombs," 446–48; Dasen, "Les amulettes d'enfants," 280; eadem, "Protéger l'enfant," 124 (all above, n. 110).

133   See G. Lankester Harding, "A Roman Family Vault on Jebel Joffey 'Aman,'" *Quarterly of the Department of Antiquities in Palestine* 14 (1950): 89 and pl. 28.

the Acrocorinth.[134] It is uncertain, however, whether the rattle served originally as a toy or was placed in the grave for an apotropaic purpose. In children's burials from the middle Byzantine period, bells were either suspended from a necklace or sewn to garments. Many examples can be drawn from funerary contexts in central Europe and the Balkans.[135] One specimen was found together with two medallions in an eleventh-century child's grave from the medieval necropolis of Krstevi, near the fortified town of Prosek on the Demir Kapija gorge, or Iron Gate, in the Republic of Macedonia. Both the pear-shaped bell and the medallions have tiny pebbles inside that make a rattling noise.[136]

The *lunulae* and pendant bells reflect the continuity of popular beliefs from the Graeco-Roman past. Their use was not eradicated by the introduction of the cross, which was believed to be the most powerful agent against evil. As early as the fourth century, John Chrysostom urged parents to teach young children how to make the sign of the cross on their foreheads.[137] He also spoke of the cross as "a miraculous gift," which could be found on beds and on clothes, and which protected bodies besieged by demons.[138] Only during the sixth and seventh centuries did the use of the pectoral cross become commonplace. In this period, tiny metal crosses were also suspended from children's necks. A small silver cross with an inset of glass paste at the intersection of the arms was found in Kjulevča on the lower Danube in a young girl's grave dated to the second half of the seventh century.[139] Several other crosses from funerary contexts were also found in Greece in graves of female children. For example, in the tenth-century burial of a little girl in Makri, Hebros district, Thrace, a glass bracelet was unearthed and a small bronze cross on the chest. The cross arms have small spherical knobs at the ends.[140] Similar crosses, dated to the tenth or eleventh century, have been discovered in Corinth. Their average height is 3 centimeters.[141] Another example that

134   N. Bookidis and J. E. Fisher, "Sanctuary of Demeter and Kore on Acrocorinth: Preliminary Report V; 1971–1973," *Hesperia* 43, no. 3 (1974): 285.

135   Fiedler, *Studien zu Gräbefeldern*, 194–95.

136   E. Maneva, *Krstevi: Medieval Necropolis* (Skopje, 2000), 141 (grave no. 29), fig. 3, pl. 22.

137   PG 61:106. See Dickie, "Fathers of the Church" (above, n. 112), 32.

138   PG 48:826. For a discussion on this passage, see Maguire, "Garments Pleasing to God" (above, n. 48), 218.

139   Fiedler, *Studien zu Gräbefeldern*, 185, pl. III.7.

140   Laskaris, *Monuments funéraires*, 248, no. 440, after N. Kallintzi and N. Eustratiou, Τὸ ἀρχαιολογικὸ ἔργο στὴ Μακεδονία καὶ Θράκη (= *ΑΕΜΘ*) 2 (1988): 501; N. Kallintzi, *ΑΕΜΘ* 4 (1990): 617; idem, *ΑΕΜΘ* 10 (1996): 907, and 916, fig. 31.

141   G. R. Davidson, *Corinth: Results of Excavations Conducted by the American School of Clas-*

Figure 12   Gold pectoral reliquary cross, obverse (left) and reverse (right), ninth or tenth century, Dumbarton Oaks, Byzantine Collection (acc. no. 53.12.22), scale 1:2 (photo: courtesy of The Image Collections and Fieldwork Archives, Dumbarton Oaks Research Library and Collection)

may have belonged to a young girl is a tiny gold reliquary cross in the collection of Dumbarton Oaks, dated to the ninth or tenth century (fig. 12).[142] The cross is only 2.5 centimeters high and 1.5 centimeters wide. The cruciform inscription reads: Θεοτόκε βοήθι Ἑλένης Ἀμ(ήν), "Theotokos [Mother of God], help Helen. Amen." Its small suspension loop may originally have been sewn onto the clothing of a baby for protection, as is common today.

Food, Childbirth, and Childhood

"Every family rejoices at the birth of a child, but how much greater is the celebration when the child is born to a noble family!" So proclaims Theodoros

─────────

sical Studies at Athens, vol. 12, *The Minor Objects* (Princeton, N.J., 1952, repr. Meridien, Conn., 1987), 258, nos. 2075, 2076.

142   Dumbarton Oaks, Byzantine Collection. Inv. no. 53.12.22. M. C. Ross, *Catalogue of the Byzantine and Early Medieval Antiquities in the Dumbarton Oaks Collection* (Washington, D.C., 2005), 23, no. 17, pl. 23. Ross proposes a date in the sixth or seventh century for this cross. However, the epigraphic form of the beta with an open loop, like a Latin capital R, rather points to the ninth or tenth century. See discussion in Pitarakis, "Female Piety in Context" (above, n. 107), 155 and fig. 13.3, 164.

Prodromos at the beginning of his poem to Alexios, the son of the *sebastokrator* Andronikos, brother of Manuel I.[143] The row of dancing women with ribbons hanging from their hands, a unique occurrence in the banquet scene from the cycle of the blessing of the infant Virgin by the priests, in the church of the Virgin Peribleptos in Mistra (third quarter of the fourteenth century), for instance, may be viewed as an illustration of the celebrations that accompanied the birth of a child into an aristocratic family in Byzantium.[144] To illustrate the value of a child within a Byzantine family, I focus here on the central role of food in the celebrations of childbirth; I then examine food as a medium through which parents, especially mothers, expressed their feelings toward their children.

Antique Tradition and Food in Celebrations of Childbirth

The study of the material culture of childhood in Byzantium opens a rich seam for the exploration of social customs rooted in antiquity. References to antiquity in the art produced during the reigns of the Macedonian and Palaiologan emperors, for example, should be understood not only as quotations from older literary and artistic works, but also as an evidence of *longue durée* in customs related to childhood. Archaeological evidence on the material environment of the newborn Byzantine child is scarce. By contrast, the iconography of the birth of the Virgin, which inspired other birth scenes of holy children and biblical figures, contains precious details on the ceremonies surrounding the birth of a child and its material expressions.[145] The emphasis on the intimate domestic reality, with

---

143   Theodore Prodromos, *Historische Gedichte,* 406, no. 44.1–5; Kazhdan and Epstein, *Change in Byzantine Culture* (above, n. 30), 108.

144   See G. Millet, *Monuments byzantins de Mistra* (Paris, 1910), pl. 128.4; M. Chatzidakis, *Μυστράς: Η μεσαιωνική πόλη και το κάστρο* (Athens, 1993), 67; Lafontaine-Dosogne, *Iconographie de l'enfance* (above, n. 31), 130.

145   See Lafontaine-Dosogne, *Iconographie de l'enfance,* 89–121; G. Babić, "Sur l'iconographie de la composition de la 'Nativité de la Vierge' dans la peinture byzantine," *ZRVI* 7 (1961): 169–75; A. Katsioti, *Οι σκηνές της ζωής και ο εικονογραφικός κύκλος του Αγίου Ιωάννη Προδρόμου στη Βυζαντινή τέχνη* (Athens, 1998), 48–60; I. Ševčenko and N. Patterson-Ševčenko, *The Life of Saint Nicholas of Sion: Text and Translation* (Brookline, Mass., 1984), 21–23, fig 1; Patterson-Ševčenko, *The Life of Saint Nicholas* (above, n. 20), 66–69; S. Dufrenne, "À propos de la naissance de David dans le Ms. 3 de Dumbarton Oaks," *Hommage à M. Paul Lemerle, TM* 8 (1981): 125–34.

a rich body of evidence from material culture, suggests that the inspiration for such scenes is drawn from everyday reality.[146]

The constant features of the images of the birth of the Virgin in their period of crystallization, from the tenth to the twelfth century, are a procession of women (servants or visitors) bringing food to the mother in childbed, and the traditional bathing of the newborn baby, often including a depiction of its cradle.[147] Studies devoted to the iconography of the birth of the Virgin have pointed out that the procession of women, usually three in number, bringing food to the mother in childbed is drawn from a popular tradition rooted in Greek antiquity.[148] A more contemporary textual reference that may explain the procession of women in the iconography of the birth of the Virgin is the chapter on the birth of a *porphyrogennetos* in the tenth-century *Book of Ceremonies*. According to the text, on the eighth day following the child's birth, the empress's bedroom was specially hung with cloth of gold and *polykandela*. Following the benediction ceremony in the atrium of the church and the public announcement of the name of the newborn infant, the baby was set in his cradle, and both mother and child were covered with gold-woven spreads. The wives of the court dignitaries passed through the empress's bedroom bringing their good wishes and gifts. From the day of birth of the *porphyrogennetos* onward, another custom was to distribute a beverage called *lochozema* (a nourishing soup given to women who had just given birth) at the portico of the triclinium of the Nineteen Couches and at the crossroads of the central avenue of the city, which led from the Chalke to the Forum Bovis. People would drink the *lochozema* over a seven-day period to wish the empress good health.[149] The modern Turkish tradition of the *lohusa şerbeti*

146   See discussion in Kalavrezou, *Byzantine Women and their World* (above, n. 3), 15–16; Parani, *Reconstructing the Reality of Images* (above, n. 41), 192–93, 225.

147   The cradle is found in the iconography of the birth of David in the ninth-century ivory box in the Palazzo Venezia and in eleventh-century representations of the birth of John the Baptist, such as that in Saint Sophia, Ohrid; the first dated examples of the cradle in the iconography of the birth of the Virgin are not earlier than the twelfth century. See discussion in Lafontaine-Dosogne, *Iconographie de l'enfance* (above, n. 31), 104–5, 109. For the origins of the iconography of the first bath of the newborn, see P. J. Nordhagen, "The Origin of the Washing of the Child in the Nativity Scene," *BZ* 54 (1961): 333–37; V. Juhel, "Le bain de l'Enfant Jésus: Des origines à la fin du douzième siècle," *CahArch* 39 (1991): 111–32. For a recent discussion on the introduction of the cradle next to the bath scene of the newborn, see also M. Meyer, "On the Hypothetical Model of Childbearing Iconography in the Octateuchs," Δελτ. Χριστ. Ἀρχ. Ἑτ. 26 (2005): 316–17.

148   Lafontaine-Dosogne, *Iconographie de l'enfance*, 96; Babić, "Sur l'iconographie," 174.

149   *Constantini Porphyrogeniti imperatoris De cerimoniis aulae byzantinae*, 2, 21, ed. J. J. Reiske (Bonn, 1829–30), 1, 618–19 (hereafter *DeCer*). On this ceremonial and on the gifts brought for

(sherbet of the woman in childbed), a beverage made from cubes of red, clove-flavored sugar (*lohusa şekeri*) and offered to visitors in the homes of newborn babies, most probably derives from the Byzantine *lochozema*. The belief in the apotropaic value of the color red, especially in protecting children, in conjunction with its imperial connotations, suggests that the *lochozema* had the same red coloring as the *lohusa şerbeti*.[150]

In the absence of textual evidence on the celebration of childbirth in Byzantine families, one can refer to religious rituals that were probably mirrored by current secular tradition. An interesting example is the early Christian ritual that consisted in the preparation of a dish made with boiled flour, known as *semidalis*, that was exchanged in honor of the childbed of the Virgin. This celebration, which took place on the Sunday after Christmas, was strongly denounced and prohibited by canon 79 of the Council in Trullo (692) on the grounds that because the Virgin had given birth miraculously and suffered no pain, she could not be celebrated as a normal mother was.[151] Another ritual of similar character, in which the offering made to Mary is bread, is listed among the heresies that were denounced by the church father Epiphanius of Salamis in his *Panarion*.[152]

---

the birth of imperial children, see also P. Grierson, "The Date of the Dumbarton Oaks Epiphany Medallion," *DOP* 15 (1961): 224.

150   The red coloring was probably obtained from cochineal or carmine dye. In Byzantium, sugar was chiefly used for medicinal preparations. See *Byzantine Monastic Foundation Documents,* vol. 2, ed. J. Thomas and A. Constantinides Hero (Washington, D.C., 2000), 761, 825; A. Dalby, *Flavours of Byzantium* (Blackawton, Totnes, Devon, 2003), 227, s.v. *sakhar*. During the Ottoman period, at least until the seventeenth century, sugar was a luxury sweetener available only to the highest strata of society. See the description by Evliya Çelebi (ca. 1646) of the outstanding dishes at the table of the Governor (Vali) of Erzerum, Defterdârzâde Mehmet Paşa, which are said to be made with sugar (Z. Kurşun, S.A. Kahraman, and Y. Dağlı, eds., *Evliya Çelebi Seyahatnamesi,* 2. Kitap [Istanbul, 1999], 190).

151   "Therefore, whereas certain persons are known to boil flour and give this to one another in honour, as it were, of the childbed of the immaculate Virgin-Mother, we decree that no such thing should be done by the faithful." See G. Nedungatt and M. Featherstone, eds., *The Council in Trullo Revisited* (Rome, 1995), 159–60. For a discussion of this canon, see also J. Herrin, "'Femina Byzantina': The Council in Trullo on Women," *DOP* 46 (1992): 104–5; Congourdeau, "Regards sur l'enfant nouveau-né" (above, n. 3), 166.

152   This heretical practice was performed by the women of a fourth-century group in Arabia, commonly called the Kollyridians, who had brought it from Thrace and Upper Scythia. On a specified day of the year, certain women would decorate a square stool, spread a cloth on it, set out bread, and offer it in Mary's name, and then all would partake of the bread. To strengthen his denunciation of the worship of Mary as a goddess, Epiphanius draws a biblical parallel with the women of Judea who made offerings of cakes to the queen of heaven (Jeremiah 7:16–19). See K. Holl, ed., *Epiphanius,* vol. 3, *Panarion haer. 65–80, De Fide* (Berlin, 1985), chs. 79.1 and 79.8. See English translation by F. Williams, *The Panarion of St. Epiphanius, Bishop of Salamis: Books II and III (Sects 47–80, De Fide)* (Leiden, 1994), 620–21, 627. See also discussion in V. Limberis, *Divine Heiress: The Virgin Mary and the Creation of Constantinople* (London, 1994), 118–20. On

BRIGITTE PITARAKIS

Despite their condemnation by church officials, sacrificial food offerings to the Virgin Mary persisted among Greek Orthodox populations in late nineteenth- and early twentieth-century Cappadocia. We may assume that they were practiced throughout the history of the Byzantine Empire. Valuable information may be drawn from the Archives of Oral Tradition of the Center for Asia Minor Studies in Athens,[153] from which we learn, for example, that a Christmas ritual (that is, for the feast of the Nativity) in the region of Niğde involved a dish made with unboiled cracked wheat, commonly called *erse* (or *herise*), *korkot,* or *dolazi of the Panagia.*[154] *Dolazi* may be understood as a corrupted version of the Turkish *dölaşı,* literally meaning "food for fecundity." In popular belief, this special dish was brought to the Virgin Mary when she gave birth to Christ. It was also the traditional gift brought to the homes of women in childbed. A variant of the same ritual in neighboring Caesarea was to prepare *kaygana,* a kind of pancake made with flour and eggs. *Kaygana* was prepared in the homes of the faithful following the celebration of the Christmas liturgy. But, once again, it was also the traditional gift to women in childbed.[155]

It appears therefore that whether pagan or Christian, the celebration of fecundity involved the preparation and gift offering of wheat-based foods. The long-standing tradition of food offerings for childbirth may be reflected in the production of clay figurines discovered during the excavations of the pilgrimage shrine of Abu Mina in Egypt. The figurines, dated to the fifth through the seventh century, include a series of pregnant women, some of whom are shown holding a deep dish with both hands as if presenting it as an offering. These statuettes were probably used as votive offerings in the crypt to promote a woman's fertility or a healthy pregnancy.[156]

---

the practice of eating *kolluria* and variants in the Orthodox church, see M. Gedeon, "Ἐγκρίδες ἢ λαλάγγια," Ἐκκλ. Ἀληθ. (1905): 595–97.

153   Many thanks to Marianna Yerasimos, who has generously shared her documentation from the Center for Asia Minor Studies in Athens.

154   Center for Asia Minor Studies, Archives for Oral Tradition, interviews: envelope 301, district of Niğde, informants Eleni Zamboglu and Polikseni Ioannidi, interview by H. Samulidis, February 6, 1958; envelope 301, district of Niğde, informant Polikseni Ioannidi, interview by E. Andreadis, November 11, 1960; envelope 229, district of Niğde, Enehil/Dikilitaş, informant Maria Topaloğlu, interview by E. Andreadis, May 11, 1960.

155   Centre for Asia Minor Studies, Archives for Oral Tradition, envelope 53, district of Kayseri, Ağırnas, informant Evlon Ananiadu, interview by L. Tomi, December 11, 1957.

156   On these figurines, see J. Engemann, "Eulogien und Votive," in *Akten des XII. Internationalen Kongresses für Christliche Archäologie, Bonn 22.-28. September 1991, Teil 1,* Jahrbuch für Antike und Christentum Ergänzungsband 20.1 (Münster, 1995), 231–33, pl. 17a, b; P. Grossmann, "The Pilgrimage Center of Abû Mînâ," in D. Frankfurter, ed., *Pilgrimage and Holy Space in Late*

In the light of these rituals, the function of the vessels held by the procession of women in the iconography of the birth of the Virgin takes on a new meaning. The central motif in compositions dated from the tenth to the twelfth century is a deep circular dish containing oval foodstuffs. Sometimes the dish is protected with a white towel, which implies purity or sacredness. Rather than eggs, as has been tentatively suggested,[157] the contents are probably bread rolls.[158] The same type of vessel filled with bread rolls recurs in a less common allegorical composition, labeled as "Thank-Offering for the Queen" (εὐχαριστία περὶ τῆς βασιλίδος), in the twelfth-century illustrations of the Homilies of James Kokkinobaphos.[159] Here the vessel is presented to the infant Virgin, who lies in a richly decorated cradle and is dressed in the blue *maphorion* of her adulthood. The woman who presents the vessel, which is protected by a white towel, is accompanied by a second one holding a *flabellum* made of flowers and leaves. The image illustrates the text of the homilies referring to the meal given to all in honor of the Virgin, which is distinct from the banquet held on her first birthday.[160]

Another type of vessel presented to Anna in representations of the birth of the Virgin from the Komnenian era is a deep pot covered with a lid. In this case, we may speculate that it contained a warm dish of boiled flour, or *semidalis,* which a weakened woman in childbed could eat with a spoon. Precisely this detail is found in the birth of the Virgin at the church of Saint Panteleimon, Nerezi (1164),[161] and recurs at Saint Achilleus in Arilje, Serbia (1295/96).[162]

Offerings of beverages become standard features of the iconography of the birth of the Virgin during the thirteenth and fourteenth centuries. The large, long-necked jar held by the one of the women who approach Anna in the mosaic

Antique Egypt (Leiden, 1998), 299–301; L. Wamser, ed., *Die Welt von Byzanz: Europas Östliches Erbe; Glanz, Krisen und Fortleben einer Tausendjährigen Kultur,* exhibition catalogue (Munich, 2004), 206, nos. 294–95.

157   Lafontaine-Dosogne, *Iconographie de l'enfance* (above, n. 31), 93, 101, 107, 111.

158   Such an identification is proposed in Dufrenne, "À propos de la naissance de David" (above, n. 145), 130–31.

159   Vat. Gr. 1162, fol. 38 v. See C. Stornajolo, *Miniature delle Omilie di Giacomo Monaco (Cod. Vatic. gr. 1162) e dell'Evangeliario greco Urbinate (Cod. Vatic. Urbin. gr. 2)* (Rome, 1910), pl. 14; I. Hutter and P. Canart, *Das Marienhomiliar des Mönchs Jakobos von Kokkinobaphos: Codex vaticanus graecus 1162* (Zurich, 1991), 33 (here also, the contents of the dish are identified as eggs).

160   PG 127:568. See discussion in Lafontaine-Dosogne, *Iconographie de l'enfance,* 101–2.

161   See D. Bardzieva Trajkovska, *St. Panteleimon at Nerezi: Fresco Painting* (Skopje, 2004), fig. 77.

162   G. Millet and A. Frolow, *La peinture du Moyen-Âge en Yougoslavie (Serbie, Macédoine, Monténégro),* vol. 2 (Paris, 1957), pl. 78.1 and 79.3; B. Todić, *Serbian Medieval Painting: The Age of King Milutin* (Belgrade, 1999), 113, fig. 54.

Figure 13 Chora Church, Constantinople (1316/21), birth of the Virgin, inner narthex, eastern lunette of the second bay (photo: courtesy of The Image Collections and Fieldwork Archives, Dumbarton Oaks Research Library and Collection, neg. no. K86-58-59)

panel from the Chora Church (1316/21; fig. 13) in Constantinople,[163] for example, may have been intended for the distribution of *lochozema* as it is described in the *Book of Ceremonies*.[164] The size, oval body, narrow base, blue color, and gold banding of the jar admit its comparison with a distinctive group of giant lusterware known as Alhambra vases, usually thought to be merely decorative. The occurrence of such a jar in the Chora mosaic suggests that these were also functional; it also strengthens the links of the image with secular reality.[165] Indeed, offerings

163 Underwood, *Kariye Djami* (above, n. 40), 1:66–7; ibid., vol. 2, *Plates 1–334, Mosaics,* pls. 98–99; R. Ousterhout, *The Art of Kariye Camii* (London, 2002), figs. 18, 39.
164 *DeCer* (above, n. 149), 619.
165 E. Dauterman Maguire, "Byzantine and Medieval Ceramics from the Kariye Camii," in *Restoring Byzantium: The Kariye Camii in Istanbul and the Byzantine Institute Restoration,* ed. H. A. Klein and R. G. Ousterhout, exhibition catalogue (New York, 2004), 65.

of food and beverages, intended to restore the health of the woman who gives birth, have always been the central element of the celebration of childbirth.

Food as an Illustration of the Bond between Parents and Children

The nurture of a child entails the creation of emotional bonds between the child and the caregiver. The word *anatrophe* used by the Greeks for both nurturing and raising suggests that the nurture of a child could be viewed as the first stage of education.[166]

The sentimental bond of a child with its mother, or its wet nurse, finds its first expression at the moment of breastfeeding. Individual representations of the Virgin Galaktotrophousa, or "she who nourishes with milk," first appear in the early Christian period. Images of a child suckling at the mother's breast are also attested in infancy cycles devoted to the products of miraculous births, such as the Virgin and John the Baptist, but they are much less frequent.[167] Among the rare examples of the Galaktotrophousa in the scene of the Nativity of Christ, we can mention the images from Omorphe Ekklesia (1282) in Aegina, in the Saronic Gulf, Greece (fig. 14),[168] and the fourteenth-century paintings of the Cypriot church of Saint Nicholas of the Roof in Kakopetria.[169] Although the image has obvious symbolic meaning, it may also allude to the intimacy between mother and child in contemporary reality.[170] The natural and intimate gesture of

166   As an allegorical figure, Anatrophe is associated with the scene of the first bath of newly born mythological heroes such as Dionysos and Achilles in fourth- to fifth-century mosaic floors from Nea Paphos, Cyprus. See A.-L. Rey, "Autour des nourrissons byzantins et de leur régime," in Dasen, *Naissance et petite enfance dans l'Antiquité,* 365 (above, n. 95); M. Corbier, "La petite enfance à Rome: Lois, normes, pratiques individuelles et collectives," *Annales: Histoire, Sciences Sociales* 54, no. 6 (November–December 1999): 1280–84.

167   Anna breastfeeding the Virgin is mentioned twice in the *Protevangelion of James,* once after the Nativity (*Protevangelion* 5:2) and a second time following the benediction of the priests in the context of the banquet given at her first anniversary (*Protevangelion* 6:2–3). See Lafontaine-Dosogne, *Iconographie de l'enfance,* 130, 133; S. E. J. Gerstel, "Painted Sources for Female Piety in Medieval Byzantium," *DOP* 52 (1998): 97–98. The texts are silent about Elizabeth breastfeeding John the Baptist. This iconographic composition was probably inspired by that of the birth of the Virgin. See Katsioti, *Οι σκηνές* (above, n. 145), 57.

168   V. Foskolou, "The Virgin, the Christ-Child and the Evil Eye," in Vassilaki, *Images of the Mother of God* (above, n. 107), fig. 21.1 and color pl. 16. See also G. Soteriou, "Η Όμορφη Ἐκκλησιὰ Αἰγίνης," Ἐπετηρὶς Ἑταιρείας Βυζαντινῶν Σπουδῶν 2 (1925): 254–56.

169   A. Stylianou and J. A. Stylianou, *The Painted Churches of Cyprus: Treasures of Byzantine Art,* 2nd rev. ed. (Nicosia, 1997), 70 and fig. 28.

170   Christ suckling at his mother's breast is mentioned in the *Protevangelion* (19:2) and in Luke (11:27). For the early images in Egypt and their symbolic function as a metaphor of the Eucharist,

the Virgin in the Nativity scene from Omorphe Ekklesia (fig. 15), shown holding her breast in the palm of her hand while pressing it from above with her thumb to facilitate the extraction of milk, in conjunction with the vernacular elements in this composition, support this hypothesis. The rocky mass of the cave of Bethlehem is fringed by a broad band inscribed with a row of six eyes, reflecting an interesting symbiosis of magic, folk tradition, and Christian religion.[171]

Although wet-nursing was a common practice, especially among the upper strata of society, not all children thrived with wet nurses. Pleas for maternal breastfeeding appear in the writings of philosophers and moralists from the Roman Empire as well as in Byzantine hagiographic literature.[172] The writers argue that it strengthens family cohesion by creating durable emotional bonds and also favors the transmission to the child of the mother's values. The importance of maternal breastfeeding in late antique society finds an evocative illustration in a fourth-century funerary epitaph praising the moral virtues and piety of a young Christian woman from Athens. The tragedy of her death is heightened by the observation that her infants will go unsuckled after her death.[173] A later discussion of maternal breastfeeding can be found in the sixth-century Life of Simeon Stylite the Younger. Early signs of the ascetic career of the holy man are seen during his infancy: the saint refused to suckle the milk of his mother whenever she had eaten meat. Consequently, he remained without food the whole day long.[174] Maternal breastfeeding was also valued among the high levels of middle

---

see E. Bolman, "The Enigmatic Coptic Galaktotrophousa and the Cult of the Virgin Mary in Egypt," in Vassilaki, *Images of the Mother of God,* 13–22; E. Bolman, "The Coptic Galaktotrophousa Revisited," in *Coptic Studies on the Threshold of a New Millennium: Proceedings of the Seventh International Congress of Coptic Studies,* ed. M. Immerzeel and J. van der Vliet (Louvain, 2004), 1173–84. The Constantinopolitan origins of this iconographic type in the early period are discussed in A. Cutler, "The Cult of the Galaktotrophousa in Byzantium and Italy," *JÖB* 37 (1987): 335–50.

171 The association of the eye motifs with the Nativity may be understood in relation to the popular beliefs about the demoness Gello. See Sorlin, "Striges et Géloudes" (above, n. 3), 426, 434–35; R. P. H. Greenfield, "Saint Sisinnios, the Archangel Michael and the Female Demon Gylou: The Typology of the Greek Literary Stories," *Byzantina* 15 (1989): 105, 107–8, 110, 112, 122–23.

172 V. Dasen, "L'allaitement maternel," in Gourevitch, Moirin, and Rouquet, *Maternité et petite enfance en Gaule romaine* (above, n. 110), 110–12. See also G. Coulon, *L'enfant en Gaule romaine,* 2nd rev. ed. (Paris, 2004), 51–52; Corbier, "La petite enfance à Rome" (above, n. 166), 1274–80. For a survey of Byzantine sources, see J. Beaucamp, "L'allaitement: Mère ou nourrice?" *JÖB* 32, no. 2 (1982): 549–58, and a recent discussion in Rey, "Autour des nourrissons byzantins" (above, n. 166), 369–75.

173 Papanikola-Bakirtzi, *Everyday Life in Byzantium* (above, n. 5), 484–85, no. 658.

174 *La vie ancienne de saint Syméon stylite le Jeune (521–592),* ed. P. Van den Ven (Brussels, 1962), 7, chap. 6, lines 1–4.

Figure 14   Omorphe Ekklesia, Aigina, Greece (1289), Nativity scene (photo: courtesy of the Byzantine and Christian Museum, Basiliko Idryma Ereunon Archives, inv. BIE 8-18)

Byzantine society. From Michael Psellos's encomium for his mother, we understand, for example, that it was considered a good sign if a baby did not accept a wet nurse but only its mother's nipple.[175]

The expression of Byzantine parents' feelings toward their children is also illustrated by their concern about their food. In the Life of Theodore of Sykeon, we find lengthy descriptions of his mother's anguish because the young Theodore did not eat properly and, instead of returning home for lunch after school, preferred to go through the day without eating anything. Once back home in the evening, after having attended church and received communion, he would eat pancakes of boiled wheat with water.[176] The priority given by Byzantine mothers to their infants in the related matters of food and health is eloquently

175   Sathas, *Bibliotheca graeca Medii Aevi* (above, n. 23), 5:5; Kaldellis, *Mothers and Sons* (above, n. 16), 19, 59.
176   *Vie de Théodore de Sykéôn* (above, n. 68), 5–6, ch. 6. See discussion in Kiousopoulou, *Χρόνος καὶ ἡλικίες* (above, n. 1), 67.

BRIGITTE PITARAKIS

Figure 15 Detail of fig. 14: the nursing Virgin surrounded by eyes (photo: courtesy of the Byzantine and Christian Museum, Basiliko Idryma Ereunon Archives, inv. BIE 8-19)

Figure 16 Chora Church, Constantinople (1316/21), playing children, scene of the multiplication of the loaves, outer narthex, third domical vault, southeastern pendentive (photo: courtesy of The Image Collections and Fieldwork Archives, Dumbarton Oaks Research Library and Collection, neg. no. 28-106-1951)

expressed in the mosaic decoration of the Chora Church in Constantinople. In the front row of the multitudes who are given bread in the scene of the multiplication of the loaves, we see a mother pushing her baby toward Christ (fig. 16). A mother reproducing the same gesture is introduced in the scene of Christ healing a multitude.[177]

In contrast to examples of mothers striving to feed their children, one might mention a horrible episode of cannibalism illustrated in the ninth-century miniatures from the Sacra Parallela in the Bibliothèque nationale de France, Paris (Paris. gr. 923). The illustrations accompany the account by Flavius Josephus of an incident that occurred during Titus's siege of Jerusalem. Driven to despair during the famine, a woman committed the abomination of slaying her own child after

---

177   Underwood, *Kariye Djami* (above, n. 40), vol. 2, pls. 242, 279; C. Mango and A. Ertuğ, *Chora: The Scroll of Heaven* (Istanbul, 2000), 141, pl. 55, and 155, pl. 62; Ousterhout, *The Art of Kariye Camii* (above, n. 163), 69, fig. 62.

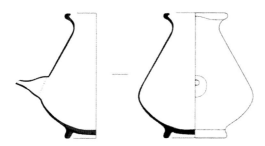

Figure 17 Glass baby feeder from Néris-les-Bains (Allier) (after the drawing by Anna Moirin in Rouquet, "Les biberons, les tire-lait," [see n. 181], 117, fig. 2)

nursing him. After having roasted the body, she ate half of it herself and offered the remnants of the meat to the rebel soldiers, who departed trembling.[178]

Abandoned and orphaned infants who could not be fed by their mothers were reared on alternative foods, such as gruels made from cereals.[179] An interesting testimony is in a passage from the Life of Theodore Tiron about his infancy. Following the death of his wife during labor, Theodore's father fed his son with a gruel made from wheat, barley, and honey that he administered to the baby in a glass vessel provided with a nipple-shaped tip. When the baby's teeth started to appear, he started eating bread, made of the finest wheat flour and soaked in white wine, that his father fed him with a spoon.[180] It has been argued that this passage might be a later addition to the Vita of the saint, but its mention of a glass baby feeder is noteworthy. The shape of the vessel is difficult to determine. Its description recalls the well-known group of late antique spouted glass goblets commonly identified as baby feeders, some of which were found in children's burials (fig. 17).[181] However, this identification is disputed, and other, similarly

178   K. Weitzmann, *The Miniatures of the Sacra Parallela, Parisinus Graecus 923* (Princeton, N.J., 1979), 246–47, fol. 227r, fig. 715.

179   On weaning, see also the article by Chryssi Bourbou and Sandra Garvie-Lok in this volume.

180   See A. Sigalas, "Βίος καὶ ἀνατροφὴ τοῦ ἁγίου μάρτυρος Θεοδώρου," Ἐπετηρὶς Ἑταιρείας Βυζαντινῶν Σπουδῶν 2 (1925): 225; *AASS* Nov. IV, 49:3. On the biography of Theodore, see also C. Walter, *The Warrior Saints in Byzantine Art and Tradition* (Aldershot, 2003), 46 and n. 9. For a discussion on this passage, see Kiousopoulou, *Χρόνος καὶ ἡλικίες* (above, n. 1), 67, and Rey, "Autour des nourrissons byzantins" (above, n. 166), 373.

181   From the second century C.E. onward, glass baby feeders replaced vessels made of baked clay. This shift seems to have been dictated by hygienic concerns. For a typology of the shapes and a discussion of their function, see N. Rouquet, "Les biberons, les tire-lait ou les tribulations

shaped pieces have been classified as lamp fillers.[182] Chemical analysis of the residues contained in clay and glass baby feeders from Gallo-Roman necropolises has revealed the presence of fatty acids with a composition identical to that found in human and animal milk. It has been recently suggested that these were used not as feeding bottles but as breast pumps.[183]

As in modern societies, food served as a reward in the education of young children during late antiquity. A letter addressed by Saint Jerome to Gaudentius in Rome on the rearing of his infant daughter Pacatula provides a vivid insight into the daily life of children, balancing educational activities with moments of tenderness and the pleasures of food and play.[184] Through offerings of food, mothers could also become involved in their children's games. One of Saint George's miracles tells about the boys of the village of Phatrynon in Paphlagonia, one of whom promised Saint George a *sphongaton,* a sort of omelet, if the saint helped him win at his games. After his prayer, he went back to his games and won, not once but several times. Then the boy went to his mother and asked her to prepare the promised gift for the saint. The woman, who loved both her little child and the martyr, immediately made the omelet and gave it to the child to take to the church.[185] This offering to Saint George also shows how children reproduced the

---

d'une tubulure peu commune," in Gourevitch, Moirin, and Rouquet, *Maternité et petite enfance en Gaule romaine* (above, n. 110), 116–22. On the same subject, see also Coulon, *L'enfant en Gaule romaine,* 60–64; D. Gourevitch and J. Chamay, "Femme nourrissant son enfant au biberon," *Antike Kunst* 35, no. 1 (1992): 78–81.

182   See, for example, Dauterman Maguire et al., *Art and Holy Powers* (above, n. 53), 63, no. 11.

183   Rouquet, "Les biberons, les tire-lait," 118–20.

184   Gaudentius had written to Jerome for advice on the rearing of his daughter, whom he had already dedicated to a life of virginity. The response is dated 413 C.E.:

> For how can you speak of self-control to a child who is eager for cakes, who babbles on her mother's knee, and to whom honey is sweeter than any words? . . . Meanwhile let her learn the alphabet, spelling, grammar, and syntax. To induce her to repeat her lessons with her little shrill voice, hold out to her as rewards cakes and mead and sweetmeats. She will make haste to perform her task if she hopes afterwards to get some bright bunch of flowers, some glittering bauble, some enchanting doll. She must also learn to spin, shaping the yarn with her tender thumb; for, even if she constantly breaks the threads, a day will come when she will no longer break them. Then when she has finished her lessons she ought to have some recreation. At such times she may hang round her mother's neck, or snatch kisses from her relations. Reward her for singing psalms that she may love what she has to learn. Her task will then become a pleasure to her and no compulsion will be necessary. (Jerome, letter 128, trans. New Advent Catholic Encyclopedia, www.newadvent .org/fathers/3001128.htm.)

185   *Sainte Thècle: Saints Côme et Damien: Saints Cyr et Jean (extraits): Saint Georges,* ed. A.-J. Festugière (Paris, 1971), 315, miracle 10.

devotional patterns of their parents. Variants of this story, enriched with anecdotal details, continued to circulate in the oral tradition of Greek Orthodox populations in modern Cappadocia, the region from which the saint was believed to originate. In one such story, from the town of Nevşehir, for example, the game the children were playing is described as knucklebones.[186] In another instance, we are told that the *sphongaton* was offered to Saint George as a thanksgiving by a woman who was delivered from a difficult childbirth. The woman placed the *sphongaton* in front of the icon of the saint in his sanctuary.[187] Another kind of food mentioned by Byzantine authors that expresses the sentimental bond of mothers toward their children is a honey cake named *melittouta*. In one of the poems Theodore Metochites wrote to himself after his reversal of fortune, he described infants in tears and crying when someone took away the *melittouta* given to them by their loving mothers.[188]

Together with sweets, children were also fond of the fruits that their parents, grandparents, or other close relatives or friends gave them. In an account of Empress Theodora's daughters visiting their grandmother, the latter gave them presents and fruits before secretly teaching them to venerate icons that she kept concealed in a chest.[189] Another interesting episode is that of Omurtag (or Koutragon), king of the Bulgarians, who summoned the young Basil while he was affably smiling and running around, and he kissed the child before giving him an enormous apple. The twelfth-century illustration of this episode in the Skylitzes manuscript shows the little child with his apple gently sitting on the lap of Omurtag, who holds him in a gesture of affection, pressing his face against the rounded cheeks of the child.[190] Beyond its highly symbolic content, the composition offers a beautiful illustration of the emotional links created through the gift of a delicacy.[191]

---

186   Center for Asia Minor Studies, Archives for Oral Tradition, envelope 28, Aravisos Neapolis, informant Sophia Debletoglou, interview by C. Pioudaki, January 13, 1954.

187   G. P. Maurochalybides, *Αξέχαστες Πατρίδες: Η Αξό Καππαδοκίας,* vol. 1, ed. O. Maurochalybides, P. Maurochalybides, and A. Maurochalybides (Athens, 1990), 261, no. 16.

188   Featherstone, *Theodore Metochites's Poems,* 108, poem 18, line 336.

189   Theophanes Continuatus, *Chronographia,* ed. I. Bekker (Bonn, 1838), 90–91; *Ioannis Scylitzae Synopsis historiarum,* ed. I. Thurn (Berlin, 1973), 52; *Jean Skylitzès: Empereurs de Constantinople,* French trans. B. Flusin, with notes by J.-C. Cheynet (Paris, 2003), 50. See discussion in W. Treadgold, *The Byzantine Revival: 780–842* (Stanford, Calif., 1988), 310 and n. 427.

190   *Ioannis Scylitzae Synopsis historiarum,* 118; *Jean Skylitzès,* 103. The illustration is on fol. 82r of the Madrid manuscript. See V. Tsamakda, *The Illustrated Chronicle of Ioannes Skylitzes in Madrid* (Leiden, 2002), 125, fig. 200.

191   For the symbolism of the apple, see A. R. Littlewood, "The Erotic Symbolism of the Apple

Toys and Playthings

Toys and playthings are the most representative category of the material culture of children. This is also the only category that provides an image of childhood that is not primarily adult-oriented. Indeed, alongside the organized production of clay toys by adults, children themselves used to construct their toys of "unshaped matter," to borrow the expression of the Vita of Nikephoros of Medikion.[192] The shaping of clay or mud into various playthings and toys was a beloved children's pastime. A frequently cited story of the child Jesus in the apocryphal Gospel of Thomas tells us that, while playing beside a brook with many other children, he fashioned twelve sparrows out of soft clay. When Joseph came to accuse him of not keeping the Sabbath, Jesus clapped his hands, and the sparrows flew away chirping.[193] Yet toys made by children are rarely found in archaeological excavations. One curious clay figurine of crude workmanship found in a late eleventh-century house in Berroia, Chalkidike, has been tentatively identified as a toy fashioned by a child,[194] as has a small toy dish modeled in mud that was found in late medieval layers during the excavations of Qasr Ibrim in the Nubian desert in Egypt. The same contexts have also yielded some examples of dolls' clothing (without actual dolls) and two small rag balls. The authors describe Nubian children making crude dolls from crossed sticks, sometimes with the addition of a head modeled in mud. These figures were then clothed in garments sewn from discarded rags. It also appears that two miniature weavings, crudely woven from brightly colored yarns, are the work of children. Their small size and irregular edges suggest that one or two girls had an early lesson in a useful skill.[195]

Because toys were often presented to children as gifts, they served as an important mechanism of bonding between adults and children. Here I mainly focus on

---

in Late Byzantine and Meta-Byzantine Demotic Literature," *BMGS* 17 (1993): 83–103; S. Trzcionka, "Calypso's Cauldron: The Ritual Ingredients of Early-Byzantine Love Spells," in *Feast, Fast or Famine: Food and Drink in Byzantium,* ed. W. Mayer and S. Trzcionka, Byzantina Australiensia 15 (Brisbane, 2005), 161–66. Earlier sources on this symbolism are discussed in E. Stock McCartney, "How the Apple Became the Token of Love," *Transactions and Proceedings of the American Philological Association* 56 (1925): 70–81.

192 F. Halkin, "La Vie de Saint Nicéphore: Fondateur de Médikion en Bithynie († 813)," *AB* 78 (1960): 401, chap. 1, lines 1–2.

193 Gospel of Thomas 2:1–4.

194 Papanikola-Bakirtzi, *Everyday Life in Byzantium* (above, n. 5), 494, no. 677.

195 See N. Adams, "Textile Materials and Weaves," in *Qasr Ibrim: The Late Medieval Period; 59th Excavation Memoir,* ed. W. Y. Adams (London, 1996), 200–201, figs. 61a, c, e.

the manufactured toys, which reflect the existence of an organized crafts indus-try for children. After considering the toys of the earliest years of Byzantine his-tory, I examine those of older children and present an overview of their outdoor activities and collective games, as well as their privileged relationship with ani-mals. This section ends with a presentation of the role of dolls in the lives of little girls and a discussion of the ambiguity between a toy and a ritual object.

The Basket of Toys of the Byzantine Child

RATTLES AND PULL TOYS

Throughout antiquity, the distinctive possessions of young children were a rattle and a basket of toys. An evocative passage from the *Politics* of Aristotle describes the restlessness of little children: "Besides, children should have something to do, and the rattle of Archytas, which people give to their children in order to amuse them and prevent them from breaking anything in the house, was a cap-ital invention, for a young thing cannot be quiet. The rattle is a toy suited to the infant mind."[196] A beautiful counterpart to the above statement is offered by John Chrysostom, who he observes that "when the toy basket, the rattle, or any other of the toys are taken away, children suffer and are dissatisfied. They become upset and they stamp upon the floor."[197] These two observations, made eight hundred years apart, illustrate the universality and timelessness of chil-dren's play.

The word commonly used for rattle is *seistron,* which also refers to an ancient percussion instrument often associated with fertility rites. A *seistron* is illustrated in the well-known miniature from the sixth-century Vienna Genesis depict-ing the lively episode of Joseph and Potiphar's wife (Gen. 39:9).[198] The sequence includes the figure of a woman standing next to a baby's cradle, holding a rattle. Although miniature in size, the rattle is drawn with precision. It appears to be made of two hemispherical discs mounted on a square frame with a long handle, which could be operated by clapping the discs together. The model for this rattle

---

196   Aristotle, *Politics,* book 8, part 6, 1340b, in *The Complete Works of Aristotle,* ed. J. Barnes (Princeton, N.J., 1984).

197   PG 61:38.

198   See B. Zimmermann, *Die Wiener Genesis im Rahmen der antiken Buchmalerei: Ikonogra-phie, Darstellung, Illustrationsverfahren und Aussageintention* (Wiesbaden, 2003), fol. 6r, fig. 31, 155–60.

Figure 18 Seated Maltese dog, terracotta rattle, mid-fourth century, Agora excavations, Athens (inv. T 1422), scale 1:1 (photo: courtesy of the American School of Classical Studies at Athens)

would have been made in painted wood, or more probably metal, and offers a simpler version of the crotals used by adults and made of copper alloy.[199]

A more common material for the manufacture of rattles was baked clay. These toys were mass-produced in double-sided molds. The sound was made by small pellets of clay, pebbles, or grains inside the hollow container. To appeal visually to a small infant, clay rattles were often made in the shape of domestic animals and painted in bright colors. Several examples yielded by the excavations of the Athenian Agora offer a valuable guide to the study of clay toys

---

199 E.g., a pair of copper alloy crotals from Egypt of unknown date (Roman or Byzantine) in Paris, musée du Louvre, département des Antiquités égyptiennes. Inv. AF 6874 and AF 6875. Height 32.5 cm. See C. Ziegler, *Catalogue des instruments de musique égyptiens: Musée du Louvre* (Paris, 1979), 68–69; *L'art copte en Égypte,* 227, no. 286 (above, n. 44); *Au fil du Nil* (above, n. 44), 158, no. 117. See also an example dated to the third century in Museu Nacional Archeològic in Tarragona, Spain. Inv. no. MNAT 45426. Height 24.5 cm. *Jouer dans l'Antiquité,* exhibition catalogue (Marseille, 1991), 53, fig. 15, and 191, no. 7.

Figure 19   Rooster, terracotta rattle, mid-fourth century, Agora excavations, Athens (inv. T 1423), scale 1:1 (photo: courtesy of the American School of Classical Studies at Athens)

from late antiquity. Animal-shaped figurines, many of which served as rattles and toys, are reportedly more frequent in the period after 267 C.E.[200] This evolution from objects mainly intended for a religious purpose to a secular one illustrates the transformation of the agora from a public to a residential area. The last stages of production during the late fourth and fifth centuries are characterized by clay artifacts wrung out of exhausted molds. The Maltese lapdog and the rooster are among the most popular shapes for the rattles from the Athenian Agora.[201] Two intact examples, both dated to the mid-fourth century, are on display in the Museum of the Ancient Agora in the stoa of Attalos. The seated

200   Grandjouan, *Athenian Agora* (above, n. 130), 6:25.
201   Ibid., 26, 29, and pls. 18, 20–21.

Maltese dog in buff clay has traces of red paint and still has a pebble inside. On this object the left mold is different from the right (fig. 18).[202] The rooster, in pinkish buff clay, also has traces of red paint and a pebble inside (fig. 19).[203] Bird-shaped clay rattles and figurines were common throughout the ancient world. They are equally attested in Roman and Byzantine Egypt. The nonrattling examples may also have functioned as toys.[204] We may imagine that the child would have supplied vocally the mimetic sound of the bird.

A fragmentary clay rooster found during the excavations of Saint Polyeuktos in Constantinople raises the issue of continuity in the production of popular types from late antiquity.[205] The rooster comes from a layer that has yielded a coin of John II Komnenos (1118–43), but it is mixed with Ottoman pottery. Inventoried among the miscellaneous items, the object was given the general label of a figurine. The rooster, of pale orange clay with matte surface, is 6.9 centimeters tall. The eyes, feathers, and wings are clearly indicated. Because the feet and tail are missing, it is hard to determine the figure's original function. If the missing parts formed a closed shape, it could have been a rattle: the hollow interior could perfectly well have held clay grains. However, the clay rooster might instead have served as a whistle, a category of toy discussed below. The appropriate spots for the mouthpiece and the whistling hole would be the missing tail and the feet. Although stylistically different, whistles of a similar type continued to be manufactured throughout the Ottoman period. One such example, dated to the first half of the seventeenth century, was yielded by the same excavations.[206]

Next to rattles, the most popular clay toy for small children, from archaic Greece to the Roman and Byzantine period, is the pull toy in the shape of a horse on wheels or saddled with a rider.[207] Once again, John Chrysostom speaks of children of his time who, he says, are happy when they see clay models of chari-

---

202   Ibid., 66, no. 750, pl. 18.

203   Ibid., 68, no. 832, pl. 21.

204   L. Török, *Coptic Antiquities I* (Rome, 1993), 53, no. K5, pl. 74; C. Fluck, "Puppen–Tiere–Bälle: Kinderspielzeug aus dem spätantiken bis frühislamzeitlichen Ägypten," in Froschauer and Harrauer, *Spiel am Nil* (above, n. 6), 19 and 96, no. 13.

205   Harrison, *Excavations at Saraçhane in Istanbul,* 1:275, no. 724 and pl. 457.

206   J. W. Hayes, *Excavations at Saraçhane in Istanbul,* vol. 2, *The Pottery* (Princeton, N.J., 1992), 298, 343, pl. 50j.

207   For a range of clay pull toys throughout antiquity, see M. Andres, *Hessisches Puppenmuseum Hanau-Wilhelmsbad: Die Antikensammlung; Griechische, römische, altorientalische Puppen und Verwandtes* (Hanau, 2000), 30, 32–33, 46, 132–33, 203–5; *Jouer dans l'Antiquité,* 68 and fig. 46, 193, no. 59; 26 and fig. 4, 193, no. 78; 72 and fig. 56, 193, no. 79.

Figure 20 Terracotta wheeled horse (wheels restored), fourth century, Agora excavations, Athens (inv. T 1364), 11 cm high (photo: courtesy of the American School of Classical Studies at Athens)

ots or carts, horses, mule drivers, and wheels.[208] The clay finds from the Athenian Agora include several examples of horses on wheels, together with separate examples of terracotta wheels.[209] In one example, dated to the fourth century, made of grayish buff clay, traces of yellow and red painting over white slip, or liquefied clay, are preserved, and the harness is clearly outlined in relief (fig. 20). The legs are pierced with holes intended for an axle to which wheels were attached, and another hole at the horse's muzzle accommodated the string with which the child could pull the figure.[210] The wheels of the toy are restored.

Another handsome horse on wheels in painted clay, dated to the fourth century C.E., was yielded by the excavations conducted during the recent construction of the Athenian metropolitan railway.[211] The horse-shaped pull toy was

208   PG 59:440.
209   Grandjouan, *Athenian Agora,* 6:28, pl. 19.
210   Ibid., 66–67, no. 781, pl. 19.
211   Athens, Acropolis Metro Station. Inv. No. M. 2535. Height 10.7 cm; length 18.8 cm; maximum width 8 cm. See *The City beneath the City: Antiquities from the Metropolitan Railway Excavations,* exhibition catalogue (Athens, 2000), 79, no. 53.

found alongside an anthropomorphic rattle dressed in a hooded cloak, a well-known attribute of the *genii cucullati* (good demons) venerated as protectors of infants and fertility. The rattle contains small clay balls. Both toys are brightly painted in red and black.[212] A fragmentary clay horse with a pierced muzzle, indicating its use as a pull toy, was found together with other clay artifacts of the fourth to the sixth century during the excavations of the necropolis of Bawit in Egypt in 1901–2.[213] This find can be paralleled by the discovery at a child's grave from Deir al-Nasara, near Antinoe, of a doll's dress together with a wooden horse on wheels.[214] The association of these two toys is interesting, as it seems to indicate that horses on wheels were popular among little girls as well as boys.[215] Clay horses were usually fabricated in double-sided gypsum molds. Two examples attributed to the late antique and early Christian period are in the Hessisches Puppenmuseum in Hanau-Wilhelmsbad, Germany (figs. 21 and 22).[216]

In addition to clay toys mass-produced in molds, late antique archaeology has also yielded hand-modeled examples. Both categories are illustrated among the finds from Egypt but were also common throughout the Mediterranean.[217] Two hand-modeled, horse-shaped clay pull toys were also found during the excavations of Deir Dusawi, a sixth- to seventh-century C.E. site near Gaza, Palestine. The horses are sketchily shaped, and the legs are shaped into loops that were initially intended for the insertion of an axle and wheels, which are lost. On one example, the sides bear the names Leontakis and Stephanos, incised before firing. Leontakis may be a diminutive form of Leontakios. It has been suggested that the two names might refer to the donor and recipient, or to siblings to whom the toy was given. The excavators stress the historic continuity in the production

---

212   Athens, Acropolis Metro Station. Inv. no. M. 2524. Height 14.4 cm, in *City beneath the City,* 85, no. 62.

213   C. Palanque, "Notes sur quelques jouets coptes en terre cuite," *Bulletin de l'Institut Français d'Archéologie Orientale* 3 (1903): 101, pl. 2.4.

214   Calament, *La révélation d'Antinoé* (above, n. 43), 292, n. 952; Gayet, *Le costume en Égypte* (above, n. 59), 244–45, nos. 586–88.

215   An earlier example is the discovery in a child's burial at Corinth of a terracotta horse on wheels together with a coin of Nero; see T. L. Shear, "Excavations in the North Cemetery at Corinth in 1930," *AJA* 34 (1930): 430–31 and fig. 20. A fragmentary earthenware find from an early Christian child's burial in the chapel of Misokampos on Samos has been identified as a toy, without further discussion as to its shape. W. Wrede, "Ein frühbyzantinisches Klostergut vom Misokampos auf Samos," *Mitteilungen des deutschen archäologisches Instituts, athenische Abteilung* 54 (1929): 70; Laskaris, *Monuments funéraires* (above, n. 88), 68.

216   Andres, *Hessisches Puppenmuseum* (above, n. 207), 223–24, nos. 144–45.

217   See Török, *Coptic Antiquities I* (above, n. 204), 53, nos. K4–K6, pl. 74.

Figure 21   Two-sided gypsum mold for a clay horse, late antique–early Christian period, probably from Egypt, Hessisches Puppenmuseum Hanau-Wilhelmsbad, Antikensammlung (inv. MAZ 970 ab) (after Andres, *Hessisches Puppenmuseum* [see n. 207], 223: no. 144)

Figure 22   Right side of a double-sided mold for a clay horse, late antique–early Christian period, probably from Egypt, Hessisches Puppenmuseum Hanau-Wilhelmsbad, Antiken-sammlung (inv. MAZ 515) (after Andres, *Hessisches Puppenmuseum,* 224: no. 145)

of clay pull toys by introducing examples yielded by Iron Age contexts in the same region.[218]

Pull toys for Byzantine children were made from wood and bone as well as clay. A deluxe example is a wheeled horse made from bone in the collection of the Benaki Museum, Athens. The horse is stained with red pigment, but the wheels are left in the natural color of bone, creating an interesting contrast. The small hole in the horse's head would have been used to attach a string by which a child could pull the toy.[219] The archaeology of Egypt provides a rich variety of wooden horses on wheels. In children's graves at Antinoe, for example, two wooden horses were found.[220] Another small group of wooden horses from Antinoe is in the collection of the Louvre. One of the best-preserved examples carries a rider. The circular drill marks on the legs indicate that the horses originally had wheels, which have since been lost. The harness, the saddles, and the manes of the horses are highlighted with red, black, and white paint, traces of which are still preserved.[221] The Coptic wooden toys in the Louvre also include a fine horse with its original wheels as well as the figure of a rider (fig. 23).[222] The object is made from two flat horse-shaped pieces of wood between which the rider is inserted. The three pieces are attached with pegs. A closely related object, similarly fashioned out of two flat pieces of wood and with its original wheels, is in the collection of the Papyrusmuseum of the Österreichische Nationalbibliothek, Vienna.[223] The same collection includes two other examples made of a single flat piece of wood. One of them is distinctive for its interesting painted decoration, which replaces the figure of a rider. A sketchy human figure painted in black, probably the rider, appears on the side of the horse, and the harness is outlined in red.[224] The second example is a horse-shaped piece of wood without

218   L. Y. Rahmani, "Finds from a Sixth to Seventh Centuries Site near Gaza, I: The Toys," *Israel Exploration Journal* 31, no. 1 (1981): 72–76, pls. 12 C–D.

219   Papanikola-Bakirtzi, *Everyday Life in Byzantium* (above, n. 5), 493, no. 674; Georgoula, *Greek Treasures* (above, n. 51), 103, no. 64.

220   A. Gayet, *Notice des objets recueillis à Antinoé pendant les fouilles exécutées en 1899–1900 et exposées au Musée Guimet du 12 décembre 1900 au 12 janvier 1901* (Paris, 1900), 13. See discussion in Calament, *La révélation d'Antinoé*, 292.

221   M.-H. Rutschowscaya, *Musée du Louvre: Catalogue des bois de l'Égypte copte* (Paris, 1986), 86–87, nos. 291, 293–94.

222   Paris, musée du Louvre, département des Antiquités égyptiennes. Inv. no. E 27134. Height 15.8 cm; length 14.8 cm. See Rutschowscaya, *Musée du Louvre,* 86, no. 290; *Au fil du Nil,* 67, no. 37; *Jouer dans l'Antiquité* (above, n. 199), 194, no. 89 and 67, fig. 43.

223   Froschauer and Harrauer, *Spiel am Nil* (above, n. 6), 92–93, no. 8.

224   Vienna, Papyrusmuseum, Österreichischen Nationalbibliothek. Inv. H 44. Height 10 cm; length 19 cm. See Froschauer and Harrauer, *Spiel am Nil,* 94–95, no. 9; C. Fluck, "Kinder-

Figure 23 Wooden horse on wheels, late Roman or Byzantine Egypt, musée du Louvre, département des Antiquités égyptiennes (inv. E 27134) (copyright musée du Louvre / G. Poncet)

a rider. It bears two holes for the wheels, which are lost, and a third, on the muzzle, for the pulling string.[225] Several other examples of wooden horses on wheels from Egypt are now in the Hessisches Puppenmuseum.[226] One example from Akhmim is in the British Museum,[227] and another, found in el-Hibe during the German excavations of 1913–14, is kept in the Ägyptologisches Institut der Universität Heidelberg.[228]

Among the intact pieces remaining in Egypt are two horses on wheels dated to the fifth through the seventh century in the Coptic Museum in Cairo, found in Karanis and Oxyrhynchos/Bahnasa, respectively. The same collection also includes a rare example of a wooden bird-shaped pull toy fitted with a pair of wheels, unearthed in Byzantine levels in Gerzah (the ancient Philadelphia) in the Fayyum.[229] The bird-shaped toy may attest to the continuity within the Byzantine period of a production of clay birds on wheels, popular during the first and second centuries C.E.[230]

Toys and Games of Older Children (the "Second Age")

WHISTLES

For older children, the most popular toys were whistles carried along during outdoor activities. In a well-known passage from the fourteenth-century satirical poem, the *Poulologos* or "Rooster's Wedding," the hero refers to the time "when I was still a child out of Klaretsa and I wore the κατάκοπτα and held a whistle (σφυρίστρια)."[231] Whistles were usually made of clay and, like other toys, they were often shaped like animals. Whistles that survive from antiquity are rela-

---

spielzeug aus dem römischen bis frühislamischen Ägypten," *Kemet* 14, no. 2 (April, 2005): 58, fig. 11.

225   Froschauer and Harrauer, *Spiel am Nil,* 95, no. 10; Fluck, "Kinderspielzeug," 58, fig. 12.

226   Andres, *Hessisches Puppenmuseum,* 229, no. 150 and 235 (without number).

227   *Jouer dans l'Antiquité,* 193, no. 57, 70, fig. 51.

228   *Ägypten Schätze aus dem Wüstensand,* 191, no. 184 (above, n. 45).

229   G. Gabra, *Le Caire: Le musée copte et les anciennes églises* (Cairo, 1996), 98; *L'art copte en Égypte,* 218, nos. 270a–b, 271 (above, n. 44); G. Gabra and M. Eaton-Krauss, *The Treasures of Coptic Art in the Coptic Museum and Churches of Old Cairo* (Cairo, 2006), 143, no. 89a–c.

230   For an example dated to the late first century or the early second century C.E. found in a Roman tomb in Palestine, see J. Zias, "A Roman Tomb at 'Ar'ara," in *'Atiqot: English Series* 14 (1980): 63–65.

231   *Ὁ Πουλόλογος,* ed. and German trans. S. Krawczynski (Berlin, 1960), verses 649–50. In his review of this edition, Linos Politis reassesses the definition of the κατάκοπτα. Rather than "Manschetten," he proposes to understand them as slashed garments, *taillades* in French (although *crevés* seems more accurate). See L. Politis, "Βιβλιοκρισίαι," *Ἑλληνικά* 19 (1966): 178.

tively rare and are therefore difficult to date accurately. One find from the Upper City of Amorion, Phrygia, is shaped like a horse; it is hollow, with a hole in the top of its back, and its rear is modeled into a flattened disc with another hole. It is made of fine reddish clay and bears patches of white slip. The findspot was occupied during the later stages of the Byzantine era and the late Seljuk period (thirteenth to early fourteenth century). Unfortunately, however, the whistle comes from an undated context. The authors suggest it may be residual Phrygian or Roman.[232] Stylistically, the Amorion whistle is quite different from the one in the Hessisches Puppenmuseum, which is identified as Phrygian on the basis of dated parallels.[233] It may be related to a group of animal-shaped whistles and figurines recently found during the excavations conducted from 1995 to 2001 of the area of the Great Palace in Constantinople, on the site of the former Sultanahmet prison. Unfortunately, once again these examples are not associated with a dated context. They come from rubbish pits, together with objects from all historical periods of the city.[234]

Another example from Constantinople, comparable to the zoomorphic whistles from the area of the Great Palace, was found in September 1993 at the imperial harbor of the Boukoleon during the restoration and cleaning of the maritime walls from Phanar to Kumkapı.[235] The whistle has the shape of a dog and has a mouthpiece (fig. 24). It is manufactured from red clay covered with white slip and highlighted with red brushstrokes. Once again, the dating of this find is uncertain. It could be archaic Greek, late medieval, or Ottoman. The Great Palace excavations have also yielded a wide range of kiln materials that were attributed to the Ottoman period on the basis of parallels from Iznik/Nicaea.[236] The development of a craft industry in a specific location is often the result of an

232   Amorion, terracotta toy whistle from the Upper City (Trench L, Context 337). Neg. AM93/08/32. Height 4.9 cm; length 6.8 cm. See C. S. Lightfoot et al., "Amorium Excavations 1993: The Sixth Preliminary report," *AnatSt* 44 (1994): 111–13, 125, pl. 24b.

233   Andres, *Hessisches Puppenmuseum,* 42, no. 19.

234   The finds from the Great Palace excavations are currently being studied by the archaeologists of the Istanbul Archaeological Museums. For a preliminary report, see A. Pasinli, "Büyük Saray bölgesinde Sultanahmet eski cezaevi bahçesindeki 1997–98 kazı çalışmaları / Excavation in the Courtyard of the Former Sultanahmet Prison (in Turkish with English summary)," *Istanbul Arkeoloji Müzeleri Yıllığı / Annual of the Archaeological Museums of Istanbul* 17 (2001): 56–101. A selection of finds was recently published in *Gün Işığında: Istanbul'un 8000 yılı: Marmaray, Metro, Sultanahmet Kazıları,* exhibition catalogue (Istanbul, 2007), 126–63. The chronology ranges from the eighth century B.C.E. to the eighteenth century C.E. and covers all the periods of the Byzantine Empire.

235   Istanbul, Arkeoloji Müzeleri. Inv. no. 94.20 (excavation no. 4). Height 7 cm; length 8.6 cm.

236   Pasinli, "Büyük Saray," no. 23, 73, 101.

Figure 24   Terracotta whistle found at the Boukoleon harbor, Constantinople, date uncertain, Istanbul Arkeoloji Müzeleri (inv. no. 94.20) (photo: courtesy of Istanbul Arkeoloji Müzeleri/T. Birgili)

earlier tradition. The production of these clay whistles may be connected with the place name Tzykalareia (potters' quarter), attested in the text of the *Patria* of Constantinople, a sixth-century account revised in the tenth century.[237] The text refers to the eight columns in latticework of the Tzykalareia (εἰς τοὺς πλεκτοὺς κίονας τῶν Τζυκαλαρείων) located south of the Milion.[238]

---

237   *Scriptores Originum Constantinopolitanarum,* ed. T. Preger, vol. 2 (Leipzig, 1907), P I 52, 141 and P II 104, 207. The passage refering to the Tzykalareia is also mentioned by Petrus Gyllius. See *Pierre Gilles: Itinéraires byzantins,* French trans. and ed. J.-P. Grélois (Paris, 2007), 275. I thank Cyril Mango, who drew my attention to the mention of the Τζυκαλαρέα in the *Patria.* For a definition of the Byzantine *tsoukalia,* see C. Bakirtzis, Βυζαντινά Τσουκαλολάγηνα. Συμβολή στη μελέτη ονομασιών, σχημάτων και χρήσεων πυριμάχων μαγειρικών σκευών, μεταφορικών και αποθηκευτικών δοχείων (Athens, 1989), 130.

238   On the Tzykalareia and their location, see A. Berger, *Untersuchungen zu den Patria Konstantinupoleos* (Bonn, 1988), 203–4, fig. 5, 206, 275–76, 551, 553.

BRIGITTE PITARAKIS

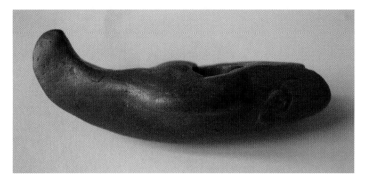

Figure 25 Dolphin-shaped terracotta whistle, seventh century (?), private collection, Istanbul, scale 1:1.5 (photo: courtesy of Garo Kürkman)

To this group of zoomorphic whistles of uncertain date from the archaeology of Istanbul we can add a dolphin-shaped example in a private collection in the same city (fig. 25). The shape of the tail brings to mind the pinched handles of terracotta lamps produced in the fifth through the seventh century in the region of Izmir and Aphrodisias in Caria, which also use the same type of micaceous slip.[239] A seventh-century date can be suggested for the dolphin-shaped whistle. Once again, the establishment of a more secure chronology for the production of clay whistles from late antiquity to the Byzantine era awaits the publication of wider groups of comparanda.

Another popular type of clay whistle attested among the finds from the area of the Great Palace, as well as from several other findspots in Istanbul, takes the shape of a cup that, when filled with water, produces the sound of a bird. The nozzle with a mouthpiece has a small hole on the top that generates the whistling

239   I owe this information to Dominique Pieri, to whom I offer many thanks.

Figure 26   Terracotta whistle, late medieval (?), Istanbul Arkeoloji Müzeleri (inv. no. 75. 21) (photo: courtesy of Istanbul Arkeoloji Müzeleri/T. Birgili)

sound. Several examples are kept in the collections of the Istanbul Archaeological Museums (fig. 26).[240] This type belongs to a tradition that extends from late antiquity to modern times. A whistle of this shape was also found in a third- to fourth-century context in Thessalonike.[241] The cup-shaped whistle is also the trademark of the clay workshops from the neighborhood of Eyüp on the Golden Horn, known for its manufacture of toys from the Ottoman period until the recent past. The activity of the pottery workshops in this neighborhood is attested from the fifteenth century onward.[242]

240   Istanbul, Arkeoloji Müzeleri. Inv. no. 75. 21. Height 4.3 cm; length 4.8 cm. Provenance: bought.
241   The whistle from Thessalonike was found during the excavations on the north side of the Evangelistria cemetery. See Papanikola-Bakirtzi, *Everyday Life in Byzantium* (above, n. 5), 494, no. 676.
242   See T. Yalçınkaya, "Çocukların sevinci Eyüp oyuncaklarıydı," in *Tarihi, Kültürü ve Sanatıyla V: Eyüpsultan Sempozyumu, Tebliğler, 11–13 Mayıs 2001* (Istanbul, 2002), 98 and

BRIGITTE PITARAKIS

The enduring popularity of this type of whistle is beautifully illustrated in the novel *Birds without Wings* by Louis de Bernières, in which bird-shaped whistles are the central element of the life of a group of children from a mixed Greek and Turkish village in Pamphylia in the early twentieth century.[243] The novel is also an interesting testament to the central role of mimesis in children's games throughout history.

BALLS, HOOPS, AND KNUCKLEBONES

Both adults and children played ball games in Byzantium.[244] However, children also juggled with small, colorful, hard balls that allowed them to develop their motor skills. Some examples have been yielded by the archaeology of Egypt. These are hollow balls made from interlaced bands of fabric, wool, or painted leather, secured with cords, and stuffed with straw, animal hair, rushes, and other organic materials. Their diameter varies between 3 and 15 centimeters. Like the previously mentioned examples from Qasr Ibrim in the Nubian Desert, made from bundles of rags sewn or tied together, these balls were often fashioned by

---

fig. 2. On the Ottoman tradition of pottery workshops in the area of the Golden Horn, see F. Yenişehirlioğlu, "Istanbul Tekfur Sarayı Osmanlı Dönemi Çini Fırınları ve Eyüp Çömlekçiler Mahallesi Yüzey Araştırmaları," in *T.C: Kültür Bakanlığı, Araştırma Sonuçları Toplantısı* (Ankara, 1995), 535–566; idem, "Eyüp'te bir Çömlekçi Ailesi," in *Tarihi, Kültürü ve Sanatıyla V,* 66–71; idem, "L'archéologie historique de l'empire ottoman: Bilan et perspectives," *Turcica* 37 (2005): 256–57. See also J. Raby, "Terra Lemnia and the Potteries of the Golden Horn," *ByzF* 21 (1995): 330–31.

243   Iskandar the potter, one of the heroes of the novel, provides an interesting testimony on how these whistles were made and used:

> What he gave them appeared at first sight to be a small amphora, except that he had moulded the neck so that it resembled the head of a bird, with a beak and two small holes for eyes. . . . Instead of a handle he had made a hollow tail whose extremity was skilfully pierced so that it became a whistle, and he had placed two simple loops of clay upon the shoulders of the pot on either side of the neck, so that they resembled wings. "I have made you musical birds," he said. "Give them back to me, and I'll show you. You half fill them with water, like this, and then you blow down the whistle" (L. de Bernières, *Birds without Wings* [London, 2005], 60).

I thank Robert Ousterhout, who drew my attention to this novel.

244   Adults playing ball, called σφαῖρα, are mentioned in the Life of Saint Nikon of Sparta, a city where the area for ball players was also popular among lovers of horseback riding. *The Life of St. Nikon,* text, translation, and commentary by D. F. Sullivan (Brookline, Mass., 1987), 135, chap. 39, line 14. The *tzykanisterion,* a field built in the precincts of the Great Palace of Constantinople, was used for a ball game similar to polo, which was popular at the imperial court. See *Ioannis Cinnami Epitome rerum ab Ioanne et Alexio Comnenis gestarum,* ed. A. Meineke (Bonn, 1836), 263.17–264.11; R. Janin, *Constantinople byzantine: Développement urbain et répertoire topographique,* 2nd ed. (Paris, 1964), 118–19.

the children themselves, or by their parents.[245] The late medieval examples from Qasr Ibrim do not differ much from those dated to late antiquity. A ball in a good state of preservation, acquired in 1896 in Achmim, formerly in the Museum für byzantinische Kunst in Berlin, was lost during World War II but is illustrated in the archives of the museum. The surface of the ball, which has a diameter of 9.5 centimeters, is entirely covered with multicolored woolen yarns that form a pattern of alternating concentric triangles and squares. Its date is uncertain.[246] A few examples dating from the Byzantine period have been preserved and are in the British Museum,[247] the Louvre,[248] the musée des Beaux-Arts in Lyon,[249] and the Hessisches Puppenmuseum.[250] One of the smallest specimens, 3.2 centimeters in diameter, now in the Victoria and Albert Museum, was found together with a small hat that was part of a doll's wardrobe in Oxyrhynchos/Bahnasa in 1897. The ball is plaited with multicolored bands of red, green, blue, cream, and black wool and stuffed with papyrus.[251]

Among the playthings he describes as dear to young children, John Chrysostom mentions balls, hoops, knucklebones, and pebbles.[252] The most popular type of hoop was a single ring propelled by a stick. This was also a popular gymnastics apparatus in antiquity. A well-known composition from the mosaic of the Great Palace in Constantinople depicts four youthful figures, each trundling a pair of hoops; this appears to be part of a common circus act for adults rather than an illustration of children's games. However, the scene may also be viewed as part of the well-attested repertory of late antique circus-game representations in which the players are children.[253]

---

245   Adams, "Textile Materials and Weaves," 200–201, fig. 61b (above, n. 195).

246   Berlin, Museum für Byzantinische Kunst. Inv. no. 9812. See Fluck, "Puppen–Tiere–Bälle" (above, n. 204), 20; C. Fluck, P. Linscheid, and S. Merz, *Textilien aus Ägypten: Staatliche Museen zu Berlin-Preußischer Kulturbesitz, Skulpturensammlung und Museum für Byzantinische Kunst,* Bestandkataloge vol. 1, part 1 (Wiesbaden, 2000), 197, no. 129.

247   London, British Museum, Department of Egyptian Antiquities. Inv. no. 46709. Height 5.5 cm; diameter 6 cm. See *Jouer dans l'Antiquité* (above, n. 199), 195, no. 110, and 93, fig. 77.

248   Paris, Musée du Louvre, Département des Antiquités égyptiennes. Inv. no. AF 1218. Calament, *La révélation d'Antinoé* (above, n. 43), 292, n. 952.

249   Durand and Saragoza, *Égypte, la trame de l'histoire,* 61, no. 31 (above, n. 45). In the catalogue entry, this "ball," strikingly similar to the other examples, is defined as a canopic package and dated to the late pharaonic period (ca. 644–332 B.C.E.) or later.

250   Andres, *Hessisches Puppenmuseum,* 195, no. 121.

251   Kendrick, *Catalogue of Textiles from Burying-Grounds in Egypt* (above, n. 61), 2:91, nos. 613 and 614, pl. 32.614; Janssen, "Soft Toys from Egypt" (above, n. 4), 237 and fig. 8.

252   PG 58:486; PG 59:386.

253   G. Brett, G. Martiny, and R. B. K. Stevenson, *The Great Palace of the Byzantine Emper-*

Games using knucklebones, *astragaloi,* were played by people of both genders and all ages from antiquity to Byzantium.[254] But it is mainly young boys and girls that Greek poetry celebrates as "lovers of *astragaloi,*" φιλαστράγαλοι.[255] Several games were played with knucklebones.[256] An amusing passage from the chronicle of George Akropolites, in his account of the rise of Michael Palaiologos to imperial power, observes that "it was not proper for the Roman Empire, being so great, to be governed by a fruit-picking and knucklebones-playing infant."[257] This passage may be contrasted with the humorous anecdote reported by John Skylitzes about Michael VI's order to clean the Strategion because, it was said, he was looking for the knucklebone he had lost while playing.[258]

Knucklebones were primarily a game of skill, but bones were also used as dice in a game of chance, wherein a particular value was attributed to each of the four distinct sides of the bone. The concave side had the value of four; the opposite, convex side a value of three; the narrower, indented side a value of six; and its opposite, fuller side a value of one. Thus opposite sides add up to seven, just as on a modern die.

Written testimonies show that children continued to play with knucklebones in early twentieth-century Anatolia and Greece as well. We learn of the different names and sizes of knucklebones, taken from the ankle joints of sheep, goats,

---

ors: *Being a First Report on the Excavations Carried out in Istanbul on Behalf of the Walker Trust (The University of St. Andrews), 1935–1938* (Oxford, 1947), 69–70, pls. 29–30; W. Jobst, B. Erdal, and C. Gurtner, *Istanbul: Büyük Saray Mozaiği, Istanbul/Das grosse byzantinische Palastmosaik, Istanbul/The Great Palace Mosaic* (Istanbul, 1997), 50, fig. 36; Antonopoulos, "Prolégomènes à une typologie de l'enfance" (above, n. 39), 274; C. Vendries, "L'enfant et le coq: Une allusion à la gladiature sur la mosaïque des 'enfants chasseurs' de Piazza Armerina," *Antiquité Tardive* 15 (2007): 159–79.

254   On the uses of knucklebones in antiquity, see *Coming of Age in Ancient Greece* (above, n. 2), 277–78; Andres, *Hessisches Puppenmuseum,* 89–90, nos. 60–61, 105, no. 74; P. Amandry, "L'antre corycien II," *BCH* suppl. 9 (1984): 347–78. See also a rich discussion with bibliography in M.-J. Chavane, *Salamine de Chypre,* vol. 6, *Les petits objets* (Paris, 1975), 185–89.

255   See Chavane, *Salamine,* 186. A votive epigram from the Palatine Anthology tells of a schoolboy who received eighty knucklebones as a prize for his good work. *Anthologie Palatine,* 6.308, ed. P. Waltz (Paris, 1960), 2:154.

256   See *Coming of Age in Ancient Greece,* 276–79.

257   ὀπωριζομένου ἢ καὶ ἀστραγαλίζοντος. *Georgii Acropolitae Opera,* ed. A. Heisenberg, vol. 1, Bibliotheca Scriptorum Graecorum et Romanorum Teubneriana (Leipzig, 1978), 157, chap. 76, lines 3–4; ed. and Greek trans. S. I. Spyropoulos (Thessalonike, 2004), 449; *George Akropolites: The History,* trans. and comm. R. Macrides (Oxford, 2007), 343, chap. 76 (where the translation proposed for ἀστραγαλίζοντος is "dice-playing").

258   ὡς τὸν οἰκεῖον ἀστράγαλον ἀναζητῶν, ὃν ἐκεῖσε παίζων ἀπώλεσεν. Skylitzes, ed. Thurn (above, n. 189), 482; *Jean Skylitzès,* 398.

and young calves and painted with various colors.[259] Games using knucklebones, such as the fivestones or *pentelithoi,* could also be played with pebbles or nuts, which are the antecedents of modern marbles.[260] Niketas Choniates mentions the young Alexios II, son of Manuel I, who was eleven years old when his father died, "playing with nuts or casting pebbles."[261]

Natural knucklebones or imitations in clay, metal, or glass are often found in adults' and children's graves from Greek antiquity to the Roman period.[262] A lead knucklebone in a child's burial from medieval layers in Rhodes illustrates the persistence of this practice in Byzantium.[263] Its longevity, together with the use of materials that are not appropriate for playthings, suggests that knucklebones in burials had an apotropaic meaning. Their use in ancient divinatory practices known as *astragalomanteia* would supports this hypothesis.

Such an apotropaic message may shed a new light on the famous mosaic of the multiplication of the loaves in the Chora Church, Constantinople, in which a group of playing children are shown scrambling about on the ground and snatching up what may be identified as knucklebones, nuts, pebbles or, less probably, pieces of bread (see fig. 16).[264] The children, totally absorbed in their play, seem unconcerned with the sacred event taking place above them. Their inclusion in this iconographic composition, at the southeastern pendentive of the third domical vault of the outer narthex, appears to be specific to the decorative program of the Chora Church. Two other young boys who are playfully wrestling on the bank of the Jordan River (see fig. 2) are introduced in the corresponding pendentive of the first domical vault of the outer narthex, to complement scenes related to John the Baptist bearing witness to Christ.[265]

259   K. I. Karalidis, *Τσαριχλί, Νίγδης Καππαδοκίας* (Athens, 2005), 47. Τούμακα (ram); γιάνακα (ram).

260   Among the playthings beloved by children, Neilos the ascetic mentions nuts along with knucklebones and balls (PG 79:386, 796).

261   Καρυατιζόμενον εὑρὼν ἢ ῥιμμῷ λιθιδίων. Niketas Choniates, *Historia,* ed. J.-L. van Dieten (Berlin, 1975), 229.72.

262   Thousands of knucklebones were retrieved in Olynthus from both adults' and children's graves of the Roman period. See D. M. Robinson, *Excavations at Olynthus, Part XI: Necrolynthia: A Study in Greek Burial Customs and Anthropology* (London, 1942), esp. 67, 198.

263   Papanikola-Bakirtzi, *Everyday Life in Byzantium* (above, n. 5), 209, no. 238.

264   Underwood, *Kariye Djami* (above, n. 40), 1:123; vol. 2, pls. 228, 239, 243; Mango and Ertuǧ, *Chora,* 140–41 (above, n. 177). The objects held by the playing children in this mosaic could also be paddles used to propel knucklebones, marbles, pebbles, or other game counters by pressing on them as in tiddlywinks or by pushing them to make them roll. I owe this remark to an anonymous reader.

265   Underwood, *Kariye Djami,* 1:110–111; vol. 2, pls. 211, 214. Wrestling children in a similar

The playing children may be understood as part of the general tendency in Palaiologan art to introduce children's activities into scenes such as the baptism and Christ's entry into Jerusalem, which are inspired by antique models.[266] However, beyond their picturesque value, the recurrence of childhood scenes at fixed locations in Chora may be considered as part of a general scheme intended to neutralize evil or envy. In the image which corresponds to that of the playing children, on the diagonal axis of the third vault, whose northern half is devoted to the miracle at Cana, the subject is the slaying of the white bullock, which conveys the idea of purification. The two images offer a contrast between a scene of violence and a scene of peace. We can also consider these scenes of children in the southeastern pendentives of the first and third vaults in relation to those inserted into the eastern pendentives of the second vault, which are devoted to episodes of Christ being confronted by the devil. Interestingly enough, the image selected for the triangular portion of the southeastern pendentive is the allegorical representation of the kingdoms of the world with which the devil tempts Christ.[267] The image of the kingdoms is juxtaposed with that of a heron eating a serpent in the northeastern pendentive of the second vault. The attack on the serpent, a motif often found on amulets, illustrates the cancellation of the power of the devil.[268] The program thus alternates images of children with images illustrating the fight between good and evil. The motif of playing children in the prominent scene of the outer narthex, set on the main axis of the building above the entrance, in combination with the images set at the same

---

attitude are found in the vertical axis of the scene of Christ's entry into Jerusalem in the paintings of the church of Pantanassa in Mistra, dated around 1430. In the same axis is an infant held by a woman, probably its mother, who thrusts it toward Christ. The groups of playing children in this scene are thought to derive from antique models and reflect the desacralization of religious painting. However, their distribution in this scene and their interaction suggest a symbolic meaning that may be understood in light of the battle between good and evil. Their presence may thus have an apotropaic significance. See D. Mouriki, "The Wall Paintings of the Pantanassa at Mistra: Models of a Painter's Workshop in the Fifteenth Century," in *The Twilight of Byzantium: Aspects of Cultural and Religious History in the Late Byzantine Empire, Papers of a Colloquium held at Princeton University, 8–9 May, 1989,* eds. S. Ćurčić and D. Mouriki (Princeton, N.J., 1991), 221–23, figs. 16, 18; M. Chatzidakis, *Mistra: La cité médiévale et la forteresse; Guide des palais, des églises et de la forteresse* (Athens, 1995), 106, fig. 66; M. Aspra-Bardabaki and M. Emmanouil, *Η Μονή της Παντάνασσας στον Μυστρά: Οι τοιχογραφίες του 15ου αιώνα* (Athens, 2005), 122–28.

266   See Mouriki, "Revival Themes with Elements of Daily Life" (above, n. 39), 458–87.

267   Underwood, *Kariye Djami,* 1:115–16; vol. 2, pls. 216, 223, 226; Mango and Ertuğ, *Chora,* 137; Ousterhout, *Art of Kariye Camii,* 58 (above, n. 163).

268   See E. Dauterman Maguire and H. Maguire, *Other Icons: Art and Power in Byzantine Secular Culture* (Princeton, N.J., 2006), esp. 61, 66, 81–82 and fig. 60.

location on the first two adjoining vaults, may be viewed as part of Theodore Metochites's scheme of warding off the evil eye from the church, which he vividly describes in one of his poems devoted to Chora, written soon after the monastery's restoration in the 1320s.[269]

Collective Games and Outdoor Activities

Some important children's activities have left no material evidence because they were performed outdoors, in the company of other children. In the Life of Saint Nikon from Sparta, for example, we learn that children delighted in playing with pebbles and stones on the seashore.[270] The Life of Saint Luke of Steiris refers to children who take pleasure in toys, jokes, games, lively activity, and running.[271] References to children's games in hagiographic literature are usually intended to contrast with the outstanding maturity and seriousness of the future saint, who follows the model of the *puer senex* and eschews childish activities.[272] The mother of Nikephoros of Medikion, for example, who gave her three sons a good education, found teachers to "teach them holy letters" and kept them away from amusements tainted by association with the old cults, such as carnivalesque dances, races at the hippodrome, and plays in the theaters—all the sorts of things, says the hagiographer, that delight young children.[273] Similar language is found in the Life of Saint Nikon, where we read that when the holy man was a child, "he did not have the mind of a child. Nor did he devote himself to toys and sports and races and horses and other things desirable and beloved by the young."[274]

Children's imaginations created a multitude of games out of their natural surroundings. Such representations are sometimes included among the genre scenes in Byzantine iconography. Children climbing a tree to pick its fruits, playing

269   M. Treu, ed., *Dichtungen des Gross-Logotheten Theodoros Metochites* (Potsdam, 1895), poem A, lines 1020–26. For an English translation of this passage, see J. M. Featherstone, "Parisinus graecus 1776: Theodore Metochites's Poems and the Chora," in *The Kariye Cami Reconsidered,* ed. H. A. Klein, R. Ousterhout, and B. Pitarakis, Istanbul (forthcoming).

270   *Life of St. Nikon* (above, n. 244), 54, 55 (English translation), chap. 10, lines 33–34.

271   *The Life and Miracles of St. Luke of Steiris,* text, translation and commentary by C. L. Connor and W. R. Connor (Brookline, Mass., 1994), 9.

272   See Hatlie, "Religious Lives of Children" (above, n. 7), 189–92; Kalogeras, "What Do They Think about Children?" (above, n. 1), 6–7, 9–19; Moffatt, "Byzantine Child" (above, n. 16), 706–7. For the iconography of the *puer senex,* see Antonopoulos, "Παιδαριογέρων" (above, n. 20), 215–31.

273   Halkin, "La vie de Saint Nicéphore" (above, n. 192), 406, chap. 5, lines 25–29.

274   *Life of St. Nikon,* 32 and 33 (English translation), chap. 2, lines 20–22.

with dogs, birds, or monkeys, or pushing each other in a swing suspended from
a tree (fig. 27) are among the genre scenes in the illustrations of the Paris manuscript of the Homilies of Gregory of Nazianzos, dated to the twelfth century.[275]
Playing with animals was apparently a favorite pastime. The Great Palace mosaics from Constantinople include several representations of children interacting
with animals either in play or for work. Among them are scenes depicting two
boys, one leading, the other driving two geese; a boy who tries to come to the
aid of two hares that are pursued by dogs; a child who holds his little dog in his
lap to prevent him from getting near a griffin eating a lizard; and two other boys
who are given a ride on a dromedary.[276]

Descriptions of children playing with birds and animals are also found in
written sources. The miracle accounts of Saint Thecla include stories of groups of
young children accompanied by their nurses, enjoying themselves in the atrium
of the shrine of Hagia Thecla in Seleukia, and running after and playing with
various kinds of birds.[277] One miracle concerns a toddler at the age of weaning

275   Paris gr. 550; G. Galavaris, *The Illustrations of the Liturgical Homilies of Gregory Nazianze-
nus,* Studies in Manuscript Illumination 6 (Princeton, 1969), 167–68, fols. 6r–v, figs. 403–4; fol.
9v, fig. 406; fol. 204r, fig. 416; fol. 100r, fig. 420; fol. 251r, fig. 426.
276   Brett, Martiny, and Stevenson, *Great Palace* (above, n. 253), 74–76, pls. 32, 33, 34; Jobst,
Erdal, and Gurtner, *Istanbul: Büyük Saray Mozaiği* (above, n. 253), figs. 30, 32, 38.
277   *Vie et miracles de Sainte Thècle,* ed., trans., and commentary by G. Dagron (Brussels, 1978),
133–34.

who was suffering from an eye disease said to have been provoked by his inces-sant crying. His wet nurse brought him to Hagia Thecla, imploring the compas-sion of the saint for the child, whose charming face was disfigured by the disease and who had lost half of his sight. The healing miracle took place in the atrium of the church, where it was customary to throw grain to the doves and the many birds that were brought as sacrificial offerings to the saint. While the little boy was happily chasing the birds, one of the cranes, which was probably disturbed by the child (or, as the hagiographer says, ordered by the saint), flew into his face and gouged out the afflicted eye with its beak. The nurse was faint with appre-hension until she realized that the thick and opaque humor which had darkened the pupil of the eye had immediately poured out, as if the membrane had been pierced and skillfully cut by a surgeon's lancet. The child recovered his sight and the light in his eye.[278] Many centuries later, when referring to the famous giraffe that had arrived in the capital as a gift from the Mamluk Sultan of Egypt to the Byzantine emperor, George Pachymeres gives a charming account of children who amused themselves by leading the animal by the nose. He adds that the giraffe followed them obediently in every direction they wanted it to go.[279]

Another interesting theme that recurs in written sources concerns children who, during their games, discover a troublesome secret, a forbidden practice, or a plot. We learn, for example, that during his childhood, while fishing in the Orontes, John Chrysostom caught a magic book that someone had discarded out of fear of condemnation.[280] George Pachymeres mentions another testimony from the period of the patriarchate of John XII, in late thirteenth-century Con-stantinople.[281] A group of young people had set up a ladder in order to capture little doves from a nest in the *katechoumeneia* of Hagia Sophia. One of them climbed the ladder, and, while holding the little doves, was attracted by a hole in the nearby column. There he found two vases between which was inserted a leaf-let. The leaflet bore the signature of the former patriarch Athanasios, who, on his first abdication from the patriarchal throne, had hidden it there. It contained an anathema against the people who had slandered him, including the emperor. The discovery of the letter allowed the emperor to appeal to Athanasios to lift

278   Ibid., 350–53, miracle 24.
279   *Georges Pachymérès: Relations historiques,* vol. 1, *Livres I–III,* ed. A. Failler and trans. V. Laurent, CFHB 24, no. 1 (Paris, 1984), 239, book 3, chap. 4.
280   PG 60:275.
281   *Georges Pachymérès: Relations historiques,* vol. 3, *Livres VIII–IX,* ed. A. Failler, CFHB 24, no. 3 (Paris, 1999), 276–77, book 9, chap. 24.

the curse.[282] The pivotal role of children in this story perhaps parallels their presence in the decorative program of the outer narthex of Chora (see above). In both instances, young children serve to neutralize evil.[283]

Byzantine boys were also keen on imitating adult roles, especially the roles of leadership and public office.[284] In the Vita of Athanasios of Athos, for instance, children simulate the roles of army generals, the emperor, and a bridegroom.[285] They were no doubt fascinated with the costume and attributes of the role models. A sophisticated and premonitory game from the childhood of Patriarch Eutychios of Constantinople (d. 582), which the latter played in church school with his classmates, consisted in a child's writing down on the wall his name and a title that would supposedly indicate his future profession. While the other boys chose the titles of high clerics and chief magistrates, Euthychios hoped for the title of patriarch.[286]

Byzantine boys were also fascinated by priests conducting church services; indeed, acting out the liturgy was a popular pastime among Byzantine children. Descriptions of such games in hagiographic tales are often drawn from the lives of important churchmen. An important source is the *Pratum Spirituale* of John Moschos and later versions of its tales. In it we are told, for example, that during his childhood, Athanasius, patriarch of Alexandria, used to play at liturgy and perform the sacrament of baptism.[287] From this tale, we understand that the performance of the liturgy in children's games was deemed acceptable when the

---

282   Ibid., 276–84, book 9, chap. 24. On the letter, see also ibid., 186–94, book 8, chaps. 22–23. See discussion on this document in A. Failler, "La première démission du patriarche Athanase (1293) d'après les documents," *REB* 50 (1992): 156–62.

283   According to Hatlie, "Religious Lives of Children," 192 (above, n. 7), children were used in divination ceremonies employing hypnosis, sleep deprivation, suggestive incantations, and other techniques producing altered psychological states. The author concludes that these practices reflected a belief in children's special ability to act as vessels for visiting spirits, both good and evil. On this subject, see R. Greenfield, *Traditions of Belief in Byzantine Demonology* (Amsterdam, 1988), 292–97. See also S. I. Johnston, "Charming Children: The Use of the Child in Ancient Divination," *Arethusa* 34, no. 1 (2001): 97–118.

284   See examples in Horn, "Children's Play as Social Ritual" (above, n. 7), 112–14.

285   *Life of Athanasios of Athos,* ed. J. Noret, *Vitae Duae Antiquae Sancti Athanasii Athonitae* (Turnhout, 1982), vita A, 6, chap. 8, lines 17–22; vita B, 129, chap. 2, lines 32–34.

286   *Life of Patriarch Eutychius,* ed. C. Laga, *Eustratii presbyteri vita Eutychii patriarchae Constantinopolitani* (Turnhout, 1992), chap. 1, lines 241–48. See discussion of this passage in Kalogeras, "What Do They Think about Children?" (above, n. 1), 16–17.

287   PG 87.3:3084–85. See discussion and bibliography in J. Duffy, "Playing at Ritual: Variations on a Theme in Byzantine Religious Tales," in *Greek Ritual Poetics,* ed. D. Yatromanolakis and P. Roilos (Cambridge, Mass., 2004), 201–2. For other versions of this story, see Horn, "Children's Play as Social Ritual," 113.

actors were destined to become priests or monks. Otherwise, children's enactment of the ritual of the Eucharist or baptism was considered dangerous. The *Pratum Spirituale* includes other beneficial tales in which children's performances of the Eucharist and baptism are ended by natural disasters such as fire, probably caused by divine anger.[288] In all likelihood, these stories were intended to illustrate the efficacy of rites performed by church officials in accordance with church custom and remind believers of the tremendous mystery and power of the Eucharist.

Dolls in the Lives of Byzantine Girls

The doll is a universal toy for little girls. When he speaks of clay carts and horses for boys, John Chrysostom also refers to dolls manufactured in the same material.[289] The doll is a toy through which the girl can project herself into the role of her mother. It can function as the girl's double as she matures. Playing with and caring for dolls in imitation of motherhood prepares a girl for her destiny of marriage and child rearing.[290] A passage from the Life of Agatha by the patriarch Methodios (843–847) speaks eloquently about teenage girls "striving to breastfeed even figuratively in their childish play."[291] The fascination that the act of breastfeeding held for these young girls may be contrasted with a much earlier testimony, Plutarch's letter of consolation to his wife after the death of their two-year-old daughter. The author reports with tenderness how his little girl used to invite her nurse to offer the breast and suckle not only other infants, but even the inanimate objects and playthings the child took pleasure in.[292]

288 See the tale about the boys from Apamea who recited the prayer of consecration in a game: PG 873:3080–84 and discussion in Duffy, "Playing at Ritual," 203. Another tale about children from a mixed Christian-Jewish village from Palestine who imitated the baptism of a Jewish child is edited in T. Nissen, "Unbekannte Erzählungen aus dem Pratum Spirituale," *BZ* 38 (1938): 361–65, chap. 8.

289 PG 59:440.

290 On the role of the doll in maturation rites in antiquity, see discussion in V. Dasen, "Les lieux de l'enfance," in *Gender Studies in den Altertumswissenschaften: Räume und Geschlechter in der Antike,* ed. H. Harich-Schwartzbauer, T. Späth, and and J. Hindermann (Trier, 2005), 67–71; M. Argyriadi, *La poupée dans la vie et l'art grecs de l'antiquité à nos jours* (Athens, 1991), 11–18, esp. 17; Horn, "Children's Play as Social Ritual," 102–4.

291 E. Mioni, "L'Encomio di S. Agata: Di Metodio Patriarca di Costantinopoli," *Mélanges Paul Peeters II, AB* 68 (1950): 58–93; D. Krausmüller, "Divine Sex: Patriarch Methodios' Concept of Virginity," in *Desire and Denial in Byzantium: Papers from the Thirty-First Symposium of Byzantine Studies, University of Sussex, Brighton, March, 1997,* ed. L. James (Aldershot, 1999), 62.

292 Consolation to His Wife, line 608. *Plutarch's Moralia,* 7, English trans. by P. H. de Lacy and B. Einarson (Cambridge, Mass., 1959), 583.

The hundreds of finds from funerary contexts raise the question of how we differentiate between a fertility idol or amulet and a little girl's toy. Bone figurines have been found massed together in female burials as well as in domestic contexts in Egypt and Palestine and are dated between the seventh or eighth and the late tenth century.[293] Recent studies conducted on the textiles from the garments of these dolls suggest an extension of this chronology until the Mamluk period.[294] The function of these figurines appears to relate to fertility and childbirth. However, we know that objects intended to enhance fertility, such as the pendant *lunulae,* for example, were also believed to be beneficial for children. Transforming such figurines into dolls that would prepare a little girl for motherhood is arguably a natural extension of this function.

One example is a bone doll from Egypt in the collection of the Benaki Museum in Athens, which is dressed in an extraordinary costume (fig. 28).[295] The figurine, dressed in delicate and precious garments, has prominent breasts and flat folds on the abdomen, the lower part of which is outlined by a large protruding triangle symbolizing the reproductive powers of women (fig. 29).

293   See discussion in Török, *Coptic Antiquities I* (above, n. 204), 60; *Ägypten Schätze aus dem Wüstensand,* 202, no. 203 (above, n. 45); Andres, *Hessisches Puppenmuseum* (above, n. 207), 225–27, nos. 146–48. A bone figurine very similar to the Benaki doll was found in a seventh- to eighth-century context at el-Burj (between Ramla and Ramallah) in Palestine. See Rahmani, "Finds from a Sixth to Seventh Centuries Site near Gaza" (above, n. 218), 77 and pl. 15A. During the Polish excavations conducted at the site of Kom el-Dikka, in the heart of modern Alexandria, such bone figurines were yielded by layers dated from the ninth to the late tenth century. See E. Rodziewic, "Reliefs figurés en os des fouilles de Kom el-Dikka," *Études et travaux (Travaux du Centre d'Archéologie médiévale)* 10 (1978): 317–36. See also G. Pinch, "Childbirth and Female Figurines at Deir el-Medina and el-'Amarna," *Orientalia* 52 (1983): 405–14. Several examples are illustrated in J. Strzygowski, *Catalogue général des Antiquités égyptiennes du Musée du Caire: Koptische Kunst* (Vienna, 1904), pl. 18; Wulff, *Altchristliche und mittelalterliche, byzantinische und italienische Bildwerke, I* (above, n. 63), pl. 22.

294   See C. Fluck, "Eine Koptische Puppentunika," in *Ägypten und Nubien in spätantiker und christlicher Zeit: Akten des 6. Internationalen Koptologenkongresses Münster, 20.–26. Juli 1996,* vol. 1, *Materielle Kultur, Kunst und religiöses Leben,* ed. S. Emmel, M. Krause, S. G. Richter, and S. Schaten (Wiesbaden, 1999), 139–40; C. Fluck, "Ägyptische Puppen" (above, n. 4), esp. 389, 398.

295   Athens, Benaki Museum. Inv. no. 10737. Height 13.5 cm; width 3 cm. See Argyriadi, *La poupée,* 20 and fig. 25; S. Tsourinaki and R. Cortopassi, "Οι Αιγυπτιακές κούκλες του Μουσείου Μπενάκι," *Αρχαιολογία* 74 (2000): 74–75, no. 3 and figs. 3–4; R. Cortopassi, "Les poupées dans l'Antiquité," *Archeologia* 373 (December, 2000): 47; *L'art copte en Égypte,* 217, no. 267 (above, n. 44); Fluck, "Ägyptische Puppen," 397–98 and pl. 24. We may recall the modern Greek folk tradition of the so-called bride-dolls, commonly named *koutsounes,* which were dressed in the local bridal costume and bedecked with coins as amulets. They symbolized a girl's future wedding and were kept among her dowry goods. M. Argyriadi, "The Influence of Christian Ritual and Tradition on Children's Play: Religious Toys and Games," *Εθνογραφικά* 9 (1993): 215; Argyriadi, *La poupée,* 23.

Figure 28   Bone doll dressed in fourteen layers of tunics, front and back views, Fatimid period, Benaki Museum, Athens (inv. no. 10737) (photo: courtesy of the Benaki Museum)

Figure 29   Naked bone figurine without the dresses shown in fig. 28, front and back views

Pregnancy and breastfeeding, the two essential functions of a woman's body, are thus emphasized. Two holes drilled at the level of the arms suggest that the figurine was initially fitted with articulated arms, allowing it to be dressed and undressed. On a similar example in the British Museum, the arms are attached with strings.[296] The Benaki figurine is an attractive female figure with real hair, dark and long, fastened with a dark, pastelike substance (resin or wax). The restoration work conducted on its garments has revealed that it is dressed in fourteen layers of sleeveless tunics. Five are made of linen cloth, five of cotton (one of them is dyed blue), two of alternating red and dark green woolen fabric, and two of a vegetal material, dyed dark blue and resembling raffia, possibly of hemp. The first and the fourteenth tunics bear a decorative brocade strip made up of a row of octagons inscribed with star motifs. Remains of silks in different colors have been preserved. The band was originally bordered with red lines, while the octagons stood on a blue ground, and golden silk was inserted in the points of the stars. The commonly accepted date for this doll, on the grounds of its costume, is the Fatimid period (eleventh–twelfth centuries). According to a study by Cäcilia Fluck, however, the brocade pattern resembles examples from Mamluk Egypt (thirteenth–fourteenth centuries). In this case, one should question whether the bone figurine is contemporary with its garments.[297]

Probably not all the bone figurines of this type were designed to be dressed. The remains of other figurines, however, suggest that they were usually clothed: in another category of bone figures, equally numerous, only the head is carved, and the remaining parts of the body are limited to an elongated triangle. The spiked end of the triangle was probably intended to be fastened to a body made of cloth and stuffed with rags, papyri, or vegetal materials.[298] On one such example in the Benaki Museum, dated to the eighth or ninth century, the large eyes are outlined with black paint.[299] The doll has real hair attached with a black paste (bitumen). The body is stuffed with rags, which also give plasticity to the breast. The arms are wooden sticks attached to the body with linen thread. The outer casing of the rag doll is made of linen cloth with a blue checked pattern in

296 Argyriadi, *La poupée*, fig. 34.
297 Fluck, "Ägyptische Puppen," 398.
298 Argyriadi, *La poupée*, figs. 32–33.
299 Athens, Benaki Museum. Inv. no. 10390. H. 11 cm; W. 8 cm. Argyriadi, *La poupée*, fig. 28; Tsirounaki and Cortopassi, "Οι Αιγυπτιακές κούκλες," 76, no. 5, figs. 8–9; Cortopassi, "Les poupées dans l'Antiquité," 47–48; *L'art copte en Égypte*, 217, no. 269; Fluck, "Ägyptische Puppen," 395–97 and pls. 22–23.

indigo blue. A doll of similar type, with a bone head and a body made of rags, was found in seventh- to eighth-century layers in Nessana, Palestine.[300] Another parallel to the Benaki doll is in the Kelsey Museum of Archaeology, University of Michigan, Ann Arbor. Its body, which is a tapering extension of the head, was inserted through a hole in the cloth and tied at the back with green yarn. A mass of tricolored yarn hair (blonde, red, and black) is attached to the doll's head. The object is not dated.[301]

The archaeology of Egypt has also yielded several examples of rag dolls entirely fashioned with fabric and stuffed with vegetal materials. On these dolls, the sexual parts are usually accentuated. On an example in the Benaki Museum (fig. 30), for instance, dated to the Fatimid period, the sex is indicated by a triangle painted with black ink.[302] The same ink has been used for drawing the features of the face (eyebrows, nose, and mouth). The breasts are emphasized by two irregular circles made with folded fragments of checked canvas. The arms are made with an articulating piece of wood at the level of the shoulders. The doll is fabricated from cloth crudely sewn together and stuffed with vegetal materials. It is dressed in three tunics, two made of hemp canvas, the third of blue and white checked cotton.

The Greek word *nymphe* that the Byzantines commonly employed for a doll also has the meaning of *bride,* and thus may connote the role of the doll as companion in the young girl's transition from maiden to woman. The presence of dolls in young female burials may therefore acquire a new meaning. Because death before marriage involves a disruption of the transition from maiden to woman, in the burial the doll may act as the symbol or substitute for the deceased girl as a bride and future mother. Young girls were often buried with their favorite doll, which was sometimes accompanied by its wardrobe as well as by miniature furniture and tools, as an allusion to the unfulfilled destiny of the girl as a housewife.[303] In the sarcophagus of the young Creperia Tryphaena, from Trastevere, Rome, a beautiful ivory doll was found with accessories such as little combs,

300   Rahmani, "Finds from a Sixth to Seventh Centuries Site near Gaza" (above, n. 218), 76 and pl. 14E.
301   Kelsey Museum of Archaeology, University of Michigan, Ann Arbor. Inv. no. 66.1.113. Height 12.5 cm; width 6.8 cm. See Dauterman Maguire et al., *Art and Holy Powers* (above, n. 53), 228, no. 145.
302   Athens, Benaki Museum. Inv. no. 16535. Height 18.5 cm; width 14 cm. Argyriadi, *La poupée,* fig. 29, Tsirounaki and Cortopassi, "Οι Αιγυπτιακές κούκλες," 73–74, no. 2 and fig. 2; Cortopassi, "Les poupées dans l'Antiquité," 46; Fluck, "Ägyptische Puppen," 391–95 and pls. 18–19.
303   See discussion in Dasen, "Les lieux de l'enfance" (above, n. 290), 67–71, esp. 71.

Figure 30   Rag doll, front and
back views, Fatimid period, Benaki
Museum, Athens (inv. no. 16535)
(photo: courtesy of the Benaki
Museum)

mirrors, bracelets, and a miniature jewel box, together with a ring, which is also the key to the jewel case. The ensemble is dated between 150 and 170 C.E.[304]

A rich range of artifacts of similar character were found in Egypt in graves that appear to have belonged to young girls. In his journal recording the discovery in 1888 of a tomb at Hawara, Fayum, dated to the second century C.E., William Flinders Petrie mentions the presence of an extraordinary quantity of toys, including a terracotta doll equipped with miniature jewels, a large number of spindles and hairnets, a wooden miniature bedstead, a wooden comb, and sandal soles.[305] Two other graves from the same settlement, dated to the fourth century, yielded a similar range of objects reflecting the world of a little girl. Two rag dolls were accompanied by a separate wardrobe, a range of miniature feminine accessories such as a copper mirror, fragments from jewels, a wooden comb, some hairnets, and sandals, as well as spindle whorls, reed needles, and a bag containing unspun dyed wool.[306] Another fourth-century burial from Rome that has yielded two precious ivory dolls is believed to be that of Empress Mary, the young bride of Honorius, who died a virgin.[307]

Even if in later periods the range and quantity of grave goods diminishes, the practice of placing a doll in young girls' burials is widely attested in Egypt during the Byzantine and Fatimid periods. The excavation of a necropolis near the monastery of Jeremiah in Saqqara in 1905–6 uncovered the grave of a little girl holding a rag doll in her hand. The textiles from the little girl's clothing allowed a dating between the sixth and the eighth centuries. The doll belongs to a category of tiny rag dolls made of strips of cloth in alternating colors, which are wrapped to form a round face.[308]

The illustration of the Saqqara doll in the original publication of James Edward Quibell (1907) permits a comparison with another doll from Egypt, said

---

304   K. M. Elderkin, "Jointed Dolls in Antiquity," *AJA* 34 (1930): 471–72; Argyriadi, *La poupée,* 19 and figs. 16 A–B; E. Salza Prina Ricotti, *Vita e costumi dei romani antichi 18: Giochi et giocattoli* (Rome, 1995), 54–56.

305   S. Walker and M. Bierbrier, *Ancient Faces: Mummy Portraits from Roman Egypt* (London, 1997), 210–14, nos. 304–36.

306   The finds from the first burial are in the Petrie Museum in London; those from the second are in the Ashmolean Museum, Oxford. See W. M. F. Petrie, *Hawara, Biahmu and Arsinoe* (London, 1889), 12, pls. 20.22, 21.3; Janssen, "Soft Toys from Egypt" (above, n. 4), 231–33.

307   Elderkin, "Jointed Dolls in Antiquity," 475; Ricotti, *Vita e costumi,* 58–59; Horn, "Children's Play as Social Ritual" (above, n. 7), 104.

308   The doll's present location is unknown. J. E. Quibell, *Excavations at Saqqara 1905–1906* (Cairo, 1907), 34, pl. 39.4; Fluck, "Eine koptische Puppentunika" (above, n. 294), 141; eadem, "Puppen–Tiere–Bälle" (above, n. 204), 2.

to have been found in the necropolis from Akhmim. This doll was once housed in the Museum für angewandte Kunst in Vienna but has since been lost. Fortunately, an illustration is available in a publication on dolls by Fritz Hoeber (1912), who proposes a date in the eighth or ninth century.[309] However, judging from the technique and decorative patterns on the textile fragment that covers the body of the doll, Fluck suggests a later date, perhaps in the Fatimid or early Mamluk period.[310] The new datings proposed for the rag dolls found in funerary contexts in Egypt are interesting because they illustrate the continuity of ancient practices related to the burial of maiden girls. This doll may have been intended to protect and accompany the little girl during her soul's journey to its last abode. With its symbolic function as a bride and mother, the doll would also appease the frustrated soul of the little girl and prevent her from returning to the world to harm newborn children, like the demoness Gello, who died a virgin.[311] This belief reflects an enduring fear of the ἄωροι (prematurely dead) who, deprived of the joys of life by an early death, killed the living out of revenge or jealousy.[312]

Conclusion

The study of objects made for children reveals important aspects of Byzantine material culture. Some children's objects offer a miniature version of the material culture of adults. Depending on the status of the owners, these objects incorporate materials varying widely in value, from gold to copper, and from silk to wool and cotton. Other fabricated objects, especially toys, were specifically intended for a child's world. The materials commonly used for the manufacture of toys are clay and wood, often enhanced with gaudy colors. The use of bone in the manufacture of horses on wheels suggests in turn that toys made from more precious materials, such as ivory, also existed among the wealthy.

309   F. Hoeber, "Alte Puppen," *Kunst und Kunsthandwerk* 15 (1912): 416–17 and fig. 15.
310   This reappraisal is based on the eleventh-century date provided by the C¹⁴ analysis of two closely related textiles in the Ashmolean Museum, Oxford, as well as other parallels from the excavations of Quseir al-Qadim, a port city on the Red Sea, occupied first during the Roman period and again from the second half of the thirteenth to the late fourteenth century. See Fluck, "Ägyptische Puppen," 388–89. On this doll, see also eadem, "Puppen–Tiere–Bälle," 2 and fig. 2; eadem, "Eine Koptische Puppentunika," 141–42.
311   See discussion in N. Baills, "Statut et place de l'enfant dans la société romaine," in Gourevitch, Moirin, and Rouquet, *Maternité et petite enfance en Gaule romaine*, 63–64; V. Dasen, "Les poupées," in ibid., 144; eadem, "Protéger l'enfant," 123.
312   Sorlin, "Striges et Géloudes" (above, n. 3), 413, 419.

BRIGITTE PITARAKIS

My approach to material culture has provided new data that improve our understanding of childhood in Byzantine society and enables us to suggest a new reading of some images of childhood in Byzantine iconography. Iconography compensates for the scarcity of written testimonies on the role of children in the Byzantine life. Persistent features in the iconography of the birth of the Virgin and other birth scenes may be viewed as reflections of deeply rooted ancient secular rituals. One of the most fascinating aspects of the study of childhood in Byzantium is the insight that it affords into distant historical periods and societies, from Graeco-Roman antiquity to modern Greece and Turkey. However, it also yields a deeper and more detailed understanding of family life in early Christianity and Byzantium.

This essay has raised several questions that cannot be resolved with the present state of research, although the publication of new archaeological data may yield answers. Thorough publication of the finds from children's graves will shed new light on burial rites related to subadult deaths in Byzantium, and archaeologists may discover objects related to children that have hitherto been unidentified as such. Like the freshness of a child's mind, the study of the material culture of Byzantine children still needs time and attention before reaching maturity.

Collège de France, Centre national de la recherche scientifique
(UMR 8167—Orient et Méditerranée)

CHILDREN IN BYZANTINE MONASTERIES
Innocent Hearts or Vessels in the Harbor of the Devil?

Richard Greenfield

I N 2001 THE PRIME MINISTER OF SRI LANKA, Ratnasiri Wickra-
manayake, who also held the portfolio of minister for Buddhist affairs,
promoted a campaign to recruit several thousand children into Buddhist
monastic orders. Promising to cope with a shortage of monks that was causing
temples to close and allegedly even threatening the viability of the clergy, the
campaign apparently received an enthusiastic initial response; but it was not
without controversy, and a debate was soon raging about the orthodoxy and
desirability of the plan. The distinguished Princeton anthropologist Gananath
Obeyesekere lent his voice to the opposition, arguing that children as young as
five were being recruited in violation of a prohibition in Buddhist doctrine on
admitting children under the age of fifteen to monasteries. Obeyesekere and
other opponents of the plan also raised the specter of child abuse. In a statement
published in the Sri Lankan press, he described institutionalized monasticism
as "notoriously associated" with sexual abuse and warned of the difficulties of
preventing it. As the debate pushed on to extremes, the prime minister's office
responded by accusing Obeyesekere of being part of a conspiracy to wipe out
Buddhism in Sri Lanka.[1]

I thank Alice-Mary Talbot for her invitation to prepare the original version of this paper for the
Dumbarton Oaks 2006 Spring Symposium and, as always, for her careful and helpful editorial
suggestions. My thanks are also due to the anonymous readers of the manuscript for their advice
and encouragement, and to my student Megan Arnott for her assistance with some of the initial
research.

1   "Princeton Prof. Says 'No' to Sri Lanka Child Monks," *Kyodo News,* 23 July 2001. www
.buddhismtoday.com/english/world/facts/104-notochildmonk.htm.

This paper is not, of course, about contemporary Buddhist monasticism, but this Sri Lankan controversy does make an appropriate starting point for the present discussion, because the arguments being rehearsed and the foundations being claimed for them in the twenty-first century would have been very familiar to those dealing with the same sort of question in the Byzantine world. There, too, doctrinal ambiguity and a variety of traditional practice prevented the establishment of a universal rule defining the appropriate relationship between children and monasteries. Even if some could dismiss the potential dangers of placing children in close proximity to celibate monastics, many others found the threat unconscionable.

The protagonists in the Sri Lankan debate clearly represent extreme views on the issue. Having started at the outer edges, this paper continues by defining the same sort of extreme parameters in the Byzantine context before moving on to a more detailed description and discussion of the general situation that seems to have obtained there. In doing so it focuses primarily on evidence from the ninth through the fifteenth centuries and uses the term *children* to include a loose range from infancy to the mid-teens.[2]

First, then, on the pro-children side, I cite the mid-thirteenth-century scholar and cleric Nikephoros Blemmydes. Certainly not a stranger to controversy or one who always followed the herd, Blemmydes argues in the *typikon* for his monastery near Ephesus for the legitimacy, indeed desirability, of exposing young children to the monastic life, provided the circumstances are right:

> Those who come to the monastery with the intention of adopting
> the monastic life should be received, provided they are at least ten years

2 The sources used here are generally unspecific as to the point at which childhood ends; the only commonly accepted delimiter is the growth of a boy's first beard, which marks him as eligible for membership in a monastic community. Although sources are often unambiguous concerning the age of the children to whom they refer, at other times there may be some overlap in terminology with that used for novices or spiritual children, who may be considerably older. I do my best to avoid basing any discussion on passages where there is obvious doubt. Given the necessary limitations to this essay, I leave a close and technical definition of childhood in Byzantium to others: see, for example, the essay by Günter Prinzing in this volume. I also leave to others consideration of the ongoing debate about broader conceptions of childhood and adolescence in the Middle Ages and the continuity of such conceptions in relation to both ancient and early modern worlds. A most helpful recent survey article on the subject, although it does not consider Byzantine evidence, is B. A. Hanawalt, "Medievalists and the Study of Childhood," *Speculum* 77 (2002): 440–60; wider-ranging, if briefer, is Hugh Cunningham's chapter "Children and Childhood in Ancient and Medieval Europe," in his *Children and Childhood in Western Society since 1500,* 2nd ed. (Harlow, 2005), 18–40.

old, on condition that they appear to have the type of character that is suitable for a life consecrated to God. The fortieth canon of the Sixth Ecumenical Council stipulates: Anyone who wishes to take upon himself the monastic yoke should not be under ten years of age. Therefore such candidates should not be sent away because of their extreme youth, nor should their own parents be allowed to drag them away by force. Nor does the civil law permit this: "We forbid," it says, "that parents remove their own children from holy monasteries when the children have chosen the monastic life."[3] Children should be accepted and everything possible should be done for their care; anyone who teaches them to live according to Christ becomes the mouthpiece of Christ. In general, those who have learned the rudiments of the spiritual life from a tender age are found to be more adept than the others, just as we see happening in all other professions and branches of science. However they should be trained with great sobriety and educated to practice self-discipline in the use of food, sleep, conversation, custody of the eyes, and all else that pertains to this virtue. They should not be too forward either with one another, or with their elders, nor ever enter [another's] cell. They should live apart, but should not form private groups. They should always be where they can be seen, and they should keep to themselves. They should be trained in quick understanding and in asceticism. Earlier they should have agreed to renounce completely all intercourse and contact with their parents and other relatives.[4]

Blemmydes goes on to describe in some detail his very positive experiences with the "many such candidates, whom I trained in this way with the help of God," and he waxes lyrical about the desirability of working with youthful candidates for the monastic life:

> It is obviously a good thing for a man to take upon himself the yoke of virtue in his youth. Therefore one should conscientiously accept such youths and not turn them away because of the work required for their education and custody, nor because of the danger that may arise if one is

3 CIC *Nov,* 3:41.
4 Typikon of Nikephoros Blemmydes for the Monastery of the Lord Christ-Who-Is at Ematha near Ephesos, ch. 9, trans. J. Munitiz in *Byzantine Monastic Foundation Documents,* ed. J. Thomas and A. C. Hero (Washington D.C., 2000), 3:1202–3 (hereafter *BMFD*).

lazy or negligent. On their innocent hearts, which are pure as fresh new writing tablets, one should inscribe with great diligence the different letters and signs that constitute salvation, out of respect for the Savior and Teacher, the one common to us all, or at least out of fear of the account to be demanded of us.[5]

A very different perspective is gained, however, from another typikon, that of the Monastery of Saint John the Forerunner of Phoberos, which dates to the early to mid-twelfth century, around 150 years before Blemmydes.[6] The founder, John, states that it is his wish "in accordance with the instructions of the saints that beardless youths should not be accepted, so that you may be free and untroubled by the harm that comes upon you from them." He then continues, "If there are some who disagree and say that such persons do not cause harm especially in the mountains, they talk foolishly . . . whatever [reason] they put forward is invalid and feeble." He then launches into an astonishingly forceful and graphic diatribe, borrowed from the much earlier (and now notorious) writer Paul Helladikos, a superior of the Elusa monastery in Idumaea in the early sixth century:

5   Compare to Blemmydes' views the rather similar attitude expressed in "The First Greek Life of Pachomius," ch. 49, ed. F. Halkin, *Sancti Pachomii Vitae Graecae*, SubsHag 19 (Brussels, 1932), trans. A. Veilleux, *Pachomian Koinonia*, Cistercian Studies Series 45–46 (Kalamazoo, Mich., 1980), 1:331.

> It is easier for children to reach this degree, that, being obedient from their earliest age, they may eagerly *strain ahead to the things that are before,* (Phil. 3:13) until they *reach perfection,* (Eph. 4:13) like Samuel in the Temple. For ground that has been cleared is ready to be planted with vines step by step, but fallow land can scarcely be planted with good seed after it has been cleaned with great toil. But we know that even clean ground, if it is neglected, will become fallow, as it is written, (Prov. 24:31) even if it was planted with good seed. Just as with fallow land then, purity is attained by care and proper zeal. So let us watch over the children as God wills, so that He who watches over the little ones, as it is written, (Ps. 116[114]:6) may keep watch over our souls *like the apple of his eye.* (Ps. 17[16]:8) Let no one dare to harm a soul, even if [only] in thought, lest he tear out the apple of an eye which sees God the *righteous judge.* (2 Tim. 4:8) As for the manner of keeping [the children], there is no need to say many words; one word is sufficient. The man *who cleanses his own conscience* (Heb. 9:14) to perfection, in the fear of God and in truth, he it is who can keep the little ones with the Lord's help—for he needs his help.

Cf. "The Tenth Sahidic Life of Pachomius," fragment 2, trans. Veilleux, *Pachomian Koinonia*, 1:451–52.

6   Rule of John for the Monastery of Saint John the Forerunner of Phoberos, ch. 58, trans. R. Jordan, *BMFD*, 3:939–43. C. Galatariotou, "Byzantine Ktetorika Typika: A Comparative Study," *REB* 45 (1987): 121–23, comments on the "unparalleled" nature of this passage.

Those who say that they associate with women and children and are not harmed in their souls by this pleasure but are greatly strengthened and face, with resistance, the temptations of fornication and the titillations of the flesh are entirely possessed by the deceit of demons. For the stratagems and devices of the devil are many, as the blessed apostle Paul says (cf. Eph. 6:11), and one of two explanations apply. Either such people are foolish and inexperienced in the evil and devious nature of our unseen enemies, or in reality they are fond of pleasure and are subject to their passions, and with an appearance of reverence and chastity they satisfy their vanity and desire for popularity, while they secretly engage in much evil and lawless pleasure, and will be counted with fornicators and adulterers and sodomites and will be punished with them on the day of judgment, even if, as they say, they carry out nothing shameful that causes harm to their bodies. For if he who has looked on a woman to desire her has committed adultery already with her in his heart (cf. Matt. 5:28), it is much more the case with the one who associates with younger males, whether he is an old man or a younger man in the prime of life and at the height of his powers and seething with fleshly passion.[7]

John then provides a wide-ranging account of how the relentless demon of fornication has been known to lead even the most advanced ascetics astray, like pigs "rolling in mud," not just by obvious heterosexual temptations but by the whole gamut of sexual orientations, from various homoerotic attractions through incest to bestiality, and including the sexual capacity of eunuchs. "For the eye of a man is like a shameless dog running in a frenzy over the faces of those it sees, and always the demons use this weapon against us." If this is the case, he argues, children do not belong anywhere near monks or nuns, however well-intentioned these monastics may be, and he concludes: "Therefore hearing all these things, my fathers and brothers, let us pay close attention to how we walk our road following God and how we live with our younger brothers, lest we find ourselves instead in the harbor of the devil, a prey and delight to our enemies, the demons I mean, who never cease tempting us."

The parameters of the debate and many of the key points are thus clearly set out by these two authors, one arguing that it is both legitimate and perhaps

7   Paul Helladikos, *Epistole,* ed. V. Lundstrom, *Anecdota byzantina e codicibus Upsaliensibus cum aliis collatis* (Uppsala, 1902), 15–23. See further *BMFD* 3:948 n. 77.

desirable for children to be in monasteries, the other that it is the last thing any true monastic should want. As in so many circumstances in human history, the debate plays out between those who are optimistic about our nature and its strength to overcome obstacles on the path to goodness and happiness and those who are pessimistic, seeing instead the frailty of human nature and a profound propensity for evil. It is also true, however, that, because Blemmydes and John stand at two extremes, neither reveals the more commonly accepted views and practices concerning children and monasteries that obtained in Byzantium in this period. In the rest of this paper I attempt to develop an understanding of these more common attitudes and situations.

Certainly children had a legal right to be in monasteries. As Blemmydes points out, the Sixth Ecumenical Council, which met in the late seventh century, had set the age of ten as the minimum for entry.[8] In doing so it was evidently endorsing earlier Christian practice and sentiment, which accepted the presence of children in monastic institutions while taking something of a middle ground between those who wanted to place very young children in monasteries and those who approved of admission only for older youths and girls.[9] Support for this practice was found in biblical exemplars and sayings, in particular the story of Samuel's childhood in the temple[10] and Jesus' admonitions, "Let

8   G. A. Rhalles and M. Potles, Σύνταγμα τῶν θείων καὶ ἱερῶν κανόνων (Athens, 1852–59; repr. Athens, 1966), ch. 40, 2:398.

9   Some examples of children entering or being placed in monasteries in the early Byzantine period are cited below: see especially nn. 30, 40, 54. See also Basil of Caesarea, *Regulae fusius tractatae* 15, PG 31:952–58, which sets out his ideas on the organization and functioning of monastic schools for both boys and girls. These ideas had a direct influence on schools and other related institutions throughout the Byzantine period. Évelyne Patlagean has suggested that the ruling of the sixth council represents a lowering of the age of monastic consent, citing Basil's criticism of relatives who placed very young girls in convents and his endorsement of sixteen or seventeen as the minimum age for entry: see her "L'enfant et son avenir dans la famille byzantine," in her *Structure sociale, famille, chrétienté à Byzance* (London, 1981), X. There seems, however, little evidence that Basil's position on this matter was widely accepted or followed, any more than was the ruling of the council, and it is probably to be seen as yet more evidence of the doctrinal ambiguity that surrounds the issue throughout the Byzantine period.

10   1 Sam. 1–3, cited, e.g., in "First Greek Life of Pachomius," ch. 49, Veilleux, *Pachomian Koinonia*, 1:331 (above, n. 5); John Moschos, *Pratum Spirituale,* ch. 197 (on Athanasios of Alexandria's childhood), PG 87:3085A, trans. J. Wortley, *John Moschos: The Spiritual Meadow (Pratum Spirituale),* Cistercian Studies Series 139 (Kalamazoo, Mich., 1992), 176; and the Vita of Peter of Atroa, ch. 2, *La vie merveilleuse de saint Pierre d'Atroa († 837),* ed. V. Laurent, SubsHag 29 (Brussels, 1956), 71, lines 27–28. The reference is also made explicitly in a number of documents detailing donations of children to Egyptian monasteries in the eighth century; see A. Papaconstantinou, "ΘΕΙΑ ΟΙΚΟΝΟΜΙΑ: Les actes thébains de donation d'enfants ou la gestion monastique de la pénurie," in *Mélanges Gilbert Dagron,* Travaux et Mémoires du Centre d'Histoire et Civilisation

the children come to me" (Matt. 19:14; Mark 10:14; Luke 18:16) and "Whoever receives one such child in my name receives me"(Matt 18:5).[11] Despite frequent prohibitions and dire warnings of the consequences, it seems clear that the tradition of accepting quite young children did not completely evaporate in the later Byzantine period. As I show, children of all ages thus appear regularly within the fabric of Byzantine monastic life, albeit usually in small numbers and under carefully controlled circumstances.

First, however, the opposing view needs to be considered, for a substantial number of passages in the sources, especially the regulatory ones, are concerned with prohibiting children from admission to monasteries and warning of the dangers they pose. Children, the authors of these passages stress, should not be allowed to test vocations in monastic institutions until they have reached a suitable level of maturity (or unattractiveness). This threshold was usually designated for boys as the growing of the first beard, but might also be set at a particular age: sixteen, eighteen, or even the early twenties. Isaac Komnenos, in his mid-twelfth-century typikon for the Kosmosoteira monastery, thus states plainly: "Young men less than twenty-four years old shall not dwell in the monastery, even if they happen to be relatives or friends or acquaintances of the superior or of [any of] the other monks, or in any way especially dear to them, on the pretext of [their] service or instruction or of some expertise or skill, whether theoretical or practical, or of [their] being reared or educated."[12]

As this passage illustrates, all manner of apparently valid justifications for the presence of children are also ruled out. Some regulators and administrators are thus at pains to make sure the prohibition is applied to children who might come or be brought to an institution out of need (such as orphans or beggars), for education, in the course of everyday life (on errands or on feast days, perhaps), or in the course of work (such as apprentices or the offspring of manual laborers). Bishop Neilos, the author of the early thirteenth-century typikon for the Cypriot Machairas monastery, rules that beardless boys "shall neither be

---

de Byzance 14 (Paris, 2002), 522–23, 525. See also T. G. Wilfong, *Women of Jeme: Lives in a Coptic Town in Late Antique Egypt* (Ann Arbor, 2002), 104. Cf. the account of Jesus in the temple at Luke 2:41–51.

11   The whole passage, Matt.18:1–14, is relevant. Cf. Mark 9:36–37; Luke 9:47–48. See also the reference and commentary in "The Tenth Sahidic Life of Pachomius," fragment 2, trans. Veilleux, *Pachomian Koinonia,* 1:451–52.

12   Typikon of the *sebastokrator* Isaac Komnenos for the Monastery of the Mother of God Kosmosoteira near Bera, ch. 39, trans. N. P. Ševčenko, *BMFD* 2:818. Note that in ch. 3 the age is set at thirty.

brought in for the sake of carrying water or another service, nor will they work as servants."[13]

But what was the problem? Why were these attempts to prohibit children so common and so wide-ranging? Clearly the temptations of sexual misconduct were always prominent in the minds of Byzantine ascetics and monastic regulators, and it is no surprise to find that the extreme attitude of John in the Phoberos typikon is echoed in numerous other sources: children, especially boys, pose a potentially deadly spiritual threat because of the sexual temptation they may offer to the celibate. In particular, a fear that the presence of beardless youths will prove too much for monks seems to lie behind most attempts to exclude them. Paul of Latros in the tenth century, for example, ordered "that never any smooth-looking beardless fellow under twenty years of age be admitted into the community of Lavra," paralleling his command with a similar prohibition on women and continuing by speaking of the need to "resist intemperate impulses . . . [to] keep most carefully free from evil thoughts."[14] In the first years of the thirteenth century, Theodosios Goudelis, the author of the Life of Leontios, the twelfth-century patriarch of Jerusalem, explains his young and still beardless hero's seclusion from the rest of the brethren when he was first admitted to the monastery of Saint John on Patmos, "because of the snares that are produced for many by the evil one on account of smoothly-cheeked youths."[15] Two hundred years later, in the early fifteenth century, the patriarch Matthew I echoes the same fears in his prescriptions for the Charsianeites monastery in Constantinople: "You should never receive youths below the age of sixteen, precisely on account of their tender years and their tendency to loose behavior and the scandal produced therefrom by the devil."[16]

Interesting in this context, if tantalizingly vague, is the evidence provided by the case of a monk that came before Demetrios Chomatenos in the early thirteenth century. One Niphon Gerbenites, who had evidently committed serious sexual crimes against children that culminated in murder, was instructed to live as a solitary for the rest of his life to avoid any further temptation that might

---

13   *Rule* of Neilos, Bishop of Tamasia, for the Monastery of the Mother of God of Machairas in Cyprus, ch. 115, trans. A. Bandy, *BMFD* 3:1155.

14   *Testament* of Paul the Younger for the Monastery of the Mother of God tou Stylou on Mount Latros, chs. 9–10, trans. G. Fiaccadori, *BMFD* 1:141.

15   *Life of Leontios,* ch. 18, ed. and trans. D. Tsougarakis, *The Life of Leontios Patriarch of Jerusalem* (Leiden, 1993), 52–55. I am grateful to an anonymous reader for this reference.

16   *Testament* of Patriarch Matthew I for the monastery of Charsianeites, [C] 2, trans. A.-M. Talbot, *BMFD* 4:1652.

be produced by seeing or speaking with children, or, for that matter, with his former associates and friends.[17] Somewhat similarly, the danger posed by the presence of young girls is vividly illustrated by a cautionary tale included in the eleventh-century Life of Lazaros of Mount Galesion but evidently circulating for centuries in monastic circles. A distinguished ascetic, named Paphnoutios, is tricked by the devil into allowing a possessed girl to be left alone in his care. Alas, runs the story, "As soon as the demon saw that the parents had gone away and had left the girl alone with the holy man, it left off convulsing her and instead entered into him. . . . It started to trouble him with illicit thoughts and then it attacked him more and more violently until, after it had broken down the strength of his resistance to the idea, it persuaded him to have sexual intercourse with the girl and then actually to murder her."[18] The fear of "beardless youths" was not entirely homoerotic either: worries were also expressed that women or eunuchs might be able to slip into a monastery undetected in this guise, a point made clearly by the emperor Manuel II in his early fifteenth-century typikon for Athos: "No eunuch or beardless youth should be received by the monks . . . for in that way even a woman might escape notice if she dared to enter into the monastery disguising herself as a man and playing the role of a eunuch or beardless youth."[19]

Although sexual temptation may have been their prime concern, monastic regulators and administrators were evidently also keen to prevent the kind of disruptions to tranquility and concentration that normally active children and

17   Demetrios Chomatenos, *Ponemata Diaphora,* 119, ed. G. Prinzing, CFHB 38 (Berlin, 2002), 384–86. I am grateful to both Günter Prinzing and Alice-Mary Talbot for this reference.
18   Chs. 37–38, *Vita S. Lazari,* ed. H. Delehaye, *AASS* Nov. 3:520–21; trans. R. P. H. Greenfield, *The Life of Lazaros of Mt. Galesion: An Eleventh-Century Pillar Saint* (Washington, D.C., 2000), 123–24. To atone for his sins, the fallen monk takes himself off to a solitary and miserable place where he eventually meets a suitably violent, if accidental, death. For another legendary example of the potentially fatal consequences of bringing children into too close contact with monks or holy men, see the story attributed to Moschos: Mioni 6, ed. E. Mioni, "Il Pratum Spirituale di Giovanni Mosco: Gli episodi inediti del Cod. Marciano greco II.21," *OCP* 17 (1951), trans. Wortley, *Spiritual Meadow* (above, n. 10), ch. 237, p. 221. An angel disguised as a monk, while traveling with a (human) monastic elder, strangles rather than blesses the only son of the man with whom they have been staying, an action later justified on the grounds that the child would have grown up to be a tool of Satan. For another story of a sick girl being left alone with a holy man, on this occasion with happier results, see n. 82 below.
19   Typikon of Manuel II Palaiologos for the Monasteries of Mount Athos, ch.13, trans. G. Dennis, *BMFD* 4:1621. For further discussion of the link between the prohibition of women and that of boys and eunuchs in monastic typika, see A.-M. Talbot, "Women and Mt. Athos," in *Mount Athos and Byzantine Monasticism,* ed. A. Bryer and M. Cunningham (Aldershot, 1996), 68–69; and Galatariotou, "Byzantine Ktetorika typika" (above, n. 6), 121–23. On girls as a source of homoerotic temptation to nuns, see n. 22 below.

teenagers might be expected to cause—the sort of "loose behavior" cited above.[20] The Vita of Lazaros thus includes an episode in which the *parekklesiarches* Germanos, after a disagreement with a young monk, angrily complains to his unusually tolerant superior, "It's you who cause these problems . . . because you welcome and tonsure these youths [νέους] and let them stay in the monastery in this disorderly way, causing problems and disturbances, and you don't discipline them or make them learn self-control. Wouldn't it be better if you expelled them, and your flock thus lived in peace?" Lazaros's answer is no, for the same sort of reasons that Blemmydes gives, but the point is made.[21] Others were evidently afraid that having children around, especially lay children, would hinder or prevent monks and nuns from making the important break from worldly and especially family attachments. Euphrosyne Palaiologina, writing in the fourteenth century, is quite firm on this point, although she will permit girls in her convent who plan to become nuns.

> I absolutely forbid the admission of lay children for the sake of being educated and learning their letters or anything else. For I find that it is a pernicious influence on the morals and habits of the nuns. For anyone who has renounced the world once and for all, and then comes into contact again with lay people and assumes responsibilities incongruous with our vows, and thus causes confusion within himself and obscures the light of understanding, and violates the commandments of the holy Fathers, and follows his own desires and wishes, should not have entered a monastery nor donned monastic habit in the first place.[22]

20   Basil, in *Regulae fusius tractatae* 15, PG 31:952–58, does not mention the danger of sexual corruption as a reason for his requirements that the children in his monastic schools should be accommodated in separate buildings and that older and younger children should normally be kept apart. As suggested by Timothy Miller in *The Orphans of Byzantium: Child Welfare in the Christian Empire* (Washington, D.C., 2003), 116–19, the latter separation, at least, probably had more to do with traditional two-tier patterns of education in the ancient world.
21   *Life of Lazaros,* ch. 152, *AASS* Nov. 3:553; Greenfield, *Life of Lazaros,* 241.
22   Typikon of Theodora Synadene for the Convent of the Mother of God Bebaia Elpis in Constantinople, ch. 148, trans. A.-M. Talbot, *BMFD* 4:1564. Blemmydes, in the passage cited in n. 4 above, requires that his young trainees "should have agreed to renounce completely all intercourse and contact with their parents and other relatives." Cf. *Testament* and typikon of Neilos Damilas for the Convent of the Mother of God Pantanassa at Baionaia on Crete, ch. 7, *BMFD* 4:1471, and *Testamentary Rule* of Neophytos for the Hermitage of the Holy Cross near Ktima in Cyprus, ch. 9, *BMFD* 4:1353.
      It has been suggested to me that, in light of the preceding section of this paper, Euphrosyne's warning that the presence of lay children (almost certainly girls) might prove a "pernicious influ-

Before moving on to the evidence for a more positive attitude toward children in Byzantine monasteries, it is worth pointing out one interesting and important difference between the Byzantine world and our own that emerges from these negative sources. As is clear from the Sri Lankan debate mentioned at the start of this essay, in our world it is the children who are the focus of concern. People's primary concern today is most likely to be the effect on a child of being confined in a monastery and the risk of abuse by monastics. But, interestingly, in the Byzantine sources cited so far, attention falls squarely on the temptation the children may pose to the monks or nuns, on the problems and distractions they may cause to the adults. Put even more bluntly, the authors of these sources seem much more worried about the potential damage to the eternal well-being of those we would now term the abusers than about the mental or physical harm done to the abused. Children, as is so often the case with women (and eunuchs) for these sorts of writers, are seen not as ends in themselves but as means to an end for the devil.[23]

Thus, for a clearly influential and important group within Byzantine monasticism, the orthodox position on children was a very negative one: children

---

ence on the morals and habits of the nuns" could be construed as an oblique reference to the temptations of female homoeroticism. If so, the passage would be significant. I have, however, been unable to detect any other clear indication in the sources of such fears for nuns, in the way that boys were obviously considered a temptation to monks, and the passage can be read more straightforwardly as a reference to the danger that nuns might be drawn back into more general worldly concerns by the presence of lay children. The only clear reference to female homoeroticism in the monastic context of which I am aware, and that not involving children, is made, perhaps not unexpectedly, in the extract from Paul Helladikos quoted by John in his *Rule* for the Phoberos monastery, ch. 58, *BMFD* 3:942: "For Satan often encourages a woman to desire a woman, and for that reason reverent mothers superior of communities instruct the nuns under them not to gaze at each other's faces simply and naturally, lest through the act of seeing they should slip into passion and harm, but to lower their eyes and look at the ground and in that way speak virgin to virgin." Note that this passage does not specifically refer to children.

23   This is unfortunately not the place for a detailed consideration of explanations for this attitude, which probably belongs in the broad context of Byzantine understandings of gender and sexuality. It is, however, worth noting here the attitudes that were evidently pervasive in the Greco-Roman world and that also persisted in contemporary Islamic culture, which saw the receptive partner in sexual intercourse, irrespective of gender, as weak and, in inappropriate liaisons, even "depraved" and responsible for leading the penetrative partner astray. For Byzantine Christian moralists following this traditional outlook, those who allowed themselves to serve as the devil's instruments of sexual temptation (woman, man, or eunuch; adult or child) were thus as bad as those who succumbed to the temptations, if not even more despicable. For instances of the devil appearing as a child or using children for nefarious purposes, see N. Kalogeras, "What Do They Think about Children? Perceptions of Childhood in Early Byzantine Literature," *BMGS* 25 (2001): 11–12, and R. P. H. Greenfield, *Traditions of Belief in Late Byzantine Demonology* (Amsterdam, 1988), 81, 85, 106–7.

should be neither heard nor seen in monasteries. But how widely accepted was this orthodoxy? How generally were these prohibitions enforced? How rigorously were children excluded from monasteries or convents? In each case the answer seems, in fact, to be "Not very." Despite all the efforts of the hard-liners, as is so often the case in Byzantine society, the reality, the "lived religion," seems to be substantially different from the theory. In almost every case the urgency, the vehemence, and the repetition of these prohibitions probably say more about the situation that was provoking them than about their effectiveness.

As I have already suggested, attempts to exclude children ran counter to at least one prominent strand in the practice and sentiment evident in monastic institutions of the early Byzantine period, and it is clear that many individuals and communities in later centuries, even during the period of reform, still saw no need to comply with the wishes of the rigorists. Indeed, an ideal of preserved innocence lies behind stories of monastic inmates raised within the walls of the community who have thus never known, and therefore have never been corrupted by, the outside world. A key exemplar of this ideal was provided in the first half of the fifth century by Theodoret of Cyrrhus in his account of Simeon Stylites the Elder. There mention is made of the *hegoumenos* Heliodoros, who had entered the monastery at the age of three "without ever beholding the occurrences of life" and who "claimed not even to know the shape of pigs or roosters or the other animals of this kind." Significantly, Theodoret stresses Heliodoros's "simplicity of character" and "purity of soul."[24] This ideal is extended by the later sources both as an object of emulation and as a justification for admitting children to monasteries: Simeon the Theologian's favored fourteen-year-old servant, Nikephoros, for example, is described as ἄκακον and ἀπόνηρον.[25]

---

24   Theodoret of Cyrrhus, *Histoire des moines de Syrie: Histoire Philothée/Theodoret de Cyr,* ed. P. Canivet and A. Leroy-Molinghen, SC 234, 257 (Paris, 1977–79), ch. 24.4; trans. R. M. Price, *A History of the Monks of Syria* (Kalamazoo, Mich., 1985), 162. This example, together with a small number of the others mentioned in the following pages, is included by Évelyne Patlagean in her broad consideration of the age at which fundamental decisions were made concerning children's lives in the Byzantine world: see Patlagean, "L'enfant" (above, n. 9), 89. For her discussion of the age at which children were placed in monastic institutions in relation to the ages at which engagement, marriage, and initial education took place, see esp. 88–90.

25   *Life of Simeon,* ch. 117, *Un grand mystique byzantin: Vie de Syméon le Nouveau Théologien par Nicétas Stéthatos,* ed. I. Hausherr, with French trans. G. Horn, *OrChr* 12, no. 45 (1928): 164–65, line 5. One might also note the story of the art historian Kurt Weitzmann's meeting an Athonite hermit in the 1930s who, having been taken to the Holy Mountain as a child, claimed never to have seen a woman. The story, from Weitzmann's memoir, *Sailing with Byzantium from Europe to America* (Munich, 1994), 135, is cited by G. Constable in his preface to *BMFD* 1:xviii–xix.

Hagiographies as well as foundation documents abound with accounts of saints and monastic founders who fled their families at a very early age and found a welcome in the monastic communities for which they pined. While this is definitely something of a topos, some of the references are so matter-of-fact and capable of substantiation by the original audience that they would seem to contain at least some core of truth.[26] Christodoulos of Patmos, for example, speaks in his *Rule* of his Bithynian origins (in the first half of the eleventh century) and continues:

> From an early age I was tossed to and fro by conflicting thoughts and, still a small child, I thought of leaving home, parents, and family, and fleeing to refuge with Christ. . . . This is exactly what I did—going to a flock of monks [in a monastery on Mount Olympus] to whom I surrendered myself, and finding a teacher and educator in the superior of this holy band. But it was God, and he alone, who, through his ineffable mercy, opened my eyes, at that early, unformed and malleable age, well before my reasoning powers were firm. This was indeed worthy of his great works, for, of old, "Out of the mouths of babes and sucklings he perfected praise" (cf. Ps. 8:2).[27]

The final stress on God's will here may be read as something of an excuse, for later in the same document Christodoulos speaks of his attempt to ban, among other undesirables, "young men in their boyish prime, before their beard appears . . . For," he says, "I strove, from the word 'go,' as they say, to remove any occasion of devilish abuse, to eliminate utterly all occasions of trouble, to cut away the roots of error."[28] Like the Buddha, who ordained his own son, Rahula, at the

26   Compare, however, the testaments of Gregory for the Monastery of Saint Philip of Fragala in Sicily [A1], trans. P. Karlin-Hayter, *BMFD* 2:628, "Gregory, the above signed humble sinner, renounced the world and all things worldly from my earliest childhood and dedicated myself to the monastery of Saint Philip, which was completely deserted." It seems impossible that Gregory could have joined and refounded a deserted monastery as a child.

27   *Rule, Testament,* and *Codicil* of Christodoulos for the Monastery of Saint John the Theologian on Patmos, A2, trans. P. Karlin-Hayter, *BMFD* 2:579.

28   *Rule* of Christodoulos A10, *BMFD* 2:583. Not that Christodoulos's words evidently carried much weight. Youths were already working in the monastery at the end of his life, and a century later, Theoktistos, one of Christodoulos's successors as *hegoumenos* on Patmos, was happy to admit the still-beardless future patriarch of Jerusalem, Leontios, when he turned up at the monastery, although he ensured that the boy remained secluded from the rest of the brethren. In this instance, the author of the Vita stresses Theoktistos's great spiritual discernment, which allowed

age of five but later specified, after being taken to task by his father, that children entering monasteries must be fifteen or have the physical maturity of a fifteen-year-old, as well as the consent of their parents, a good number of Byzantine monastic founders evidently believed in the policy of "Do what I say, not what I do [or did]."

Another monastic leader who banned beardless youths from his establishments, Paul of Latros, was taken as a young orphan to the monastery of Karya on Latros by his brother, probably near the end of the ninth century.[29] The adoption of orphaned siblings or relatives by established monastics seems to be another fairly common and long-established route by which young children found their way into monastic institutions, although in other cases no mention is made of a relative in the establishment to which the orphan was entrusted. On the female side, the fourth-century Life of Anthony the Great provided an early and influential precedent in recounting how Anthony placed his young sister in a community of virgins after their parents' death;[30] and Theoktiste of Lesbos is said to have been placed in a nunnery by her relatives after being orphaned as a very young child, ostensibly in the ninth century.[31] On the male side, Neophytos the

---

him to see past Leontios's physical appearance: Tsougarakis, *Life of Leontios* (above, n. 15), ch. 18, 52–55.

29   *BMFD* 1:135.

30   *Life of Anthony,* chs. 1–5, ed. G. J. M. Bartelink, *Athanase d'Alexandrie: Vie d'Antoine* (Paris, 1994), trans. R. C. Gregg, *Athanasius, the Life of Antony and the Letter to Marcellinus* (New York, 1980). Also in the fourth century, the martyr Febronia was raised from the age of two in her aunt Bryene's monastery after being orphaned in her infancy: see *Passio Febroniae,* chs. 5 and 7, ed. P. Chiesa, *Le versione latine della* Passio sanctae Febroniae: *Storia, metodo, modelli di due traduzioni agiografiche altomedievali* (Spoleto, 1990), 158, 159, 301, 302, 370, 372. See also Miller, *Orphans of Byzantium* (above, n. 20), 130. Other female examples from earlier in the Byzantine period are found in the Vita of Elizabeth the Wonder-Worker, who lived in the fifth century (ed. F. Halkin, "Sainte Elisabeth d'Héraclée, abbesse à Constantinople," *AB* 91 [1973]: 257, trans. V. Karras in *Holy Women of Byzantium,* ed. A.-M. Talbot [Washington, D.C., 1996], 127); in the Vita of Theodore of Sykeon, who, in the mid-sixth century, placed his sister Blatta in a convent at the age of twelve (ch. 25, ed. and French trans. A.-J. Festugière, *Vie de Théodore de Sykéôn,* SubsHag 48 [Brussels, 1970], 1:22, 2:24, English trans. [summary] E. Dawes and N. Baynes, *Three Byzantine Saints* [New York, 1977], 105); in the more or less legendary sixth- or seventh-century Life of the female saint Mary/Marinos, who brought her abandoned infant "son" into the monastery with her and raised him there (chs. 13–17, ed. M. Richard, "La Vie ancienne de sainte Marie surnommée Marinos," in *Corona Gratiarum: Miscellanea patristica, historica et liturgica Eligio Dekkers O.S.B. XII Lustra complenti oblata,* 1 [Brugge, 1975], 91–92, trans. N. Constas in Talbot, *Holy Women,* 9–10); and in the case of Theodosia of Constantinople, who in the early eighth century was taken by her mother to a convent to be tonsured at the age of seven after her father died (Synaxarion notice for Theodosia of Constantinople, *Synaxarium CP,* 828, trans. N. Constas in *Byzantine Defenders of Images: Eight Saints' Lives in English Translation,* ed. A.-M. Talbot [Washington, D.C., 1998], 5).

31   *Life of Theoktiste of Lesbos,* ch. 18, *AASS* Nov. 4:229, trans. A. C. Hero in Talbot, *Holy Women,*

recluse, who himself adopted the monastic life at the relatively early (but still respectable age) of eighteen, in his *Testamentary Rule,* written in the early thirteenth century, entrusted his monastery to his nephew Isaiah, who was in his "still flourishing youth." Presumably to counter charges of nepotism, Neophytos says that he did so "not, indeed, out of a feeling of family affection, but because he was raised here from a tender age and I have had good hopes for him."[32] Similarly, Joachim, who became metropolitan of Zichna and wrote the typikon for the monastery of John the Baptist on Mount Menoikeion near Serres, recounts how he was adopted by his uncle, the founder of the monastery, after being orphaned before he was two in the later thirteenth century. His uncle, he continues, "met every physical need and nourished me with care. Then, vesting me with the monastic habit, he ordered me to live continuously with him and be trained in the monastic discipline, although I myself was able to grasp nothing of his angelic way of life and conduct. Therefore I settled down in his cell and was educated and trained by him."[33] One is led to wonder how happy his experiences with his uncle were, for he, too, is adamant in his *Rule* that boys and youths under twenty should not to be allowed to live in the monastery, "even if they should be friends or relatives of the superior of the monastery himself or of one of its monks, not even under the pretext of performing some service or of receiving theoretical or practical instruction. I totally reject such an idea as contributing to many scandals and to spiritual injury."[34]

It was not only orphans who were placed by parents or relatives in monasteries.

---

110. See also A.-M. Talbot, "The Byzantine Family and the Monastery," *DOP* 44 (1990): 121–23; A. Laiou, "Observations on the Life and Ideology of Byzantine Women," *ByzF* 9 (1985): 75–76.

32   Testamentary typikon of Neophytos, ch. 16, trans. C. Galatariotou, *BMFD* 4:1358.

33   Typikon of Joachim, metropolitan of Zichna, for the monastery of Saint John the Forerunner on Mount Menoikeion near Serres, ch. 1, trans. T. Miller, *BMFD* 4:1592–93.

34   Ibid., ch. 14, *BMFD* 4:1601. See also here the typikon of Gregory, superior of the monastery of Saint Philip of Fragala in Sicily, who designates as his primary successor his nephew Blasios, who "has been raised in this most pious monastery from childhood and is learned and observes scrupulously all a monk should" (Fragala, [B7], trans. T. Miller, *BMFD* 2:632; cf. [A7], 2:629). Athanasios, the author of the mid-twelfth-century typikon of the monastery of Saint Mamas in Constantinople of which he was superior, had evidently been raised, educated, and tonsured in another Constantinopolitan monastery, that of the Philanthropos Savior, of which he subsequently became steward: see typikon of Athanasios Philanthropenos for the Monastery of Saint Mamas in Constantinople, *BMFD*, 3:993. On Peter of Argos, who entered a monastery (probably in Constantinople), along with his brother, after their parents died when both were still very young, and who later became bishop of Argos and founded a school for orphans, see Miller, *Orphans of Byzantium* (above, n. 20), 122–23, 268–69. For an example of an unhappy experience with a monastic relative, see the *Life of Lazaros,* ch. 3, *AASS* Nov. 3:510; Greenfield, *Life of Lazaros* (above, n. 18), 80, where the problem is the child's dismay at his uncle's lack of Christian charity.

A variety of reasons are cited for taking such a decision, which was obviously not always an easy one nor simply a relatively kind way of getting rid of unwanted offspring. Among the more common reasons are that the child was promised to God as a result of a birth following difficulties in conception or after the earlier deaths of siblings, or after surviving a nearly fatal illness; that one or both parents wished to enter monastic life themselves; or that the relatives simply wanted to create a better opportunity for the child than they could provide at home. In the ninth century, for example, the infant Theopiste, the daughter of a key supporter of Theodora of Thessalonike, was placed in the saint's convent by her father when she was only one year old, as a thank offering for her miraculous recovery from a life-threatening illness.[35] In precocity she thus outdid the saint's own daughter Theopiste (after whom she was named), who was placed in the convent of one of her mother's relatives at the age of six as an offering to God following the death of her two younger siblings.[36] Toward the end of the tenth century, Lazaros of Galesion seems to have lived in no less than four different monasteries by the time he was fourteen, placed in them by his parents at the advice of his monastic uncle, and benefiting in each from different opportunities for education.[37] In the fourteenth century, Niphon of Athos, at the age of

---

35   "Narrative [of Gregory the Cleric] about the translation of the Venerable Relics of Our Blessed Mother Theodora," chs. 13–15, ed. S. A. Paschalides, Ὁ βίος τῆς ὁσιομυροβλύτιδος Θεοδώρας τῆς ἐν Θεσσαλονίκῃ: Διήγησῃ περὶ τῆς μεταϑέσεως τοῦ τιμίου λειψάνου τῆς ὁσίας Θεοδώρας (Thessalonike, 1991), 214–20, trans. A.-M. Talbot in Holy Women (above, n. 30), 228–30. See also A.-M. Talbot, "Family Cults in Byzantium: The Case of St. Theodora of Thessalonike," in Leimon: Studies Presented to Lennart Rydén on his Sixty-Fifth Birthday, ed. J. O. Rosenqvist (Uppsala, 1996), 57–58, 60.

36   Life of Theodora of Thessalonike, chs. 8–9, Paschalides, Θεοδώρας, 78–84; Talbot, Holy Women, 169–71. The child is said to have been (irregularly) tonsured at once, but this does not seem to have caused any problems, as she went on to become superior of the convent and thus spiritual mother to her own mother, the saint, who entered the same establishment at the comparatively ripe age of twenty-five.

37   Life of Lazaros, chs. 3–4; Greenfield, Life of Lazaros, 79–81 (above, n. 18). See also Maximos, the founder of the monastery of the Theotokos at Skoteine near Philadelphia, who, while still in grammar school, came under considerable pressure to enter monastic life from his father and the devout monk who ran the small monastery that had been established in the family vineyard. Maximos succumbed, despite his youth and apparent reluctance, to the constant good advice and dire warnings he received; see Testament of Maximos for the monastery of the Mother of God at Skoteine [Boreïne] near Philadelphia, [7], BMFD 3:1181–82. Elisabeth the Wonder-Worker entered the Constantinopolitan nunnery where her aunt was superior when probably in her mid-teens, succeeding her aunt while probably still only in her late teens; see Halkin, "Sainte Elisabeth" (above, n. 30), 256–58, Talbot, Holy Women, 126–28. Peter of Atroa's spiritual father, Paul, had been placed in the Monastery of Mantineion in his childhood; see Laurent, Pierre d'Atroa (above, n. 10), ch. 5, 76–79. On parents trying to improve their children's

ten, entered the monastery in which his uncle was sacristan.[38] Precedents in earlier hagiography reveal that these later Byzantine families were following long-established patterns. At the end of the fourth century, for example, Theodoret of Cyrrhus was dedicated by his parents to God in thanks for his conception after thirteen years of childlessness,[39] and early in the following century Daniel the Stylite's parents tried to place him in a monastery when he was only five— although without success, the superior of the monastery refusing "because the child was still so very young."[40]

Hagiographic ideals and historical precedents thus clearly worked to encourage young would-be ascetics to seek entry to the monastic life as early as possible. However, the doors of monasteries and convents did not always open to them; nor were all parents keen for them to fulfill their dreams, especially when they had an eye to more practical outcomes, such as marriage, estate management, and support in old age. The case of Luke the Younger in the early tenth century provides a particularly vivid example of parental resistance to childhood

---

lot in life through adoption, see R. Macrides, "Kinship by Arrangement: The Case of Adoption," *DOP* 44 (1990): 111.

38   *Life of Niphon of Athos,* ch. 1, ed. F. Halkin, "La vie de S. Niphon, ermite au Mont Athos (XIVe s.)," *AB* 58 (1940): 12–13, cf. 6. The monastery was that of Saint Nicholas at Mesopotamos in Epiros.

39   Theodoret was certainly in close contact with monastics from a very early age, if not actually resident in a monastery: see Canivet and Leroy-Molinghen, *Histoire des moines* (above, n. 24), 13:16–17, trans. Price, *Monks of Syria,* 105–6; see further I. Pásztori-Kupán, *Theodoret of Cyrus* (New York, 2006), 3–4.

40   *Life of Daniel the Stylite,* ch. 3, ed. H. Delehaye, *Les saints stylites,* SubsHag 14 (Brussels, 1923), 4; trans. Dawes and Baynes, *Three Saints,* 8. In the third quarter of the eighth century, Simeon of Lesbos's aged mother is said to have taken him, at the age of eight, to join the community led by his brother David: see *Lives of David, Symeon, and George of Lesbos,* ch. 9, ed. J. Van den Gheyn, "Acta graeca ss. Davidis, Symeonis et Georgii Mitylenae in insula Lesbo," *AB* 18 (1899): 218, trans. D. Domingo-Forasté in Talbot, *Byzantine Defenders of Images* (above, n. 30), 162. There are, however, serious problems concerning the alleged age of Simeon in this story: in the previous chapter he is implied to be "a teen-aged boy on the verge of manhood," and there are also difficulties over his mother's age. Also to be noted here is the collection of eighth-century Coptic contracts concerning the donation of young boys, often in thanks for recovery from serious illness, to the monastery of the holy man Apa Phoibammon near the town of Jeme in Egypt. However, although there are many parallels to the examples cited above, the children who are the subjects of the Jeme donations are, significantly, to become not monks but servants in the monastery. See especially Papaconstantinou, "ΘΕΙΑ ΟΙΚΟΝΟΜΙΑ" (above, n. 10), and eadem, "Notes sur les actes de donation d'enfants au monastère de Saint-Phoibammon," *Journal of Juristic Papyrology* 32 (2002): 83–105. See also Wilfong, *Women of Jeme,* 99–104 (above, n. 10). I am grateful to Alice-Mary Talbot, Arietta Papaconstantinou, and Caroline Schroeder for drawing my attention to this material. Schroeder's forthcoming work on children in Egyptian monasticism will be important in casting light on the earlier Byzantine period not covered in this essay.

monastic ambitions. After an initial attempt, which failed miserably when he ended up being thrown in jail and undergoing a brutal interrogation as a suspected runaway slave, Luke, at the age of fourteen, eventually duped two monks who were staying with his widowed mother into thinking he was an unattached stranger and persuaded them to take him along on their pilgrimage to Jerusalem. The monks left the boy in a monastery at Athens, where the superior, despite failing to elicit any real information about his origins, tonsured him. However, Luke's distraught mother had her prayers answered when she was permitted by God to appear in the superior's dreams, or perhaps nightmares, and berate him so fiercely that he was persuaded to send her son home. Only after Luke had returned to his mother and made his peace with her was he finally able to leave and start the life of asceticism for which he became so famous.[41] In the later fourteenth century, the future patriarch Matthew I received a similarly unsupportive reaction when, at the age of twelve, he revealed his desires for the ascetic life to his parents:

> My parents were sorely distressed and grieved at my words, overcome
> by their natural affection, as a result of which they "left no stone
> unturned," as the proverb says, in the hope that they might weaken
> somewhat the intensity of my desire and my stubborn resolution. They
> recounted the arduous life of monks, the mortification of the body, and
> the extreme hardship and ill-treatment, all of which were difficult and
> scarcely tolerable for immature adolescents like myself. But although they
> posed these objections, I managed to avoid being persuaded by them, or
> being affected with any of their timidity, to such an extent that I became
> even more eager, as if I had heard encouraging words.[42]

At least the story had a happy ending for Matthew, who got his way at the ripe old age of fifteen.

Others who went on to distinguished monastic careers were also thwarted in their youthful ambitions by those within the system who doubted the legality or wisdom of admitting children to monasteries, however determined or devoted the children might be. In the mid-tenth century, Simeon the Theologian, age

---

41 *Life of Luke the Younger (of Steiris),* chs. 8–16, ed. and trans. C. L. and W. R. Connor, *The Life and Miracles of St. Luke of Steiris* (Brookline, Mass., 1994), 14–27.

42 Matthew I, *Testament* for Charsianeites, [A] 2, trans. A.-M. Talbot, *BMFD* 4:1633–34.

RICHARD GREENFIELD

thirteen, was turned away from the Stoudios monastery by his future mentor Simeon Eulabes,[43] and the Lives of three fourteenth-century saints all recount similar rebuffs. Athanasios of Meteora went to the Holy Mountain as a young teenager and spoke with some of the fathers, "but he was not allowed to remain there because of his youth and beardlessness."[44] Dionysios of Athos was reluctantly persuaded to remain at home until his beard grew, after learning of the rule which banned beardless men from Athos,[45] and Germanos Maroules failed to persuade John of Athos, whom he met in Thessalonike, to take him back with him to the Holy Mountain, although he was later able to abandon his home and the study of classical poetry, in which he had meanwhile been engaged, and enter John's community when "the signal was given in that his beard began to grow."[46]

Whatever their intentions, legislative attempts by rigorists and their supporters to ban children from monasteries reveal how persistent the practice of admitting them seems to have been, as well as some of the abuses connected with it. The monastic mountain of Athos seems to have developed a reputation by the fourteenth century as a place that really did not tolerate children. But it is equally evident that this was not always the case. The typikon of Constantine IX Monomachos, which dates to 1045, reveals that rulings by both John I Tzimiskes (969–976)[47]

43 Hausherr, *Un grand mystique byzantin* (above, n. 25), ch. 4, 6–7. The reason cited is that Simeon Eulabes was "experienced in the monastic life and the wiles of the Devil."

44 *Life of Athanasios of Meteora,* ch. 3; ed. N. A. Bees, "Συμβολὴ εἰς τὴν ἱστορίαν τῶν μονῶν τῶν Μετεώρων," *Byzantis* 1 (1909): 240–41. Despite being rejected at Athos, Athanasios then went to Constantinople and lived with two monks who allegedly wanted to make him their superior, despite his youth and continuing beardlessness.

45 *Life of Dionysios of Athos,* ch. 14, ed., B. Laourdas, "Βίος τοῦ ὁσίου Διονυσίου τοῦ Ἀθωνίτου," *Ἀρχ. Ποντ.* 21 (1956): 49. Dionysios,

> while still a youth in his homeland, was seized with a love of the monastic life and, learning from others of the holy men of God who lived on Athos, and hearkening to those inspired and virtuous men, he greatly desired to go there and to embrace and grasp that life. However the law and the ruling of the synod against young and beardless men prevented him from accomplishing this, for the law ordered that beardless men should not be allowed to live on the mountain on pain of banishment and curse. Respecting this law, since he was intelligent, Dionysios remained at home, bearing the delay with difficulty, as if blaming his age.

46 *Life of Germanos Maroules,* chs. 8–9, ed. D. G. Tsames, *Φιλοθέου Κωνσταντινουπόλεως τοῦ Κοκκίνου ἁγιολογικὰ ἔργα* (Thessalonike, 1985), 1:108–9.

47 Typikon of the Emperor John Tzimiskes, ch. 16, trans. G. Dennis, *BMFD* 1:238:

> We must strictly enjoin that boys, beardless youths, and eunuchs who journey to the Mountain to be tonsured should not be received at all. But in case it cannot be avoided,

and Athanasios of Athos[48] some seventy years before had failed to stem the problem of eunuchs and beardless youths on the Holy Mountain. Monomachos's typikon recounts how his agent, Kosmas Tzintziloukes, had asked for a list of problems that needed to be fixed. This one was at the top: "Before all else they said that some [of the monks] showed no respect for the provisions laid down in the typikon, namely, that the monks should not accept and tonsure either eunuchs or beardless youths, nor have these in the fields or the monastery."[49] The subsequent purge shows that not only were there plenty of boys (and eunuchs) on Athos at this time, but that their admission had been a persistent practice, opposed by some but with enough support from others to permit it to flourish.[50] Fifty years later again, in the first decade of the twelfth century, apparently nothing much had changed, for two documents among the acts of the patriarch

and the situation becomes urgent, we order that nothing should be done, and nobody should be admitted or tonsured unless the *protos* and all the superiors of the Mountain have investigated the case and freely consent. But if one of the superiors or *kelliotai* out of contempt for these stipulations should introduce into his field or cell a eunuch or a child, and after being denounced for this once and then twice, [and] should give no evidence of changing his ways, then we consider it best simply to drive him away from the Mountain.

Cf. ch. 25, p. 240, which also deals with the possibility of construction workers' bringing youthful apprentices onto the mountain.

48   Typikon of Athanasios the Athonite for the Lavra Monastery, ch. 48, trans. G. Dennis, *BMFD* 1:263: "I order the superior and the brothers who have positions of leadership after him never to receive a eunuch in our Lavra, even if he be an old man, nor [should they receive] a young boy, even though he should be the son of the man who holds in his hands the imperial scepter." Earlier, ch. 34, *BMFD* 1:259, Athanasios rules against "having a disciple in your cell out of affection, for this can harm the unstable." He is here paraphrasing an injunction by Theodore Studites that makes clear that the disciple in mind is an adolescent, see *Testament* of Theodore the Studite for the Monastery of Saint John Stoudios in Constantinople, ch. 18, *BMFD* 1:78. Further on these passages, see Galatariotou, "Byzantine Ktetorika typika" (above, n. 6), 121–22.

49   Typikon of Emperor Constantine IX Monomachos, ch.1, trans. T. Miller, *BMFD* 1:285.

50   "The monks said that such evil demanded correction. Therefore, we together with the monks were immediately roused to condemn this and correct what pertained to it and we found that all [the monks] from the great down to the small were convinced and were ready to offer fervent promises that they would expel all such persons from the Mountain. Their expulsion, then, was carried out by the most devout monks—the superiors, the overseers, and the elders who were dispatched with these men—in accord with the collective will" (ch. 1, trans. Miller, *BMFD* 1:285). This was not the only related problem, for Tzintziloukes was later told that "led by stupidity, silliness, or ignorance of the canons, some monks and superiors had ordained boys who had not entered their twentieth year not only to the office of deacon, but also that of priest. On account of some family relationship or some unsuitable attachment, others leave wills in which they designate young men of such an age as superiors—an unlawful act" (ch. 15, *BMFD* 1:290). See also here the example cited in n. 34 above; and that of Peter of Atroa, who was apparently ordained before he was twelve: Laurent, *Pierre d'Atroa* (above, n. 10), ch. 3, 70–73.

Nicholas III Grammatikos once more condemn the presence of children and beardless youths on the mountain.[51]

In the case of Athos, the emperors Tzimiskes and Monomachos seem to have been on the side of the rigorists, but things could be different when a member of the imperial family was in charge of a monastery. The typikon of the monastery of the Theotokos Kosmosoteira, written by the *sebastokrator* Isaac Komnenos in 1152, shows that he was very concerned about the continued well-being of his foster son Konstitzes, who had evidently grown up in the monastery and was still under eighteen.[52]

Most of the children mentioned so far in this essay have been rather special individuals, either because of their subsequent achievements in Byzantine monasticism and spirituality or because of their relationships to important people. It seems clear, however, that many ordinary children lived in monastic institutions, or at least in close proximity to them. The great majority of such children probably fell into three categories: orphans or foundlings being cared for by monks or nuns, those receiving an education in a monastery, and those training for the religious life. These categories appear frequently to have overlapped and merged, both in the vision of monastic founders and administrators for their communities and in practice. Basil of Caesarea, in the fourth century, had established an influential precedent for monastic involvement in the care and education of children by ruling that his monks should run a school. This was meant primarily for orphans, although it also catered to children brought by their parents. As well as providing an education for these children, the school was clearly intended to serve as a recruiting and training ground for future members

51   V. Grumel and J. Darrouzès, *Les regestes des Actes du patriarcat de Constantinople,* 2nd rev. ed. (Paris, 1989), 1: nos. 975, 983. The first document is apocryphal but still makes the point. The reiteration of the ban on beardless youths and eunuchs in the typikon of Manuel II for Athos (chs. 13 and 15, *BMFD* 4:1621–22), written three and a half centuries later, in 1406, may indicate an even longer-term persistence of the problem, but its wording, coupled with evidence for the upholding of a strict ban on such boys in the fourteenth century, could instead suggest that it is primarily addressing the more particular issues of workers bringing their apprentices with them and the possibility of females entering the confines of the Holy Mountain in disguise, or simply repeating earlier strictures. Further on the typika of Constantine IX and Manuel II in this context, see Talbot, "Women" (above, n. 19), 69.

52   Isaac Komnenos, typikon for Kosmosoteira, chs. 86, 107, 110, 117, *BMFD* 2:837, 845, 846, 848. Further on Konstitzes, see P. Magdalino, "The Byzantine Aristocratic *oikos*," in *The Byzantine Aristocracy, IX to XIII Centuries,* ed. M. Angold (Oxford, 1984), 103–4; and R. Macrides, "Substitute Parents and their Children in Byzantium," in *Adoption et fosterage,* ed. M. Corbier (Paris, 2000), 6.

of the community.[53] Significantly, Basil required his school to be physically separate from the main monastery. Later Byzantine monastic institutions, which appear often to have played a role in the care and education of orphans and other children, seem to have followed this stipulation also. Thus a good number of the children mentioned in the sources in connection with monastic education and training may never have actually been allowed inside the community proper, at least until they were old enough to take formal vows. However, at least some monks and nuns came into close and regular contact with children outside the community, and in other instances children obviously did receive care and education inside the monastery.

In *The Orphans of Byzantium,* Timothy Miller provides an extensive catalogue of the evidence for the care and education of orphaned or abandoned children in Byzantine monasteries in sources dating from the fourth to the fourteenth century. He demonstrates how monasteries, along with other episcopal, imperial, and private foundations of one sort or another, played an important part in the loosely organized but apparently quite comprehensive system of institutional care for orphans and abandoned children. Many of the examples he cites involving special individuals have already been mentioned above, but other references to the general care of orphans include the school established by Theophanes, superior of the Stoudios monastery, in the tenth century; Alexios Komnenos's use of monastic schools in the twelfth century to assist orphaned or abandoned refugee children from Asia Minor; and the baby girl raised by a nun in the monastery of Theodora of Thessalonike in the fourteenth century, in the hope that she would become a servant in the community.[54]

Evidence for monastic care of orphaned children is also found in three late Byzantine typika. In her typikon for the convent of Lips in Constantinople, written at the turn of the fourteenth century, Theodora Palaiologina clearly envisages the care of orphans and other young girls as an important function of the establishment: "If a girl is brought to the convent during infancy or as a child (I do not care whether she is of noble or common birth), on account of some misfortune such as is wont to occur, or on the other hand because of her love

<hr/>

53 Basil of Caesarea, *Regulae fusius tractatae* 15, PG 31:952–58. See also Miller, *Orphans of Byzantium* (above, n. 20), 114–20.

54 Also to be noted from the earlier Byzantine period is the work of Gregory of Nyssa's sister Macrina and her nuns in caring for children abandoned in Cappadocia, and the monastic school in Palestine in which George of Choziba ended up after being orphaned in the late sixth century. For all these examples see Miller, *Orphans of Byzantium,* esp. 127–32, 157–60, 270–71.

RICHARD GREENFIELD

for God, she should wait until her sixteenth year, and then, after being openly examined and making responses in the presence of all the nuns, she should be consecrated in the customary manner. Otherwise she should be dismissed to do as she wishes."[55] Some thirty years later, Theodora Synadene, in her typikon for the Convent of the Theotokos Bebaia Elpis in Constantinople, writes of casting "all my thoughts, all my hopes, all my anxiety, all my concern for myself and my orphaned children upon the Lord, the Father of orphans, the protector of the defenseless, the great hope and succor of those in despair."[56] Theodora's daughter, Euphrosyne Palaiologina, cited above for her prohibition of lay children, who may herself have been brought to the monastery by her mother as a child, also permits the presence of young girls in the convent who have expressed at least some sense of vocation: "But if certain girls should wish to be enrolled among the nuns, but want first to be educated, and learn lessons which contribute to the monastic rule, with the intention of being tonsured years later and numbered among the nuns, I fully approve and consent."[57] John Thomas has concluded from this evidence that the convent may actually have relied on orphan girls for its staffing.[58]

I have cited Nikephoros Blemmydes' enthusiastic attitude to his young novices at Ematha as exceptional, but others, as we have seen, were prepared to allow the routine presence of child trainees (if sometimes begrudgingly and only in very controlled circumstances). The example of a childhood and education like that enjoyed by Lazaros of Galesion in the late tenth century shows that this practice was perhaps not unusual.[59] Certainly the possibility of children who showed potential for an ecclesiastical career being eligible for early enrollment in a monastery was envisaged in Christian legend. Thus, in both versions of John Moschos's early seventh-century account of the children who were struck down by heavenly fire while playing at celebrating the liturgy, the local bishop sends the boys to a monastery as soon as they have recovered.[60] More concretely,

55 Typikon of Theodora Palaiologina for the Convent of Lips in Constantinople, ch. 18, trans. A.-M. Talbot, *BMFD* 3:1271.

56 Theodora Synadene, typikon for Bebaia Elpis, ch. 10, trans. Talbot, *BMFD* 4:1526.

57 Euphrosyne Palaiologina, typikon for Bebaia Elpis, ch. 148, trans. Talbot, *BMFD* 4:1564.

58 J. Thomas, "Independent and Self-Governing Monasteries of the Fourteenth and Fifteenth Centuries," *BMFD* 4:1486.

59 Further on the role played by monastic institutions in the education of children in Byzantium, see N. Kalogeras, "Byzantine Childhood Education and Its Social Role from the Sixth Century until the End of Iconoclasm" (PhD diss., University of Chicago, 2000).

60 Moschos, ch. 196, PG 87:3084A, Wortley, *Spiritual Meadow,* 174 (above, n. 10); and Nissen 8, ed. T. Nissen, "Unbekannte Erzählungen aus dem Pratum Spirituale," *BZ* 38 (1938); 351–76,

Gregory Pakourianos speaks vehemently in his late eleventh-century typikon of the danger of "granting wickedness an entry" and the "irreverent disobedience" of allowing young boys (and eunuchs) into the monastery, but nevertheless makes provision for a number of boys, six of whom will be candidates for the priesthood, to be taught reading and writing in the monastery of Saint Nicholas, a *metocheion* of the main monastery.[61] At the Kecharitomene convent, provision was made in the early twelfth century for two girls to "be reared in the convent and brought up and educated and prepared and be tonsured at the appropriate time."[62]

That not all those raised in monastic surroundings might turn out as well as their guardians might hope is shown in a colorful story recounted in the mid-eleventh-century Vita of Nikon. Here a young boy (μεῖραξ), who was "cared for and left in the holy monastery of the saint," becomes so obsessed with desire for the fruit he can see being sold in the marketplace outside that he slips into the cell of one of the brothers to steal his money. The brother returns and catches the

Wortley, *Spiritual Meadow,* ch. 227, 209–10; cf. Moschos, ch. 197, PG 87:3084D–3085A, Wortley, *Spiritual Meadow,* 175 (on Athanasios of Alexandria's legendary early start in life as a bishop).

61   Typikon of Gregory Pakourianos for the Monastery of the Mother of God Petritzonitissa in Bačkovo, chs. 17 and 31, trans. R. Jordan, *BMFD* 2:541, 550–51. Cf. the *Rule* of Manuel, bishop of Stroumitza, for the Monastery of the Mother of God Eleousa, ch. 17, *BMFD* 1:186, which similarly denies entry to any youth under eighteen but does allow such boys to be admitted to one of its *metocheia;* also Neilos, *Rule* for Machairas, ch. 115, *BMFD* 3:1155, which has rather similar provisions but perhaps excludes younger boys. Compare the treatment of Leontios, future patriarch of Jerusalem, who, as a still-beardless boy, was admitted by the *hegoumenos* of the monastery of Saint John on Patmos but was instructed "not to mix with the brotherhood, nor to frequent the common assembly, but to pass the time in his cell and by himself and to perform the canon as he had learnt it" (Tsougarakis, *Leontios* [above, n. 15], ch. 18, 52–53).

62   Typikon of Empress Irene Doukaina Komnene for the Convent of the Mother of God Kecharitomene in Constantinople, ch. 5, trans., R. Jordan, *BMFD* 2:671. Miller, *Orphans of Byzantium* (above, n. 20), 132, notes that although two orphans would seem a very small number to take care of, the community itself numbered only twenty-four. He also claims that if all the many female communities in the Byzantine world had taken in a small number of orphaned girls, the need for support would have been met. Ruth Macrides, however, commenting on this passage, suggests that such institutional provisions probably accounted for only a small number of orphans: see her "Kinship by Arrangement" (above, n. 37), 112. Cf. Neilos Damilas's typikon, ch. 5, trans. A.-M. Talbot, *BMFD* 4:1470: "Under no circumstances should you admit a woman with a little girl under the age of ten; but even then only if the child wishes to learn her letters and become a nun; for I forbid her to learn any other skill until she dons the novice's habit at the age of thirteen." Christodoulos, [B. 6], trans. Karlin-Hayter, *BMFD* 2:596, mentions "any children I reared from infancy." Miller, *Orphans of Byzantium,* 129, wonders if these children on Patmos were provided for on traditional Basilian lines or if they were maintained "merely to perform labor services for the community."

unfortunate youth, but when he goes off to report him, the boy leaps from the window in an attempt to avoid punishment. Despite falling more than thirty feet in front of all the people in the busy marketplace, he is virtually uninjured.[63] This is obviously the miraculous point to the story in its original context, but one should also note the evidence this episode provides not just for the presence of such boys in a monastery,[64] but also for the author's underlying fear that, had the youth been seriously injured, the public would have suspected that behind his dramatic leap lay the worst possible motives.[65]

Children might also find their way into monasteries as workers or servants. John Tzimiskes' typikon for Athos, which dates to 971–72, shows that construction workers employed on the Holy Mountain were in the habit of bringing with them young apprentices or assistants, thus violating the strict ban on beardless youths he hoped to enforce.[66] A century later, in the 1090s, Christodoulos of Patmos was also struggling with the threats to the spiritual well-being of his monks posed by the wives and children of manual laborers. His initial attempt to manage without skilled lay workers failed, and he was forced to allow them onto the island. Despite his attempt to enforce strict segregation for their families, the codicil of his will shows that even before he died, youths were working in the monastery, for the document specifies that "the servants working for the monastery may not sit at table or drink wine until they get a beard; if it is scant the decision is to rest with the *charistikarios* and the monks responsible for

63   *Life of Nikon,* ch. 75, D. F. Sullivan, ed. and trans., *The Life of Saint Nikon* (Brookline, Mass., 1987), 258–63.
64   In another story, a boy living in the monastery is miraculously healed (ibid., ch. 63, 213–17).
65   Every evil wishing person would have been glad and malign men would have chattered greatly over the fall; they would have been excessively glad at our affliction and loss and in their excess of evil not ashamed to bedrudge [*sic*] the very miracles of the holy man. For the word then went forth at that hour that the child had a violent fall and was crushed and had a bitter end to his life. And the report furnished material to the malign and to those in whose hearts evil and wickedness always lurk to say these things, or rather to stammer and ridicule such things as the passion residing in them suggested. This event, together with others, brought them to this.

Ibid., ch. 75, 261–63. For another example of a "troubled" orphan, although in an episcopal rather than monastic institution, see the story of John the thief contained in John Apokaukos, *Epistola* 100, ed. N. A. Bees, "Unedierte Schriftstücke aus der Kanzlei des Joannes Apokaukos," *BNJ* 21 (1971–74): 151, on which see further Miller, *Orphans of Byzantium* (above, n. 20), 125–26 and 269–70.
66   Tzimiskes, ch. 25, *BMFD* 1:240. See also ch. 16, 1:238. As noted in n. 51 above, the same point is made by Manuel II in the early fifteenth century: ch. 15, *BMFD* 4:1622.

propriety."[67] Even John, the author of the early to mid-twelfth-century Phoberos typikon cited at the start of this essay for its extremely negative attitude toward the presence of young boys, reveals that such youths might be allowed to work in his establishment, although they were to live off the premises:

> But if the superior is obliged from time to time either for service or
> for the comfort of the old to accept some such person, when perhaps the
> brothers are hard pressed and do not have people to minister to them,
> I give you the instruction that these should reside on the estate of the
> monastery, which is called St. Peter . . . , and minister to the brothers until
> they grow a beard, and then they should be accepted into the monastery
> along with the fathers. For otherwise it is not a good thing that such
> persons should spend their time with the old men inside the monastery.[68]

The mention here of employing boys to help care for elderly monks recalls the role played by Nikephoros, the fourteen-year-old sent by his parents to Simeon the Theologian. The boy became the saint's closest and most trusted servant, helping him in his old age in the first quarter of the eleventh century.[69] Labor of a different sort is mentioned in the Vita of Lazaros of Galesion: boys are employed to carry water to the various communities on the barren mountain in the mid-eleventh century,[70] confirming that the practice of using boys for such tasks, banned in the early thirteenth-century typikon for the Machairas monastery, was probably quite common.[71]

The sources also show that, consistently throughout the Byzantine period, children went or were taken to monasteries as visitors for a wide variety of reasons, spiritual and mundane. Long before the period covered in this essay, a touchingly fresh account of such behavior is provided by Theodoret of Cyrrhus, who remembers making weekly visits, around the turn of the fifth century, to receive the blessing of the holy man Peter the Galatian. Peter would sit the little boy on his knee and feed him grapes and bread.[72] A similarly vivid episode can,

---

67 Christodoulos [C4], trans. Karlin-Hayter, *BMFD* 2:599.
68 Phoberos, ch. 58, trans. Jordan, *BMFD* 3:939.
69 *Life of Simeon*, chs. 116–17, Hausherr, *Un grand mystique byzantin* (above, n. 25), 162–67.
70 *Life of Lazaros*, ch. 45, *AASS* Nov. 3:523; Greenfield, *Life of Lazaros*, 130–31 (above, n. 18).
71 Neilos, *Rule* for Machairas, ch. 115, *BMFD* 3:1155.
72 Theodoret of Cyrrhus, ch. 9.4, Price, *Monks of Syria*, 83 (above, n. 24). Theodoret's mother used to send him on these visits and seems to have accompanied him on trips to see other neighborhood monastics when he was an adolescent: see chs. 8.15, 12.4, and 13.18, Price, *Monks of Syria*,

however, be found in the eleventh-century Vita of Lazaros, which tells how the young son of a local priest was sent up the mountain with a honeycomb for the venerable stylite. The boy could not resist furtively eating some of the sweet delicacy on his journey.[73] Another story in the same life recounts how the young nephew of one of the monks on Galesion was going up to visit the monastery in the middle of the day when he was terrified by the apparition of a headless man.[74]

Less happily, one of the more common reasons children were brought to monasteries was evidently in the hope of finding relief from serious disability or sickness. For example, Peter of Atroa, in the ninth century, is said to have worked several miracles on visiting children, curing two severely disabled seven-year-old boys who were brought to him in his monastery by their fathers.[75] He also healed another seriously ill five-year-old boy, although this cure took place in a nearby chapel because the child was accompanied by his mother, who was not allowed to enter the monastery itself.[76] Again in the ninth century, Simeon of Lesbos cured a young boy suffering from a grotesque hernia after the child had been brought to him by his father, who lived near the monastery and knew the saint.[77] Children might also be taken to the graves or relics of saints located

---

79, 97, 107. At roughly the same time, in the first years of the fifth century, the future stylite Daniel was taken by his parents to a monastery at the age of five with offerings of fruit; this was the occasion on which he was given his final name. *Life of Daniel the Stylite,* ch. 3; Delehaye, *Saints stylites,* 3–4; Dawes and Baynes, *Three Saints,* 8 (above, n. 40). Later, when he himself had become a renowned holy man, Daniel was visited by streams not only of men but also "of women with their children"; ch. 16, Delehaye, *Saints stylites,* 16; Dawes and Baynes, *Three Saints,* 16. See also the account of the heretic and his wife and children who visited Daniel to ridicule him, ch. 59, Delehaye, *Saints stylites,* 57–58; Dawes and Baynes, *Three Saints,* 42.

73   *Life of Lazaros,* ch. 65, *AASS* Nov. 3:530; Greenfield, *Life of Lazaros,* 153–54. Lazaros, with his gift of insight, knows that the boy has eaten some of the honey on the way to the monastery.

74   *Life of Lazaros,* ch. 155, *AASS* Nov. 3:554–55; Greenfield, *Life of Lazaros,* 245.

75   *Life of Peter of Atroa,* chs. 20, 29; Laurent, *Pierre d'Atroa,* 112–15, 132–35 (above, n. 10).

76   *Life of Peter of Atroa,* ch. 51, Laurent, *Pierre d'Atroa,* 168–71.

77   *Lives of Saints David, Simeon, and George of Lesbos,* ch. 19, Van den Gheyn, "Acta graeca ss. Davidis, Symeonis et Georgii," 240 (above, n. 40); Talbot, *Byzantine Defenders of Images* (above, n. 30), 205–6. Some frequent visitors to Lazaros of Galesion once brought with them a possessed youth (νεανίσκος) who immediately lost control and went running inside the monastery; *Life of Lazaros,* ch. 219, *AASS* Nov. 3:575; Greenfield, *Life of Lazaros,* 312–14. There is also plenty of evidence for such visits and cures from before the period under study here. A distraught mother brought her possessed nine-year-old to Stephen the Younger in exile on the island of Prokonnesos in the eighth century; *Life of Stephen the Younger,* ch. 50, ed. and trans. M.-F. Auzépy, *La vie d'Étienne le Jeune par Étienne le Diacre,* Birmingham Byzantine and Ottoman Monographs 3 (Aldershot, 1997), 151–52, 249. When Theodore of Sykeon stayed at a monastery in Galatia, in the late sixth or early seventh century, he is said to have been besieged by people seeking cures, among

within the confines of a monastic institution. A series of children are said to have been healed by the remains of Athanasia of Aegina, which were evidently on display in her convent church by the early tenth century.[78] Others were being cured at the sarcophagus of Theodora of Thessalonike and at the tomb of Mary the Younger at roughly the same time,[79] and, later in the century, at the tomb of Luke the Younger.[80] Most of these visits seem to have been brief, and the sick children were accompanied by their relatives; but, despite the circulation of cautionary tales (like the one about Paphnoutios and the possessed girl), there is also evidence that children were sometimes left unattended while a cure was pursued. The Vita of Peter of Atroa recalls a possessed boy being left by his father in the monastery of Saint Zacharias, apparently for some considerable time,[81] and that of Simeon the Theologian records how a disabled four-year-old, abandoned on the doorstep of the monastery by his impoverished mother, was miraculously healed after being carried into the saint's cell.[82]

---

them parents with their sick children; *Life of Theodore of Sykeon,* ch. 65, Festugière, *Théodore de Sykéôn* (above, n. 30), 1:54–55, 2:58, Dawes and Baynes, *Three Saints,* 133. On another occasion he was visited in his own monastery by two aristocratic ladies bringing their disabled children to be healed, one of whom was an eight-year-old girl; ch. 110, Festugière, *Théodore de Sykéôn,* 1:87–88, 2:90–91, Dawes and Baynes, *Three Saints,* 160–61. In the early fifth century, Theodoret of Cyrrhus records a number of healings performed by holy men after young children have been brought to them by distraught parents; Theodoret of Cyrrhus, chs.14.3, 21.14, Price, *Monks of Syria,* 111, 138–39 (above, n. 24). In the same period, various people also brought children to Daniel the Stylite to be cured: a lawyer with his very young possessed son, a man with his seven-year-old crippled son, and a woman with her twelve-year-old mute son; *Life of Daniel the Stylite,* chs. 29, 33–34, 86, 89, Delehaye, *Saints stylites,* 29–30, 31–33, 80–81, 83–84; Dawes and Baynes, *Three Saints,* 24, 26–27, 59–60, 61–62 (above, n. 40).

78   Life of Athanasia of Aegina, chs. 16–18, ed. F. Halkin, "Vie de sainte Athanasie d'Egine," in *Six inédits d'hagiologie byzantine,* SubsHag 74 (Brussels, 1987), 192–94; trans. L. F. Sherry in Talbot, *Holy Women* (above, n. 30), 154–57.

79   *Life of Theodora of Thesssalonike,* ch. 50, Paschalides, Θεοδώρας, 166–68; Talbot, *Holy Women,* 207–8; "Narrative," ch. 10, Paschalides, Θεοδώρας, 208–10; Talbot, *Holy Women,* 226; *Life of Mary the Younger,* ch. 29, *AASS* Nov 4:703, trans. A. E. Laiou in Talbot, *Holy Women,* 283.

80   *Life of Luke the Younger,* chs. 69–70; Connor and Connor, *Luke of Steiris,* 113–19 (above, n. 41). In the mid-eleventh century a young boy was healed at the tomb of Nikon; Sullivan, *Life of Nikon* (above, n. 63), ch. 68, 232–35.

81   *Life of Peter of Atroa,* ch. 60, Laurent, *Pierre d'Atroa,* 182–83 (above, n. 10).

82   Life of Simeon, ch. 118, Hausherr, *Un grand mystique byzantin* (above, n. 25), 166–69. Simeon of Lesbos had invited a girl who had been struck dumb to stay with him for a week, possibly alone and apparently in close proximity. Although the girl in this case is said to have already reached maturity (τελείαν ἡλικίαν), the narrative and the fact that the holy man uses the term τέκνον of her imply that she was still young; *Lives of Saints David, Simeon, and George of Lesbos,* ch. 19; Van den

---

280   RICHARD GREENFIELD

In conclusion, then, there is clear evidence that children were present in Byzantine monasteries, not only as occasional visitors, like sick children seeking cures, but also on a fairly regular, indeed permanent basis. They were not present in all monastic institutions, and it may be that their absence was more common than their presence—Byzantine monasteries were not day-care centers or schools—but, in spite of the rhetoric of those who saw in children (as in women and eunuchs) a terrible danger to the spiritual well-being of monks and nuns, the textual evidence demonstrates that they were actually permitted in far more establishments than one might expect from listening only to the doctrinalists. Giles Constable may be technically correct in saying, in his introduction to the *Byzantine Monastic Foundation Documents* collection, that there are no references to child members in the typika except in the passage from Blemmydes, and in emphasizing the rather late ages (in comparison to Western practice) at which monastic profession was permitted,[83] but one should not be misled into drawing a more general inference from this statement that children were rigorously excluded from Byzantine monasteries. Similarly, I believe, one should not be enticed into concluding that general attitudes and practices concerning children and monasteries changed significantly over the long time span encompassed by this essay. Although the very positive attitude of Blemmydes in the mid-thirteenth century, or the provisions made by such women as Theodora Palaiologina and Theodora Synadene in the fourteenth century for the care of orphans in their monasteries, might, in isolation, be taken as indicative of a movement toward the acceptance of children in monastic contexts in the late Byzantine period, evidence from the same period, in, for example, the apparently uniform refusal to accept boys on Mount Athos in the fourteenth century, surely indicates an ongoing lack of consensus in thought or conformity of practice. Material from the earlier periods shows equal inconsistency. Further study might usefully be devoted to a search for evidence in particular types of monastic communities, for instance in convents as opposed to male establishments, or in urban as opposed to rural foundations, either for unwavering attitudes toward children or for clear shifts in attitude over time. Unfortunately the relatively scattered evidence considered here does not allow me to predict

---

Gheyn, "Acta graeca ss. Davidis, Symeonis et Georgii" (above, n. 40), 234–36; Talbot, *Byzantine Defenders of Images* (above, n. 30), 193–96.

83   Preface, *BMFD* 1:xx.

with any confidence that such patterns may be found. Instead we seem to be left with yet another example of persistent and typically individualized Byzantine ambivalence. Behind the rhetoric of principled declarations and legal documents requiring the exclusion of children from monastic establishments lies a rather different reality, in which children flit through the shadows of the courtyard and peep from the doorways of the outbuildings and dependencies of the religious community.

Queen's University, Kingston

RICHARD GREENFIELD

THE DEATH AND COMMEMORATION
OF BYZANTINE CHILDREN

Alice-Mary Talbot

"What shall I say of the sudden mortal end of both my dearest
younger children, remarkable for their beauty and intelligence,
upon whom I looked with sweetness, good hopes for them
being poured round my heart?"

Theodore Metochites, Poem XV

THIS LAMENTATION OF Theodore Metochites, the fourteenth-century
writer and statesman, reminds us of the realities of family life in Byzantium, a society in which the death of infants and children was an all-
too-common phenomenon, even among the elite. His anguished cry demonstrates that even in a culture where children often died young, parents still
suffered greatly from their loss. This essay examines the surviving archaeological
and written evidence for the mortality of infants and children and the causes for
their premature deaths. It then surveys parental attitudes toward the death of
children, funerary and burial rituals, and ways in which parents commemorated
their prematurely deceased offspring. The essay focuses on the geographical
regions of Greece and Anatolia, and evidence is drawn primarily from sources
for the middle and late centuries of the Byzantine Empire, although reference is
occasionally made to earlier material for comparative purposes.

Death in Childhood
Evidence from Archaeology

The excavations of Byzantine cemeteries in recent decades are generating significant new data on subadult (usually defined as age 0–15) burials that indicate
high death rates among infants and children in the middle and late centuries of
Byzantium. Children's skeletons represent a substantial percentage of the individuals whose remains have been excavated, even though immature bones are

less likely to be preserved and are more difficult to recover.[1] As a number of physical anthropologists have noted, the bones of infants and children are probably underrepresented in archaeological publications because their small size and fragility makes them more likely to decompose or be confused with animal bones.

With regard to the late Byzantine burials at Saraçhane in Constantinople, mostly in the atrium area of the church, for example, Don Brothwell comments that the "scarcity of infant skeletal remains . . . does suggest some form of social or burial differential working against their survival and recovery."[2] The remains of only two skeletons could be identified as those of babies age 0–1, a clear anomaly and underrepresentation of this age group. Brothwell further proposes that an additional factor in this low number of infant skeletons could be the burial of newborns and infants in a different location.[3] Nonetheless, the proportion of burials of older children is striking: out of a total of 125 individuals to whom an age could be ascribed, 14 were age 1–4, 20 age 5–9, and 14 age 10–19. Thus 40 percent died before the age of 20.[4] Recent excavations in Thebes and its vicinity have also uncovered numerous childhood burials from the middle and late Byzantine periods. Analysis of tenth- to eleventh-century tombs found in the narthex of the church at Xeronomi (southwest of Thebes) and in areas outside the church has identified 55 skeletons, of which 36 (55.5 percent) were of infants, children, or teenagers. At a twelfth- to thirteenth-century cemetery site within the city, 151 individuals were unearthed, of whom 23 (15.2 percent) were sub-

1   On the skeletal data, see, for example, C. Bourbou, *The People of Early Byzantine Eleutherna and Messene (6th–7th Centuries A.D.): A Bioarchaeological Approach* (Athens, 2004), esp. 64–72 and fig. 11.

2   D. Brothwell, "The Human Bones," in R. M. Harrison, *Excavations at Saraçhane in Istanbul* (Princeton, N.J., 1986), 1:374. Harrison does not provide a specific date for the burials, describing them only as "late Byzantine" (1:27–30).

3   Brothwell, "The Human Bones," 1:380. A similar phenomenon can be observed at a predominantly twelfth-century cemetery at Kalenderhane, where, out of a sample of 163 individuals, only 2 were infants; the investigators concluded that "infants are underrepresented due to differential preservation and/or different burial practices for children under one year of age." See J. L. Angel and S. C. Bisel, "Human Skeletal Remains," in *Kalenderhane in Istanbul: Final Reports on the Archaeological Exploration and Restoration at Kalenderhane Camii 1966–1978*, vol. 2, *The Excavations*, ed. C. L. Striker and Y. D. Kuban (Mainz, 2007), 373, 375. I am indebted to Lee Striker for sending me an advance copy of this chapter.

4   Brothwell, "The Human Bones," 1:381, table 2. The data from Kalenderhane are less helpful in this regard. The relative numbers of children are skewed at this monastic cemetery because so many of the burials appear to have been of monks; the figures are 2 infants (age 0–1), 15 children (age 1–9), and 13 adolescents (age 10–14), 32 women, and 100 men. See Striker and Kuban, *Kalenderhane* 2:373, 384. There is a slight discrepancy in statistics between text and the table in fig. 101.

ALICE-MARY TALBOT

adult.[5] The discrepancy between the percentages is noticeable, but it is impossible to say whether it represents higher mortality among children in rural areas or a difference between two chronological periods.

The osteological analysis of a twelfth- to thirteenth-century cemetery population at Abdera/Polystylon in northern Greece confirms the high morbidity and mortality of children in the later Byzantine period. Out of 60 excavated skeletons from the ΞA 2 site, 27, or almost half, were of infants, children, or teenagers: thirteen age 0–6, ten age 7–12, and four age 12–18.[6]

At late Byzantine Panakton in Boeotia, 41 percent of the skeletons were from infants, children, or adolescents.[7] Despite local variations, it is clear that the early childhood years were perilous ones, especially up to age 5.[8]

Evidence from Written Sources

Some autobiographical sources provide gripping testimony about the premature death of children. Thus George Sphrantzes, a fifteenth-century courtier, diplomat, and historian, provides precise and sorrowful evidence about the brief life spans of his five sons and daughters. One son, born in 1440, survived for thirty days; another, born in 1445, lived only eight days. Yet another, born in 1442, did not reach his sixth birthday.[9] His two other children perished as teenagers

5   For a preliminary abstract on these findings, see P. Tsitsarole, "Οι παιδικές ταφές δύο βυζαντινών Βοιωτικών νεκροταφείων (Ξηρονόμη, 100ς -110ς αι. καί Θήβα, 120ς-130ς αι.) καί η σημασία τους για την ανάλυση των ταφικών εθίμων," Χριστιανική αρχαιολογική εταιρεία: Εικοστό έβδομο συμπόσιο βυζαντινής καί μεταβυζαντινής αρχαιολογίας καί τέχνης; Πρόγραμμα καί περιλήψεις εισηγήσεων καί ανακοινώσεων (Athens, 2007), 112–13. I thank Sophia Kalopissi-Verti for sending me a copy of this abstract.

6   A. Agelarakis, "Excavations at Polystylon (Abdera), Greece: Aspects of Mortuary Practices and Skeleton Biology," Ἀρχ. Δελτ. 47–48 (1992–93): 293–308.

7   S. Gerstel and M. Munn, "A Late Medieval Settlement at Panakton," Hesperia 72 (2003): 216, table 1.

8   Statistics from late Roman and early Byzantine burial grounds in Greece confirm similar high levels of infant and child mortality. Thus, 18 out of 74 skeletons studied at Messene and 45 out of 151 studied at Eleutherna were subadult (age 0–14); cf. Bourbou, People of Early Byzantine Eleutherna, esp. 64–72 and fig. 11. Similar percentages of children's bones are reported from excavations of early Byzantine graves at Gortyna in Crete (45 percent) and the Lerna Hollow at Corinth (29 percent); ibid., 32–33 (table 1), 35. At late antique Isthmia, where subadults constitute 29 percent of the excavated skeletons, 21.5 percent of the total studied population died in the first four years of life; see J. Rife, The Roman and Byzantine Graves and Human Remains [Isthmia, vol. 9] (forthcoming).

9   Georgios Sphrantzes: Memorii, 1401–1477, ed. V. Grecu (Bucharest, 1966), 24.5, p. 62, 26.10, p. 68, 38.6, p. 72; English trans., M. Philippides, The Fall of the Byzantine Empire: A Chronicle by George Sphrantzes, 1401–1477 (Amherst, Mass., 1980), 52, 55, 56–57.

following the Ottoman capture of Constantinople in 1453; his son John was murdered by the sultan Mehmed II at the age of "fourteen years and eight months less a day," and his daughter Thamar, who had been conscripted into the sultan's harem, died two years later "of an infectious disease in the sultan's seraglio" at the age of "fourteen years and five months."[10] Thus, two of Sphrantzes' children died in infancy and one at the age of five from disease, and two died as teenagers, under admittedly abnormal circumstances.

Equally poignant are the brief notes of the scribe Demetrios Leontares, recording the birthdays of his twelve children, five girls and seven boys, over an approximately thirty-year period in the early fifteenth century. Next to the names of six of the children is the terse marginal annotation ἐτεθνήκει, "s/he has died."[11] This attested 50 percent mortality rate in the children of a single family should not be considered atypical: Angeliki Laiou's study of tax registers in fourteenth-century Macedonia suggests that 50 percent of the children in rural villages died by the age of five.[12]

The evidence for high infant and childhood mortality found in the historical notices of Sphrantzes and Demetrios Leontares can be supplemented by hagiographical texts, as can be seen in three texts of the ninth century. Although certain elements of these saints' Lives are certainly fictional and must be used with caution as sources, the commonplaces or topoi they include must reflect the realities of daily life in Byzantium and the expectations and experiences of readers. The Life of Saint Evaristos, for example, tells of a cobbler named Demetrios who "was fortunate in the procreation of children, but unfortunate in what happened thereafter. For death immediately and suddenly snatched away the infants at birth, and did not even provide an opportunity for them to receive holy baptism." Four of his children in a row died at birth. Finally, thanks to the saint's blessing of his wife, Demetrios's fifth child, a son, lived to maturity.[13] A topos of hagiography is for parents to dedicate to monastic life a child who manages

10   *Sphrantzes,* 37.3, 9, pp. 104, 106; trans. Philippides, *Sphrantzes,* 74–75.

11   P. Schreiner, *Die byzantinischen Kleinchroniken,* 1 (Vienna, 1975), no. 98a, pp. 643–45.

12   A. E. Laiou-Thomadakis, *Peasant Society in the Late Byzantine Empire: A Social and Demographic Study* (Princeton, N.J., 1977), 295. For similar statistics for the earlier Byzantine period, see the study of Évelyne Patlagean, who has used a series of late antique funerary epitaphs from al-Kerak in Jordan to show that only 50 percent of the children in her sample survived to age 15; see her *Pauvreté économique et pauvreté sociale à Byzance, 4e–7e siècles* (Paris, 1977), 96.

13   C. van de Vorst, "La vie de s. Evariste, higoumène à Constantinople," *AB* 41 (1923): 317, ch. 34 (my translation).

to survive after siblings born earlier have all died.[14] In the Vita of Saint Peter of Atroa, for instance, we read of a couple whose first thirteen children all died prematurely; but thanks to the prayers of the holy man, the fourteenth survived and became a monk.[15] Saint Theodora of Thessalonike had three children, of whom only one lived past infancy; this child was dedicated to a convent at the age of 6.[16] Similarly, Theodotos, a benefactor of Theodora's monastery, saw four of his children die young: "As long as the infant was an embryo in his wife's womb or was breastfeeding, Theodotos was a father and was so called. But when the child grew and reached its second or third year, the child would die and Theodotos would again be childless." When his fifth child, a girl, was stricken with a serious illness at the age of 1 year, Theodotos promised her to the convent if she should survive; and so after her miraculous recovery she was raised in Theodora's nunnery.[17]

Causes of Infant and Childhood Mortality
Evidence from Archaeology and Medical Textbooks

In recent years bioarchaeologists and, to a lesser extent, historians of medicine have begun to explore the causes of high infant and childhood mortality in the Byzantine period. Osteologists who study the skeletal remains of subadults have found evidence of scurvy and iron-deficiency anemia (cribra orbitalia), as well as malnutrition (enamel hypoplasia), which made children more vulnerable to infectious disease.[18] One of Brothwell's striking findings at Saraçhane was that 69.2 percent of his sample showed at least slight underdevelopment (hypoplasia) of the tooth enamel, suggesting that more than two-thirds of the Saraçhane population suffered from malnutrition or infectious disease in childhood sufficient to prevent proper tooth calcification.[19]

---

14   See T. Pratsch, *Der hagiographische Topos: Griechische Heiligenviten in mittelbyzantinischer Zeit* (Berlin, 2005), 72–74.

15   V. Laurent, *La vie merveilleuse de saint Pierre d'Atroa († 837)* (Brussels, 1956), ch. 59, 181–83.

16   S. Paschalides, Ὁ βίος τῆς ὁσιομυροβλύτιδος Θεοδώρας τῆς ἐν Θεσσαλονίκῃ: Διήγησις περὶ τῆς μεταθέσεως τοῦ τιμίου λειψάνου τῆς ὁσίας Θεοδώρας (Thessalonike, 1991), Vita, ch. 8–9, 78–84.

17   Paschalides, *Βίος, Translatio*, ch. 13–14, pp. 214–20; English trans. A.-M. Talbot, in A.-M. Talbot, *Holy Women of Byzantium* (Washington, D.C., 1996), 228–30.

18   Bourbou, *People of Early Byzantine Eleutherna* (above, n. 1), 55–56, 64–71. Cribra orbitalia is a term describing pitting of the upper frontal plate of the ocular orbit of the skull.

19   Brothwell, "The Human Bones" (above, n. 2), 1:392.

At Abdera/Polystylon evidence of growth retardation and cessation was found at ages 2 and 5. Hypoplastic defects in dental enamel were very frequent in subadult skeletons, with calculated onsets again at ages 2 and 5. Such defects indicate nutritional deficiencies and diseases such as jaundice and gastroenteritis. The presence of porotic hyperostosis, as manifested in cribra orbitalia, was detected in 40 percent of the skeletons of children age 0–12, suggesting the prevalence of malnutrition, infectious and opportunistic diseases, and iron-deficiency anemia resulting from weaning and the shift to a cereal diet.[20] Isotopic analysis that indicates age at weaning around the ages of 2–3 corresponds with a relatively high incidence of mortality at this age, suggesting the dangers from diarrhea caused by the introduction of goat's milk and honey into an infant's diet.[21]

Pediatric textbooks of the Byzantine era recount the numerous diseases that afflicted children, many of them still all too common today, especially in the developing world. Thus, we read about intestinal problems such as diarrhea, dysentery, cholera, and worms, as well as convulsions and fevers. In such books, long sections are devoted to skin problems as well as to infections and inflammations of the tonsils and throat. The medical books focus, however, on the descriptions of symptoms and methods of treatment, with few comments on mortality.[22]

Evidence of Literary Sources

Findings from the archaeological record and medical texts can be supplemented with information on childhood disease and accidental death drawn from literary and hagiographic sources. First, many mothers were unable to carry their babies to term for a variety of reasons, ranging from maternal illness to congenital abnormalities. One tragic example of fetal death in the year 1443 is recorded by a grieving father who lost on the same day his sixteen-year old daughter, who died of the plague, and his prematurely born granddaughter. Five hours before her death, the unfortunate young mother gave birth to a fetus of five or six months' development. The infant was able to breathe on its own but died shortly

20 Agelarakis, "Excavations at Polystylon" (above, n. 6), 293–308.
21 See, for example, Bourbou, *People of Early Byzantine Eleutherna*, 67–68; on weaning and diarrhea, see the essay by C. Bourbou and S. Garvie-Lok in this volume. The death of Theodotos's first four children in their second or third year (see above) suggests an association with weaning and its dangers; in fact, the hagiographer specifically notes that the children tended to die when they stopped breastfeeding.
22 C. Hummel, *Das Kind und seine Krankheiten in der griechischen Medizin: Von Aretaios bis Johannes Aktouarios (1. bis 14. Jahrhundert)* (Frankfurt, 1999).

after birth; there was time only to administer perfunctory baptism with lamp oil to the dying baby.[23]

Other babies were stillborn, or died during difficult deliveries. Many a saint's Life recounts the successful intervention of a holy man or relic in the travails of a woman undergoing protracted labor, enabling the safe birth of the baby. The Vita of the patriarch Ignatios recounts the particularly vivid case of a laboring woman whose baby was in an abnormal position, with its feet emerging from the womb first and obstructing the birth canal. The woman was in agony, and in order to save her life the surgeons were preparing to perform an embryotomy, an operation in which the fetus was cut into pieces in order to extract it from the uterus. Fortunately someone had access to a fragment of cloth from a garment worn by the recently deceased patriarch. As soon as he placed the cloth on the woman's abdomen, the baby turned and was born head first, without further incident.[24] Other such cases did not end as well, as can be seen from a female skeleton found at Corinth in which the fetus was lodged crossways in the pelvis: evidently the mother died in childbirth.[25]

Many of the miracles performed by living holy men and women or by relics involved the healing of infants or small children brought by despairing parents. The afflictions of these children give us some idea of the congenital abnormalities from which they suffered: blindness, deafness, crippled legs, and nervous disorders. A five-year-old boy was described as having some sort of a growth disorder: from birth, his body was composed only of bones and sinews, with virtually no flesh.[26] A seven-year-old boy also had a congenital malformation: from the waist down he had no bones at all, only flesh and skin.[27] Another boy was so crippled that he could only crawl on all fours, supporting his hands on blocks of wood.[28] Children also are described as suffering from fevers, convulsions, leprosy, dropsy, paralysis, cancer, and smallpox.[29]

---

23   P. Schreiner, "Eine Obituarnotiz über eine Frühgeburt," *JÖB* 39 (1989): 209–16. This form of emergency baptism is not mentioned by J. Baun in "The Fate of Babies Dying before Baptism in Byzantium," in *The Church and Childhood,* ed. D. Wood, Studies in Church History 31 (Oxford, 1994), 115–25.

24   PG 105:564B–C.

25   E. Barnes, "The Dead Do Tell Tales," in *Corinth: The Centenary, 1896–1996,* ed. C. K. Williams II and N. Bookidis (Athens, 2003), 438 and fig. 26.6.

26   Laurent, *La vie merveilleuse* (above, n. 15), ch. 51, 169–71.

27   Ibid., ch. 29, 133–35.

28   I. van den Gheyn, "S. Macarii monasterii Pelecetes hegumeni acta graeca," *AB* 16 (1897): 149–50.

29   Fevers: Vita B of Theodore of Stoudios by Michael the Monk, ch. 49 (PG 99:305B).

Children were also at high risk of fatal accidents. Among the dangers they faced were falling off walls[30] and being bitten by snakes.[31] Some children suffered these injuries while performing household tasks, such as foraging for wild greens or fetching water;[32] others were injured at play, when hit by a thrown rock or falling and breaking a leg.[33] In one tragic instance, a father was responsible for the accidental killing of his son during an informal archery contest, when he shot an arrow at the target without realizing that his son had gone to retrieve the previously shot arrows.[34]

Popular Beliefs about Gello/Gyllo

The high incidence of infant mortality was attributed in popular belief to the female demon Gello (also variously spelled Gyl[l]o[u] or Gillo), who was accused of murdering newborn and suckling infants.[35] She may have been held responsible in particular for sudden and inexplicable deaths, such as would today be attributed to sudden infant death syndrome (SIDS). She was believed to enter into women who were then transformed into evil spirits capable of passing through solid walls and locked doors to suffocate infants. In a case reminiscent of the Salem witch hunts, some poor women in eighth-century Constantinople were charged with passing through cracks in the walls or closed doors and clandestinely killing newborn children. The father of the future patriarch Tarasios took it upon himself to defend these women and managed to get them acquit-

---

Convulsions: Paschalides, *Βίος, Translatio,* ch. 10; trans. Talbot, *Holy Women* (above, n. 17), 226. Leprosy: Laurent, *La vie merveilleuse,* ch. 35, p. 141. Dropsy: I. Cozza-Luzzi, *Historia et laudes ss. Sabae et Macarii* (Rome, 1893), ch. 31, pp. 46–47. Paralysis: F. Halkin, "Vie de sainte Athanasie d'Egine," in *Six inédits d'hagiologie byzantine* (Brussels, 1987), ch. 17–18, trans. L. F. Sherry in Talbot, *Holy Women,* 156. Cancer (tumor on head): V. Laurent, *Vita retractata et les miracles posthumes de saint Pierre d'Atroa* (Brussels, 1958), ch. 92. Smallpox: Paschalides, *Βίος, Translatio,* ch. 16–19; trans. Talbot, *Holy Women,* 232–35.

30   D. F. Sullivan, *The Life of Saint Nikon* (Brookline, Mass., 1987), ch. 26.

31   Cozza-Luzi, *Historia et laudes ss. Sabae et Macarii,* 21–22.

32   Ibid.; Vita of Ioannikios by Sabas, *AASS* Nov. 2.1:352C–353A.

33   E. Sargologos, *La vie de saint Cyrille le Philéote moine byzantin* (Brussels, 1964), ch. 13.1; *Periegesis of Andrew Libadenos,* ed. O. Lampsides, Ἀνδρέου Λιβαδηνοῦ βίος καὶ ἔργα (Athens, 1975), 43.

34   G. Prinzing, *Demetrii Chomateni Ponemata Diaphora* (Berlin, 2002), no. 131, pp. 403–5. In the account of the case brought before the court, the boy is called his father's "dearest and beloved" (φίλτατον, ἐγκάρδιον) son (404.22).

35   For more on Gello, see the essay by M.-H. Congourdeau in this volume, and the bibliography in her n. 52, to which should be added an article by Richard Greenfield: "Saint Sisinnios, the Archangel Michael, and the Female Demon Gylou," *Byzantina* 15 (1989): 83–142.

ted.[36] Amulets were often used to protect newborn children against Gello during the especially dangerous period between birth and baptism.

Parental Attitudes toward the Death of Children

Were Byzantine parents as devastated by the death of their children as parents are today? Two factors might lead one to believe that Byzantines faced the premature deaths of their offspring with greater resignation and equanimity than their modern counterparts. First, as Antony Littlewood argues, because only about 50 percent of children survived to adulthood, parents were fully cognizant of the risks involved in bearing children and therefore more resigned to their early deaths.[37] Second, because Byzantines were a people of strong faith, who believed that death represented a passage to a better world and afterlife, one might expect them to grieve less for innocent children whose salvation seemed assured.

The Evidence of Hagiography

A stoic attitude toward the death of a child is found more often in the ideal world of hagiography than in historical narrative.[38] For example, Mary of Bizye (d. ca. 902/3), a future saint, is depicted in her Vita as refraining from an excessive display of grief at the death of her firstborn son, Orestes:

> When the child was five years old, it was cut down by the scythe of death, before its time. The others [probably referring to family members] wept disconsolately and mourned in a disorderly fashion. As for her, her mother's heart was broken and torn asunder, as one would expect; but she kept to herself, sighing and openly weeping, without, however, displaying unseemly behavior. She did not tear out her hair, nor did she disfigure her cheeks with her hands, nor did she rend her clothes, nor did she throw ashes on her head, nor did she utter blasphemous words. She almost conquered nature and, weeping just enough to show she was a mother,

36 S. Efthymiadis, *The Life of the Patriarch Tarasios by Ignatios the Deacon (BHG 1698)* (Aldershot, 1998), ch. 5, pp. 72–74.
37 A. Littlewood, "The Byzantine Letter of Consolation in the Macedonian and Komnenian Periods," *DOP* 53 (1999): 37.
38 Unfortunately this topic is not discussed in Pratsch, *Der hagiographische Topos* (above, n. 14).

gave thanks to the guardian of our souls and . . . cried out in a calm voice with greatness of soul [the words of Job], '*The Lord gave and the Lord has taken away . . . blessed be the name of the Lord . . .*' In this manner she bore what happened with patience and thanksgiving.[39]

The hagiographer's description reveals the expectations for normal behavior at the time of a child's death: pulling one's hair, rending one's flesh with fingernails, tearing one's clothes, and throwing ashes over one's head—in other words, time-honored and ritualized expressions of grief in eastern Mediterranean society. Mary, as a holy woman of unusual faith, is depicted as overcoming her natural tendencies and accepting her child's death as the will of God. Similarly, when her second child died, "she bore the suffering with thanksgiving."[40] Fortunately, her third and fourth children, twin boys, survived into maturity.

The Evidence of Historical Narrative

Mary's restraint was no doubt uncommon. There is persuasive evidence, especially in historical narratives of the Palaiologan period, but in earlier funerary orations as well, that Byzantine parents felt keen anguish at the loss of their offspring. Like their modern counterparts, Byzantine mothers and fathers not only had powerful emotional bonds to their children but also hoped they would live into adulthood to bear grandchildren and inherit property, to look after their parents in their old age, and to ensure the parents' proper burial and posthumous commemoration.[41] As Metochites wrote, "Through our children we mortal men still live even after we have left this life. . . . When we ourselves are dead, they are yet alive and immortal, for in them we live an immortal life."[42]

---

39   Vita of Mary the Younger of Bizye, *AASS* Nov. 4, 693; English trans., A. Laiou in Talbot, *Holy Women* (above, n. 17), 258–59.
40   Vita of Mary the Younger of Bizye, *AASS* Nov. 4, 694; English trans., A. Laiou in Talbot, *Holy Women*, 261.
41   Photios remarked in a letter that his brother's grief at the death of his newlywed teenage daughter was compounded by the fact that she had not yet brought forth a grandchild. "Now all hope is lost that this girl's child would ever enter the house and rush to the open arms of the grand-parents, play and dance and talk with them in its babyish way." See Photios, ep. 234, ed. B. Laourdas and L. G. Westerink, *Photii Patriarchae Constantinopolitani epistulae et Amphilochia*, 2 (Leipzig, 1984), 150.10–12; trans. D. S. White in "Photios' Letter to his Brother Tarasios on the Death of his Daughter," *GOTR* 18 (1973): 49.
42   J. M. Featherstone, *Theodore Metochites's Poems "To Himself"* (Vienna, 2000), poem XV, lines 348–57.

ALICE-MARY TALBOT

The testimony of two fifteenth-century Byzantine fathers whose offspring died young illustrates the grief of bereaved parents. Here are some notations from the *History* of George Sphrantzes, who had five children: "On March 27 of the . . . year [1440], on a bright Sunday, my second son, Alexios, was born; he survived for only thirty days." "On August 15 of the . . . year [1445], my son Andronikos was born; he lived for only eight days." "On August 15 of the . . . year [1448], my son Alexios passed away. He was five years and eleven months old. I was extremely affected by his death, but I did not suspect what sadder misfortunes were in store for the future."[43] Sphrantzes is alluding to the impending tragic deaths of his two surviving teenage children, mentioned above. The murder of his son John prompted Sphrantzes to utter the laconic lament, "Alas for me, his unfortunate and wretched father."[44]

A contemporary of Sphrantzes, a secular cleric whose name is unknown, also left notes on the deaths of two of his four children. George, born in March of 1428, died at the seventh hour on Friday, 8 October, in the second indiction, at the age of six months: "His death touched me to my bones and marrow and I almost went out of my mind from my great grief." In 1435, just before midnight on Sunday, 4 September, of the fourteenth indiction, his daughter Mary died of the plague: "My most cherished and beloved daughter, Lady Mary, who surpassed many honored maidens in all virtues, has died of a pestilential disease; and her death has caused me many misfortunes and has rendered me half dead. And I live a bitter and painful life, myself differing in no way from those who have died."[45]

The fourteenth-century patriarch Philotheos Kokkinos, whose biographical writings demonstrate particular interest in the childhood years of his subjects,[46] also gives vivid insight into two fathers' close ties to their children and fears for their death in his lengthy account of the life of Gregory Palamas. He characterizes Gregory's father, Constantine Palamas, as a man who, against his natural instincts, deliberately avoided playing with and hugging his small children

---

43   *Sphrantzes,* ed. Grecu, 24.5, p. 62; 26.10, p. 68; 28.6, p. 72; *Sphrantzes,* trans. Philippides, 52, 55, 56–57 (above, n. 9).

44   *Sphrantzes,* ed. Grecu, 37.3, 9, pp. 104, 106; trans. Philippides, *Sphrantzes,* 74–75.

45   S. Kougeas, "Notizbuch eines Beamten der Metropolis in Thessalonike aus dem Anfang des XV. Jahrhunderts," *BZ* 23 (1914/19): 151, no. 77 (my translation). We do not know Mary's age at death, but as she is called a virgin, it is likely that she was a young teenager.

46   A.-M. Talbot, "Children, Healing Miracles, Holy Fools: Highlights from the Hagiographical Works of Philotheos Kokkinos (1300–ca. 1379)," *Bysantinska Sällskapet Bulletin* 24 (2006): 48–64.

because, knowing the likelihood of their early death, he feared becoming too attached to them.[47] Also memorable is Philotheos's description of Andronikos Tzimiskes,[48] a man from Berroia, with a gravely ill son. Tzimiskes could not bear to remain in the room as the dying child drew his final breath, so he withdrew outside. "As if consumed by grief, [he] withdrew, avoiding the very sight of the child and seeing him separated from his soul, and sat by himself, . . . placing his right arm on his knees and his head in his right hand, in the posture of mourners."[49]

The Evidence of Funeral Orations and Letters of Consolation

Other evidence about the reaction of Byzantine families to the death of a child is found in funeral orations commissioned by members of the elite and in letters written by highly educated individuals. One of the best-known examples of an *epitaphios logos,* or funerary oration, was composed by the eleventh-century courtier Michael Psellos on the death of his nine-year-old daughter Styliane. She was the apple of his eye, a well-behaved and beautiful girl, who was pious, intelligent, and skilled at weaving. He had hopes of arranging a fine marriage for her until she was struck down by a dread disease, probably smallpox. After a full month of suffering from loathsome sores that covered her entire body, she succumbed, surrounded by her family and the household servants. Her father's lamentation on her premature departure from life seems to have been written some time after her death, perhaps for the first anniversary of her passing. His grief is overwhelming: "My innards are all twisted up, my heart is rent asunder, and I am everywhere falling to pieces, pushed deeper into depression by the memory of her. . . . I now go about life dejected and gloomy and, hardly differing from a dead man, lament the loss of one so dear to me. I go to her grave and call upon the one who lies there. Then I return, striking my chest, and am quite beside myself."[50]

His consolation is that her death was God's will, and that God took her before

---

47 *Logos on Gregory Palamas,* ch. 6 in Φιλοθέου Κωνσταντινουπόλεως τοῦ Κοκκίνου ἁγιολογικὰ ἔργα, vol. 1, Θεσσαλονικεῖς ἅγιοι, ed. D. Tsames (Thessalonike, 1986), 432–33. I view this text, a *logos* rather than a *bios,* as much closer to historical biography than to hagiography.

48 *Prosopographisches Lexikon der Palaiologenzeit,* 11 (Vienna, 1990), no. 27950.

49 *Logos on Gregory Palamas,* ch. 131, pp. 584–85. The story had a happy ending, as the boy was miraculously cured after the apparition of Gregory to Andronikos in a dream vision.

50 Michael Psellos, Funeral Oration on his daughter Styliane, ed. K. Sathas, Μεσαιωνικὴ βιβλιοθήκη, 5 (Paris, 1876), 63, 85; English trans., A. Kaldellis, *Mothers and Sons, Fathers and Daughters in Byzantium* (Notre Dame, Ind., 2006), 119, 136–37.

her purity and innocence were defiled by marriage and sexual intercourse.[51] One feels, however, that Psellos is not wholly comforted by this rationalization. Although he states that one must not "contest divine decisions," he protests to God nonetheless, asking why an innocent child should die when some wicked people recover from serious illnesses and live into old age. Why have the family's prayers to the saints been ineffective? Why did God not show compassion for the young girl's suffering and reward her for her forbearance?[52] In his sorrow, Psellos is sustained by one hope of consolation: that his daughter will appear to him and his wife in their dreams, with unblemished face, as she was before her final terrible illness.

At some point during the last decade of the twelfth century, the historian Niketas Choniates was devastated by the unexpected loss of his firstborn son, a toddler not yet able to speak, who died from a constriction of his throat and high fever, perhaps diphtheria. His funerary oration likens his son's brief time on earth to the flash of a comet or lightning bolt. He also compares his short-lived child to a rose that had not yet unfurled its petals. Only at the end does he shift gears and attempt to console himself and his family with the reminder that his child now dwells in heaven, a pure innocent unsullied by the sins of the world.[53]

A number of other surviving funeral orations and letters of consolation on the death of children shed further light on the reaction of parents to their loss and the efforts of friends and relatives to alleviate their despair and sorrow. Although the orations were intended for public delivery and the letters for more private family reading, the sentiments expressed are much the same. It is taken for granted that the parents are anguished and inconsolable: in the words of Theodore of Stoudios, "Truly your limb is severed, your flesh is cut off … gloom is upon the household, sorrow upon the servants, grief upon the relatives, and above all upon the grandmother … and grandfather."[54] The orator or correspondent seeks ways to persuade the grieving family that they should accept God's will and see the positive aspects of their children's early passing. A few of the monodies are so phrased as to shock our modern sensibilities, including Gregory

---

51   Psellos, Funeral Oration, ed. Sathas, 81–82, 77; trans. Kaldellis, *Mothers and Sons,* 133–34, 130.

52   Psellos, Funeral Oration, ed. Sathas, 80–82; trans. Kaldellis, *Mothers and Sons,* 132–34.

53   Niketas Choniates, oration 6, ed. J. L. van Dieten, *Nicetae Choniatae orationes et epistulae* (Berlin, 1972), 46–53. The oration is tentatively dated between 1192 and 1200 in J. L. van Dieten, *Niketas Choniates: Erläuterungen zu den Reden und Briefen nebst einer Biographie* (Berlin, 1971), 36, 59.

54   G. Fatouros, *Theodori Studitae epistulae,* 1 (Berlin, 1991), ep. 18.22–27 (my translation).

Antiochos's oration on a youth of the Komnenian family killed in a riding accident. His grisly rehearsal of the details of the boy's fall from his horse and his trampling underneath its hooves, as well as allusions to his bloodied clothing, might seem to bring little consolation to bereaved parents, but they may have been intended to encourage cathartic tears.[55]

A particular challenge was faced by the exiled bishop of Athens, Michael Choniates, who in 1208 needed to write words of consolation to his nephew George the *sebastos,* whose young teenage son had just been cruelly murdered by the tyrant of Corinth, Leo Sgouros.[56] The boy, who was Michael's namesake, had led a tragic life. His mother had died in childbirth, and he was nurtured on "stranger's milk" by a wet nurse. As a young child, he developed a tumorous swelling on his forehead that had to be removed in a surgical operation. Worst of all, in 1204 he was taken hostage by Leo Sgouros and forced to undergo complete castration, a procedure that nearly killed him. For the next four years he served the tyrant as his cupbearer, until the day when he accidentally broke a wineglass. The infuriated Sgouros immediately hit the boy over the head with an iron club and killed him.

As in the oration of Gregory Antiochos cited above, a number of passages in the bishop's two letters of consolation rehearse the tragedy in vivid outlines. He keeps reviewing the details of the murder, stressing the inequality in value between human life and a cheap wineglass. He muses on exactly where the fatal blow fell on the skull and wonders whether the child expired immediately or died later of gangrene. He laments the fact that out of fear of the tyrant's wrath, none of the bystanders would have dared to tend the child's wounds, mourn his death, prepare his body for proper burial, or dig a grave for him.

In a more positive vein, the bishop reassures the bereaved father that Sgouros will surely go straight to hell, while the boy Michael will go to heaven. In one touching passage he asks the child to appear to him and his father in a dream to reassure them of his present whereabouts. Is he in the garden of Eden, in the bosom of Abraham, or in the company of Abel, who was murdered by his brother Cain? Bishop Michael urges the father to accept the will of God, imitating the example of David and Job, to be strong like a man, and not succumb to

---

55   A. Sideras, *25 Unedierte byzantinische Grabreden* (Thessalonike, 1990), 75–87; see also idem, *Die byzantinischen Grabreden: Prosopographie, Datierung, Überlieferung; 142 Epitaphien und Monodien aus dem byzantinischen Jahrtausend* (Vienna, 1994), 204–6. I thank an anonymous reader for this insight.
56   *Michaelis Choniatae epistulae,* ed. F. Kolovou (Berlin, 2001), epp. 100, 101.

womanly grief.[57] Most unusually, he develops the theme that the boy is a martyr, like the infants massacred by Herod, a holy child now crowned with a wreath. When praising the boy's character, he emphasizes qualities very similar to those ascribed to youthful saints: the young Michael did not laugh out loud, but only smiled; he was mature and intelligent beyond his years (echoing the *puer senex* theme so often found in hagiographic texts);[58] he did not run and jump like other children, but walked with a serene gait; he was serious at his lessons and never rode his horse at a gallop.

Words of comfort in other letters or orations may have been more soothing. A commonplace, already seen in the oration of Psellos, was that the dead child or teenager remained an innocent, untainted by knowledge of the evils or sorrows in this world, unsullied by sexual activity, and uncorrupted by wickedness. Thus salvation and reception into paradise and the bosom of Abraham were assured.[59] Theodore of Stoudios expressed similar sentiments in a letter to Leo the *orphanotrophos,* who had lost two successive children in infancy and the third at age three. He should be reassured that his deceased children were pure and uncorrupted by sin because of their tender years, and assuredly were reposing with the holy infants in the bosom of Abraham.[60] To assure another bereft father, he paraphrased the words of Job 11:2: "Blessed is that one among the offspring of women who is short-lived, and whom the Lord has chosen and taken to Himself at a young age, since he has not experienced the bitter sins of this life."[61] Or, as Photios explained in a letter to his brother Tarasios, who had just lost his teenage daughter, the shorter one's life, the less time one has to sin![62]

Other arguments for the benefits of early death seem more contrived: in the same letter, Photios argued that his niece was better off dying young, before she had given birth to a baby, as she would not leave behind an orphaned child to mourn her; and because she died before her parents, she would not have to mourn their passing.

57 Photios, ep. 234.171–73, 218–26 (trans. White, "Photios' Letter," 54–55; above, n. 41), also urges his brother not to grieve like a woman, and to follow the example of David, who ceased to mourn once his child had died.
58 See the essay by Béatrice Caseau in this volume.
59 See, for example, the monody and letter of consolation on the death of a child emperor, probably Andronikos V Palaiologos, "An Unknown Byzantine Emperor, Andronicus V Palaeologus (1400–1407?)" ed. G. T. Dennis, *JÖBG* 16 (1967): 180–87; for the bosom of Abraham, see Photios, ep. 234, trans. White, "Photios' Letter," 55.
60 Fatouros, *Theodori Studitae epistulae,* 1: ep. 29.24–29.
61 Ibid., ep. 18.52–55 (my translation).
62 Photios, ep. 234.82–98, trans. White, "Photios' Letter," 51.

Another type of consolatory advice was to focus on the child's happiness in paradise. Photios reassures Tarasios that if he could hear his daughter speak, she would tell him how delightful it was to live in paradise and how she looked forward to welcoming her parents there.[63]

Another tack was to remind the bereaved parents that they should not question God's will by complaining that their children were taken too soon. As Photios reminded his brother, God, not man, is the timekeeper who decides the length of human life.[64] It is also important for Christians to keep in mind the example of Old Testament models such as David and Job and the mother of the Maccabees, who did not protest against God's decision to take their children from them and who realized that grieving changes nothing.[65] No doubt having in mind the high rate of child mortality, Photios further commented that Christians needed to recognize the fact that certain children who died young were intended as an offering to God, whereas others were chosen to live and perpetuate the family line.[66]

The Funerals and Burial of Children
Preparations for Burial and Funeral Ceremonies

Psellos's oration on the death of Styliane provides one of the most detailed descriptions we have of the preparation of a Byzantine child's body for burial and the attendant funerary ceremonies.[67] On her deathbed, the girl was surrounded by family members and retainers, who were weeping and beating their chests. As she breathed her last, they cried out in lamentation, and fell upon her body to give it a final embrace. After a suitable period for tearful wailing, her body was washed, dressed in funerary garments, and placed on a bier. Her corpse was then carried to its burial place, hymns were sung, and the Eucharist celebrated. Finally her body was placed in the tomb and covered with a slab.[68]

63   Photios, ep. 234.123–51, trans. White, "Photios' Letter," 52 .
64   Photios, ep. 234.99–108, trans. White, "Photios' Letter," 52.
65   Photios, ep. 234.218–41, trans. White, "Photios' Letter," 55; letter of Philetos of Synada to Nikephoros Balanites, ed. J. Darrouzès, *Epistoliers byzantins du Xe siècle* (Paris, 1960), ep. 4, pp. 251–53.
66   Photios, ep. 234.179–81, trans. White, "Photios' Letter," 54.
67   The most recent description of the ceremonies attendant on death and burial can be found in N. Constas, "Death and Dying in Byzantium," in *Byzantine Christianity*, ed. D. Krueger (Minneapolis, 2006), 124–45, 230–32 . Although this article provides a very useful overview, it contains little material specifically related to children.
68   Psellos, Funeral Oration, ed. Sathas, 79–80, 82, trans. Kaldellis, *Mothers and Sons,* 132–34.

A few additional details on final rites can be found in Psellos's description of the funeral of his sister, who died probably in her late teens. After she drew her last breath, her mother closed the girl's eyelids and began her lamentations. Those who prepared her body for burial cut off her long blond hair and suspended the tresses from the foot of the catafalque. As the funeral procession passed through the streets, men dismounted from their horses, and men and women alike descended from the upper floors of their houses to join the cortege.[69] Psellos also describes the ritual commemoration on the seventh day after the funeral, when members of the girl's extended family gathered around the grave to mourn.[70]

Funerary Liturgy

Although rarely mentioned, there was a special funeral liturgy for very young children, the κανὼν ἀναπαύσιμος εἰς νήπια τελευτήσαντα, with moving words of consolation and reassurance for grieving parents.[71] Its prayers, alternately addressing Christ and the Virgin, echo some of the themes we have seen already in funerary orations for children and letters of condolence, for example a supplication to Christ, who had deigned to take the form of an infant, to place the deceased baby in the bosom of Abraham. Another prayer entreated the Savior to vouchsafe that the child, who had not lived long enough to enjoy earthly delights, might enjoy the pleasures of the afterlife. These infants who suffered a premature death are compared to tender blades of grass, harvested before their time, or to tender branches cut by the sword of death. The canon acknowledges that nothing is more pitiable than bereaved parents committing their child to the grave, especially when the child had been old enough to speak, and describes mothers standing before the tomb beating their breasts. The parents are reminded, however, that although they may grieve at their loss, death is a cause of joy for their pure and innocent child, who will inherit eternal life.

69   Psellos, encomium for his mother, ed. C. Sathas, Μεσαιωνικὴ Βιβλιοθήκη, 5 (Paris, 1876), 32–33, trans. Kaldellis, *Mothers and Sons*, 78–80.
70   Psellos, ed. Sathas, 29, trans. Kaldellis, *Mothers and Sons*, 76.
71   P. de Meester, *Rituale-benedizionale bizantino* [= Liturgia bizantina 2.6] (Rome, 1930), 92–93; J. Goar, *Euchologion sive Rituale Graecorum* (Venice, 1730; repr. Graz, 1960), 474–78; see also P. J. Fedwick, "Death and Dying in Byzantine Liturgical Traditions," *Eastern Churches Review* 8 (1976): 152–61. Nicholas Constas points out that unbaptized infants were denied Christian burial, but he gives no source for this statement; see his "Death and Dying in Byzantium," 136. J. Baun does not discuss the issue of burial in her article (above, n. 23) but emphasizes that babies who died before baptism had no hope of salvation.

Children's Graves

On the actual procedures for the digging of graves and burial of children, literary texts are virtually silent, so we must turn to archaeological and art historical evidence.[72] Most subadults were buried in simple cist graves, either individually or in family graves that held multiple burials.[73] The children, dressed in their own clothes and/or in a shroud,[74] were either placed directly in the ground or occasionally laid to rest in wooden coffins.[75] Small infants might be buried in amphorae that had been cut in half.[76] Skeletal remains of children are also found in ossuaries, that is, storeplaces for bones that had been exhumed from a primary burial and moved to a secondary location.[77]

Children's bodies were usually laid out in the same way as their parents'. Typically the bodies were aligned in an east-west direction, with the head to the west but propped up by earthen pillows or a tile or stone so as to face east. The head might be held in position by fragments of roof tiles on either side, and another piece of tile might be placed under the chin to hold the jaw in place as the body decomposed. Alternatively, the jaw was held shut with a cord tied under the chin. Often the arms were folded over the chest or abdomen.[78] The bodies might be partially covered with roof tiles.[79]

Grave goods are rarely associated with subadult burials, but there have been occasional finds of jewelry, such as bracelets, earrings, finger rings, and necklaces, as well as toys.[80] Eric Ivison has hypothesized that the beads found occa-

---

72   I express my appreciation to three colleagues, Chryssi Bourbou, Sarah Brooks, and Joseph Rife, who have generously provided bibliographic information on a subject outside my range of competence. I am particularly grateful to Dr. Rife, who permitted me to read the manuscript of his forthcoming book, *The Roman and Byzantine Graves and Human Remains* [Isthmia, vol. 9], in advance of its publication.

73   Rife, *Roman and Byzantine Graves* (forthcoming).

74   Rife, *Roman and Byzantine Graves* (forthcoming); Gerstel and Munn, "Panakton," *Hesperia* 72 (2003): 217.

75   C. K. Williams, "Frankish Corinth: 1996," *Hesperia* 66 (1997): 21.

76   Rife, *Roman and Byzantine Graves* (forthcoming).

77   On ossuaries, see E. Ivison, "Mortuary Practices in Byzantium (c. 950–1453): An Archaeological Contribution" (PhD diss., University of Birmingham, 1993), 106–8.

78   Rife, *Roman and Byzantine Graves* (forthcoming); Gerstel and Munn, "A Late Medieval Settlement at Panakton" (above, n. 7), 217–18; Williams, "Frankish Corinth: 1996," 22–23.

79   C. K. Williams, "Frankish Corinth: 1997," *Hesperia* 67 (1998): 240.

80   For example, a bronze ring was associated with one infant burial at Isthmia and a necklace with beads and a bone pendant with another; see Rife, *Roman and Byzantine Graves* (forthcoming). A bell-shaped rattle was found in a child's burial in the sanctuary of Demeter and Kore on Acrocorinth: see N. Bookidis and J. E. Fisher, "Sanctuary of Demeter and Kore on Acrocorinth:

sionally in child graves may have been amulets with an apotropaic function.[81] In a Frankish-era graveyard at Corinth, three infants were found buried with unbroken eggs, a practice attested in classical Greek burials as well.[82] Fragments of broken earthenware jugs found on top of the graves suggest the pouring of ritual liquids, while glass shards indicate that lamps were lit at the tombs, perhaps on the anniversary of death.[83]

Occasionally infants and children were buried in a segregated area, as in the Frankish-era burial ground at Corinth, where a group of twenty-six graves dating to the early fourteenth century may indicate an epidemic that decimated the youngest members of society.[84] Very recently, an extremely important child cemetery of the middle Byzantine period has come to light at Amorion. In 2007, shallow graves containing the remains of sixty-two infants were uncovered to the north of the basilica and in the vicinity of the apse of the baptistery. The majority were infants ranging from fetuses to babies up to six months old. The graves lay just beneath the surface, and grave goods were found only with the skeletons of older infants.[85] It is possible that this cemetery area was reserved for unbaptized children. Recent finds in the Agora at Athens suggest that some stillborn fetuses and newborns may have been buried beneath the floor of the house.[86]

The Commemoration of Deceased Children

Bereaved parents remembered their deceased children in many ways. George Sphrantzes and the anonymous secular cleric carefully noted the dates of death of their sons and daughters; the latter even included the time of the day and the indiction. These precise notations may have served to ensure that liturgical commemorations of the child were held on the appropriate day. Demetrios

---

Preliminary Report V; 1971–1973," *Hesperia* 43 (1974): 285. Finds of toys were evidently so rare that they are not even discussed in Ivison, "Mortuary Practices." For jewelry, see, for example, S. Ercegović-Pavlović, *Les nécropoles romaines et médiévales de Mačvanska Mitrovica* [Sirmium, 12] (Belgrade, 1980), 18 (tomb 2), 27 and pl. 21 (tomb 193), 28 and pl. 24 (tomb 218). See also Eric Ivison's discussion of the finds at Hattusas in "Mortuary Practices," 186. For the most recent discussion of this topic, see the article by Brigitte Pitarakis in this volume.

81   Ivison, "Mortuary Practices," 184.
82   Williams, "Frankish Corinth: 1997," 241.
83   Cf. ibid., 241; Rife, *Roman and Byzantine Graves* (forthcoming).
84   Williams, "Frankish Corinth: 1996," 22–23.
85   Eric Ivison, personal communication, May 2008.
86   Cf. J. M. Camp, "Excavations in the Athenian Agora: 2002–2007," *Hesperia* 76 (2007): 629, 646. I am grateful to Christopher Lightfoot for this reference.

Leontares named some of his children after their deceased siblings.[87] Wealthier families memorialized their departed children with more permanent monuments, of which a tantalizingly small number are preserved.

Inscriptions on Tombstones

Relatively few tombstone inscriptions for children have survived: those that have are all from late antiquity, as far as I can determine. They indicate that bereaved parents with the necessary means often went to considerable expense to purchase a suitable slab of limestone or marble and to hire a stonecutter to engrave a brief memorial record; on occasion they might even commission a poet to write an epitaph for placement on the tomb. A fourth- to fifth-century example of such a marble gravestone, preserved on Thasos, bears a twelve-line epigram in dactylic hexameter. The father, Eugenios, laments the death of his 3-year-old daughter Dalmatia, struck down by a "baneful disease." She is compared to a rose or lily destroyed by a storm. Although Eugenios concludes by mentioning his tears, he also alludes to the consolation for bereaved Christians of the promise of eternal life for the departed.[88] In the church of the Panagia Dexia in Berroia, a marble slab in the floor of the north aisle near the templon preserves the fifth- to sixth-century funerary inscription of John, the young son of Zenobios, who died at the age of 8.[89] In the sixth century the *komes* Athenaios and his wife, Phidelia, commissioned a marble slab commemorating the brief life of their daughter, also named Phidelia, who died at the age of 3; the prose inscription includes the precise date of death, presumably so that she might be remembered in perpetuity on the anniversary of her passing.[90] Around the same time, the young daughter of the priest Alypios, named Theodora, who died at the age of 5, was commemorated with an epitaph on a marble plaque that also provides the exact date of death; she is compared to a sun that set soon after its rising.[91]

87   Schreiner, *Die byzantinischen Kleinchroniken* (above, n. 11), 1, no. 98a, 643–45. This subject might be worthy of special study within a larger monograph on naming practices in Byzantium.
88   D. Feissel, *Recueil des inscriptions chrétiennes de Macédoine du IIIe au VIe siècle* (Paris, 1983), 219–20, no. 265.
89   L. Gounaropoulou and M. B. Hatzopoulos, Ἐπιγραφὲς κάτω Μακεδονίας: Μεταξὺ τοῦ Βερμίου Ὄρους καὶ τοῦ Ἀξιοῦ ποταμοῦ, vol. 1, Ἐπιγραφὲς Βέροιας (Athens, 1998), 375, no. 439; Feissel, *Recueil*, 75, no. 71.
90   C. Mango and I. Ševčenko, "Some Recently Acquired Byzantine Inscriptions at the Istanbul Archaeological Museum," *DOP* 32 (1978): 18, no. 21.
91   The epitaph is of the fifth to sixth century: see C. Asdracha, *Inscriptions protobyzantines et byzantines de la Thrace orientale et de l'île d'Imbros (IIIe–XVe siècles)* (Athens, 2003), no. 222;

ALICE-MARY TALBOT

Funerary Monuments for Elite Children

Children of the elite were sometimes buried in the privileged space of churches, as we know from both literary and material evidence. For example, the account of miracles at the Pege monastery located just outside the walls of Constantinople reports that in the late ninth century Helena Artavasdina, the *magistrissa* and a benefactor of the monastery, arranged for her two children to be interred just outside the church sanctuary, next to an icon of the Virgin Episkepsis.[92] This location close to the altar was particularly desirable and reflects Helena's position as a special patron of the Pege church.[93] Turning to material remains, small rock-cut arcosolia in Cappadocia, as in the narthex of the tenth-century church of Saint Daniel at Göreme, testify to the burial of infants and young children in the sacred space of a church.[94] At the eleventh-century Karşı Kilise in Gülşehir, two adolescent girls are depicted in a frescoed niche with their mother Irene; the mother rests one hand on the head of each teenage daughter. Both girls have their arms crossed over their chests and are clearly deceased.[95] Funerary monuments for children have been identified in narthexes,[96] next to nave walls,[97]

Mango and Ševčenko, "Byzantine Inscriptions," 13–14, no. 17. For other marble tombstones of children, see the seventh-century epitaph of the nephew of Isaac, exarch of Ravenna, who died at age 11; Isaac claimed to have loved the boy as his own son (A. Guillou, *Recueil des inscriptions grecques médiévales d'Italie* [Rome, 1996], 114–15, no. 108). Noteworthy also are the tombstone of Kyrilla, age 3, which was made of the prized marble from her hometown of Dokimion (R. Merkelbach, *Die Inschriften von Kalchedon* [Bonn, 1980], no. 116), and the fifth- or sixth-century tombstone of Stephanos (G. Dagron and D. Feissel, *Inscriptions de Cilicie* [Paris, 1987], 103, no. 57).

92 *De sacris aedibus deque miraculis Deiparae ad Fontem*, ch. 15, *AASS* Nov. III: 883BC.

93 On the hierarchy of locations for church burials, see Ivison, "Mortuary Practices" (above, n. 77), 66–81, esp. 74.

94 U. Weissbrod, *"Hier liegt der Knecht Gottes . . .": Gräber in byzantinischen Kirchen und ihr Dekor (11. bis 15. Jahrhundert); Unter besonderer Berücksichtigung der Höhlenkirchen Kappadokiens* (Wiesbaden, 2003), 213.

95 Ibid., 221–22.

96 See Ivison, "Mortuary Practices," 72: at the church of the Koimesis at Nicaea, the child Manuel Angelos (d. 1211) was buried in the narthex, as shown by an epitaph observed in the seventeenth century.

97 One example is at the church of the Koimesis of the Virgin at Longanikos in Lakonia, where a fourteenth-century frescoed tomb niche on the west wall of the nave depicts a monk presenting a young boy to a standing Virgin and Child. The boy raises his hands in supplication. Olympia Chassoura hypothesizes (in *Les peintures murales byzantines des églises de Longanikos—Laconie* [Athens, 2002], 219–23) that it is a commemorative funerary panel: the monk is the father, and the boy is deceased; this hypothesis is accepted in S. T. Brooks, "Commemoration of the Dead: Late Byzantine Tomb Decoration (Mid-thirteenth to Mid-fifteenth Centuries)" (PhD diss., Institute of Fine Arts, New York University, 2002), appendix A.11, 361–66.

and in exedrae, as at the church of Hagios Nikolaos at Phountoukli on Rhodes. Here a frescoed pseudo-arcosolium, probably of the fifteenth century, depicts the three deceased children of the logothete and *pansebastos* Nicholas Bardoanes, male and female adolescents and a younger boy. All three have their hands crossed over their chests. In this case it seems likely that the bereaved parents commissioned the entire church in memory of their three children.[98]

In the early thirteenth century, Nikephoros Kounales of Berroia restored a church dedicated to the Virgin Eleousa in memory of his son, who died as a toddler shortly after his mother's death. He also established a small male monastery there with a hieromonk to perform services of commemoration.[99] Likewise at Berroia, ca. 1325, the *sebastos* Theodore Sarantenos and his wife constructed a church and monastery dedicated to Saint John the Baptist in memory of their numerous children, who had all predeceased them.[100]

Other children were buried just outside the church and commemorated with paintings on the exterior walls. At Kastoria, for example, at the church of the Taxiarchs, an array of early fifteenth-century frescoed pseudo- and real niches on the south exterior facade adorned a series of funerary monuments, including the depiction of three deceased children. One beardless young man stands alone; one is next to his father, who touches his shoulder; and a girl is next to her mother, who raises both arms in supplication. All three children have their arms crossed over their chests.[101]

Funerary Icons and Epigrams

Other families of aristocratic or imperial lineage commissioned funerary icons of their deceased children for placement on the tomb (presumably inside a church); the icon frames bore verse epitaphs lamenting the premature passing of these youths. Such an icon was recorded in the early part of the twentieth century

---

98 M. Acheimastou-Potamianou, "Οι τοιχογραφίες της οικογενείας Βαρδοάνη στον Άγιο Νικόλαο στο Φουντουκλί της Ρόδου," *Θωράκιον· Αφιέρωμα στη μνήμη του Παύλου Λαζαρίδη* (Athens, 2004), 247–62, followed by Brooks, "Commemoration of the Dead," appendix A. 19, 423–28; see also A. Orlandos, "Βυζαντινοὶ καὶ μεταβυζαντινοὶ ναοὶ τῆς Ρόδου, Β: Αἱ τοιχογραφίαι," *ABME* 6 (1948): 194–96.

99 Prinzing, *Demetrii Chomateni Ponemata Diaphora* (above, n. 34), 176–80, no. 48.

100 J. Bompaire et al., *Actes de Vatopédi, I: Des origines à 1329* (Paris, 2001), 354.23ff.

101 E. Drakopoulou, *Η πόλη της Καστοριάς τη βυζαντινή και μεταβυζαντινή εποχή (12ος–16ος αι.)· Ιστορία—Τέχνη—Επιγραφές* (Athens, 1997), 128–29, followed by Brooks, "Commemoration of the Dead," appendix A.16, 394–406.

at the monastery of Megaspelaion in the northern Peloponnesos, but unfortunately it was destroyed in the fire that ravaged the monastic complex in 1934. An early photograph shows that the one-meter-high icon had a semicircular top and depicted a youth in imperial dress facing forward, with his hands turned in supplication toward an enthroned Virgin and Child. The Christ Child is blessing the boy with his hand. Titos Papamastorakis has argued that the flat rendering of the boy's pallid face, in contrast to the modeled features of the Virgin and Child, is meant to indicate that he is dead.[102] The boy is identified in a painted inscription as John Doukas Angelos Palaiologos Raoul Laskaris Tornikes Philanthropenos Asan, who was the son of Manuel Raoul Asan, brother of the empress Irene, wife of John VI Kantakouzenos.[103] An epigram of at least twelve lines that originally adorned the now-lost frame was copied in the nineteenth century onto the icon itself; it laments the death of the child who, as so often, is described as a flower cut down before its time.[104]

Such funerary icons for children are attested in the twelfth century also, as we learn from epigrams of Nicholas Kallikles, composed to be inscribed on icons standing on the tomb of Andronikos Palaiologos Doukas, the son of George Palaiologos. The tomb was located in the monastic church of Saint Demetrios of the Palaiologoi, founded by George in Constantinople. In this case the poet has put words into the mouth of the grieving mother:

FOR AN ICON PLACED ON A TOMB

An ear of wheat cut down by suffering and a bunch of grapes cut down
    by disease,
O child of my womb snatched away from life,
I place you now beside the all-pure Virgin.
May you be everything for him, light, salvation,
Eden, a place of delight or a place of fresh grass,

---

102   T. Papamastorakis, "Ioannes 'Redolent of Perfume' and His Icon in the Mega Spelaion Monastery," *Zograf* 26 (1997): 71.

103   *Prosopographisches Lexikon der Palaiologenzeit,* ed. E. Trapp (Vienna, 1976), vol. 1, no. 1502, following the earlier bibliography, placed John in the fifteenth century, but Papamastorakis, in "Ioannes 'Redolent of Perfume'," has convincingly dated him to the mid-fourteenth century and identified him as the nephew of the empress Irene Kantakouzene.

104   In addition to the Papamastorakis article, see earlier articles on this icon by G. Sotiriou, "Ἡ εἰκὼν τοῦ Παλαιολόγου τῆς μονῆς τοῦ Μεγάλου Σπηλαίου," *Ἀρχ. Δελτ.* 4 (1918): 30–44, and for the epigram A. Philippidis-Braat, "Inscriptions du Péloponnèse, 2: Inscriptions du IXe au XVe siècle," *TM* 9 (1985): 354–56, no. 91.

And living water and adornment for a divine marriage.
O Maiden, the mother of the deceased [says] these words to you,
Adorning your image, O adornment of our lineage.[105]

The eight-line poem was no doubt engraved on a silver-gilt frame surrounding
an image of the dead boy standing next to the Virgin, perhaps in a pose similar to the one in the icon of John Asan. A second icon, showing the youth being
blessed by Christ, had a golden frame bearing an eight-line epigram, again purportedly the words of the mother:

I would have wished that the shoot of my womb,
The glorious Andronikos, should remain uncut,
And that the root should be cut before the branch.
But since as a result of your incomprehensible decisions,
O Word, untimely death has cut him down,
And the tomb unexpectedly contains him,
Receive the wretched entreaty of the one who bore him
And accept him like a fragrant flower.[106]

From two additional poems of Kallikles, we learn that the youth had just been
married and was therefore perhaps 15 years old. He is described as having golden
hair that fell in waves over his neck, a piercing gaze, and skin that was white as
milk and ruddy as a rose.[107]

Conclusion

My conclusion can be brief: infant and childhood mortality in Byzantium was
very high, paralleled in our day and age only by that of sub-Saharan Africa. But
despite the frequency of premature death, Byzantine families keenly felt the
loss of their youngest members. They took care to bury them properly, noted
their death dates so as to perform anniversary ceremonies at their graves or in

---

105   R. Romano, *Nicola Callicle: Carmi* (Naples, 1980), no. 11 (my translation). I am grateful to
Edmund Ryder for calling my attention to these poems of Kallikles, as well as to the Papamastorakis article cited above.
106   Romano, *Nicola Callicle: Carmi,* no. 12 (my translation).
107   Ibid., nos. 9–10.

ALICE-MARY TALBOT

church, and sometimes kept their memory alive by giving their names to subsequent children. The anguish experienced by families with dying children is conveyed, for example, by Gregory the Cleric, who recounts Saint Theodora of Thessalonike's unexpected and miraculous healing of his young sister Martha from smallpox. He vividly recalls his own childhood grief and that of his family during her severe illness, as they shared in the girl's suffering and were convinced that her death was imminent. As Gregory wrote years later, "Tears come to me as I summon up in my mind the image of that child, with most of her limbs lifeless and hanging limp from every part of her body . . . and it is no wonder that I am affected in this way by my sister. For . . . in this case where there is . . . kinship and natural bonds and brotherly love, how could I possibly remain untouched in these circumstances and not share in her circumstances as best I could?"[108] Thanks to the intervention of Saint Theodora and the extraordinary nursing care of Martha's family, Gregory's worst fears were not realized, and his sister survived; but the memory of her narrow escape remained with him always and became the motivation for his composition of a Vita of the holy woman who had saved Martha's life.

Michael Psellos is another author who attests to a brother's fierce sorrow at the death of his slightly older sister. As he recounts the tale, as a youth of sixteen he was residing not far from Constantinople when his sister died. His parents were reluctant to send him the bad news by letter, because they were aware of the close bonds of affection between the siblings; they preferred to inform him in person so that they could immediately embrace and comfort him. So they wrote asking him to return home, giving no reason. Although it is not clear why Psellos could not be notified in time to attend the funeral, the burial ceremonies were held without him. He learned of his sister's death only when he came to Constantinople one week after the funeral, and by coincidence encountered a group of mourning relatives assembled at her tomb for seventh-day commemoration ceremonies. When Psellos learned the news, as he writes, "I know not what came over me. Just as though I were burned by holy fire, I was struck senseless and speechless." He fell from his horse in a dead faint. When he recovered his senses, his lamentations combined the expectation that his sister was reposing in a paradise of meadows, beds of roses, flowing rivulets, and singing nightingales

---

108   Paschalides, *Βίος* (above, n. 16), *Translatio* of relics, ch. 17, pp. 224–26; trans. Talbot, *Holy Women,* 233.

with gloomy thoughts about the decomposition of her body. He expressed the hope to be buried eventually in the same grave so that their bodies could dissolve together, and they would be reunited in death.[109]

Both Gregory and Michael Psellos write as adults recalling their youthful grief for their sisters. Unfortunately, it is virtually impossible for us to retrieve the words or sensibilities of children facing their own imminent departure from this world. The closest we can come is in Psellos's oration on the death of his daughter, when he purports to recount her deathbed vision of the life hereafter. Styliane reported that she had dreamed of traveling on a long road in the company of a man with keys (no doubt Saint Peter); eventually they reached a locked garden door, which he opened. "We both went inside and beheld a shady garden with trees ripe with fruit, thickly planted with all the other varieties of flora and exceedingly delightful. Neither roses nor lilies nor any species of fragrant flower was missing." In the garden was a giant man whose head reached to the sky. Two youths dressed in white handed him a tiny, sickly infant, whom he rocked in his bosom until "it regained its health and strength and seemed to be reborn. Then, he placed it on the ground beside him in a spot graced by every kind of flower."[110] Such was Psellos's account of the dying vision of his nine-year-old daughter, an expectation of paradise that may have brought some consolation to a grieving father.

Dumbarton Oaks

---

109   Psellos's encomium for his mother, ed. Sathas, 29–31, trans. Kaldellis, *Mothers and Sons,* 76–78 (above, nn. 69, 50).
110   Psellos's oration on Styliane, ed. Sathas, 82–84, trans. Kaldellis, *Mothers and Sons,* 134–35.

ABBREVIATIONS

AASS	*Acta sanctorum,* 71 vols. (Paris, 1863–1940)
AB	*Analecta Bollandiana*
ABME	*Ἀρχεῖον τῶν Βυζαντινῶν Μνημείων τῆς Ἑλλάδος*
AJA	*American Journal of Archaeology*
AJPA	*American Journal of Physical Anthropology*
AnatSt	*Anatolian Studies*
AnnalesDH	*Annales de démographie historique*
ArtB	*Art Bulletin*
Ἀρχ. Δελτ.	*Ἀρχαιολογικὸν Δελτίον*
Ἀρχ. Ποντ.	*Ἀρχεῖον Πόντου*
BCH	*Bulletin de correspondance hellénique*
BHG	*Bibliotheca hagiographica graeca,* 3rd ed., ed. F. Halkin, 3 vols. (Brussels, 1957)
BHL	*Bibliotheca hagiographica latina antiquae et mediae aetatis,* ed. Socii Bollandiani, 2 vols. (Brussels, 1898–1901 [1949]); supplement (Brussels, 1911 [1984])
BHO	*Bibliotheca hagiographica orientalis,* ed. Socii Bollandiani (Brussels, 1910)
BMGS	*Byzantine and Modern Greek Studies*
BNJ	*Byzantinisch-neugriechische Jahrbücher*
BSl	*Byzantinoslavica*
ByzF	*Byzantinische Forschungen*
BZ	*Byzantinische Zeitschrift*
CahArch	*Cahiers archéologiques*
CCAG	*Catologus Codicum Astrologorum Graecorum*
CCSG	Corpus Christianorum Series Graeca
CFHB	Corpus fontium historiae byzantinae
CIC	Corpus iuris civilis, 3 vols. (Berlin, 1928–29; Dublin–Zurich, 1972)
	CI *Codex Iustinianus,* ed. P. Krüger (Berlin, 1929)
	Dig *Digesta,* ed. Th. Mommsen and P. Krüger (Berlin, 1928)
	Inst *Institutiones,* ed. P. Krüger (Berlin, 1928)
	Nov *Novellae,* ed. F. Schoell and G. Kroll (Berlin, 1928)

CSHB	Corpus scriptorum historiae byzantinae
Δελτ. Χριστ. *Ἀρχ. Ἑτ.*	*Δελτίον τῆς Χριστιανικῆς Ἀρχαιολογικῆς Ἑταιρείας*
DOP	*Dumbarton Oaks Papers*
Ἐκκλ. Ἀλήθ.	*Ἐκκλησιαστικὴ Ἀλήθεια*
FM	*Fontes minores*
GCA	*Geochimica et Cosmochimica acta*
GOTR	*Greek Orthodox Theological Review*
GRBS	*Greek, Roman, and Byzantine Studies*
JArS	*Journal of Archaeological Science*
JbAC	*Jahrbuch für Antike und Christentum*
JÖB	*Jahrbuch der Österreichischen Byzantinistik,* vol. 18– (Vienna, 1969–) (Before 1969, *Jahrbuch der Österreichischen Byzantinischen Gesellschaft, JÖBG*)
JTS	*Journal of Theological Studies*
LBG	*Lexikon zur byzantinischen Gräzität, besonders des 9.–12. Jahrhunderts,* vol. 1, *A–K,* ed. E. Trapp, with W. Hörandner et al. (Vienna, 2001)
Littré	Émile Littré, *Dictionnaire de la langue française,* 5 vols. plus suppl. (Paris, 1859–72)
OCP	*Orientalia christiana periodica*
ODB	*The Oxford Dictionary of Byzantium,* ed. A. Kazhdan et al., 3 vols. (New York, 1991)
OrChr	*Orientalia christiana*
OrSyr	*L'Orient syrien*
PG	Patrologiae cursus completus, Series graeca, ed. J.-P. Migne, 161 vols. in 166 pts. (Paris, 1857–66)
RAC	*Reallexikon für Antike und Christentum*
REB	*Revue des études byzantines*
ROC	*Revue de l'Orient chrétien*
SC	Sources chrétiennes
Settimane	*Settimane di studio del centro italiano di studi sull'alto medioevo*
SicGymn	*Siculorum gymnasium*
TM	*Travaux et mémoires*
ZRVI	*Zbornik radova Vizantološkog instituta, Srpska akademija nauka*

ABOUT THE AUTHORS

DIMITER G. ANGELOV is University Research Fellow and Lecturer at the Centre for Byzantine, Ottoman and Modern Greek Studies, Institute of Archaeology and Antiquity, University of Birmingham, U.K. He is a historian with wide-ranging interests, mostly in late Byzantium. His most recent publication is *Imperial Ideology and Political Thought in Byzantium* (2007).

CHRYSSI BOURBOU is currently Research Associate at the 28th Ephorate of Byzantine Antiquities, Hellenic Ministry of Culture, and temporary lecturer at the Department of Mediterranean Studies, University of the Aegean. Her book *The People of Early Byzantine Eleutherna and Messene, 6th–7th centuries A.D.: A Bioarchaeological Approach* was published in 2004.

BÉATRICE CHEVALLIER CASEAU is Associate Professor in Byzantine History at the University of Paris–Sorbonne and a member of the Centre d'Histoire et Civilisation de Byzance. Her publications explore religious anthropology and sacred spaces of the late antique and Byzantine periods and include *Euodia: The Use and Meaning of Fragrances in the Ancient World and their Christianization (100–900 AD)* (1994). She is coeditor of *Pèlerinages et lieux saints dans l'Antiquité et le Moyen âge (2006)* and of *Pratiques de l'eucharistie dans les Églises d'Orient et d'Occident (Antiquité et Moyen Âge)* (2009).

MARIE-HÉLÈNE CONGOURDEAU is researcher at the Centre national de la recherche scientifique, Centre d'histoire et civilisation de Byzance (UMR 8167 Orient et Méditerranée). She has a longstanding interest in classical and Byzantine attitudes toward the embryo and recently published *L'embryon et son âme dans les sources grecques (6e s. av. J.-C.-5e s. ap. J.-C.)*, (2007). She serves as secretary of the Comité français des Etudes byzantines and is a member of the editorial board of the *Revue des études byzantines*.

SANDRA J. GARVIE-LOK, a bioarchaeologist, is currently Assistant Professor of Anthropology at the University of Alberta, Canada. Her research interests include weaning and associated illnesses in archaeological populations and regional variation in diet and health in the late Roman Aegean.

RICHARD GREENFIELD is Professor of Middle and Late Byzantine History at Queen's University in Kingston, Ontario. He has special interests in Byzantine magic and demonology, explored in his *Traditions of Belief in Late Byzantine Demonology* (1988), and in Byzantine hagiography and monasticism. His translation of the Vita of St. Lazaros of Mt. Galesion was published by Dumbarton Oaks in 2000.

ARIETTA PAPACONSTANTINOU is currently Marie Curie Fellow at the Oriental Institute, University of Oxford. She is the author of *Le culte des saints en Égypte des Byzantins aux Abbassides* (2001) and of various articles on aspects of late antique and early Islamic social history and material culture. Her research focuses on the history of Near Eastern Christian communities during the transition from Roman to Islamic rule and on the history of childhood and the family in the eastern Mediterranean.

BRIGITTE PITARAKIS, chargée de recherche at the Centre national de la recherche scientifique / Centre d'histoire et civilisation de Byzance in Paris, is a specialist in the material culture of Byzantium. Among her particular interests are the typology of early Christian bronze vessels and the terminology for art objects in archival documents. She is author of *Les croix-reliquaires pectorales byzantines en bronze* (2006) and coeditor of *Kariye: From Theodore Metochites to Thomas Whittemore; One Monument, Two Monumental Personalities* (2007).

GÜNTER PRINZING has been Professor of Byzantine Studies at the Johannes Gutenberg-Universität Mainz since 1986. His wide-ranging research covers such topics as relations between Byzantium and east-central Europe, the geography and history of Albania, and most recently a critical edition of the works of Demetrios Chomatenos (2002) for the Corpus Fontium Historiae Byzantinae.

ALICE-MARY TALBOT is Director of Byzantine Studies at Dumbarton Oaks. Her research has focused on Byzantine monasticism and hagiography, and women's studies. Her most recent book, an annotated translation of the *History of Leo the Deacon*, coauthored with Denis Sullivan, was published by Dumbarton Oaks in 2005.

INDEX OF GREEK WORDS

INDEX

avoided by holy children, 124n159

hunting with bow and arrow, 110

arcosolia, 303

Ariès, Philippe, 1–9 *passim*, 13–14, 86–87, 104, 123, 125, 165, 171

Aristotle, 12, 13, 40

armbands, for children, 190, 200

Arsenios Autoreianos, patriarch of Constantinople

education of, 119 and n142

omen of future patriarchal status, 115n123

prophecy of imperial accession of Andronikos II, 99

testament with autobiographical information, 93–94

art. *See under* children

Artavasdina, Helena, *magistrissa*, 303

Asan, John Doukas Angelos Palaiologos Raoul Laskaris Tornikes Philanthropenos, son of Manuel Raoul Asan, 305–6

Asan, Manuel Raoul, 305

Askepsimas, St., 133

Asklepios, St., 134

astrologers, 40, 42

Athanasia of Aegina, St., tomb of, 280

Athanasios, patriarch of Alexandria, playacting as cleric, 152, 153, 241

Athanasios I, patriarch of Constantinople

education of, 116–17 and n135

enters monastery as child, 121–22

filial affection of, 121–22

Athanasios of Athos, St.

differing depictions of his childhood in two vitae, 164–65

playacting as monastic leader, 152

as *puer senex*, 152

typikon of, 272

Athanasios of Lavra, St. *See* Athanasios of Athos, St.

Athanasios of Meteora, St., 271

Athanasios Philanthropenos, *hegoumenos* of St. Mamas monastery, 267n34

Athenaios, *komes*, 302

Athos, Mount (Holy Mountain), 261, 271, 273, 277, 281

Auxentios, St., 142–43

Axouch, Alexios, 46

baby feeder, glass, 215–16, n181 and fig. 17

balls, 233–34

of leather, 233

of rags, 218, 233

of wool, 233–34

Balsamon, canonist, 54, 59, 60, 63

on children's liability to punishment, 27 and n60

baptism, infant, 289 and n23, 291, 299n71, 301

age at, 24

of imperial princes, 100 and n57

Baradatos, St., 134

Bardoanes, Nicholas, logothete and *pansebastos*, 304

barley meal, kneaded, as infant food, 71

barrenness, 38, 52, 196–97, 269

as heavy burden for women, 36

as unnatural and unhealthy for women, 50–51

women viewed as responsible for, 37, 51

Basil I, emperor, 92, 94–95, 96, 115

divine omens at his birth, 98

gift of apple from king of Bulgarians, 112–13, 217

Life of. *See Vita Basilii*

mother's dream of his imperial destiny, 99n55

playful behavior, 112–13

Basil II Kamateros, patriarch of Constantinople

education of, 120 and n148

omen at birth, 115

Basil, brother of Paul of Latros, 146

Basil, pseudo-, author of *Hortatory Chapters*, 94–95 and nn38–39, 106, 108

Basil of Caesarea, 258n9, 273–74

canons of, 54, 59–60, 63

claim of avoidance of topoi of rhetoric, 136–37

views on minimum age for girls to enter monastery, 131–32

Basil the Younger, St., Vita of, 74, 78

beads, 194, 300

beard, first, 254n2, 259

beardless youths, 256, 259–60, 261, 265 and n28, 266, 271–73, 276n61, 277, 278

beggar children, 259

bells, as protective devices for children, 200, 201–2

emperors (*continued*)

    Vitae of, 91

    See also encomia *and individual emperors*

empresses, Vitae of, 90

encomia, of emperors, 88–90, 96

    rules for composition of, 92–93, 135

enkyklios paideia. See education, secondary

Ephodia, therapeutic manual, 47–48

epigrams, funerary, 304–6. *See also* inscriptions, funerary

epitaphios logos. See orations, funerary

epitaphs, funerary. *See* inscriptions, funerary

eunuchs, 257, 263n23, 280

    prohibition of in monasteries, 261 and n19, 271n47, 272, 273n51, 276

Eusebia, wife of Constans II, 49

Eusebios, SS., 133

Eustathios of Antioch, heretic, 30

Eustathios of Thessalonike, praise of Alexios II Komnenos, 102

Euthymios of Sardis, 9th-c. iconodule saint, 127, 156

Euthymios the Great, St., miraculous conception of, 143–44

Euthymios the Younger, St., military service as child, 142

Eutychios, patriarch of Constantinople

    education of, 117

    omen of future patriarchal status, 115 and n122, 241

    playacting at celebrating liturgy, 153

Evaristos, St., 286

evil eye, 197 and n112, 198, 200, 237

exercises, gymnastic, 108

    avoided by holy children, 124 and n159

eyes, as magic symbol, 211 and n171 and fig. 15

fasting, among saintly children, 147–49, 211

Febronia, St., 266n30

fertility. *See* barrenness *and* conception

fetus, 55, 59–60, 287, 288, 301

    death of, 55, 196, 288

fevers, 288, 289

fishing, as childhood activity, 240

flowers, as bridal wreath, 195

folic acid deficiency, 74, 75n41

food

    baby, 9, 67–75, 77.

children's reward, 216 and n184

    See also barley meal, bread, butter, cereals, eggs, fruit, goat's milk, gruel, honey, hydromel, nosesmart, pap, porridge, southernwood, spelt soup, *and* wine

footwear, for children, 169 and n5, 186–87.

    See also boots, sandals, shoes, slippers, *and* socks

foundlings. *See* abandoned children

fractionation, 66

Frankish Greece, burials in, 80–82. *See also* Corinth

fruit

    children picking, 238

    favorite food of children, 148, 217, 276

funerals. *See under* children *and* orations

Galen, 48

Galesion, Mount, 279

games, 1, 149–53, 216–17, 233–41

    avoidance of, by holy children, 116, 124 and n159, 129, 151–52, 164

    ball, 233 and n244

    for western medieval children, 87

    See also balls, play, playacting, *and* toys

garden, 308

garments, for children, 169, 177, 178–86

    luxurious, studded with jewels, 178

    See also caftans, caps, girdles, mantles, *and* tunics

gastroenteritis, 288

Gatteliusi, ruling family of Lesbos, 81

Gello/Gyllo, female demon, 197–98, 200, 211n171, 250, 290–91 and n35

    causes miscarriages, 44

    smothers newborn infants, 44

George II Xiphilinos, patriarch of Constantinople, education of, 119n145

George, St., thank offerings to, 216–17

George, son of anonymous cleric, 293

George of Choziba, St., 274n54

George the *sebastos*, nephew of Michael Choniates, 296

Gerbenites, Niphon, monk, 260

Germanos I, patriarch of Constantinople, 38

Germanos, *parekklesiarches* on Mount Galesion, 262

Giles of Rome, author of *De regimine principum*, 95–96
giraffe, 240
girdles, to facilitate conception, 44–45
gospel books, miniature, worn as protective device, 200
Goudelis, Theodosios, author of Vita of Leontios of Jerusalem, 260
grapes, 278
Gratian, emperor, as *puer senex*, 102n67
grave goods, for children, 191–95, 201, 243–50, 300–301. *See also* amulets, bells, ceramic pitchers, coins, crosses, dolls, eggs, goblets, jewelry, *lunulae*, perfume flasks, *and* toys
graves/tombs, of children, 284–85, 296, 298, 299, 300–301, 306, 308. *See also* burial, cemeteries, churches, *and* death
Gregory II, patriarch of Constantinople, 94
education of, 117, 119n145, 120n149, 122
Gregory, founder of monastery of St. Philip of Fragala (Sicily), 265n26, 267n34
Gregory of Cyprus. *See* Gregory II, patriarch of Constantinople
Gregory of Nazianzos, patriarch of Constantinople, 116
education of, 118 and nn137–38, 122
use of rules of rhetoric, 139
Gregory of Nyssa, St.
author of Life of sister Macrina, 274n54
avoidance and use of rhetorical topoi, 135–36, 137, 139
Gregory Thaumaturgus, St., 136
Gregory the Cleric, 9th-c. hagiographer, 307, 308
gruel, as infant food, 73, 215
guardians of children, 12, 18 and n16, 33
Gyllo. *See* Gello

Hagia Sophia, church of, in Constantinople, site of divine omen at birth of Alexios II Komnenos, 98–99
hagiography
evidence for childhood mortality, 286–87
evidence for parental attitudes towards children's death, 291–92
relationship with biography and encomium, 93

as source for ideals of imperial and patriarchal childhood, 87, 88, 90–91, 96–97
as source for ideals of saintly childhood, 5, 96–97, 127–66
Hannah, mother of Samuel, 37, 38, 143–44
Helena, mother of Constantine I, 98, 107 and n93, 111–12
Helena, sister of Constans II, 49
Heliodoros, *hegoumenos*, 264
Helle, Egyptian holy man, 130
hematite, 43
Hermogenes, author of textbook on *progymnasmata*, 92 and n28, 135 and n32
hernia, 279
Herod, king, 297
hikanatoi, cadet corps, minimum age of 15 for enrollment, 103
Hippocrates, 40, 47, 54, 55
Holobolos, Manuel, orator, 7, 102n68, 109, 113–14
Holy Mountain. *See* Athos, Mount
Holy Rider. *See* amulets
homosexuality, 12, 263n23
juvenile passive homosexuals, 12, 27
among monks, 257, 261
honey. *See also* hydromel
harmful for infants, 74, 288
as infant food, 71, 73, 279n73
honeycomb, 279
Honorius, emperor, education of, 106, 107
hoops, for play, 234
horse races, avoidance by holy children, 124n159, 238
horseback riding, 97, 108, 109–10, 116, 233n244, 296, 307
Hortatory Chapters by pseudo-Basil, 94–95 and nn38–39, 106, 108
hunting, by children and teenagers, 103, 108 and n97, 109, 110–11, 124
avoidance by holy children, 124n159
hydromel, solution of honey and water, as infant food, 71, 72
hypoplasia of tooth enamel, 287, 288

Iakobos, St., 134
Iakobos of Nisibis, St., 133

iatrosophia, manuals of medical therapy, 40, 41, 45, 46, 47, 61

icons
    funerary, 304–6
    of Virgin Episkepsis at Pege, 303

Ignatios, patriarch of Constantinople, 38, 39, 289
    appointment as military commander at age ten, 103
    education of, 117 and n135

illnesses and afflictions, childhood, 6, 11, 16. *See also* anemia, blindness, botulism, cancer, cholera, congenital abnormalities, convulsions, deafness, demonic possession, diarrhea, diphtheria, dropsy, dysentery, fevers, folic acid deficiency, gastroenteritis, hernia, jaundice, leprosy, paralysis, plague, scurvy, skin problems, smallpox, snakebite, sudden infant death syndrome, throat infections, *and* worms, intestinal

incest, in monasteries, 257

incubation, 38

infanticide, 37, 46, 49–50, 56, 214–15. *See also* cannibalism
    condemnation of, 13
    legislation regarding, 57

inscriptions, funerary, 286n12, 302

Ioannes. *See* John

Ioannikios, St., pigherder as child, 155

Ioubes, John, *illoustrios*, 196

Ioulianos, St., 133

Irene, empress, wife of John VI Kantakouzenos, 305

Isaac II Angelos, emperor, 102n70

Isaac, exarch of Ravenna, 303n91

Isaiah, nephew of Neophytos the Recluse, 267

Isidore I, patriarch of Constantinople, 93–94
    avoidance of childish games, 116
    education of, 119
    piety as child, 115

Isocrates, author of ancient Greek mirror of princes, 106

isotopic anlysis, 65, 288. *See also* nitrogen isotype analysis

jaundice, 288

javelin throwing, 109

Jeme, town in Egypt, 269n40

Jeremiah, model of holy destiny from time of birth, 144–45

Jerome, St., advice on raising saintly child, 158, 184

Jerusalem, 270

Jesus, infancy and miracles of, 131

jewelry, for children, 169, 177–78, 187–95, 300
    as grave goods, 191–95
    See also armbands, beads, belts, bracelets, earrings, finger rings, *and* necklaces

Joachim, father of Virgin Mary, 175–76
    caressing of daughter in mosaic at Chora, 176

Joachim, metropolitan of Zichna, 267

Job, stoicism at death of child, 292, 296, 297, 298

John I Tzimiskes, emperor, typikon of, 271, 273, 277

John II Komnenos, emperor, 109

John III Vatatzes, emperor, 91, 93n32, 96n45, 104, 108

John V Palaiologos, emperor, 103

John VIII Palaiologos, emperor, addressee of *Foundations of Imperial Conduct*, 95, 108

John VIII Xiphilinos, patriarch of Constantinople, secular education of, 120n149

John X Kamateros, patriarch of Constantinople, education of, 119n145, 120n147

John, founder of monastery of Phoberos, 256–57, 258, 260, 278

John, 14th-c. monk on Mount Athos, 271

John, St., holy man, 134

John, son of Zenobios, 302

John Chrysostom, 37, 49, 63
    advice on raising saintly child, 158–59
    attacks on magical practices, 200
    education of, 117, 118 and nn138–39, 120
    Encomiastic Oration of, by Leo VI, 97
    humility as child, 116
    postponement of entrance into monastery, 121n153
    praises role of women in childrearing, 187

recommends cross as protection for
children, 202
John Moschos, author of *Spiritual Meadow*,
150, 153, 241, 261n18, 275
John the Almsgiver, St., 131, 142
John the Baptist, church of, in Berroia,
constructed in memory of deceased
children, 304
John the Baptist, St.
conception of, 36
grants prayers for conception of Simeon
Stylites the Younger, 38
John the Faster, author of penitential, 61
John the Hesychast, St., 140–41
Julius Africanus, author of *Kestoi*, 42, 46
jumping, 110
in full armor, 109
Justin, martyr saint, 142
Justinian I, emperor, 49
as addressee of *Ekthesis* of Agapetos, 94
legislation on birth control and abortion,
51–52, 56–57
legislation on disinheritance of children,
30–31
legislation on legal status of children, 23

Kallikles, Nicholas, poet, 305–6
Kekaumenos, Basil, funerary poem on a
friend's son, 174–75
Kinnamos, John, 46
knucklebones (*astragaloi*)
as playthings of imperial children, 235
used for games, 169n5, 217, 234–36
Koiranides, medical-magical collection, 41,
45, 47
Komnenos, Isaac, *sebastokrator,* typikon of,
259, 273
Konstitzes, foster son of Isaac Komnenos,
273
Kouka, Cappadocia, church of the Virgin
at, 38
Kounales, Nikephoros, restorer of church at
Berroia, 304
Kyrilla of Dokimion, 303n91

labor, maternal
difficult, 38, 39, 43–45, 53
drugs for, 43
stones to facilitate, 43–45

Lampenos, Nicholas, court orator of
Andronikos II, 99
lamps, glass, 301
lapidaries, 42–43 and n47, 45, 47
Latros, Mount, 146
Lazaros of Mount Galesion, St.
childhood of, 268, 275
influence of monastic uncle, 160–61, 268
omens of future sanctity, 146
Vita of, 261, 262, 278, 279 and n77
lector (ἀναγνώστης)
minimum age to become, 24, 34
ordination of, 160
legislation. *See specific issues and emperors*
Leo VI, emperor
addressee of *Hortatory Chapters*, 94–95
author of *Encomiastic Oration* on John
Chrysostom, 97
education of, 106, 108
legislation on abortion, 57–58, 63
legislation on age of admission to
monastery, 30
legislation on betrothals, 28–29
legislation on magic, 52
Leo the *orphanotrophos*, 297
Leontares, Demetrios, scribe, 286, 301–2
Leontios, patriarch of Jerusalem
as child monk, 260, 265n28, 276n61
healing of sexual impotence, 53
lack of information on his childhood, 163
Leontios, poet, 160
leprosy, 289
letters of consolation, 294–98, 299
Lilith, female demon, 44
lily, 302, 308
liturgical chants, memorization of, 115
liturgy, funerary, for children, 299. *See also
under* burial *and* children
Lizix, Anastasios, vestarch, 174–75
lochozema (lohusa şerbeti), broth for recent
mothers, 205–6, 209
Longanikos (Lakonia), church at, 303n97
Longin procedure (for extraction of bone
collagen), 76–77
longue durée, 170–71, 204
Luke the Stylite, St., facilitates delivery of
woman in protracted labor, 196
Luke the Younger (of Steiris), St.
avoidance of games, 151

Luke the Younger (of Steiris), St. (*continued*)
family of, 157
fasting practices, 148
leaves home as teenager to enter
monastery, 269–70
tomb of, 280
lunulae, crescent-shaped pendants, 200–201
and fig. 11, 202, 243

Maccabees, mother of, 298
Macrina, sister of Gregory of Nyssa, 274n54
burial in wedding attire, 195
secret name of Thecla, 137–38
Vita by Gregory of Nyssa, 137–39
Maesymas of Cyrrhus, St., 133
magicians, 40
Makarios the Egyptian, St., as *puer senex*,
152
Makedonios, St., 133
facilitates gestation of Theodoret of
Cyrrhus, 39, 143
Maleinos, Michael, St.
barren mother's prayer for his
conception, 38, 53
sign of his future sanctity, 156–57
malnutrition, 287, 288
mantles, for children, 179
artistic depictions of, 179 fig. 2
Manuel I Komnenos, emperor
divine omen at birth of male heir, 98–99
divine omen at his birth, 98n49
dream vision of Virgin, 99
education of, 105n84, 106
historical omen at birth, 101
military training, 109
praise, by Michael Italikos, 113n120
relative's attempt to render him sterile,
46
Manuel II Palaiologos, emperor, 105n84
author of *Foundations of Imperial
Conduct*, 95, 108
typikon of, 261, 273n51
Marana and Cyra, SS., 134
marbles, as toys, 150, 236 and n264
Marinos/Mary, St., 149, 266n30
Maris, St., 134
Mark the Deacon, author of Vita of
Porphyry of Gaza, 137
Markellos, addressee of poem by Photios, 17

Markianos, jurisconsult, 51
Markianos of Cyrrhus, St., 133
Maron, St., 133
Maroules, Germanos, St., 271
marriage
age at, 9, 21, 23n40, 28–29, 130, 138, 142
refusal of, 138, 146
marriage crowns, 195
Martha, sister of Gregory the Cleric, 307
Mary, daughter of anonymous cleric, death
from plague, 293
Mary, daughter of Manuel Xeros, funerary
icon of, 195
Mary, wife of emperor Honorius, 249
Mary of Bizye (the Younger), St.
stoicism at death of her children, 291–92
tomb of, 280
Mary of Egypt, St., 162
Matthew I, patriarch of Constantinople
autobiographical testament of, 94, 260
becomes monk as teenager, 116–17, 122,
270
opposes admission to monastery of
youths under sixteen, 260
parental opposition to his adoption of
monastic habit, 270
Maximos, founder of monastery at Skoteine
(Boreine) near Philadelphia, 268n37
Maximos Kausokalybites, St.
differing depictions of childhood in two
Vitae, 164
precocious learning abilities, 155
medical textbooks, on childhood illnesses,
288
Medusa, on amulets, 198
Mehmed II, Ottoman sultan, 286
Melania the Younger, St., 45, 130, 142
Meletios of Myoupolis, St., difficulty in
learning letters, 156
melittouta, honey cake, 217
Menander Rhetor, 92–93, 134–35
Methodios, patriarch of Constantinople
author of Vita of Euthymios, 127
education of, 117, 119, 120n149
views on causes of sanctity, 156
Metochites, Theodore, 188
death of children, 283, 292
Metrodora, midwife (7th c.) and medical
writer, 35, 40–43 *passim*, 50, 51, 71

Neilos, bishop of Tamasia (Cyprus)
forbids use of children as monastic
servants, 259–60
Neilos of Rossano, St., precocious learning
ability, 154
Neophytos the Recluse, St.
becomes monk at eighteen, 266–67
entrusts monastery to his youthful
nephew, 267
Nicholas, founder of shrine of Holy Sion,
147
Nicholas of Bounaina, St., breastfeeding of,
141
Nicholas of Myra, St.
artistic depiction of his clothing, 178
fasting from infancy, 147–48
good behavior from infancy, 140
renders his mother sterile after his birth,
46
wise choice of companions, 151
Nicholas of Sion, St.
influence of archbishop, 159–60
influence of uncle, 160, 161
precocious learning ability, 154
saintly destiny from time of conception,
145
stands upright at birth, 145–46
Nicholas of Stoudios, St., influence of
monastic uncle, 161
Nikephoros I, patriarch of Constantinople,
education of, 118 and n140, 120 and
n148
Nikephoros III Botaneiates, emperor,
102n69
Nikephoros, teenage servant of Simeon the
Theologian, 264, 278
Nikephoros of Medikion, St., Vita of,
218
Nikon ho Metanoeite, St.
mention of his fatherland, 139
as *puer senex*, 152
tomb of, 280
Vita of, 276
Niphon, hagiographer of Maximos
Kausokalybites, 164
Niphon of Athos, St., role of monastic
uncle, 161, 268–69
nitrogen (δ^{14}N and δ^{15}N) isotopic analysis,
10, 66–69, 72, 75–82

limitations of, 69–70
See also isotopic analysis
nosesmart, a kind of cress, used as infant
food, 71
novices, monastic, 121, 254–55,
276n62
parental resistance to children becoming,
121nn153–54
training of, 255–56
nuns, 262, 275
homosexuality among, 262n22
pregnancy of, 58
should avoid association with children,
257
vows of virginity, 36
nursing. *See* breastfeeding *and* wetnurse
nutrition, infant and child, 70–75. *See also*
baby food
nuts, as playthings, 236 and n260

Obeyesekere, Gananath, anthropologist,
253
Obizuth, female demon, 44
Olympus, Mount, in Bithynia, 146, 265
omens
at birth of future emperors, 97–99
of future sanctity, 144–47
of imperial destiny, 112–13, 123
Omurtag (Koutragon), khan of Bulgars,
112–13, 217
orations, funerary, for children, 9, 294–98,
299. *See also* encomia *and individual
orators*
Orestes, son of Mary of Bizye, 291–92
Oribasius, Greek medical writer, 48, 70–71,
72, 73
Origen, 88
orphans, 6, 11, 12, 277n65
adoption by monasteries, 266–67
legal terminology for stages of childhood,
20n28
monastic care of, 259, 266 and n30,
273–75, 276n62
school for, 267n34, 273–74
See also abandoned children
ossuaries, 80, 300

Pacatula, daughter of Gaudentius, rearing
of, 216

Pachomius, monastic founder in Egypt, 256n5
  as infant regurgitates pagan libation, 147
Pakourianos, Gregory, monastic founder, opposes admission of boys to monastery, 276
Palaiologina, Euphrosyne, daughter of Theodora Synadene
  admits young girls with monastic vocation, 275
  forbids education of lay girls in her convent, 262
Palaiologos, Constantine, the *porphyrogennetos,* as *puer senex,* 102, 113–14
Palaiologos, George, founder of church of St. Demetrios of the Palaiologoi, 305
Palamas, Constantine, affection for his children, 293–94
Palamas, Gregory, childhood of, 293
Palladios, St., 133
Palladios of Helenopolis, author of *Lausiac History,* 39, 53, 132
panegyric. *See* encomia *and* orations
pap (boiled flour and bread), 73
Paphnoutios, hermit on Mount Galesion, 261, 280
paradise, 298, 307, 308. *See also* Eden, garden of
paralysis, 289
Paraskeve, St., miraculous conception of, 38
parents, of saintly children, 127, 129, 156–59. *See also* affection, parental
Paris, son of Priam of Troy, exploits as teenager, 104
patriarchs
  childhood of, 114–21
  education of, 117–21, 124
  encomia of, 89, 90, 96
  omens of future patriarchal status, 114–15
  Vitae of, 90, 115–19, 121–23
  See also individual patriarchs
Paul, spiritual father of Peter of Atroa, 268n37
Paul Helladikos, superior of Elusa monastery in Idumaea, 256, 263n22
Paul of Aegina, Greek medical writer, 48, 70–71

Paul of Latros, St.
  entrance into monastery as young orphan, 266
  omens of his future sanctity, 145–46
  prohibition of beardless monks, 260
pebbles, as playthings, 150, 234, 236, 238
Pelagia, St., 162
penitentials, 60–62
peony seeds, for conception and contraception, 47
perfume flasks, as grave goods, 191
Perpetua, St., 142
pessaries
  to aid conception, 41, 51
  to prevent conception, 47
  to promote abortion, 48
pet animals, 169, 238, 239–40
Peter, *hegoumenos* of monastery of Karya on Mount Latros, 146
Peter of Argos, St., 267n34
Peter of Atroa, St.
  baptismal name of Theophylaktos, 144
  donation to monastery, 144
  facilitates delivery of stillborn child, 196
  miraculous birth of, 144
  miraculous healing of children, 279, 280
  ordination as child, 272n50
  precocious learning ability, 154
Peter the Galatian, holy man, 133, 278
Phidelia, daughter of Athenaios and Phidelia, 302
Philotheos Kokkinos, patriarch of Constantinople, interest in childhood of saints, 163–64, 293–94
Phoibammon, Apa, holy man in Egypt, 269n40
Phokas, St., dislike of school, 155
Photios, patriarch of Constantinople
  author of consolatory letters, 292n41, 297–98
  author of *Hortatory Chapters* attributed to Basil I, 94–95
  poem on nine ages of human life, 17
Phountoukli (Rhodes), church of Hagios Nikolaos, depiction of deceased children in arcosolium, 304
phylakteria, protective devices. *See* amulets

physician attitudes
  toward abortion, 55, 57, 60
  toward birth control, 50–51, 54–56, 60,
    62–63
  toward pregnancy, 50–51
pilgrimage, by children, 270
plague, 288, 293
Planoudes, Maximos, 101, 113n120
play, children's, 149–50
  artistic depiction of, 164, 234, 236–37
  avoided by holy children, 116, 129, 151–52,
    164
  running, 151, 238
  See also balls, dolls, games, *and* toys
playacting (role-playing), 149, 152–53, 171,
    242–42, 275
  celebration of liturgy, 115
  mock baptism, 152, 241–42
  monastic leadership, 152
  simulation of adult roles, 241
polo, 110, 111, 124, 233
  disapproval of, by Blemmydes, 110
Polystylon. *See under* cemeteries
Poppins, Mary, 1–2
porotic hyperostosis, 288
Porphyry of Gaza, St., 39, 137
porridge, as infant food, 72
Poseidonios of Thebes, ascetic, 39
Poublios of Zeugma, St., 133
pregnancy
  beneficial for women's health, 50–51
  determination of, 40
  See also conception
pregnant women, figurines of, from Abu
    Mina, 207 and n156
priest
  playacting as, 275
  youthful ordination, 272n50
procreation, desire for, 35–37. *See also*
    conception
prophylactics. *See* pessaries
prostitutes, 49–50, 57, 63
Psalms, memorization of, 115, 154, 156,
    216n184
Psellos, Michael
  advice on determination of sex of fetus,
    42
  advice on contraception, 46
  author of Vita of St. Auxentios, 142–43

encomium to grandson, 173, 178, 200
epitaphs on patriarchs, 120n149
funeral oration for daughter Styliane,
    173, 294–95, 297, 298, 308
funeral oration for mother Theodote,
    173–74
grief for deceased sister, 299, 307–8
letter to Konstantinos on birth of his
    son, 173n25
puer senex theme, 7, 238, 297
  among imperial children, 102–4, 113–14
  among saintly children, 152
  term coined by Curtius, 87–88
pull toys
  bird, 228
  horses on wheels, 222–28 and figs. 20–23

quadrivium, 118
Queenford Farm (Britain), child burials at,
    80
Quintilian, orator, 134

racing, as military exercise, 109
Rahula, son of the Buddha, 265–66
Raphael, archangel, 44
rattles (*seistra*), 201 and fig. 11, 202, 219–22,
    224, 300n80
  animal-shaped, 220–21 and fig. 18
  bird-shaped, 221–22 and fig. 19
reader. *See* lector
recipes, medical, 35, 40
rhetoric, rules of, 134–38, 143
rings, finger, for children, 193, 300
role-playing. *See* playacting
Romanos III, emperor, 42
Romanos from Rhosos of Cilicia, St., 133
rose, 302, 307, 308
  metaphor for deceased child, 295
running, 151, 238

Sabas, St., saintly destiny from conception,
    145
saints, childhood of, 8, 127–66
  ascetic behavior, 147–49
  topoi in, 128–29
  paucity of information on, 129–34
  precocious learning ability, 154–56
  See also under patriarchs *and*
    hagiography

Salamanes, St., 133
Samuel
  childhood in the temple, 258
  miraculous conception of, 37, 38, 143–44
sandals, for children, 169n5, 186–87
Sarah, sterility of, 36
Sarantenos, Theodore, *sebastos,* founds
    monastery at Berroia in memory of his
    deceased children, 304
sardonyx, 43
schools, monastic, 258n9, 259, 262n20,
    273–74, 276
  prohibition of admission of lay children,
    262
  See also education
scurvy, 287
semidalis, dish made with boiled flour for
    new mothers, 206, 208
sex determination of children, 42
sexual impotence, 53
Sgouros, Leo, tyrant of Corinth, 296
shoes, for children, 186 and fig. 6, 187
Simeon Eulabes, mentor of Simeon the
    Theologian, 271
Simeon Metaphrastes, hagiographer, 140
Simeon of Lesbos, St.
  cures boy with hernia, 279
  enters monastery at age eight, 269n40
  family of, 157
  heals girl who has been struck dumb,
    280n82
Simeon of Sisa, St., 134
Simeon Stylites the Elder, St.
  childhood of, 132
  lack of information on family
    background, 133
Simeon Stylites the Younger, St.
  miraculous conception of, 38
  nurses only from one breast, 147
  prevents miscarriages, 39
  refuses to suckle when mother has eaten
    meat, 73, 211
Simeon the Fool, St.
  children make fun of him, 150
  omission in his Vita of his childhood,
    130–31
Simeon the (New) Theologian, St.
  has 14-year-old servant, 264, 278
  healing of child, 280

precocious learning ability, 154–55
refused admission to monastery at age
    thirteen, 270–71
singing, 150
Sisinnios, on uterine amulets, 44
Sixth Ecumenical Council, canons of, 255,
    258
skin problems, 288
Skizenos, *oikoumenikos didaskalos* at
    patriarchate of Constantinople, 98–99,
    100
slippers, for children, 186
smallpox, 289, 294, 307
snakebite, 290
socks, for children, 184
Solomon, on uterine amulets, 44
Soranus of Ephesus, medical writer, 40, 48,
    50, 54, 55, 56, 71–73, 80
sorcery, 52, 58
southernwood, an herb used as infant food,
    71
spelt soup, as infant food, 72
sphongaton, omelet, as thankoffering to St.
    George, 216–17
Sphrantzes, Alexios, 293
Sphrantzes, Andronikos, 293
Sphrantzes, George, historian, death of his
    children, 285–86, 293, 294, 301
Sphrantzes, John, 286, 294
spinning. *See* children's work
sports. *See under* birds, discus throwing,
    fishing, horseback riding, javelin
    throwing, jumping, polo, racing,
    running, *and* wrestling
Sri Lanka, 253–54
standing upright at birth
  omen of future career as stylite saint, 146
  omen of sanctity, 146–47
Stephen the Younger, St.
  heals possessed child, 279n77
  miraculous conception of, 38, 53, 143, 196,
    197
sterility. *See* barrenness
stillbirth. *See* death, fetal
stones. *See under* conception *and*
    miscarriage
Styliane, daughter of Michael Psellos
  death of, 294–95
  deathbed vision of afterlife, 308

INDEX

329

Styliane, daughter of Michael Psellos
(*continued*)
funeral of, 298
parental affection for her, 173
sudden infant death syndrome (SIDS), 290
sugar, 206 and n150
swaddling clothes for infants, 178
swing, 239 and fig. 27
Simeon Seth, 41, 47, 48
Synadene, Theodora, foundress of convent,
275, 281
Synesius of Cyrene, 94, 108
Synkletike, St., 130

throat infections, 288, 295
tombs. *See* graves
tonsure, age at, 270, 275
topoi, of childhood, 6–7
in encomia, 6
in funerary orations, 9
in hagiography, 138, 140–56, 163, 286–87
in monastic literature, 12
toys, 169, 177, 218–33, 300
as grave goods, 193 and n88
for western medieval children, 87
See also dolls, games, knucklebones,
pebbles, pull toys, rattles, *and*
whistles
trophic levels, 67–69
tumor, surgical removal of, 296
tunics, for children, 179–86
from Egypt, 180
flared, 184–85 and fig. 5
hooded, 181–83 and fig. 3

uncles, role in spiritual upbringing of
saintly children, 159–61, 268–69

venia aetatis, 33, 34
visions. *See* dream visions
votive offerings, to promote fertility or a
healthy pregnancy, 207

weaning, 65–83
adverse effects of, 73–75, 288
age at, in Byzantium, 10, 70, 72–74,
78–83
age at, in Frankish Greece, 81–82
age at, in Western Europe, 79–82
donation of child to monastery after, 144
weaving. *See* children's work
wet nurse, 10, 71–72, 210, 211, 239–40, 296
baby's refusal of, 141
suckling of several children, 242
See also breastfeeding
whistles, 228–33
bird-shaped, 222, 233
clay, 171
cup-shaped, 232 and fig. 26
zoomorphic, 228–32 and figs. 24–25
wine
as infant food, 72
prohibition of for beardless monastic
servants, 277
womb, 40, 43, 46, 47, 51, 53
amulets for, 198–200
uterine anomaly causing problems with
pregnancy, 54, 55
women
disguised as men, 273n51
disguised as monks, 261
prohibited in men's monasteries, 260, 261
and n19
worms, intestinal, 288
wrestling, 108, 109, 179 fig. 2, 236